For the Swezeys;

You may find Twain's mature social ethics appealing.

Bill Phipps

Always do right. This will gratify some people, & astonish the rest.

Truly Yours
Mark Twain

*Postcard sent in 1901
to the Young People's Society of a Church in Brooklyn.*

Mark Twain's Religion

by William E. Phipps

Mercer University Press
September 2003

ISBN 0-86554-846-3   MUP/H638
ISBN 0-86554-897-8   MUP/P264

Mark Twain's Religion
Copyright ©2003
Mercer University Press, Macon, Georgia USA
Printed in the United States of America

The paper used in this publication meets the minimum requirements
of American National Standard for Information Sciences—
Permanence of Paper for Printed Library Materials,
ANSI Z39.48-1984.

Library of Congress Cataloging-in-Publication Data

Phipps, William E., 1930-
Mark Twain's religion / by William E. Phipps.
   p. cm.
Includes bibliographical references and index.
ISBN 0-86554-846-3 (hardcover : alk. paper) —
ISBN 0-86554-897-8 (paperback : alk. paper)
1. Twain, Mark, 1835–1910—Religion. 2. Religion in literature.
I. Title.
PS1342.R4P47 2003
818'.409—dc22
                                       2003018931

Contents

Dedication viii
Significant Dates for This Study ix
Preface xi

1. Introduction 1
   Religious or Irreligious? 1
   The Scope of Religion 3
   The Approach of This Study 4

2. Along the Mississippi 7
   Parental Influences 7
   Growing Up in Hannibal 13
   Religious Varieties 30

3. Peripatetic Journalist 41
   To the Pacific 41
   To the Mediterranean 59
   Travel Reflections 81

4. Amid Liberal Calvinists 89
   In New York State 89
   In Hartford 111
   Relations with Cable 134

5. Justice in America 143
   Economic Equity 143
   Political Morality 155
   Race Relations 162
   Women's Rights 181

6. Ambassador-at-Large 187
   In Europe 188
   Global Tour 194
   The Anti-Imperialist 202

7. Biblical Usages 221
   Jewish Scriptures 222
   The New Testament 241
   Scriptural Allusions 248

8. Theological Journey 263
   Views of God 263
   Views of Jesus 277
   Evil and Freedom 281
   Personal Immortality 299

9. Final Quest 313
   Joan of Arc and Susy 313
   Search for Healing 321
   Bittersweet Last Years 328

10. Conclusion 351
    Parallel Lives 351
    Ethics and Truth 359
    Humorist and Preacher 363
    The Tolerant Monotheist 368

    Bibliography 377
    Index 383

To Cary Anne and Laura Catherine Chapman,
beloved granddaughters.
May they carry through this century
their mother's artistic interests and
their grandmothers' caring concerns.

Significant Dates for This Study

1835 Samuel Langhorne Clemens born in Florida, Missouri
1839 Family moves to Hannibal
1847 Father John Marshall Clemens dies
1848 Apprentice printer
1853–1856 Journeyman printer
1857–1859 Apprentice pilot on Mississippi
1860–1861 Steamboat pilot
1861 Joined Missouri National Guard for two weeks
1862 Nevada journalist; adopts "Mark Twain" as pen name
1863 Unsuccessful prospector for precious metals
1865 California journalist
1866 Lecturer on Hawaii
1867 Mediterranean excursionist
1868–1869 Courtship with Olivia Langdon of Elmira, New York
1869 *The Innocents Abroad* published
1870 Marriage; newspaper editor in Buffalo, New York
1871 Settles in Hartford, Connecticut
1872 *Roughing It* published; Son Langdon dies
1873 *The Gilded Age* published
1876 *Adventures of Tom Sawyer* published
1880 *A Tramp Abroad* published
1881 *The Prince and the Pauper* published
1883 *Life on the Mississippi* published
1885 *Adventures of Huckleberry Finn* published
1889 *A Connecticut Yankee in King Arthur's Court* published
1891 Moves to Europe after financial failure
1894 *Pudd'nhead Wilson* published
1895 Global lecture tour begins
1896 *Personal Recollections of Joan of Arc* published;
    Daughter Susy dies
1897 *Following the Equator* published
1899 *Christian Science* published
1900 *The Man that Corrupted Hadleyburg* published
1904 Wife Livy dies
1904–1908 Resides in New York City
1905 *King Leopold's Soliloquy* published

1906 *What Is Man?* privately published
1908 *Captain Stormfield's Visit to Heaven* published
1909 *Letters from the Earth* completed; Daughter Jean dies
1910 Dies at his Stormfield mansion near Redding, Connecticut

Preface

What is the best way to address the one about whom this book is written? Since it will focus as much on his personal beliefs, correspondence, and practices as on his imaginative writings, "Samuel Clemens" might be appropriate. But using both given and family names is cumbersome, yet calling him "Samuel" is overly familiar for the adult figure. To refer to him as "Clemens" often lacks clarity, for there are numerous Clemenses involved in this study. He gave himself the pseudonym "Mark Twain" early in his writing career and in the generations to follow it became inextricably linked in both the author's and readers' minds with the man behind the literary mask. Even as only a "pudd'nhead" would be permitted to kill his half of a jointly owned barking dog, so it would be foolish to attempt to separate the interdependent Clemens/Twain entity. Perhaps "Twain Clemens" might be a way of dealing with the two blurred public/private persons!

Some adopt the method of address that a biblical author used in writing about the apostle Paul. Luke used the Hebrew name Saul while discussing his early activities, but the Roman name Paul after he began traveling outside the Jewish homeland. There is some justification for using one designation before the man of Missouri left his home region, and another one later. "Sam" was the way his relatives called him during his years along the Mississippi, so it will serve as a name for that period.

The young man then went to America's Far West and began to sign his newspaper and periodical articles as "Mark Twain." Since this pen name contains neither a given name nor a family name, but a number and possibly a verb, the use of one part without the other is inappropriate. The one who originated the pen name, and used it for the rest of his life, occasionally abbreviated it as "MT." Thus "Mark Twain" is not rent asunder if "MT" is used, so that is my simple, space-economizing solution. ("MT," incidentally, is also standard for the annotated bibliography in the *Mark Twain Journal*.)

The total literary corpus of MT is daunting, especially since half his writings were unpublished during his lifetime. In Everett Emerson's literary biography, 309 writings of MT are listed,[1] but only eighteen of

---

[1]Everett Emerson, *The Authentic Mark Twain* (Philadelphia: University of

them are singled out above in "Significant Dates for This Study." MT defined a classic as "a book which people praise and don't read."[2] Excepting several of his novels that are still widely sold in different editions, many of his writings—by his definition—might qualify as classics as far as the general public is concerned.

MT did not believe in the resurrection of his bodily remains, but he was determined that his literary remains would be reissued, or published for the first time, long after his physical death. Indeed, he preserved most of what he wrote, even though he insisted that many compositions he deemed controversial—often pertaining to religion—remain undisclosed for at least a generation after his burial. Dozens of his notebooks, hundreds of his unpublished manuscripts, and more than 10,000 of his letters have now been either published or are being readied for publication at the Bancroft Library at the University of California. That massive project, involving publishing his works with extensive scholarly annotations, will not be completed even by 2010, a century after his death. Those materials help those interested in MT's religion, or lack of religion, to explore ever more deeply.

Researching the vast number of relevant studies of the best-known American writer nationally and internationally is almost overwhelming for anyone. I thank the scholars and staff working with the Mark Twain Project for assisting me in that task during and after my visit to the archives in Berkeley. Available there are more than a million pages of MT papers, including a substantial amount of MT's autobiography that has yet to be published. Also, I am grateful to Gretchen Sharlow, who directed the Center for Mark Twain Studies at Quarry Farm in Elmira, New York, for offering me a research fellowship there. Lodging at the place where MT did much of his writing, and absorbing its Victorian atmosphere, has stimulated my historical imagination. Librarian Mark Woodhouse was also of invaluable assistance during the weeks I worked with the splendid Mark Twain Archives at Elmira College. In addition, I am indebted to Henry Sweets, curator of the Mark Twain Museum, for helping me ferret out some details on MT's boyhood religion when I

Pennsylvania Press, 1984) 321-26.

    [2]FE 241. [Editor's note. Works frequently referred to are cited by abbreviation only. See the first section of the bibliography, below.]

visited Hannibal. I also thank Phyllis Morris, an excellent novelist who was once my student, for helping to make this book more readable.

In appreciation, MT said of his wife Livy that "She not only edited my works, she edited me."[3] I, too, have been dependent on my wife Martha Ann, who has reorganized and improved the written and personal material I have given her for almost half a century. Moreover, her roots in Missouri and New York have provided me with more understanding of the native soils of the Clemens partners.

---

[3]Quoted in Archibald Henderson, *Mark Twain* (New York: Stokes, 1912) 183.

Chapter 1

Introduction

Religious or Irreligious?

Some MT scholars might dismiss as oxymoronic the title of this study. Maxwell Geismar refers to MT as an "eloquent and outraged atheist."[1] "He never became a Christian," writes Justin Kaplan, winner of the Pulitzer prize for his MT biography.[2] Biographer John Lauber refers to him as "a man who entirely lacked religion."[3] Another recent biography, written by Andrew Hoffman, contains virtually no treatment of his religion. Ken Burns's television documentary on MT portrays his outlook as mostly sardonic. Those works leave the reader with the impression that serious attention need not be given religion in understanding MT, even though religious imagery saturates his writings. Or, consider some who write in learned journals: Father Edward Rosenberger calls him a "blustering agnostic";[4] Max Eastman refers to him as "the great infidel";[5] William Phelps claims that "Mark Twain did not have even a grain of religious faith";[6] and an editor of a secular-humanism journal asserts that he had "a strong contempt for religion."[7] A librarian in his Missouri hometown was surprised to learn of my search for documents pertaining to his religion because she presumed he had none.

When quoted selectively, MT seems to agree with the categorical judgments of those literary critics. "I have found . . . perfect peace . . . in absolute unbelief," he wrote in 1885 to his former secretary Charles

---

[1]Maxwell Geismar, *Mark Twain: An American Prophet* (Boston: Houghton Mifflin, 1970) 354. Also, Wesley Britton states in his introduction to "Cradle Skeptic" (diss., North Texas State University, 1990) that atheism was "the only constant thread that dominated Twain's religious tendencies."

[2]Justin Kaplan, *Mr. Clemens and Mark Twain* (New York: Simon and Schuster, 1966) 80.

[3]John Lauber, *The Inventions of Mark Twain* (New York: Hill and Wang, 1990) 16.

[4]Edward Rosenberger, "An Agnostic Hagiographer," *Catholic World* (September 1928): 719.

[5]Max Eastman, *Harper's Magazine* (5 May 1938): 621.

[6]William Phelps, "Mark Twain," *Yale Review* (December 1935): 295.

[7]*Free Inquiry* (Fall 1997): 50.

Stoddard, who had converted to Catholicism.[8] In 1888, he wrote in his notebook, "I cannot see how a man of any large degree of humorous perception can ever be religious—except he purposely shut the eyes of his mind and keep them shut by force."[9] Again, he wrote, "The easy confidence with which I know another man's religion is folly teaches me to suspect that my own is also."[10] MT offered this analogy: "The cat's tail is only an incumbrance to her, yet she thinks it is the most precious thing she has got. Just so with man and his religion."[11] Appearing to be a settled apostate in his old age, he commented on a Methodist, "She has religious beliefs and feelings and I have none."[12]

A variety of interpretive reminders are needed in examining MT judiciously and avoiding stereotypes. He often used hyperbole to make a point, and that may be the case in the above quotations. Also, his emotional state at the time of writing is significant; disorienting grief or business failure sometimes prompted him to put down thoughts not intended for publication that otherwise might never have crossed his mind. Context is crucial; a sampling of more than a few words of a letter or story is needed before weighing its irony content. To accept his sentences on religion in isolation is as absurd as claiming that the Bible declares "There is no God," without acknowledging that the saying is attributed to a fool.[13] Furthermore, some do not distinguish MT's own ideas from those of characters in his novels. In particular, as will be demonstrated, I disagree with the interpretation of Henry Nash Smith in his influential book on MT's development as a writer. Smith claims that MT ended his career by identifying himself with Satan in *The Mysterious Stranger* who has contempt for belief in God and for human beings.[14]

To show that religion is also treated positively in MT's writings, several samples should suffice. He said, "Religion is the highest and holi-

---

[8]John Frederick, *The Darkened Sky* (Notre Dame IN: University of Notre Dame Press, 1969) 152.

[9]N&J 3:389.

[10]MTB 1584.

[11]MT's marginalia in his copy of Rufus Noyes, *Views of Religion*.

[12]MTL 680.

[13]Psalm 14:1.

[14]Henry Nash Smith, *Mark Twain: Development of a Writer* (New York: Atheneum, 1974) 188.

est thing on earth."[15] Late in life he affirmed: "The Being who to me is the real God is the One who created this majestic universe and rules it. . . . Everything which he has made is beautiful."[16] Also, Saint Joan of Arc's life is described endearingly and without skepticism in his longest novel. He even rated that story of religious martyrdom as his best. However, MT ever indulged in verisimiltude, so it is always difficult to weight his words on any topic for their truth content.

The Scope of Religion

Some scholars are insensitive to "the varieties of religious experience"— to borrow the title of a book by MT's friend, William James. If religion and theology are stereotyped by those researching MT, it is easy for them to assume they did not matter either to him or to the culture in which he lived. Those who narrowly define religion to mean either orthodoxy or liberalism, modernism or fundamentalism, Catholicism or Protestantism, Christianity or Judaism, pentecostal or liturgical practices, Western or Eastern faiths, sometimes rightly claim that he was not religious. Moreover, if being religious means being a sanctimonious churchman, MT was certainly antireligious. But MT recognized that the scope of religion is much wider than Christianity of any one standard or heretical variety.

A glance at some biblical views of religion should assist in avoiding caricatures. Two of the "Wisdom" books of Hebrew scriptures, Job and Ecclesiastes, show that profound skepticism is not necessarily antithetical to religion. Job has contempt for the conventional moral order in which God sees to it that the righteous get the riches and the rascals get the rags. Ecclesiastes is a philosophical essay by a person who eschews pious activity and thinks humans are no more immortal than beasts. Also, Jesus was at odds with some of his fellow Jews who interpreted a rejection of some old forms of religion as irreligion, and that conservative outlook has persisted over the centuries.

The term "religion" is rarely found in the King James Version—the version MT used. The writer of the Letter of James, who uses "religion" several times, stresses that it should pertain not to doctrine but to social ethics and personal morality: "Pure religion . . . is this, to visit the

---

[15]CT1 410.
[16]MTN 361.

fatherless and widows in their affliction, and to keep himself unspotted from the world."[17] The writer of James denounced those with faith who do not help the needy, much as Jesus did in his parable of the Good Samaritan.[18] That famous story, as well as Jesus' parable of the Last Judgment,[19] illustrates that the essence of New Testament "religion" is acting with compassion.

If criticism of a culture's prevalent religion makes someone irreligious, then denouncers of the prevailing national values in every era— from Moses to Martin Luther King, Jr.—would not be religious. If being religious is defined as pledging allegiance to the world's largest Christian church, Roman Catholicism, then MT was as irreligious as the Protestant Reformers. Or, more broadly, if religion is reduced to giving consent to a particular credal statement or devotional practice, then he was arguably not a religious person. Those who think belief in personal immortality is the sine qua non of religion will find MT, along with most ancient Hebrews, to be irreligious.

To some, religion is defined mainly as belief in supernatural beings— often limited to the one or ones worshiped in their community. To others, religion is defined principally as participation in certain awe-inspiring, guilt-arousing, or comfort-producing rituals. To still others, religion is measured by the depth of persons' mental involvement in the meaning of their existence. Of the many other definitions remaining is an ethical one: living by a moral code believed to be sanctioned by a divine power. Depending on the definition or definitions one selects, MT can be classified as either "irreligious" or "religious."

The Approach of This Present Study

For the past century interpreting MT has been largely the province of such outstanding literary critics as William Dean Howells, Bernard DeVoto, Dixon Wecter, Henry Nash Smith, John Tuckey, Hamlin Hill, Louis Budd, Alan Gribben, Laura Skandera-Trombley, Shelley Fisher Fishkin, Howard Baetzhold, and Jim Zwick. By skillful textual analysis they have produced an abundance of nuanced literary studies, and occa-

---

[17]James 1:27.
[18]Luke 10:31.
[19]Matthew 25:31-46.

sionally they have given some attention to the place of religion in MT's fiction. But those specializing in the field of American literature tend to have little interest in, or knowledge of, the breadth of American and world religions.

There is now needed, from someone whose academic field is religious studies, a thorough and careful probe of MT's changing personal religion and its effect on his public conduct. In this regard I hope to be able to provide some insights overlooked by Twain scholars into the way his religion was related to such significant issues as racism, imperialism, and materialism. Indeed, several American literature specialists, who apparently associate religion mainly with theological beliefs and private morality, read this study while it was in gestation and criticized much of it as being irrelevant to my topic because of its attention to MT's social action.

This monograph will take a close look at MT's participation in the slave culture of his parents and the radically different abolition culture in which his wife was raised. I will attempt to deal with the thorny issue of the extent to which the literary figures he created exemplify the way he lived out his personal religion. Although many pages will be devoted to an examination of religious themes in MT's imaginative literature, I am more interested in tracing in his personal life evolving religious principles and the moral actions that flowed from them. The chapter organization is mostly chronological, but a compendium is provided of his use of his most important literary source, the Bible, and another chapter treats his theological views systematically.

My cultural background in religion is similar to that of MT in spite of being separated from him by a century. Like him, I grew up in the branch of Presbyterianism that condoned slavery at the time of the "Northern Invasion" and continued to believe in WASP supremacy afterward. My mother, even as MT's mother, saw to it that her son attended church for hours each Sunday and memorized the "Westminster Shorter Catechism." We both learned by heart some denominational hymns and recited Bible verses to Sunday school teachers. Stories we read from the Bible as a boy stimulated our imaginations as much as any we discovered elsewhere. Purchasing a newspaper, swimming, fishing, and theatergoing were all forbidden on "the Sabbath." That longest day of the week began with confinement to a pew while my preacher-father droned on. I received a small relief from watching wasps light on dozing members of the congregation. The intellectual rigor of my family's

Calvinism caused me to look with condescending amusement at "hoop'n holler" cult activity in my town. Yet, like Hannibal Presbyterians, I attended revivals and camp meetings in the summertime. Like MT's boyhood church, my church expressed scorn toward the savage heathen abroad, the idol-worshiping Catholics, and the Yankees, who had the misfortune of having been born north of the Mason-Dixon line. I shared with him an inordinate pride in having noted Virginian ancestors. As a recovering Confederate Presbyterian I have found it difficult to escape from such conditioning, and I think MT might have said the same.

I have long found MT to be an insightful participant in and critic of religion, as well as a fascinating teller of moral tales. My scholarly interest in his works began when I was writing a book on *The Wisdom and Wit of Rabbi Jesus*. In it, I discussed some similarities of style and content between Jesus and MT, showing that both used humor to make criticisms more palatable and that both were contemptuous of hypocrisy. When my editor convinced me that I was dwelling too much on MT in a book focused on Jesus' teachings, I removed some of the material and used it in an article entitled "Mark Twain, the Calvinist."[20] The response to that article has encouraged me to undertake a thorough examination of MT's religion, from crib to coffin. I have also been influenced by Everett Emerson's article on MT's religion, which concludes with a call for a contextual treatment "in terms of both Clemens's life and the religious (or antireligious) spirit of the times in which he lived."[21]

Finally, I have usually opted for quoting Mark Twain's inimitable droll way of expressing his ideas rather than providing paraphrases. Whenever possible I have allowed him to speak for himself and to choose the right word. As he put it, "The difference between the almost right word and the right word is really a large matter—'tis the difference between the lightning-bug and the lightning."[22] But beware of accepting at face value the pronouncements of one who told the truth obliquely.

---

[20]*Theology Today* (October 1994): 416-20.

[21]"Religion," ENC; see also Everett Emerson, "Mark Twain's Quarrel with God," in R. W. Crump, ed. *Order in Variety* (Newark DE: University of Delaware Press, 1991) 32-48.

[22]CT1 946.

Chapter 2
Along the Mississippi

A thorough examination of Samuel Clemens's early religious influences is especially germane, since he tended to have a boy's-eye view of the world throughout life, drawing heavily from the deep well of childhood memories to write his novels and short stories. With his pervasive exaggeration, he acknowledged late in life, "All that goes to make the me in me was in a Missourian village."[1]

The birthplace of Samuel Clemens in Florida, Missouri.
He shared this two-room house with six others: his siblings
(Pamela, Orion, and Henry), his parents, and their one slave.
Photo by the author.

Parental Influences

Sam was born on November 30, 1835, during the auspicious month when Halley's comet was passing over his two-room birthplace in Florida, Missouri. A few years earlier his parents had migrated from Tennessee

---

[1]FE 352.

to Missouri because John Quarles, who had a large farm there, had invited his brother-in-law to become a partner in a general store. Sam boasted that his arrival increased the population of the nearly "invisible" frontier village by one percent.

When Sam was three, his family moved to nearby Hannibal, a rapidly developing town on the Mississippi with a population of one thousand. He was to spend his most impressionable years—a quarter of his life— along the river, and principally in Hannibal. There, the town council's decision in 1845 to ban all Sunday "games of amusement"[2] may have given young Clemens his first push toward rebellion. Family heritage may also have contributed to his religious independence, for his paternal line can be traced to ancestors who founded the Quaker meetinghouse in Lynchburg, Virginia.[3]

Sam's earliest memory regarding religion was of the log church in Florida. It had slab benches with no backs, resting on a floor of flattened logs; sounds and odors came through its unfilled cracks. When the hogs that slept beneath the church were disturbed by dogs, the preacher paused until he could again be heard. Until Sam became old enough to become employed, he spent his summers in Florida on the apple and tobacco plantation of his Uncle John, whom he much admired. Sam was fond of the plain religion of some slaves on the Quarles farm, and was charmed by their songs and by their supernatural tales of witches and ghosts.[4] After his Aunt Martha died in 1850, Sam read the sentiments placed on her gravestone, "Death is defied . . . since the Savior hath died; and looking to him who salvation hath given, I'll meet thee . . . in Heaven."

John Marshall Clemens, Sam's father, had been named for the most famous jurist of his native state. After having much difficulty providing financially for his family, Marshall Clemens succeeded in becoming a justice of the peace before his early death. Sam remembered him in this unaffectionate way:

---

[2]SCH 85.

[3]Samuel Webster, *Mark Twain, Business Man* (Boston: Little, Brown, 1946) 4. That meetinghouse is now part of the Quaker Memorial Presbyterian Church in Lynchburg, and some of MT's ancestors are buried in the cemetery there. See the (Bedford) *Bulletin-Democrat*, 11 March 1976.

[4]AMT 1-6, 14.

My father and I were always on the most distant terms when I was a boy—a sort of armed neutrality, so to speak. At irregular intervals this neutrality was broken, and suffering ensued; but I will be candid enough to say that the breaking and the suffering were always divided up with strict impartiality between us—which is to say, my father did the breaking, and I did the suffering.[5]

Regarding Marshall Clemens's religious orientation, Sam recalled, "My father was . . . a sternly just and upright man, albeit he attended no church and never spoke of religious matters, and had no part nor lot in the pious joys of his Presbyterian family, nor ever seemed to suffer from this deprivation."[6] Sam likely overstated his father's alienation from churches and religion. There is an account of his attending church and requesting the minister to include in the announcements that he had lost a cow. When this was not done, Clemens strode into the pulpit and notified the people himself.[7] Some biographers refer to Sam's father as a "freethinker," which John Frederick plausibly interprets to mean that he questioned the divinity of Jesus, rejected biblical literalism, and did not attend church regularly.[8] If that was the case, then the outlook on religion of father and mature son were similar.

The last day of his father's life impressed itself upon the memory of eleven-year-old Sam. Dying of pneumonia, Marshall Clemens displayed affection for the first time by kissing his daughter. In that extreme situation, Sam recalled in 1897, his father acknowledged his Christian faith: "The Presbyterian preacher had said, 'Do you believe on the Lord Jesus Christ, and that through his blood only you can be saved?' 'I do.' Then the preacher prayed over him and recommended him."[9]

Included in the few books Marshall Clemens left was one large Bible, two small ones, and a New Testament; most of the other books pertained to his legal profession.[10] The large Bible probably provided Sam his first

---

[5]CT1 428.

[6]FE 351.

[7]Ira Holcombe, *History of Marion County* (St. Louis: Perkins, 1884) 914.

[8]John Frederick, *The Darkened Sky* (Notre Dame IN: University of Notre Dame Press, 1969) 128.

[9]HH&T 40.

[10]Probate file #358, Palmyra, Missouri; MTLB 68.

Sam's mother, Jane Clemens (1803–1890).

glimpse of European art. Many family Bibles, like the one from his own library now at Berkeley, contained engravings illustrating biblical scenes.

Some of Sam's personality can be traced to his father, but much more to his mother, Jane Lampton Clemens. After she died at the age of eighty-eight, he wrote: "She was of a sunshiny disposition and her long life was mainly a holiday to her. She was a dancer, from childhood to the end, and as capable a one as the Presbyterian Church could show among its communicants." More generally, he commented, "It is at our mother's knee that we acquire our highest and noblest and purest ideals but there is seldom any money in them."[11] Describing his own mother, whom he called his "first and closest friend," he wrote, "She had a slender, small body, but a large heart—a heart so large that everybody's grief and everybody's joys found welcome in it, and hospitable accommodation."[12] In rejoicing with those who rejoice and weeping with those who weep, Jane Clemens embodied what the apostle Paul declared to be a basic part of Christian morality.[13]

In his autobiography, Sam claimed that he learned from his mother that "intolerance is everything for oneself and nothing for the other per-

---

[11]SCH 126.
[12]AMT 25.
[13]Romans 12:15.

son."[14] A relative wrote: "Jane Clemens took an interest in any religion, the livelier the better. They were drama to her as much as uplift."[15] Sam described his mother's "liberal sympathies" that made her a "friend to the friendless":

> Her interest in people and other animals was warm, personal, friendly. She always found something to excuse, and as a rule to love, in the toughest of them. . . . It was believed that, Presbyterian as she was, she could be beguiled into saying a soft word for the devil himself. . . . When her pity or her indignation was stirred by hurt or shame inflicted upon some defenseless person or creature, she was the most eloquent person I have heard speak. It was seldom eloquence of a fiery or violent sort, but gentle, pitying, persuasive, appealing; and so genuine and so nobly and simply worded and so touchingly uttered, that many times I have seen it win the reluctant and splendid applause of tears.[16]

The profound influence of Jane Clemens on Sam is widely recognized. Dixon Wecter comments, "Mark Twain's passionate humanitarianism, his lifelong indignation against bullies and other shapes of overmastering power, came straight from his mother Jane."[17] Abby Werlock states: "Jane Clemens bequeathed to Twain her storytelling abilities and provided him with rich inspiration. Almost certainly the source of his wit, sense of humor, and eloquence, Twain exclaimed of her, . . . 'What books she could have written!' "[18] He was no doubt alluding to the heritage received from his mother when he quipped: "I have always felt friendly toward Satan. . . . It must be in the blood, for I could not have originated it."[19] Once he planned to write about Satan's history but his Sunday school teacher stopped him.[20]

Frontier therapy included many nonmedical remedies, Sam recalled, and his mother's influence extended to health care. When she had a toothache she went to a "faith doctor" who used this technique, "She

---

[14]MTA 2:13.

[15]Samuel Webster, *Mark Twain, Business Man*, 24.

[16]AMT 26.

[17]SCH 128.

[18]"Jane Clemens," ENC.

[19]AMT 16.

[20]Charles Neider, ed. *The Complete Essays of Mark Twain* (Garden City NY: Doubleday, 1963) 413.

would lay her hand on the patient's jaw and say, 'Believe!' and the cure was prompt."[21] In her old age, his mother continued to rely on faith healers for minor illnesses.[22] During the latter years of his life, as we shall see, Sam also explored religious healing to find help for his family.

Jane Clemens was an active Presbyterian and no book interested her more than the Bible, but she applied its message temperately. Noting that her son Orion was stringently adhering to the Sermon on the Mount by not resisting when reviled, Sam wrote him that "his little Presbyterian mother was not pleased with this too-literal loyalty to the theoretical Bible-teachings which he had acquired through her agency, for . . . [she] was not of the cheek-turning sort." Their mother had asserted, "I know that a person that can turn his cheek is higher and holier than I am . . . but I despise him, too, and wouldn't have him for a doormat."[23] Jane Clemens was like Isaiah, who loathed "holier than thou" individuals.[24] Shunning self-righteousness, she said, "Religion is a jugfull; I hold a dipperfull."[25] Her comment on a theater production in St. Louis demonstrates her broadmindedness. Whereas respectable people generally considered attending a play immoral, she drolly responded, "It was allright, but not the sort of a play that a man should go to."[26]

Sam provided a clue for understanding his mother, and the religious values they shared, by disclosing that she was the prototype for the fictional Aunt Polly, Tom Sawyer's guardian. Each responded in a similar manner "when a meanness or an injustice roused her spirit."[27] Aunt Polly agonized over Tom's contrariness and prayed for him with "measureless love in her words."[28] When her nephew returned home after one of his escapades, she said, "I'm thankful to the good God and Father of us all . . . that's long-suffering and merciful to them that believe on Him and

---

[21]AMT 11.

[22]Doris Webster and Samuel Webster, "Whitewashing Jane Clemens," *Bookman* (July 1925): 532.

[23]SCH 228; Matthew 5:39.

[24]Isaiah 65:5.

[25]SCH 228.

[26]Letter of Samuel Webster, *The Twainian* (November 1948): 4.

[27]AMT 7.

[28]TS 132.

keep His word, though goodness knows I'm unworthy of it."[29] She was often amused at and indulgent in his bad conduct even though she presumed that "the Good Book" says "spare the rod and spile the child."[30] Occasionally she did whack Tom, but she had too much compassion for him to administer strong corporal punishment. He felt that her weeping over him was more painful than being whipped.[31] The family worship that Aunt Polly conducted after breakfast "began with a prayer built from the ground up of solid courses of scriptural quotations, welded together with a thin mortar of originality; and from the summit of this she delivered a grim chapter of the Mosaic Law, as from Sinai."[32]

Growing up in Hannibal

Sam's first weekday school was taught by a teacher from New England in a Hannibal log cabin. One day, he recalled, she read "Ask and it shall be given you" from the Sermon on the Mount and interpreted the verse to mean that earnest prayer would be answered. Sam coveted the slab of gingerbread the baker's daughter brought to school each day and decided to pray for it fervently. Noticing that she was looking the other way when he finished praying, he snatched it and was satisfied, but subsequent attempts failed. "I found that not even the most powerful prayer was competent to lift that gingerbread again," he said, "and I came to the conclusion that if a person remains faithful to his gingerbread and keeps his eye on it he need not trouble himself about your prayers." Perceiving her son's anxiety, Jane Clemens urged Sam to tell her what was bothering him. He confessed that he had attempted to use religion for his own purposes, "I had found out that I was a Christian for revenue only and I could not bear the thought of that, it was so ignoble." His wise mother, explaining that few, however religious, were without ulterior motives, caused him to understand "that if I would continue in that condition I would never be lonesome."[33]

In Hannibal, Sam first attended a Methodist church called "Old Ship

---

[29] TS 152.
[30] TS 19; cf. Proverbs 13:24.
[31] TS 99.
[32] TS 42.
[33] AMT 32-33.

of Zion," so named for the camp meeting song, "The Old Ship of Zion, Hallelujah! She landed many thousands, and she will land as many more." Passengers aboard this Ship included forty "colored" members.[34] He admired his Sunday school teacher but, on hearing the Garden of Eden story, expressed this skepticism: "Mr. Richmond, did you ever actually see a girl who wouldn't cut and run if she spied a snake?"[35]

Sam took advantage of an arrangement the Methodists had made for borrowing books published by the American Sunday School Union. Tickets were given for reciting Bible verses, and an accumulation of tickets could be exchanged for a book loan. According to Sam, he recited the same five verses every Sunday and his satisfied teacher supplied him with more reading material. "They were pretty dreary books," he recalled, "for there was not a bad boy in the entire bookcase."[36] Tickets representing the recitation of two thousand verses could be exchanged for a Bible. Generally it took years to earn this prize, and few children were able to amass enough tickets. However, as MT was to describe in a novel, Tom Sawyer cleverly exchanged gewgaws to obtain tickets that his friends had earned. Presented with the coveted Bible at a special ceremony, Tom was asked to show off his presumed vast knowledge by naming the first two disciples that Jesus appointed. "David and Goliath," he responded.[37]

After two years in the Methodist Church, Sam and his siblings followed their mother to the Presbyterian Church where, on February 18, 1841, she became a Presbyterian "upon profession of faith in Christ."[38] The baptism of the children of members was not recorded in the church records, but Presbyterians, following their understanding of early Christian practice, expected children in a household to be baptized along with their parent(s). Since he later wrote that he was a baptized Presbyterian,[39] he and his siblings were probably baptized in Hannibal. Walter Blair notes that "all the Clemenses except the judge became members of the

---

[34]PH 43.

[35]Oliver Howard and Goldena Howard, *The Mark Twain Book* (Marceline MO: Walsworth, 1985) 77.

[36]AMT 74-75.

[37]TS 52.

[38]Session records 1834–1859, First Presbyterian Church, Hannibal MO (unpublished) 27.

[39]CT1 208.

[Presbyterian] church" and that from about the age of ten Sam attended both the Sunday school in the church basement and listened to sermons on the first floor.[40] After participating in two "religious disorders" in Hannibal, he recalled that "the terms were easier" at the Methodist Sunday school.[41] Sam was aware of the boast of Presbyterians that they distinguish themselves by following the New Testament's admonition to "let all things be done decently and in order."[42]

The Hannibal Presbyterian Church, built in 1839,
was the first church erected in the town.
Sam attended Sunday school and church services there.

Joshua Tucker, the first regular pastor of the Presbyterian church in Hannibal, helped to finish the brick structure on Fourth Street and to install in its steeple a bell he obtained from a wrecked steamboat. His first pulpit platform, consisting of two springy planks resting on sawhorses, reminded him that he needed to be levelfooted as well as levelheaded! Tucker remembered Jane Clemens as "a woman of the

---

[40]HH&T 368.
[41]Outlook (March 1907) 651.
[42]1 Corinthians 14:40.

sunniest temperament, lively, affable, a general favorite, who little dreamed what spurts of fun and frolic would spring from the curly head of the six-year-old boy who answered her laugh with another." He also spoke of Marshall Clemens as "a grave, taciturn man, a foremost citizen in intelligence and wholesome influence."[43]

In 1837 a schism developed among American Presbyterians. The "Old School," which was concentrated in the Southern states, adhered to strict Calvinist theology, with its extreme predestination and total depravity doctrines. It was antirevival, believing that apart from an response by humans, God determined whether they would be saved or damned. The "New School" approved of revivals where converts exercised free choice, and these moderate Calvinists wanted to unite with the liberal Congregationists of New England.[44] Missouri Presbyterians convened in 1841 at Hannibal to form a New School Synod.[45] Tucker's allegiance was with the New School, and this caused a minority of the several hundred members with Old School sympathies to form the Second Presbyterian Church in Hannibal.[46] In 1857, as national sectionalism increased, the New School national leaders could not accept Missouri Presbyterians who continued to support slavery.[47] Consequently, in 1859, the congregation of Hannibal's First Presbyterian Church reverted to the Old School.[48] "The Presbyterian Church in the United States" separated from its parent denomination in 1861 to endorse the Confederate antiabolitionist position. As Sam came of age, he was no doubt exposed to vigorous winds of religious dispute between the more conservative and the more liberal Presbyterians.

Presbyterian shepherds in Hannibal kept close watch over their flock. The 1840s records of the session, the local governing body, show that its elders disciplined members for irregular church attendance, for "profane

---

[43]"Recollections of Joshua Tucker," quoted in Henry Sweets, *The Hannibal Missouri Presbyterian Church* (Hannibal: First Presbyterian Church, 1984) 51.

[44]Winthrop Hudson, *Religion in America* (New York: Scribner's, 1965) 162, 165.

[45]E. H. Gillett, *History of the Presbyterian Church in the United States of America* (Philadelphia: Presbyterian Publication Committee, 1864) 2:541.

[46]Sweets, *The Hannibal Missouri Presbyterian Church*, 5-7.

[47]George Hays, *Presbyterians* (New York: Hill, 1892) 209.

[48]Sweets, *The Hannibal Missouri Presbyterian Church*, 8.

swearing," for "acting in a revengeful manner," and for attending dances. When Sam was thirteen years old the session declared that it was "deeply grieved to witness and to hear of the frequent violations of God's commandment to keep holy the Sabbath day by some who profess to be the children of God." Violations included "hunting and sporting," "riding for pleasure," and steamboat travel. At his sixty-seventh birthday party, MT confessed that he was occasionally a Sabbath desecrater. He said, "We were good Presbyterian boys when the weather was doubtful; when it was fair, we did wander a little from the fold."[49]

Decades after Sam left Hannibal, he recalled being traumatized by the drowning one Sunday of a boy who fell out of the boat on which they were playing. "Being loaded with sin," Clemens deadpanned, "he went to the bottom like an anvil." That night a raging thunderstorm made him think that Heaven was serving this notice on the village boys: unless they repented they would also be punished. For a few days he was determined to express his remorse by carrying out these resolutions:

> I would be punctual at church and Sunday-school; visit the sick; carry baskets of victuals to the poor. . . . I would instruct other boys in right ways, and take the resulting trouncings meekly. I would subsist entirely on tracts; I would invade the rum shop and warn the drunkard.[50]

Still another event that occurred in Sam's youth haunted him. Responding to a tramp's request, he had given him matches for his pipe. Then, after being jailed for drunkenness, the tramp burned to death when a spark ignited his straw bed. For months afterward, Sam suffered from dreams that loaded the whole blame on him. In his autobiography, he offered this analysis:

> I was not responsible for it, for I had meant him no harm but only good, when I let him have the matches; but no matter, mine was a trained Presbyterian conscience and knew but one duty—to hunt and harry its slave upon all pretexts and on all occasions, particularly when there was no sense nor reason in it.[51]

Sam had his full share of youthful misbehavior. He enjoyed telling about the time he bombed his "exasperatingly good" younger brother,

---

[49]MTS 458.
[50]LM 352-53.
[51]AMT 41.

Henry, with a watermelon rind. After careful calculation, he dropped the rind from a second-story window, hollow side down, precisely on Henry's head as he walked under it.[52] Sam thought of himself as the polar opposite of a dumb boy in Hannibal who exuded godliness and proper manners: "This fellow's reproachlessness was a standing reproach to every lad in the village. He was the admiration of all the mothers and the detestation of all their sons."[53]

Speaking of George Washington, Clemens spoofed:

As a boy he gave no promise of the greatness he was one day to achieve. He was ignorant of the commonest accomplishments of youth. He could not even lie. . . . I could lie before I could stand—yet this sort of sprightliness was so common in our family that little notice was taken of it.[54]

From the age of ten, Sam was expected to attend regularly Sunday morning adult services as well as Sunday school. Presbyterians were given this official instruction regarding conduct in public worship, "Let all the people attend with gravity and reverence, . . . abstaining from all whisperings, . . . gazing about, sleeping, smiling, and all other indecent behaviours."[55] He recalled that the Sabbath was a "dreary bore" and that the benediction was "the gladdest moment" of the church service, because it signaled the end of one tiresome feature of the day.[56]

Jane Clemens did not emphasize the punitive aspects of biblical theology and practice. A granddaughter who lived with her for many years never heard her tell of God's stern retribution to sinners.[57] Sam told of the worse discipline that he could remember receiving from her when he was Tom Sawyer's age:

Whenever my conduct was of such exaggerated impropriety that my mother's extemporary punishments were inadequate, she saved the matter up for Sunday and made me go to church Sunday night—which was penalty

---

[52]AMT 92-93.

[53]LM 358.

[54]CT1 205.

[55]*The Constitution of the Presbyterian Church* (Philadelphia: Perkins, 1846) 428.

[56]LE 16.

[57]Webster and Webster, "Whitewashing Jane Clemens," *Bookman* (July 1925): *Bookman* 531.

sometimes bearable, perhaps, but as a rule it was not.[58]

Throughout Sam's teen years, Joseph Bennett was pastor of Hannibal's First Presbyterian Church. Sam may have set the type for this *Hannibal Journal* notice on October 9, 1851, "Rev. Mr. Bennett will preach at 11 a.m. and 7 p.m. on the third anniversary of his ordination." After they met again in 1869, Clemens recalled that he used to attend Sunday school as well as Bennett's church service every Sunday.[59] It is difficult to determine how he felt about churchgoing. In mid-life he told a friend that as a boy he "fear[ed] God and dread[ed] the Sunday school,"[60] but when he visited Hannibal's Presbyterian Church in 1902, he alleged that he had loved attending Sunday school.[61] By that time, the sanctuary—still the current one—had relocated several blocks away, although the steeple still held the steamboat bell he had heard ring out so often.

When Sam grew up, a national movement was underway that had changed the meaning of the term "temperance" from moderation to abstinence. It was especially prominent in frontier communities where hard drinking was a major social problem. Presbyterians joined with Methodists in urging citizens to abstain from substances that could harm the body. Hannibal Presbyterians sponsored a unit of the "Cadets of Temperance" and the name "Samuel L. Clemens" was at the top of a membership roster.[62] He wrote, "I joined the Cadets myself, although they didn't allow a boy to smoke, or drink, or swear, but I thought I never could be truly happy till I wore one of these stunning red scarfs and walked in procession when a distinguished citizen died."[63] He did not long remain faithful to the tobacco pledge, since by the age of fifteen he was addicted to nicotine and would remain so for the rest of his life.[64] He boasted that he kept until he was about twenty-seven years old the pledge he made on the Bible not to drink liquor.[65] Later he judged teetotaling to be counterproductive: "Temperate temperance is best. Intemperate

---

[58]MTA 2:95.
[59]LTR 3:134.
[60]MTHL 128.
[61]MTB 1169.
[62]PH 80, 109.
[63]MTTB 146.
[64]AMT 43.
[65]LTR 1:260; PP 112.

temperance injures the cause of temperance."[66]

The adult Clemens wrote a novel containing autobiographical features of his boyhood in Hannibal. The preface to *Tom Sawyer* states that most of its episodes were real events in which the author and his friends had participated. One indelible impression made on Sam was the worship service at the Hannibal Presbyterian Church. Its comic features later emerged in a fictional form through the *Tom Sawyer* narrator:

> The minister gave out the hymn, and read it through with a relish. . . . His voice began on a medium key and climbed steadily up till it reached a certain point, where it bore with strong emphasis upon the topmost word and then plunged down as if from a springboard: "Shall I be car-ri-ed toe the skies, on flow'ry beds of ease, / Whilst others fight to win the prize, and sail thro' bloody seas?" . . . The minister gave out his text and droned along monotonously through an argument . . . that dealt in limitless fire and brimstone and thinned the predestined elect down to a company so small as to be hardly worth the saving. . . . The minister made a grand and moving picture of the assembling together of the world's hosts at the millennium when the lion and the lamb should lie down together and a little child should lead them. But the pathos, the lesson, the moral of the great spectacle were lost upon the boy; he only thought of the conspicuousness of the principal character before the onlooking nations; his face lit with the thought, and he said to himself that he wished he could be that child, if it was a tame lion.[67]

The unctuous pulpit oratory Sam heard in Hannibal probably contributed to this parody written in 1863:

> If it [these exhortations] prove the means of restoring to health one solitary sufferer among my race, of lifting up once more the fire of hope and joy in his faded eyes, of bringing back to his dead heart again the quick, generous impulses of other days, I shall be amply rewarded for my labor; my soul will be permeated with the sacred delight a Christian feels when he has done a good, unselfish deed.[68]

At the same time, *Tom Sawyer* also reveals the positive aspects of growing up in a supportive congregation. The funeral for boys who were presumed to be dead illustrates its importance in times of grief. There is

---

[66]MTN 310.
[67]TS 54-57.
[68]CT1 37.

genuine sorrow followed by joy over the return of prodigals who, like their Gospel counterpart were "dead and . . . alive again."[69] "Old Hundred swelled up with a triumphant burst" as the Presbyterians sang "Praise God from whom all blessings flow."[70] Clemens no doubt treasured the ties made in that Presbyterian church when he returned to Hannibal years later for the funeral of his mother. Afterward her body was buried alongside the remains of her husband and son Henry in the local Mount Olivet Cemetery.[71]

Clemens's remembrance of a typical pastoral prayer also reveals the value of being part of a religious community. The "good, generous prayer" contained these elements: civic—for government officials and for those suffering under despotism; ecumenical—"for other churches of the village" and for "the heathen in the far islands"; congregational—for nurture of the children and for fruitfulness of the adults; and petitions for those in dangerous work and those who have not acted on gospel imperatives. The narrator of *Tom Sawyer* interjects, "The boy whose history this book relates did not enjoy the prayer, he only endured it."[72] Nevertheless, the experience of common prayer may have enabled the author to empathize with a broad range of peoples.

On his last visit to Hannibal, Clemens was warmly received at the Presbyterian church and participated in the Memorial Day program. Later that day, speaking to those graduating from the high school, he sentimentalized:

> Many and many a time in my boyhood days . . . I desired earnestly to stand in that Presbyterian pulpit and give instructions—but I was never asked until today. My ambition of two generations ago has been satisfied at last! . . . I noticed at the Presbyterian Church this afternoon that the style of oratory has changed. In my day the speakers made more noise. Their oratory was bombastic, full of gesticulation, pounding the pulpit, and all sorts of exterior

---

[69]Luke 15:32.

[70]TS 147. This "Long Meter Doxology" is called "Old Hundredth" because the tune (attributed to Louis Bourgeois) to which it is most-often sung appeared with William Kethe's metrical form of Psalm 100 in the *Four Score and Seven Psalms of David* (Geneva, 1561), then in later editions of the *Genevan Psalter*. (In the *Genevan Psalter* of 1551 the tune was used for Psalm 134.)

[71]Sweets 19.

[72]TS 56.

suggestions of sense, combined with the utter absence of that quality.[73]

Long after leaving Missouri, memories of his boyhood church returned when he attended a church in Paris, Illinois:

> There was the high pulpit, with the red plush pillow for the Bible. . . . There were the stiff pews; the black velvet contribution-purses attached to long poles; . . . the tall windows and Venetian blinds; . . . the gallery, with . . . six boys scattered through it, with secret spit-ball designs on the bald-headed man dozing below. . . . The choir hurled its soul into a "voluntary"—one of those things where the melodeon pumps, and strains, and groans, and wails a bit, and then the soprano pipes a reedy solo, the alto drops in a little after, then the bass bursts in, then the pealing tenor—then a wild chase, one trampling on the heels of the other—then a grand discordant confusion that sets one's teeth on edge—and finally a triumphant "Oh, praise the L-o-r-d!" in a unison of unutterable anguish—and the crime is consummated. It was Herod's slaughter of the babes set to music. Then there was a hymn. It was read . . . with strong emphasis and falling inflection . . . thus: "Come, thou fount. Of every blessing. / Tune my heart. To sing thy praise." . . . Presently he gave out another hymn, beginning, "O for a sweet, inspiring ray." And it was old times over again.[74]

The above parody illustrates Sam's keen interest in religious music. With the exception of the Bible, the Presbyterian *Psalms and Hymns* was probably the book that most influenced him as a boy.[75] Selections from the Psalms, the hymnbook of the ancient Hebrews, was central to the official collection. Over the centuries the Presbyterian favorite has been the paraphrase of Psalm 100 by William Kethe, a poet who lived in Calvin's Geneva. Originally it was sung with such a "sprightly rhythm" that Queen Elizabeth scornfully called it one of the "Geneva jiggs."[76] The spirit of the Psalter is expressed in the opening stanza:

> All people that on earth do dwell,
> Sing to the Lord with cheerful voice;
> Him serve with mirth, His praise forth tell,

---

[73]MTS 432.

[74]LTR 4:528.

[75]*Psalms and Hymns Adapted to Social, Private, and Public Worship in the Presbyterian Church in the United States of America* (Philadelphia: Presbyterian Board of Publication, 1843).

[76]Albert Bailey, *The Gospel in Hymns* (New York: Scribner's, 1950) 17.

Come ye before Him and rejoice.

The Presbyterian hymnal that Sam used included the three hymns referred to above—"Oh for a Sweet, Inspiring Ray," "Come, Thou Fount of Every Blessing," and "Am I a Soldier of the Cross." "All Hail the Power of Jesus' Name" was also in that collection and Clemens later urged its use—to the tune "Coronation"—for shipboard devotions.[77] The hymnbook included other lyrics that he appreciated. Some of his lifelong religious sentiments are expressed in these Isaac Watts classics: "I Sing the Mighty Power of God," a lyrical expression of the opening chapter of the Bible, and "Our God Our Help," a metrical paraphrase of the ninetieth psalm. Clemens writes that "Watts's Hymns," which was first published in 1707, along with a collection of church music, were among the few things that he and his comrades took with them when they went prospecting in Nevada.[78]

Included in the *Psalms and Hymns* was the "Westminster Shorter Catechism," which provided for Presbyterian children and adults the basic teachings of Calvinism. In 1898, Clemens referred to himself as a thoughtful Presbyterian and acknowledged that Catechism as the doctrine of his denomination.[79] Baptized children were expected to learn it by heart,[80] and it provided much of the theological agenda to which he responded both positively and negatively for the rest of his life.

The first and foremost Catechism statement is that "man's chief end is to glorify God and to enjoy him forever." Directions for attaining those two purposes, the Catechism continues, are contained in the Bible. God is then described as a nonphysical Spirit with these attributes: "infinite, eternal, and unchangeable in his being, wisdom, power, holiness, justice, goodness, and truth." According to the Catechism, God's good creation is governed by Providence, which preserves the natural order, and by humans, who are made in the divine image. The first humans violated their freedom by disobeying their Creator, corrupting their own nature and that of their posterity. Losing their close relationship with God, the Catechism continues, they became "liable to all miseries in this life" and

---

[77]IA 45.
[78]LMT 1:147.
[79]WM 235.
[80]*The Constitution of the Presbyterian Church*, 439.

"to the pains of hell forever." However, God has graciously saved some through the Son of God who became human "in the womb of the Virgin Mary." The Catechism's description of the work of Christ is followed by an explanation of the Ten Commandments, the sacraments, and the Lord's Prayer. To emphasize the Catechism teaching about the Fourth Commandment, the hymnbook also included a worship directory that placed first "the sanctification of the Lord's Day." One way to keep that day holy is to abstain "from those recreations which may be lawful on other days."

Protestants in the Calvinist tradition were devoted to raising the educational level of the communities in which they lived. They founded Harvard, Yale, Princeton, and Brown, along with hundreds of lesser known institutions, long before state supported educational institutions arose. Marion College, the first to be charted in Missouri, was established by Presbyterians near Hannibal in 1831. Its president was David Nelson, a physician, clergyman, and *Calvinist Magazine* editor. He may have been the widest read Missourian, for he claimed he had even studied all of Voltaire's writings.[81] To serve on his faculty, he attracted some Presbyterian scholars from the Northeast and gathered from there a large amount of funding. One distinguished member of the Marion College faculty was Dr. Ezra Ely, who had come from Philadelphia to become professor of Theology and Bible. Jane Clemens attended a camp meeting near Hannibal soon after moving to the town and became a Presbyterian on hearing Ely preach there.[82] Although the college had a program of academic merit, it only lasted one decade because of the faculty's abolitionist sympathies.[83]

In 1832, President Nelson, "a thrilling and powerful preacher," conducted a several-day outdoor evangelistic meeting in Hannibal and afterward organized the converts to Presbyterianism into a congregation, which met at the schoolhouse in the town square. Nelson was highly controversial because he condemned slavery and refused communion to

---

[81]David Nelson, *The Cause and Cure of Infidelity* (New York: American Tract, 1841) 270.

[82]Curtis Dahl, "Mark Twain and Ben Ely," *Missouri Historical Review* (July 1972): 552, 557, 559-60.

[83]Perry McCandless, *A History of Missouri* (Columbia: University of Missouri Press, 1972) 2:199; Holcombe, *History of Marion County*, 203.

slaveholders. In 1836 he was shot at while preaching that slaves should be emancipated, resulting in his fleeing to Illinois. Near Quincy he established a theological school that served as a depot on the underground railroad for conveying fugitives from Missouri to freedom.[84]

An elementary school was opened in the basement of Hannibal's First Presbyterian Church by Mary Ann Newcomb, who had emigrated from New York and had gotten to know the Clemens family when she taught in Florida, Missouri.[85] In Hannibal, the Clemenses occasionally provided compensation by boarding her. Newcomb was a teacher who influenced Sam, and she became the prototype for the severe Miss Watson in *Huckleberry Finn* and for Mrs. Bangs in his unfinished "Autobiography of a Damned Fool." In the latter writing he compared her to vinegar, and gave this description:

> She had ringlets, and a long sharp nose, and thin, colorless lips, and you could not tell her breast from her back if she had her head up a stove-pipe hole looking for something in the attic. . . . She was a Calvinist and devotedly pious, but otherwise she was a most disagreeable woman.[86]

Beside the elementary school, Presbyterian churches were often used for more advanced weekday educational programs, with a clergyman providing the instruction. Rev. Daniel Emerson was headmaster of the English and Classical School that was housed in the First Presbyterian Church.[87] At the Second Presbyterian Church, Rev. Thomas Lea established in 1848 a school for young women that offered a wide range of subjects in the humanities and sciences.[88] Occasionally the Hannibal Presbyterians sponsored artistic events, such as amateur concerts featuring stringed instruments.[89] Sam's last teacher was Scotsman John Dawson, who opened a school in Hannibal for young ladies and a few boys of

---

[84]William Sprague, *Annual of the American Pulpit* (New York: Carter, 1859) 4:685; "Nelson, David," in *Dictionary of American Biography*, ed. Dumas Malone (New York: Scribner, 1934); Andrew Murray, *Presbyterians and the Negro* (Philadelphia: Presbyterian Historical Society, 1966) 95.

[85]HH&T 361; CT1 950.

[86]S&B 140, 163.

[87]MTMW 8.

[88](Hannibal) *Journal*, 3 August 1848.

[89]SCH 193.

"good morals."[90] The school lasted for two years until Dawson joined the gold rush to California in 1849.[91]

The availability of a variety of secular as well as religious literature in Hannibal indicates that Sam did not come of age in an intellectual backwater. The several thousand citizens living there had local newspapers, bookstores, and a public library. Marshall Clemens became the first president of that library in 1844, and within the next decade it acquired 425 books. The titles of those books are unknown, but a private library of a Missouri physician at that time suggests what might have been found on its shelves. Other than his medical texts, there were more books on religion than on any other subject. These included Philips's *Life and Times of John Bunyan*, Alexander and Archibald's *Christian Evidences*, Chalmers's *A Call to the Unconverted*, Nevin's *Summary of Bible Antiquities*, Paley's *Natural Theology*, Doddridge's *Rise and Progress of Religion*, and Tooke's *Pantheon of Heathen Gods*. John Johnson, a Clemens relation and a Baptist minister who lived near Hannibal, had more than a thousand volumes covering a wide range of knowledge. Sam frequently visited that library, the largest in the region.[92]

When Clemens wrote about the Grangerfords in *Huckleberry Finn*, he displayed memories of Presbyterian homes he had known in his childhood. The *Presbyterian Observer* journal reinforced the theme of "preforeordestination" ("predestination" conflated with "foreordination") preached in the church. In addition to a big illustrated family Bible, the Grangerfords owned *Pilgrim's Progress*, a hymnal, a poetry book, a medical text, and an anthology of political speeches.[93]

In contrast to Tom Sawyer, school was more to Sam's liking. "I used to get the medal for good spelling, every week," he told Missouri's Governor David Francis.[94] His memory of dropping out of school as soon as his father died is faulty, for the 1850 census lists him in school at

---

[90]John Gerber, *Mark Twain* (New York: Twayne, 1988) 3.

[91]Kent Rasmussen, *Mark Twain A to Z* (New York: Oxford University Press, 1995) 106.

[92]Minnie Brashear, *Mark Twain, Son of Missouri* (Chapel Hill: University of North Carolina Press, 1934) 200, 205; "John Johnson," ENC.

[93]HF 137, 139, 147.

[94]MTL 756.

fourteen.[95] While still a student he probably worked part-time in a print shop. In school, McGuffey's texts were the staple of the curriculum, and since those readers contained many Bible stories, Sam studied scriptures at both Sunday and weekday schools. Moreover, he tells us that his teacher "always opened school with prayer and a chapter from the New Testament; also she explained the chapter with a brief talk."[96] A Hannibal newspaper published at that time urged children to study the Bible as life's "great textbook and wisdom's inexhaustible mine."[97]

From childhood onward, Sam had a voracious appetite for books. The first demanding volume he absorbed was the Bible, and he read it through within a decade of when he became literate. As an adult he bragged about his lifelong sensitivity to God's word and joked that he complained as an infant about being named after a biblical boy who did not quickly respond to the Lord's call.[98] Judging from his treatment of many biblical passages in his later writings, his retention of this childhood reading was great. Early on he also read other classics by authors such as Cervantes, Voltaire, and Shakespeare, but for him they lacked the charm of the Bible.

In 1902, at the Hannibal High School graduation, he told of the poetry that he had memorized as a youth, recalling from Lord Byron's "Destruction of Sennacherib" a stanza about the invasion of the Israelites' ruthless enemy and their defeat by the Lord:

The Assyrian came down like the wolf on the fold,
And his cohorts were gleaming in purple and gold;
And the sheen of their spears was like stars in the sea,
When the blue wave rolls nightly on deep Galilee.[99]

One of Sam's childhood exposures to the Bible conditioned him to associate it with divine judgment and grotesque death. After a man was shot at noon on the main street of Hannibal, "some thoughtful idiot" placed an opened family Bible on the dying person's chest, its weight adding torture to his labored breathings. "In my nightmares," Clemens

---

[95]SCH 131.
[96]AMT 32.
[97](Hannibal) *Journal*, 14 July 1853.
[98]CT1 405; 1 Samuel 3:4-11.
[99]MTS 433; 2 Kings 19:32-37.

recalled, "I gasped and struggled for breath under the crush of that vast book for many a night."[100]

By reading through the entire Bible, Sam became aware of its violent and obscene parts. In his old age he encouraged adults to do the same, "Will you examine the Deity's morals . . . and remember that in the Sunday school the little children are urged to . . . try to be as like him as they can?" He then told reading as a boy of the Israelites slaying all the male Midianites "as the Lord commanded Moses."[101] Not finding in the Torah passage a reason for the genocide, Sam searched other historical books of the King James Version and came up with this explanation:

> Some Midianite had been pissing against the wall. I am sure of it, for that was an impropriety which the Source of all Etiquette never could stand. A person could piss against a tree, he could piss on his mother, he could piss on his own breeches, and get off, but he must not piss against the wall—that would be going quite too far. . . . Take the case of Jeroboam. "I will cut off from Jeroboam him that pisseth against the wall." [1 Kings 14:10] . . . The same with the house of Baasha: everybody was exterminated, kinsfolks, friends, and all, leaving "not one that pisseth against a wall" [that is, not one male: 1 Kings 16:11]. . . . Protestant parents still keep the Bible handy in the house, so that the children can study it; and one of the first things the little boys and girls learn is to be righteous and holy and not piss against the wall. . . . The Bible has this advantage over all other books that teach refinement and good manners: that it goes to the child: it goes to the mind at its most impressible and receptive age—the others have to wait.[102]

Slavery and the Bible were inextricably intertwined in Hannibal, where about one-quarter of the population was enslaved. Clemens remembered, "The local pulpit taught us that God approved it, that it was a holy thing, and that the doubter need only look in the Bible if he wished to settle his mind—and then the texts were read aloud to us to make the matter sure."[103] The compelling texts for Southern Christians were from the New Testament: "Servants, obey in all things your masters," and "Let as many servants as are under the yoke count their own masters worthy

---

[100]AMT 41.
[101]Numbers 31:7.
[102]LE 48-51.
[103]AMT 6.

of all honour."[104] Sam's parents, who came from slaveholding families, accepted the institution without question. There was usually a slave or two in their household while he was growing up, and several hundred in the community.

Sam's awareness of the awfulness of slavery, America's great open sore, began early. He recalled his father striking the household slave boy for "trifling little blunders."[105] Sam lived on the edge of a border slave state, for Hannibal was within swimming distance of the free state of Illinois. Notices on runaway slaves appeared frequently in the local newspaper. When Sam was five years old, his father was a member of the jury that sent three students from Nelson's Mission Institute to twelve years imprisonment for their unsuccessful attempt to free some Missouri slaves. Before their arrest, a mob wanted to lynch the "nigger-stealers . . . who will pray for you at evening and steal your negro at midnight."[106] At that same time, Sam's father sold a slave girl to pay his debts, causing her mother to shriek in anguish as a steamboat took her off to the Deep South.[107] Slaves knew that plantation labor and sexual conditions were harsher there than in Missouri, so being "sold down the river" was among the worst things they could imagine.

Clemens remembered an episode involving him, his mother, and their slave boy. Irritated by the slave's incessant singing and whistling, he asked his mother to make him shut up. This request brought tears to her eyes as she explained that he was trying to sing away his sadness over having been torn away from his mother in another state. About sixty years later, he said that the incident "must have meant a good deal to me or it would not have stayed in my memory, clear and sharp, vivid and shadowless, all these slow-drifting years."[108] Significantly, his earliest memory of his mother pertains to her compassion for a motherless child a long way from home. He was so close to her that he could identify with the boy's homesickness.

Sam's religious sensitivity, like that of his mother, was much affected

---

[104]Colossians 3:22; 1 Timothy 6:1.

[105]FE 252; MTB 1040.

[106]Edwin McReynolds, *Missouri* (Norman: University of Oklahoma Press, 1962) 169.

[107]MTB 41.

[108]AMT 6-7.

by the slave culture in which they lived. When he was ten years old, he witnessed a slave being hit in the head with a lump of iron ore "for merely doing something awkwardly," and then dying an hour later.[109] The slaveowner could have been prosecuted by an 1807 Missouri statute that prohibited the mistreatment of slaves. Slaves in that state filed hundreds of cases, and were granted court-appointed attorneys. Surprisingly, "dozens won their cases, persuading juries of white men to set them free."[110] The same year that Sam saw a slave murdered with impunity, Dred Scott was freed by the St. Louis court, but subsequently the controversial verdict was reversed by higher courts. The controversial decision by the U.S. Supreme Court that Scott was a nonperson with no civil rights moved the nation closer to civil war.

For several teenage years Sam learned the printing trade from Joseph Ament in Hannibal. While at Ament's print shop Clemens gained personal knowledge of the slave culture by eating with slaves, hearing their dialect, and sleeping—as they did—on a pallet on the floor.[111] Although Sam did not at that time express disdain for slavery, there were disagreements in his family over the issue. Orion, his older brother, probably influenced by the antislavery Presbyterian clergy in Marion County in the 1840s, was an abolitionist from an early age and campaigned to get Lincoln elected.

Religious Varieties

Although Sam's religious associations in Missouri were mainly with Presbyterians, he was aware of some other Christian denominations in Missouri. Stirring there was a debate on how many would be admitted to Heaven. The *Hannibal Journal* reported on Universalist Rev. E. Manford of St. Louis, who argued against Calvinist predestination and maintained that the Bible teaches the "final holiness and happiness of all mankind" rather than the endless punishment of those "who die in disobedience to the Gospel."[112] Sam was probably attracted to the broad outlook on religion of John Quarles, his favorite uncle. Thomas Bodine, who was

---

[109]FE 352.

[110]*Richmond Times-Dispatch*, 22 March 2003, A2.

[111]Terrell Dampsey's editorial, (Hannibal) *Courier Post*, 15 November 2001.

[112](Hannibal) *Journal*, 15 July 1852.

acquainted with people who knew Quarles, has written this about him:

> The question of human destiny, the why, the whence, the whither, was always with him. Unable to reconcile it with the accepted dogmas of his people, and driven by the promptings of a vigorous mind and kindly heart, he became a "Universalist."[113]

The Campbellites, later called "Disciples of Christ," interested both Sam and his father. Hannibal historian Ira Holcombe records that Marshall Clemens "never joined any church, though he inclined to the Campbellites."[114] Its founder was Rev. Alexander Campbell, who had once been a Scottish Presbyterian. Along the western frontier, he championed this motto, "Where the Scriptures speak, we speak; where the Scriptures are silent, we are silent." His plea to reject narrow creeds and restore the unity of the New Testament church had great appeal, and the movement flourished. Sam knew Barton Stone, a famous Campbellite preacher. Once a Presbyterian, Stone had been alienated by the predestination doctrine that only "God's elect" would be saved. He was the grandfather of Will Bowen, Sam's closest friend in Hannibal, and lived in the Bowen home in his old age. When Stone surprised the boys as they were playing cards, the forbidden cards were hidden in his "baptizing robe." Clemens alleged that several aces floated out the next time the minister immersed converts in the river![115]

Campbell visited Hannibal when Sam was eleven years old, coming from Bethany College in western Virginia where he was president. Clemens remembered the "prodigious excitement" of the crowd when this celebrity preached in the public square. He noted, "That was the first time in my life that I had realized what a mighty population this planet contains when you get them all together."[116] Campbell's hearers wanted to preserve his spoken words, so an arrangement to publish his sermon was made at the print shop where Sam worked. Campbell had reproved Wales McCormick, Sam's fellow printer, for exclaiming "Great God!" ("Great Scott!" was the limit of acceptable speech, Campbell admonished.) Consequently, in setting up the type, McCormick and Sam

---

[113]Thomas Bodine, (Kansas City) *Star*, 9 May 1912.
[114]Holcombe, *History of Marion County*, 915.
[115]HH&T 32, 346; SCH 88-89.
[116]AMT 90.

replaced "Great God" with "Great Scott" in the text and also abbreviated "Jesus Christ" as "J.C." to get all the words on a crowded page. Noticing these modifications in the page proofs, Campbell stomped into the shop and insisted that Christians should always enlarge, not diminish the Savior's name. Recalling that swearers often provide enlargements in their speech, the mischievous printers, if Sam can be believed, printed the holy name as "Jesus H. Christ."[117]

Clemens remembered that during his boyhood years there was only one "unbeliever" in Hannibal, a young lawyer from Kentucky. Concerning the villagers reaction to that "fascinating cuss," he wrote:

> They expected a judgment to fall upon him at any moment. . . . He was very profane, and blasphemous. He was vain of being prayed for in the revivals; vain of being singled out for this honor by every new revivalist. . . . The young ladies were ambitious to convert him.[118]

The Campbellites, along with other Protestants living in the sparsely settled Marion County, participated in camp-meeting revivals that were held in a woods clearing several miles from Hannibal. Riding to that place in their wagons and setting up tents in order to sing and hear preaching was the principal summer outing for many.[119] Marie Windell describes those Missouri campers, "Many anticipated a profound conversion and religious experience, some came only to jest, swear, or be amused by the emotional excesses for which the meetings were known; others came to see the condition and prospects of the matrimonial market."[120] Jane Clemens allegedly forbade Sam from attending those gatherings because of the "camp-meetin' babies" that were conceived there.[121] But when Orion Clemens was editor of a Hannibal newspaper, he may have sent his brother to report on a week-long summer meeting that had a large attendance. The published report described the retreat as refreshing because it provided a break from ordinary activity and the

---

[117]N&J 3:305; AMT 91.

[118]HH&T 35.

[119]Dahl, "Mark Twain and Ben Ely," 557.

[120]Marie Windell, "The Camp Meeting in Missouri," *Missouri Historical Review* (April 1943): 256.

[121]Thomas Beer, *The Mauve Decade* (New York: Knopf, 1926) 122.

fellowship of like-minded persons.[122] As a boy, Sam noted in telegraphic style: "Campbellite revival. All converted but me. All sinners again in a week."[123]

The camp meeting account in *Huckleberry Finn* grew out of those early experiences. A passage that he cut from a draft of that novel describes a revivalist's style:

> He would lay the Bible down and weave about the platform, and work back to the Bible again, . . . bang with his fist and shout "Here it is! the rock of salvation-ah!" And so he went on a-raging, and the people groaning and crying, and jumping up and hugging one another, and Amens was popping off everywheres. Every little while he would preach right at people that he saw was stirred up: . . . "The sperrit's a workin' in you brother—don't shake him off-ah! Now is the accepted time-ah! (A-a-MEN!] The devil's holt is a weakenin' on you, sister—shake him loose. . . . Hell's a-burning, the kingdom's a-coming-ah![124]

In the novel, many Pokeville folks respond by coming to "the mourners' bench" and writhing wildly on the ground. A visiting con man gives a phony testimony of repentance and persuades the congregation to finance his efforts to convert others. After taking up a collection and embracing the pretty girls, he leaves town with much money and a stolen jug of whiskey.[125]

In "The New Wildcat Religion," one of Sam's early essays, he described the frenzied activity associated with camp meetings and revivals while acknowledging that he leaned strongly toward one of "the old legitimate regular stock religions."[126] Relevant to this is a semiserious comment he made in 1889, "I believed God was a Presbyterian."[127] A conundrum he invented also says something about his view of Protestants who were antiestablishment: "Question: If a congress of Presbyterians is a Presbytery, what is a congress of dissenters? Answer: A Dysentery."[128] Offering a mild satire on his levelheaded religion, he said:

---

[122](Hannibal) *Journal*, 4 September 1851.
[123]MTMF 88.
[124]HF 487.
[125]HF 171-74.
[126]WG 133.
[127]N&J 3:413.
[128]MTP note to Twichell, 30 December 1875.

He also noted that "their purpose was to get free—but the U.S. enclosed them. Morally we have not the same right to boss them which we have in other territories."[2]

MT's comments on the Mormons differed from the usual contempt expressed by non-Mormons who visited Utah. For example, George Pine compared Salt Lake City to ancient Sodom that lay alongside another salt lake and was destroyed by fire and brimstone. The "insufferable licentiousness" of polygamy, he declared, would be the cause of Mormon punishment.[3] By contrast, MT credited Brigham Young with "Christian charity" for marrying generally poor and unattractive women. To make his point by exaggeration, he described Young's difficulty in coping with the complaints of some twenty wives and their fifty children whenever he gave something to one without giving equally to all seventy.[4] Richard Cracroft, a devout Mormon scholar, finds "delightful" MT's treatment of Young and the church he led.[5]

MT and Orion examined the foundation of "the prodigious temple"— begun in 1853 and completed forty years later—in Salt Lake City and conversed with Heber Kimball, the apostle who was second to Young in the Mormon hierarchy. Kimball believed that the Civil War would destroy the United States and the Mormons would then "take charge of the country."[6] Joining with several other "Gentiles" (as non-Mormons were called there), the Clemens brothers paid "a state visit" to Young's residence, the "Lion House."[7] While there, MT unsuccessfully attempted to "draw him out" on some controversial political issues.[8] Impressed by Young's power, MT called him "an absolute monarch."[9] For example, he wrote, Young had ordered some Mormons, who had disregarded signed contracts and failed to erect telegraph poles when they found they were

---

[2]N&J 3:42.

[3]George Pine, *Beyond the West* (Utica NY, 1870) 315, 328.

[4]RI 97-103.

[5]Richard Cracroft, "The Gentle Blasphemer," *Brigham Young University Studies* (Winter 1971): 131.

[6]Orion's letter to the *Missouri Democrat*, 19 August 1861.

[7]Young's appointment book verifies that this visit took place. See Leonard Arrington, *Brigham Young* (Urbana: University of Illinois Press, 1992) 325.

[8]RI 92-93.

[9]RI 549.

not making money, to fulfill their commitment, and they promptly complied.[10]

As regards the *Book of Mormon*, MT was less impressed: "It is chloroform in print. If Joseph Smith composed this book, the act was a miracle—keeping awake while he did it was, at any rate."[11] After perusing it, MT frankly concluded that "the Mormon Bible is rather stupid and tiresome to read, but there is nothing vicious in its teachings."[12] "Its code of morals is unobjectionable," he judged, since it originated in the New Testament. He listed honesty, industriousness, healthiness, and neatness as Mormon virtues. Even so, he expressed criticisms. He quoted passages from the Mormon scriptures to show how the grandeur of Jesus' teaching became tedious to read and hard to comprehend. He noted a "mongrel" combination of King James English and modern English as well as plagiarism of certain Bible passages. This anachronism is cited from the *Book of Mormon*: a compass on an ancient ship. Also, he was surprised to find that it specifically prohibited polygamy and that the harems of Israel's most famous kings were called an abomination.[13]

On reaching Carson City, the territorial capital of Nevada, MT wrote his sister-in-law about aspects of his personal life that had moral significance. Mollie was such a prim Presbyterian that he enjoyed shocking her. He explained why, at the age of twenty-six, he had delayed searching for a wife:

> I never will marry until I can afford to have servants enough to leave my wife in the position for which I design her, viz.—as a companion. I don't want to sleep with a threefold Being who is cook, chambermaid, and washerwoman all in one. I don't mind sleeping with female servants as long as I am a bachelor—by no means—but after I marry, that sort of thing will be "played out," you know.[14]

MT's conscience was apparently not disturbed by contemplating fornication. Servants were easily hired for sex and prostitutes were available

---

[10]RI 94-96.
[11]RI 107.
[12]RI 115.
[13]RI 107-15; Jacob 2:27.
[14]LTR 1:145.

in the places where he lodged. Louis Budd's description of MT's virility during his bachelor years has removed previous assumptions that he was a virgin until he married.[15] Late in life, he noted: "The course of free love never runs smooth. I suppose we have all tried it."[16]

In Carson City he attended the newly formed Presbyterian church where Rev. A. F. White was pastor. That "whinny, nasal, Whangdoodle preacher" was so melancholy, MT confided, that after listening to him for an hour he had to wait for the beans he had for Sunday dinner to toot before he felt cheerful again.[17] White also served as the head of Nevada's public schools, and his incompetence, MT alleged, prompted him to place this "For Sale or Rent" advertisement in a New York journal:

> One Superintendent of Public Instruction—good as new. Understands all the different systems of teachings, and does not approve of them. It is his laudable boast that he is a self-made man. It has been said of him by his admirers that God Almighty never made such a man. It is probably so. He is the soul of honor, and is willing to take greenbacks at par. No objection to making himself useful; can preach if required.[18]

MT became associated with the Carson City Presbyterians when the congregation was meeting in the courtroom, which was over the jail. He found the arrangement appropriate "for they save men eternally in the second story of the new court house, and damn them for life in the first."[19] An intoxicated Irishman came to a worship service on the assumption that it was a meeting of the Union League, which also assembled in the courtroom. The congregation became so tickled at the Irishman's strong language that they could hardly contain themselves. MT commented that the Presbyterians came to pray and remained to laugh.[20]

Orion, who had become an elder and treasurer of the Presbyterian church in Carson City, enlisted his brother's assistance in fundraising.

---

[15]Louis Budd, "Mark Twain Plays the Bachelor," *Western Humanities Review* (Spring 1957): 157-67.

[16]MTN 392.

[17]LTR 1:171.

[18]Henry Nash Smith, ed. *Mark Twain of the Enterprise* (Berkeley: University of California Press, 1957) 125.

[19]ET 222.

[20]ET 286-87.

After MT had been elected "governor" of a mock government organized by journalists, the church trustees requested him to repeat his entertaining state-of-the-territory speech so they could charge admission. In accepting the invitation, he stated, "Although I am not a very dusty christian myself, I take an absorbing interest in religious affairs, and would willingly inflict my annual message upon the church itself if it might derive benefit thereby."[21] The "dusty" adjective refers to trudging dutifully like a soldier. The large ticket sale from his first public lecture in 1864 hastened the completion of an edifice that for two years had been in skeleton form.

To raise funds to complete this Carson City Presbyterian Church, still in use, MT lectured for the first time to an audience that paid admission.

Charles Garrison finds it noteworthy that MT maintained church ties during his years in Nevada, even though it "was probably the most

---

[21]LTR 1:272.

secular place in America during the mid-nineteenth century."[22] MT claimed that he tried to recruit a territorial assemblyman for membership in the congregation. The question he raised regarding that "old fossil" is studded with biblical allusions, "Why will a man, when he gets to be a thousand years old, go on hanging around the women, and taking chances on fire and brimstone, instead of joining the church and endeavoring, with humble spirit and contrite heart, to ring in at the eleventh hour, like the thief on the cross?"[23]

In Carson City, MT began his lifelong protest against exploitive morticians. He recommended that a municipal graveyard be established for low-cost burials "from which a man can set out for Paradise or perdition just as respectably as he can from the undertaker's private grounds."[24] At a later time he told about the widow of an army private who had been solicited by an undertaker to have her husband's body embalmed and returned to her. Embalming was a new procedure in America and she had contracted without knowing what it would cost. On receiving the enormous bill, the poor widow wondered if those who "stuffed" her husband thought she was going to start a museum.[25]

MT was fond of at least one minister in Nevada—Franklin Rising, whom he got to know during their years together at Virginia City. Both arrived there in 1862 and were about the same age. (Rising had just graduated from General Theological Seminary in New York City.[26]) MT had gone to that mile-high location of the richest silver deposit ever found to work as a reporter for the *Territorial Enterprise*. While he was living there, he wrote this tribute, "Mr. Rising is our Episcopal minister and has done as much as any man among us to redeem this community from its pristine state of semibarbarism."[27]

---

[22]Charles Garrison, "The Comstock of Mark Twain," *Nevada Historical Society Quarterly* (Fall 1995): 199.

[23]Smith, *Mark Twain of the Enterprise*, 93; Genesis 19:24; Psalm 51:17; Matthew 20:6; Luke 23:39-43.

[24]Smith, *Mark Twain of the Enterprise*, 162.

[25]CT1 407.

[26]Andrew Muir, "Notes on Twain and Rising," *California Historical Society Quarterly* (December 1955): 317.

[27]WG 63.

There is a conversion story pertaining to Rising in *Roughing It* that may have a factual basis. At the death of the operator of a sumptuous saloon in Virginia City, his friends decided he should have a classy funeral. Scotty Briggs, his gambling pal, went to make arrangements with "a fragile, gentle, spiritual new fledgling from an Eastern theological seminary." Having little education or Christian understanding, Briggs asked, "Are you the duck that runs the gospel-mill next door?" "I am the shepherd in charge of the flock," Rising replied.[28] Eventually the two learned to comprehend and appreciate each other. Briggs became MT's kind of Christian, "Making him one did not warp his generosity or diminish his courage; on the contrary it gave intelligent direction to the one and a broader field to the other." When he became a Sunday school teacher, his students had "a consuming interest" because he told Bible stories in language they understood.[29]

Rising happened to enter the *Enterprise* office one evening as MT was cussing out his fellow employees. "I know it's wicked to talk like this," MT said, "but if you had a candle, Mr. Rising, and those thieves should carry it off every night, I know that you would say . . . Goddamn their impenitent souls." Rising admitted that he might, but he would rather try to say, "Forgive them, Father, they know not what they do." MT recanted: "If you put it on the ground that they are just fools, that alters the case, as I am one of that class myself. Come in and we'll try to forgive them and forget about it."[30] He later said of Rising: "He and I were fast friends. I used to try to teach him how he ought to preach in order to get at the better natures of the rough population about him."[31]

§ § §

In 1864, MT left Nevada for California after getting into trouble for poking fun at the owner of a rival newspaper. In mock biblical language, he likened the comforts he found in San Francisco to those prepared for the weary Christian in Paradise: "To a Christian who has toiled months and months in Washoe [Nevada] . . . and whose soul is caked with a

---

[28]RI 309-10.
[29]RI 317.
[30]MTB 215; Luke 23:34.
[31]LMT 2:333-34.

cement of alkali dust— . . . unto such a Christian, verily the Occidental Hotel is Heaven on the half shell."[32] When his pious sister-in-law voiced suspicion that he had become an apostate after his move, he replied, with some irritation: "Well Mollie I do go to church. How's that?"[33]

 While he was in San Francisco, he went occasionally to the Calvary Presbyterian Church, where Dr. Charles Wadsworth was pastor. He humorously blamed his irregular attendance on Wadsworth's able preaching, "I never could get a pew, and therefore had to sit in the gallery among the sinners." Using the military term "brevet"—the bestowing of an award without an accompanying compensation—MT told San Franciscans about his upbringing:

> I was sprinkled in infancy, and look upon that as conferring the rank of Brevet Presbyterian. It affords none of the emoluments of the Regular Church—simply confers honorable rank upon the recipient and the right to be punished as a Presbyterian hereafter; that is, the substantial Presbyterian punishment of fire and brimstone instead of this heterodox hell of remorse of conscience of these blamed wildcat religions.[34]

From his experience with camp meetings and Calvinist congregations, MT was aware of the contrast between participant and spectator religion. Satirizing the stereotypical decorum and emotional apathy of "cool Presbyterians," he told how they passively watched the performances of paid professionals:

> We get up on a Sunday morning and put on the best harness we have got and trip cheerfully down town; we subside into solemnity and enter the church; we stand up and duck our heads and bear down on a hymn book propped on the pew in front when the minister prays; we stand up again while our hired choir are singing, and look in the hymn book and check off the verses to see that they don't shirk any of the stanzas; we sit silent and grave while the minister is preaching. . . . No frenzy—no fanaticism—no skirmishing; everything perfectly serene. You never see any of us Presbyterians getting in a sweat about religion.[35]

---

[32]WG 74.
[33]LTR 1:315.
[34]CR1 208.
[35]*Golden Era*, 4 March 1866.

MT entertained San Francisco's raw frontier people by advising them on appropriate church conduct. He said that deodorant should not be so heavy that the congregation cannot decide "whether you bring with you air from Heaven or from Hell." Also, it is improper to become so absorbed in meditation that you are oblivious to the offering plate when passed, and it is despicable to help yourself when it passes.[36]

More seriously, what MT especially appreciated about Wadsworth was his criticism of unrealistic Sunday school stories about "bad little boys who infallibly got drowned on Sunday."[37] For example, one story published during that time was about a boy who drowned after skipping Sunday school, and his body was brought home on a board covered by a sheet. The story concluded with this moral:

> Surely no little boy who reads this will ever leave his Sunday school to go a hunting, or fishing, or to swim in the river. If he should be tempted to do such things, or to stay away from school or the place of worship for any other sinful purpose, I hope he will remember the boy who went out so cheerfully to swim and was carried home to his parents on a plank.[38]

Stories such as this had frightened MT as a child, and infuriated him now. In 1866, he published "The Story of the Bad Little Boy Who Bore a Charmed Life" about a youth who deceived his parents and hunted on the Sabbath but in the end "got wealthy by all manner of cheating and rascality, and now he is the infernalest wickedest scoundrel in his native village, and is universally respected, and belongs to the Legislature."[39] In debunking the formula for writing Sunday school books, MT was not aiming at undermining the importance of training children to do good and shun evil. On the contrary, he was attacking the kind of artificial morality that claimed bad behavior would necessarily result in poverty, illness, and early death. Recognizing that deity was not honored by lies, MT thought religious characters should experience a mixture of failure and success, as was typical of Bible stories. Although he may not have been acquainted with the philosophy of Immanuel Kant, he discerned that true morality is doing what is right for its own sake, not for personal gain.

---

[36]ET 242.
[37]CT1 209.
[38]*Youth Magazine* (New York) in PH 37.
[39]CT1 194.

Several years later, MT wrote a companion parody entitled "The Story of the Good Little Boy Who Did Not Prosper." In the story, Jacob, who models his behavior after the heroes of Sunday school literature, is blown to kingdom come when he attempts to stop delinquents who are executing dogs by tying nitroglycerin to their tails.[40] That story has overtones of two tragedies that had vexed him. His younger brother, an exceptionally fine boy, also died after an explosion. And MT would have us believe that he himself had recovered from a swimming hole near Hannibal the corpse of an "exasperatingly good" boy who had recited three thousand Bible verses just the day before.[41] Experience had shown MT the absurdity of expecting earthly rewards or punishments to match what a person justly deserved.

During this period MT wrote still another parody entitled "Mamie Grant, the Child-Missionary," featuring a prodigy who thought of herself as "a beacon light flashing its cheering rays far over the tossing waves of iniquity." From her Sunday school library, Mamie "drew those stores of wisdom which made her the wonder of the young and the admiration of the aged." She distributed tracts with titles such as "The Gamester's Last Throw," "The Reformed Inebriate," "The Blasphemous Sailor Awfully Rebuked," "The Pains of Hell, or the Politician's Fate," and "The Slave of Gain or the Dirge of the Damned." Mamie so disgusted everyone who came to do business with her guardian uncle that his business failed. She was blissfully unaware of the deleterious effect of her self-righteousness and aspired to have her "noble work" featured in a Sunday school book.[42] The genre of model children stories was popular throughout MT's lifetime, and Horatio Alger, his contemporary, became famous from writing them.

Beside taking on Sunday school literature, MT also took a crack at worldly clergy. Hearing that a pulpit had become vacant at Grace Episcopal Cathedral, San Francisco's most prominent edifice, he published a fictitious letter announcing the opening to outstanding Eastern ministers and listed its attractions. "Sinners are so thick that you can't throw out your line without hooking several," he promised. "If you could manage

---

[40]CT1 374-76.
[41]LM 438.
[42]CT1 262-68.

to ring in a few of the popular and familiar old tunes that the people love so well you would be almost certain to create a sensation. . . . Your preaching will be easy. Bring along a barrel of your old obsolete sermons; the people here will never know the difference."[43] He then concocted an appreciative response from Bishop Hawks, D.D., of New York, who nevertheless refused the offer, explaining that while the gospel assures God's providence for ravens, his large family of Hawks had not been similarly provided for. When his vestry learned that Hawks had been offered employment elsewhere, they greatly increased his already handsome stipend. Because of that, and because he had cotton stock investments in the East needing his shepherding, Hawks decided to reject God's "call" to California.[44] In this fictitious letter exchange, MT vented his disgruntlement with hypocritical clergy who profess gospel values while being primarily interested in advancing their own material welfare.

Other clergy, however, he found admirable. Writing to his mother about clergymen he had come to know in California, MT claimed, "There are none I like better to converse with—if they ain't narrow minded and bigoted they make good companions."[45] Defending himself from one preacher who, for some undisclosed reason, blasted him from the pulpit as a "son of the Devil," he remarked: "It is only the small-fry ministers who assail me. All those of high rank and real influence I visit, dine and swap lies with, just the same as ever."[46] He claimed that he was "running on preachers" who were "regular bricks," meaning that he was energized by those admirable fellows. He mentioned several: Dr. Henry Scudder, who served a large Presbyterian church and was in demand as a speaker around San Francisco; Rev. Horatio Stebbins, a Harvard graduate who helped to establish both Stanford and the University of California; and Dr. Henry Bellows, a Unitarian. MT gave a special tribute to Bellows, whom he described as "a man of imperial intellect and matchless power—he is Christian in the truest sense of the term."[47] Bellows edited the influential *Christian Examiner* and advocated unpopular reforms. In 1868, MT spoke to a group organized by his friend Wadsworth at the

---

[43]CT1 114-15.
[44]CT1 117.
[45]LTR 3:50.
[46]LTR 2:221.
[47]LTR 1:368.

Calvary Presbyterian Church and provided literary entertainment for a Methodist church benefit in Oakland.[48]

Why did MT generally find the clergy attractive? His eminent parson friends were among the best-educated Americans. Skilled in interpreting literature and articulate as orators, they had talents he wished to emulate. Moreover, clergy generally place a low priority on the accumulation of wealth and aim at a more just society. He also admired their compassionate outlook on the unfortunate and their tenderness toward those suffering loss. In their personal dealings they were customarily unassuming and honest.

In addition to enjoying the religious culture with which he was familiar, MT developed in California an appreciation of Chinese culture, which would remain with him for life. He found the immigrants from China "patient, quick to learn, and tirelessly industrious" and he described their religious observances with respect.[49] The tolerance and compassion he had learned from his mother caused him to be alarmed by the inhumane manner in which the Chinese were treated in San Francisco. He wrote about a Chinese petty thief whose skull was cracked by a policeman's club and who soon died because medical attention was withheld. Commenting on the incident, he used irony to castigate the establishment: "The man was an infernal stranger. He had no vote. . . . If he stole flour sacks, did he not deliberately put himself outside the pale of humanity and Christian sympathy by that hellish act?"[50]

In local and national journals, MT repeatedly voiced his outrage over police racial profiling, employment discrimination, and the torment of Chinese immigrants by bigots.[51] He told a story about a boy who had learned from a newspaper that they had no rights:

> Therefore, what could have been more natural than for this sunny-hearted boy, tripping along to Sunday school with his mind teeming with freshly learned incentives to high and virtuous action, to say to himself: "Ah, there goes a Chinaman! God will not love me if I do not stone him."[52]

---

[48]LTR 2:206.
[49]RI 369-72.
[50]WG 98.
[51]CT1 196, *Galaxy* (October 1870–January 1871).
[52]CT1 381.

For much of the time that MT was in San Francisco, his regular salary came from reporting on local news for the *Morning Call*, a routine job with long hours that he soon came to dislike. One article he filed described how meat merchants sicced their dogs on a Chinaman who was quietly passing by with the wash of a Christian customer. After the alien was mutilated, a butcher added to his own enjoyment by knocking out some of his teeth with a brick. A policeman watched the scene with amusement and did nothing about it.[53] MT reported this cruelty with "holy indignation" but his editor refused to publish it because the *Morning Call*'s poor Irish subscribers hated the Chinese.[54] Realizing that MT's temperament did not match the prejudices of those on whom the newspaper's survival depended, the editor dismissed him.

A note to Mollie shows that his unemployment and failure at gold prospecting in Calaveras County caused a shift in mood:

> I have a religion—but you will call it blasphemy. It is that there is a God for the rich man but none for the poor. . . . Our religions are alike . . . in one respect—neither can make a man happy when he is out of luck. If I do not get out of debt in three months—pistols or poisons for one—exit *me*.

Mollie may have dismissed this suicide threat as a sick joke, since her brother-in-law went on to grouch that she could now preach to him on another topic, having provided her with "a text for a sermon on Self-Murder."[55] However, a note MT wrote in 1909 suggests that he suffered then from severe depression:

> I put the pistol to my head but wasn't man enough to pull the trigger. Many times I have been sorry I did not succeed, but I was never ashamed of having tried. Suicide is the only really sane thing the young or the old ever do in this life.[56]

At the age of thirty, MT pondered the different kinds of work he had done—printer, pilot, journalist, and miner—in order to decide what career he should pursue. He had previously considered becoming a minister because "it looked like a safe job." He later commented on the eternal

---

[53]CT1 381.
[54]AMT 120.
[55]LTR 1:323.
[56]MT's marginalia in his copy of *Letters of James Russell Lowell*.

protection he had anticipated, "It never occurred to me that a preacher could be damned."[57] Evidently guiding others to Heaven was supposed to guarantee one's own salvation. Writing his nephew namesake Sam, whom he hoped would become a minister, MT reminisced:

> I wanted to be a minister myself—it was the only genuine ambition I ever had—but somehow I never had any qualification for it but the ambition. I always missed fire on the ministry. Then I hoped some member of the family would take hold of it and succeed. Orion would make a preacher, and I am ready to swear he will never make anything else in the world. But he won't touch it.[58]

Out of these reflections, MT discerned more clearly what biblically oriented people refer to as a "calling," and expressed it in a letter to Orion and Mollie in 1865:

> I never had but two powerful ambitions in my life. One was to be a pilot, and the other a preacher of the gospel. I accomplished the one and failed in the other, *because* I could not supply myself with the necessary stock in trade—i.e. religion. I have given it up forever. I never had a "call" in that direction, anyhow, and my aspirations were the very ecstasy of presumption. But I *have* had a "call" to literature, of a low order—i.e. humorous. It is nothing to be proud of, but it is my strongest suit, and if I were to listen to that maxim of stern *duty* which says that to do right you *must* multiply the one or the two or the three talents which the Almighty entrusts to your keeping, I would long ago have ceased to meddle with things for which I was by nature unfitted and turned my attention to seriously scribbling to excite the *laughter* of God's creatures.

MT went on to say that he became convinced of his humorous writing talent and vocation when he was praised by "editors of standard literary papers in the distant east." He then tried to encourage his brother to become a Christian minister and discourage him from becoming a lawyer:

> I don't know how you regard the ministry, but I would rather be a shining light in that department than the greatest lawyer that ever trod the earth. What is the pride of saving the widow's property or the homicide's trivial life, to snatching an immortal soul in mercy from the "jaws of hell?" Bah!

---

[57]MTB 84.
[58]LTR 1:367.

the one is feeble glitter of the firefly, and the other the regal glory of the sun.[59]

Here, as in earlier years, MT viewed a main mission of the ministry to be the saving of souls for the hereafter. Yet he recognized that salvation had little to do with the emotional experience of conversion and much to do with assisting the needy.

The priority that MT gave to the ministry was still present five years later when he wrote Frank Walden, a boyhood friend in Hannibal. Having heard that he had become a Methodist clergyman, MT responded:

> I am glad you are in the ministry, and hope your career may be long and useful. It is the highest dignity to which a man may aspire in this life, and, when its duties are faithfully performed, the satisfaction felt must be greater than that customarily felt by men in the ordinary walks of life.[60]

§ § §

In 1866, MT went to Hawaii (then called Sandwich Islands) as a roving correspondent for the Sacramento *Union*. He had first learned about the Hawaiians from a Sunday school story he had read as a child. It told of Obookia (or Opukaheia) who had assisted the "chief cook" at the temple of god Lono, where humans were roasted and sacrificed. In 1809, the captain of a whale ship took Obookia to Connecticut; there he was educated and became a Christian before returning to Hawaii with the first missionaries.[61]

In Hawaii, MT encountered foreign missionaries in person for the first time. Descended mainly from the Calvinist Puritans who had settled New England, the missionaries arrived in the isles in 1820. During the next several decades they put the native language into writing, enrolled thousands in schools, made many converts, and encouraged the natives to enact laws to raise moral practices. Even before MT's visit, the board that sent out the missionaries decided that control by outsiders had served its purpose and that the Christians were ready for self-government.[62]

---

[59]LTR 1:322-24.

[60]LTR 4:86.

[61]RI 493.

[62]Kenneth Scott Latourette, *A History of Christianity* (New York: Harper, 1953; London: Eyre, 1954) 1299-1300.

MT praised "that Puritan spirit which subdued America and underlies her whole religious fabric today—which has subdued these islanders, and whose influence over them can never be unseated."[63] He reported his arrival in Honolulu in this rhapsodic way:

> It was Sunday morning, and about church time, and we steamed through the narrow channel to the music of six different church bells, which sent their mellow tones far and wide, over hills and valleys, which were peopled by naked savage, thundering barbarians only fifteen years ago! Six Christian churches within five miles of the ruins of a pagan temple, where human sacrifices were daily offered up to the hideous idols in the last century! We were within pistol shot of one of a group of islands whose ferocious inhabitants closed in upon the doomed and helpless Captain Cook and murdered him, eighty-seven years ago; and lo! their descendants were at church! Behold what the missionaries have wrought![64]

In the same vein, MT jotted in his notebook about Hawaii:

> Americans have given religious freedom, education, written language and Bible. . . . Missionaries have made honest men out of the nation of thieves; instituted marriage; created homes; lifted women to the same rights and privileges enjoyed elsewhere; abolished infanticide; abolished intemperance; diminished licentiousness; given equal laws, whereby a chief's power of life and death over his subjects is taken away; in a great measure abolished idolatry; have well educated the people.[65]

In an article for the New York *Tribune*, MT said of Hawaiians:

> These natives are the simplest, the kindest-hearted, the most unselfish creatures that bear the image of the Maker. . . . The natives are all Christians now . . . and are fonder of theology than they are of pie. . . . Religion is drink and meat to the native. He can read his neatly printed Bible . . . and he knows all the hymns you ever heard in your life.[66]

The American missionaries MT met in Hawaii received a mixed evaluation. On the one hand he described them as "pious; hard-working; hard-praying; self-sacrificing; hospitable; devoted to the well-being of this people and the interests of Protestantism." They infused into the peoples

---

[63]LSI 117-18.
[64]LSI 17.
[65]MTN 21, 28.
[66]LMT 5:560-61.

"the spirit of democracy and the religious enthusiasm that animated themselves." But he faulted the missionaries for making the natives "permanently miserable by telling them how beautiful and blissful a place heaven is, and how nearly impossible it is to get there; and . . . how dreary a place perdition is and what unnecessarily liberal facilities there are for going to it."[67] MT also perceived these missionaries to be "bigoted; . . . old fogy—fifty years behind the age; uncharitable toward the weaknesses of the flesh." And he disliked the way, not sanctioned by the gospel, a missionary sometimes dealt with "a stranger" such as himself:

> He weighs him and measures him and judges him (in defiance of the injunction to "judge not," etc.) by an ideal which he has created in his own mind—and if that stranger falls short of that ideal in any particular, the good missionary thinks he falls just that much short of what he ought to be in order to stand a chance for salvation; and with a tranquil simplicity of self-conceit, which is marvelous to a modest man, he honestly believes that the Almighty, of a necessity thinks exactly as he does.[68]

While MT gave more attention to the larger operation in Hawaii by American missionaries, he judged French missionaries there with generosity:

> The Catholic clergy are honest, straightforward, frank, and open; they are industrious and devoted to their religion and their work. . . . The American missionaries have no quarrel with these men. . . . There is an anomaly for you—Puritan and Roman Catholic striding along, hand in hand, under the banner of the Cross![69]

MT sided with the missionaries who were disgusted that the royal family "imported a cheap ready-made bishop from England" to officiate over state functions. He witnessed Bishop Thomas Stanley presiding over elaborate, weeks-long mourning for a princess. When "His Grace the Lord Bishop of Honolulu" justified the rites by citing that Jesus wept at the death of Lazarus, MT commented, "I could not disguise from myself that the gentle grief of the Savior was but poorly imitated here."[70]

---

[67]LSI, 41.
[68]LSI 101-102, 117.
[69]LSI 121.
[70]LSI 114; John 11:35.

Concerning this Anglican intrusion into local missions, he said, "The chagrin of the missionaries has never been comprehensively expressed to this day, profanity not being admissible."[71]

During his months in Hawaii, MT again enjoyed the companionship of Rising, who had gone there from Nevada to recover his health. They arranged to return on the same ship to California, and MT found him the only congenial companion aboard. Rising took charge of worship services for the five Sundays of the voyage but he found it difficult to get fellow passengers to sing. MT volunteered to arrange for the music, but wrote his family that his contribution was miserable: "I am leader of the choir on this ship, and a sorry lead it is. I hope they will have a better opinion of the music in Heaven than I have down here. If they don't a thunder-bolt will come down and knock the vessel endways."[72] With his tenor voice, he was the solitary singer each week of this closing hymn:

> Lord, dismiss us with Thy blessing;
> Fill our hearts with joy and peace;
> Let us each, Thy love possessing,
> Triumph in redeeming grace.
> Oh refresh us, oh refresh us,
> Traveling thro' this wilderness.

MT had learned those words from the Presbyterian hymnal that he had used in Hannibal. The hymn, a prayer to put the Gospel's main themes into practice, was composed by Baptist minister John Fawcett, and the last line alludes to *Pilgrim's Progress*.

MT continued to keep in contact with Rising in New York City after Rising became the Financial Secretary of the Church Missionary Society. Rising died several years later as a result of a collision of steamboats. MT wrote that the face of his steadfast friend would evermore come to mind when he thought of "Oh, refresh us." He recalled, "A lonely ship in a great solitude of sky and water; and in my ear comes no sound but the complaining waves and the softened cadences of that simple old hymn . . . freighted with infinite pathos!"[73] (The hymn continues to be

---

[71]RI 464.
[72]LTR 1:352.
[73]LTR 2:333-34.

widely used by various Protestant denominations, occasionally with the variant first line, "*God*, dismiss us with *your* blessing.")

§ § §

After returning to California, MT had his first taste of professional lecturing in a dozen cities and towns. In speaking on Hawaii, he pointed out that he, like many other Sunday school children, had contributed pennies to missionary efforts and that he was pleased to see the results of his investment. He was especially gratified, he said, to observe the high quality of education that Hawaiians were receiving at mission schools.[74]

Americans were then flocking to hear speakers who could be both entertaining and enlightening, and a lyceum composed of circuit-riding lecturers had developed. In the years to follow, MT would deliver hundreds of lectures, and his ability to captivate audiences shows that he could have become famous without becoming an author. That extended platform experience satisfied some aspects of his early desire to be a minister. Paul Fatout discerns:

> He would have made a dubious preacher for a straitlaced congregation, perhaps for any congregation in a century more orthodox than ours, but he could have been a most lively one, and sensible too. There may be more sincerity than meets the eye in his facetious identification of lecturing as preaching.[75]

To the Mediterranean

In 1867, MT sailed eastward, changing ships in Panama, to work as a journalist for the San Francisco *Alta California*. On the way he got to know Captain Edgar Wakeman, the ship's captain, whose fascinating stories influenced his subsequent writing. He describes him in this way:

> He was a liberal talker and inexhaustibly interesting. In the matter of a wide and catholic profanity he had not his peer on the planet while he lived. . . . He knew the Bible by heart and was profoundly and sincerely religious. He was always studying the Bible when it was his watch below and always finding new things, fresh things and unexpected delights and surprises in

---

[74]MTS 5.

[75]Paul Fatout, *Mark Twain on the Lecture Circuit* (Bloomington: Indiana University Press, 1960) 20.

it—and he loved to talk about his discoveries and expound them to the ignorant.[76]

After disembarking on the Atlantic coast, MT headed out to the Midwest to visit with his family. While there he attended several church services and spoke at a Sunday school. In St. Louis he gave a benefit lecture to raise missions funds.[77] He became aware of the Reorganized Church of Jesus Christ of Latter Day Saints, describing them as Mormons who "call Brigham a wicked imposter and his new-fangled Mormonism a swindle. That well-accepted group in Iowa claim that polygamy is not a tenet of genuine Mormonism."[78]

During the months MT spent in New York City, the most detailed description he sent to his San Francisco newspaper was of the Bible House, the headquarters of the Bible Association. Five stories high and occupying an entire city block, it was one of the largest buildings in the city. MT rated it as "one of the chief among the fountain-heads of civilization in this great city, (if not the chief)." He reported that more than one million Bibles annually were printed there in fifty languages to supply global Christian missions. He was intrigued by the many translations on exhibit there. By way of promoting his favorite book, MT wrote:

> And they will sell you a complete Bible, well bound in sheep, for forty-five cents. Therefore, why need men be ignorant of the Word? The great city of New York has within her limits no institution she has more reason to be proud of than this colossal Bible Association.

The printing operation at the Bible House fascinated the former printer, and he spent hours observing it. He watched the Gospels being set up in Arabic type, which looked "like ever so many elegant fishing-worms out on a spree." In reporting on this visit, Allison Ensor notes that MT began a new device, a "pretended ignorance about the Bible in order to get a laugh from the reader, who can congratulate himself on not being

---

[76]AMT 276.
[77]MTTB 135-36.
[78]MTTB 149.

quite so stupid as Twain."[79] He told of seeing on the counter "piles of the Books of Esau, Isaac and Jacob, Matthew, Mark and Genesis."[80]

MT reported widely on New York while swayed by "a pious frenzy." He visited the "Boot-Black Brigade Chapel" and found there some likable streetwise boys. When they were told the story of Lazarus's resurrection after being buried for four days, "there was a pretty general telegraphing of incredulity from eye to eye about the assemblage, and one boy with a shockhead and rags all over to match nudged his neighbor, and said in a coarse whisper, 'I don't go that, Bill, do you?—'cause he'd stink, wouldn't he?' "[81] Asked to name the all-powerful Being, one boy replied, "The chief of police." Cold from spending night and day in the winter out-of-doors, another boy found the description of the heat of hell inviting. "Wicked," and other preacher words, had no meaning. The growth of grass seed and lovely meadows as a part of God's beautiful creation was outside their experience.[82] MT praised Christian social workers who braved dangerous slum areas:

> The midnight mission is composed of sincere and zealous religious men who, in a good work, are ironclad against jeers and insult, and they go about these streets at dead of night, trying to rope in the prostitutes that infest the alleys and byways of this teeming hive of humanity, and bring them back to the walk of virtue. Talk about courage![83]

MT also visited congregations of the elite, in part because the usual places of public entertainment were closed on Sundays. At the Zion Episcopal Church he enjoyed the sermon as well as the music, and jibed, "I attended Bishop Southgate's matinee yesterday in pursuit of my desire to test all the amusements of the metropolis." About the preacher at another church, he said, "His eloquence is genuine, free from show and unsubstantial flummery, meant for use, not ornament."[84] He was also

---

[79]Allison Ensor, *Mark Twain and the Bible* (Lexington: University Press of Kentucky, 1969) 13.

[80]"For Christians to Read," (San Francisco) *Alta California*, 7 July 1867; MTTB 202-209.

[81]MTTB 223; John 11:39-44.

[82]CT1 253-56.

[83]MTTB 162.

[84]MTTB 92.

impressed by the Universalist pastor Dr. Edwin Chapin, whom he called "a recognized leader in all the progressive movements of the day." MT described the power of Chapin's preaching, "There is an invisible wire leading from every auditor's soul straight to a battery hidden away somewhere in that preacher's head, and down those wires travels in ceaseless flow the living spirit of words." Moreover, his utterances "were teeming with truth and wisdom."[85]

Henry Ward Beecher in the pulpit
of the Plymouth Church of Brooklyn.

But it was Henry Ward Beecher, one of "the great guns of the New York pulpit," who impressed MT the most. One of the eleven children of Lyman Beecher, Henry Ward belonged to the most influential family in the religious history of America. He had come to Brooklyn from the Midwest, where he had been pastor of a Presbyterian church in Indianapolis.

---

[85]MTTB 174-76.

His flamboyant pulpit-less eloquence at the Plymouth Congregational Church earned him the title "the Barnum of religion." Beecher attracted thousands weekly and became the most conspicuous American preacher of his day. His sermons, which a stenographer took down, were printed weekly in pamphlet form and circulated widely. On a frigid Sunday, MT arrived an hour early at his church in Brooklyn to get a good seat, but was only able to squeeze into the gallery and sit on a stool the size of a spittoon. Justin Kaplan describes the experience, "Sam Clemens was intoxicated with oratory in an age that adored it and that turned to it for entertainment as well as persuasion, and the pastor of Plymouth Church impressed him more as a showman than as a shepherd."[86] After his visit, he submitted this report on Beecher:

> The choir over his head sang charmingly, and then he got up and preached one of the liveliest and most sensible sermons I ever listened to. He has a rich, resonant voice, and a distinct enunciation, and makes himself heard all over the church without very apparent effort. His discourse sparkled with felicitous similes and metaphors; . . . satire and eloquent declamation were happily blended upon a groundwork of earnest exposition of the great truths involved in his text. Whenever he forsook his notes, marching up and down his stage, sawing his arms in the air, hurling sarcasms this way and that, discharging rockets of poetry, and exploding mines of eloquence, I could have started the audience with a single clap of the hands and brought down the house.[87]

C. J. Armstrong, a Hannibal pastor during the first part of the twentieth century, speculated on what kind of preacher MT would have made. Had he fulfilled his early career ambition, Armstrong thought he would have conducted himself like Beecher. There would have been nothing stale, and little that was conventional, as he attacked snobbery and sham with humor, compassion, and courage.[88]

§ § §

---

[86]Justin Kaplan, *Mr. Clemens and Mark Twain* (New York: Simon & Schuster, 1966) 24.

[87]MTTB 93-94.

[88]C. J. Armstrong, "Sam Clemens Considered Becoming a Preacher," *The Twainian* (May 1945): 1.

While at the Plymouth Church, MT's interest was also stimulated by reading a prospectus about an excursion being organized by members of that congregation. For five months the *Quaker City*, a paddle-wheeler steamship, would carry one of the first organized tours to sites in Europe, Asia, and Africa that could be reached from the Mediterranean Sea. However, for Twain to make the round trip from New York, he first needed to obtain underwriting for its cost. The *Alta California* agreed to pay his fare in exchange for frequent articles about the journey, even though the cost was six times that of attending that year the International Exhibition in Paris.

S.S. Quaker City leaving New York harbor.

Becoming certified for membership in the touring party was more difficult for MT. A committee of the Plymouth Church had the duty of approving those whose character and culture qualified them for joining the group. Captain Charles Duncan, who headed the committee, reportedly "never swore an oath—never drank a glass of liquor."[89] Even though

---

[89]*American Agriculturist* (March 1867): 86.

MT was deficient in propriety, wealth, and orthodoxy, he submitted his application. If accepted he thought he would enjoy the churchgoing group, having learned that "preachers are always pleasant company when they are off duty."[90] A friend accompanying him to the screening committee attempted to assist him by introducing him as "the Rev. Mark Twain, who is a clergyman of some distinction, lately arrived from San Francisco."[91] Later MT acknowledged the hoax to Duncan but he was still accepted, probably because of a shortage of applicants. Many had dropped out after bellwether Beecher and General William Sherman decided not to join the expedition. In telling about the interview much later, Duncan made mention of MT's "fume of bad whiskey." "I couldn't afford good whiskey," MT retorted; "How could I know the 'captain' was so particular about the quality of a man's whiskey?"[92]

MT appropriately called the majority of the Quaker City passengers "pilgrims," for many were descendants from the Puritans who came from England centuries earlier. Moreover, they were headed to "the land of promise" where Abraham and Sarah—the first to be called "pilgrims"— had gone.[93] Whereas the Easterners were on a spiritual journey, he was on a business trip. The average age of the passengers was twenty years older than MT, and the men greatly outnumbered the women. The one who had spent the previous decade as a pilot, miner, and Wild West journalist soon found quite uncongenial those who presumed they had already been elected to a heavenly position. He lampooned one pilgrim, probably one of the three clergymen aboard, as "a solemn, unsmiling, sanctimonious old iceberg that looked like he was waiting for a vacancy in the Trinity." In the middle of the Atlantic this pietist inquired "if the excursion would come to a halt on Sundays." MT found unacceptable the prudential basis of his ethics:

> I respected that man's repugnance to violating the Sabbath until he betrayed that he would violate it in a minute if he were not afraid that lightning would strike him, or something else would happen to him. . . . I perceived that he was not good and holy, but only sagacious, and so I turned the key

---

[90]MTTB 166.
[91]LTR 2:16.
[92]*New York World*, 18 February 1877.
[93]Hebrews 11:9-13.

on my valise and moved it out of his reach. I shall have to keep an eye on that fellow.[94]

MT was a regular at the Sunday religious services and at the daily evening prayer meetings, where hymns were sung from *The Plymouth Collection* compiled by Beecher.[95] The participants persistently beseeched the Almighty to provide favorable winds for the *Quaker City*, which amounted to requesting ill headwinds for most of the other ships they sighted. Many sailing ships moving in the opposite direction were dependent upon favorable winds, but those aboard the steamship could proceed regardless of the wind direction. MT admired the ship's executive officer who protested the prayer petition, saying, "It ain't good sense, it ain't good reason, it ain't good Christianity, it ain't common human charity."[96] Much of the daily passenger routine, MT observed, consisted of devotions and slander![97]

Captain Duncan, who was for MT the epitome of the humorless and insufferable pilgrim, usually presided over the prayer meetings. Some years after the voyage MT recalled:

> These meetings could have been made useful to the cause of religion, if the circumstances had been different; but the thought crept into many humble, seeking-hearts, that if heaven was to be populated with Duncans it might not be wise to proceed rashly in so serious a matter. . . . Barring certain defects, hell had its advantages.[98]

MT consented to lead one of the the prayer meetings.[99] In that role he encountered the disdain of William Denny, a Methodist Sunday school superintendent who had earlier helped capture abolitionist John Brown and had served as a colonel in the Confederacy. He was indignant when MT asked him to pray, because the "worldling" had just been dancing. Denny described his shipmate in his journal as "a wicked fellow that will

---

[94]MTTB 276-77.
[95]LTR 2:243.
[96]IA 46.
[97]IA 645.
[98]*New York World*, 18 February 1877. This may be the source of the maxim attributed to MT: "Heaven for climate but hell for company."
[99]Julia Millikan, ed., *Journal Letters of Emily Severance* (Cleveland: Gates, 1938) 7.

take the name of the Lord in vain." On the other hand he admitted that "he is liberal, kind, and obliging, and if he were only Christian, would make his mark."[100]

On board ship, MT had more camaraderie with the small contingent he called "sinners," distinguished by their profane speech and cigar smoke. He noted about one of them, "Man on this ship as hard a case as Paul—got to knock him endwise with a streak of lightning before he could get religion."[101] The sinners gave the name "pilgrim" to a stoop-shouldered and long-legged bird at the Marseilles zoo that strutted about looking as if it had hands under its dress coat. Finding the bird highly amusing, MT exclaimed, "Such tranquil stupidity, such supernatural gravity, such self-righteousness, and such ineffable self-complacency . . . were in the countenance and attitude of that gray-bodied, dark-winged, bald-headed, and preposterously uncomely bird!"[102] Weighed down by a lack of joyful dancing and laughing among the unctuous pilgrims, MT dryly remarked that "the pleasure trip was a funeral excursion without a corpse."[103] This description is a literal sea change from what he had reported as they disembarked. "We have got the pleasantest and jolliest party of passengers that ever sailed out of New York was what he said then, perhaps in pretended naivete."[104]

The *Quaker City*'s first stop was at the Portuguese colony in the Azores Islands. MT viewed the church there as an instrument for perpetuating ignorance, "The good Catholic Portuguese crossed himself and prayed God to shield him from all blasphemous desire to know more than his father before him."[105] When shown at the Jesuit cathedral what was alleged to be a relic of Jesus' cross, MT marveled that "these confiding people believe in that piece of wood unhesitatingly."[106] Even after the six-week Atlantic voyage in the company of "pilgrims," he was not interested in following up on what sailors told him about Azorean women, "They

---

[100]Quoted in Robert Hirst, "Sinners and Pilgrims," *Bancroftiana* (Fall 1998): 6.

[101]MTN 70.
[102]IA 101.
[103]IA 644.
[104]MTTB 166.
[105]IA 56.
[106]IA 57.

say they are not virtuous—but I cannot see how the devil they can possibly be otherwise—for fornication with such cattle would come under the head of the crime without a name."[107]

What MT said about religion on those islands was sharply different from what he had said about the Protestant-dominated Hawaiian islands. By way of explanation, he frankly admitted, "I have been educated to enmity toward every thing that is Catholic, and sometimes, in consequence of this, I find it much easier to discover Catholic faults than Catholic merits."[108] The General Assembly of the Presbyterian Church, in the year he was born, had proclaimed that "the Roman Catholic Church has essentially apostasized from the religion of our Lord and Savior Jesus Christ" and therefore cannot be recognized as a Christian Church.[109]

MT dismissed most religious relics encountered on the tour as fraudulent. He doubted that the alleged remains of John the Baptist enshrined in Genoa's cathedral were genuine because he had encountered similar claims for the same saint in another church. Sounding like skeptical John Calvin,[110] MT commented on the nails of Jesus' cross, "I think we have seen as much as a keg of these nails."[111] He was struck by the easy public acceptance of questionable evidence pertaining to holy objects. Concerning St. Veronica, the saint who allegedly wiped Jesus' brow before he was crucified and obtained an image of his face, MT remarked sarcastically, "No tradition is so amply verified as this of St. Veronica"; proof of this was his having seen that handkerchief—twice in Italy, once in France, and once in Spain.[112] In Rome he was also incredulous when shown the facial impression made by the apostle Peter when he fell against a stone in the Mamertine Prison.[113] At Naples Cathedral, the vial of St. Januarius's blood that was said to liquify miraculously twice a year prompted MT to comment, "Every day for

[107]N&J 1:344.

[108]IA 599.

[109]*Minutes of the General Assembly of the Presbyterian Church in the U.S.A.: 1821–1835* (Philadelphia: Presbyterian Board of Publication, 1835) 490.

[110]See Georgia Harkness, *John Calvin: The Man and His Ethics* (New York: Abingdon, 1931) 97-99.

[111]IA 165.

[112]IA 575.

[113]IA 275.

eight days, this dismal farce is repeated, while the priests go among the crowd and collect money for the exhibition." Angered by this profitable scam, he rated it as "one of the wretchedest of all the religious impostures one can find in Italy."[114] Concerning his sensitivities as he toured churches in southern Europe, James Wilson comments, "The commercial exploitation of religious relics he thinks profound sacrilege, and he seizes the opportunity to lampoon the gullibility of those so desperate for faith that they will accept anything to redeem their own miserable lives."[115]

At a catacomb near Rome, MT did not question the authenticity of the relics but was amazed by their description in his guidebook:

> "Here the heart of St. Philip Neri was so inflamed with divine love as to burst his ribs." I find that grave statement in a book published in New York in 1858, and written by "Rev. William H. Neligan, LL.D., M.A., Trinity College, Dublin; Member of the Archaeological Society of Great Britain." Therefore, I believe it. Otherwise, I could not. Under other circumstances I should have felt a curiosity to know what Philip had for dinner.[116]

"Priest-ridden Italy" appalled MT because the government supported a surplus of priests, leaving it no funds for diminishing the abounding poverty.[117] He claimed:

> Italy, for fifteen hundred years, has turned all her energies, all her finances, and all her industry to the building up of a vast array of wonderful church edifices, and starving half her citizens to accomplish it. She is to-day one vast museum of magnificence and misery. All the churches in an ordinary American city put together could hardly buy the jeweled frippery in one of her hundred cathedrals. And for every beggar in America, Italy can show a hundred.[118]

Arthur Scott clarifies MT's assessment of European Catholicism:

> There was no irreverence in his treatment of the Catholic Church, because he was not denouncing religion. He was denouncing, instead, a Church which seemed to have abandoned religion in its lust for wealth and power.

---

[114]IA 311.

[115]James Wilson, "Religious and Esthetic Vision in Mark Twain's Early Career," *Canadian Review of American Studies* (Summer 1986): 159.

[116]William Neligan, *Rome* (New York: Kirker, 1858) 432; IA 296.

[117]IA 256-57.

[118]IA 258.

. . . Mark Twain held the Roman Church largely responsible for the state of filth and degradation in which most Italians lived out their lives.[119]

There were some aspects of Italian Catholicism that MT admired. He commended the Dominican friars who sacrificed their lives by nursing the sick during a cholera plague, saying, "Surely the charity, the purity, the unselfishness that are in the hearts of men like these would save their souls though they were bankrupt in the true religion—which is ours."[120] He also had generous praise for St. Charles Bartolomeo, bishop of Milan several centuries earlier, whose "whole life was given to succoring the poor, encouraging the faint-hearted, visiting the sick, . . . relieving distress, whenever and wherever he found it. His heart, his hand, and his purse were always open." MT set those virtues in bold relief against the treasures lavished on the bishop's corpse—a rock crystal coffin, a crown with brilliant gems, and a solid gold cross upon his chest studded with emeralds and diamonds. He commented:

> How poor, and cheap, and trivial these gewgaws seemed in presence of the solemnity, the grandeur, the awful majesty of Death! . . . Dead Bartolomeo preached: . . . You that worship the vanities of earth—you that long for worldly honor, worldly wealth, worldly fame—behold their worth![121]

Later the excursionists were received by Greek Catholic hermits called the Convent Fathers. MT was effusive in his gratitude for their unconditional love, which to him was the essence of true religion:

> They knew we were foreigners and Protestants, and not likely to feel admiration or much friendliness toward them. But their large charity was above considering such things. They simply saw in us men who were hungry, and thirsty, and tired, and that was sufficient. They opened their doors and gave us welcome. They asked no questions, and they made no self-righteous display of their hospitality. . . . When we got up to breakfast in the morning, we were new men. For all this hospitality no strict charge was made. We could give something if we chose; we need give nothing, if we were poor or if we were stingy.[122]

---

[119]MTAL 54-55.
[120]IA 261.
[121]IA 178.
[122]IA 599.

In general, MT was unimpressed by Roman Catholic art, in part because the order of reverence appeared to be, from highest to lowest, "the Mother of God," God, Peter, canonized popes and martyrs, and then "Jesus Christ the Saviour—but always as an infant in arms."[123] Moreover, the artists depicted Mary as having the appearance of a Western Gentile, "None of them ever put into the face of the Madonna that indescribable something which proclaims the Jewess."[124] At the Vatican gallery, however, MT did extol Raphael's "Transfiguration" as "wonderfully beautiful."[125] A radiant Jesus, flanked by Moses and Elijah on a mountain, is contrasted with his disciples who, in the shadows below, are pointing a mentally ill boy and his parents to the person who can help them. MT probably identified with the existential predicament of the child's father who, in the Gospel text, cries: "Lord, I believe; help thou mine unbelief."[126]

§ § §

After the European tour, the *Quaker City* docked at Beirut and MT, along with many others, disembarked to travel over the mountains to Damascus. The pietists who dominated the group demanded that the trip be speeded up by a day in order to avoid travel on the Sabbath. Although MT pleaded on behalf of the overtaxed horses, recalling Jesus' teaching that domestic beasts should be cared for every day, they nevertheless rode thirteen hours on limping horses in blistering heat. Disgusted by this ill-treatment, he commented:

> When did ever self-righteousness know the sentiment of pity? . . . They were willing to commit a sin against the spirit of religious law, in order that they might preserve the letter of it. It was not worth while to tell them "the letter kills." [2 Corinthians 3:6] . . . They lecture our shortcomings unsparingly, and every night they call us together and read to us chapters from the Testament. . . . Apply the Testament's gentleness, and charity, and tender mercy to a toiling, worn, and weary horse? Nonsense.[127]

---

[123]IA 306.
[124]IA 195.
[125]IA 303.
[126]Mark 9:24.
[127]IA 451-52.

One of MT's close friends later observed, "He could sometimes be of an unsparingly hostile temper toward a fellow man, but he could never bear to see an animal in pain."[128]

Appropriately, the party stopped by a fountain which had provided refreshment for Balaam's ass, whom MT canonized as "the patron saint of all pilgrims." At Damascus, the pilgrims also displayed a remarkable lack of compassion for their fellowman. When one of the less-pious excursionists came down with cholera, they decided to leave him behind. MT responded: "Gentlemen, I understand that you are going to leave Dan Slote here alone. I'll be goddamned if I do."[129] In spite of his occasional bursts of anger, however, he tried to be forbearing toward the pilgrims, "None of these can say I ever took their lectures unkindly, or was restive under the infliction, or failed to try to profit by what they said to me."[130] Biographer Albert Paine has preserved what a physician among the excursionists said after the cholera incident:

> Doctor Church was a deacon with orthodox views and did not approve of Mark Twain; he thought him sinful, irreverent, profane. "He was the worst man I ever knew," Church said; then he added, "And the best."[131]

MT was filled with anticipation as he entered the region where Jesus had lived, and he reminisced on gospel events that happened at particular places. At the Sea of Galilee the excursionists wanted to cross over to the other side, but they refused to pay the boatman's high fee. "No wonder the Lord walked," MT groused.[132] Of Jesus' boyhood town, he wrote, "Nazareth is wonderfully interesting because the town has an air about it of being precisely as Jesus left it."[133] As someone who would one day entertain the public with marvelous stories from his own boyhood, he mused about the intense interest a book on Jesus' youth might have. He asked about Jesus' siblings:

---

[128]Joseph Twichell, in *Hartford Courant*, 23 April 1910.
[129]MTN 89.
[130]IA 499.
[131]MTB 336.
[132]Cyril Clemens, *Wit and Wisdom of Mark Twain* (New York: Stoakes, 1935) 15.
[133]IA 537.

Who ever inquires what manner of youth they were; and whether they slept with Jesus, played with him and romped about him; quarreled with him concerning toys and trifles; struck him in anger, not suspecting what he was? . . . Who ever gives a thought to the sisters of Jesus at all?[134]

MT examined a "quaint volume of rejected gospels,"[135] called the New Testament Apocrypha, hoping to find more stories of Jesus' boyhood to add to the one found in the New Testament. Having been previously familiar only with what orthodoxy had proclaimed to be the authentic holy scriptures, he was intrigued by some of the noncanonical gospels. However, they proved to have only entertainment value so far as his quest for the historical Jesus was concerned. The fictitious stories he found there missed the spirit of Jesus, telling as they did how he blinded his accusers, killed the companions who jostled him, and created living creatures out of clay.[136] MT related one apocryphal tale in which the king of Jerusalem ordered Joseph to build him a throne; when his construction turned out to be two spans too narrow, Jesus relieved his father's worry over the king's anger by magically stretching the boards to the right length.[137]

At Nazareth and elsewhere in Palestine, MT searched for something more genuine about the family of Jesus than anything found in the bizarre supernaturalism that had grown up in the course of church history. At a later year he planned to write a life of Jesus, but friends persuaded him that such an effort would be misunderstood.[138] Other than the Virgin's Fountain in Nazareth, where Mary probably came for water, MT found little featured in the guides that was not bogus. The "holy family," unlike other families then, were presumed to have been housed in caves in Bethlehem and Nazareth, and one of them was called "the Virgin's Kitchen." He gave them no credence, "It is an imposture—this grotto stuff."[139] Assuming that swindlers, such as those he encountered in Nazareth, had exploited others through history, he mused on a prophecy

---

[134]IA 501; Mark 6:3.
[135]IA 538.
[136](San Francisco) *Alta Calfornia*, 2 June 1867; 11 August 1867.
[137]IA 537.
[138]*North American Review* (June 1910): 830.
[139]IA 528.

of Isaiah, "How it must have surprised these people to hear the way of salvation offered to them 'without money and without price.' "[140]

While the party was on a Galilean road, an episode occurred that gave MT insight into Jesus' healing ministry. Dr. George Birch from Hannibal, using an eyewash, treated the fly-infested eyes of some children he encountered. Soon a crowd of "the lame, the halt, the blind, the leprous" swarmed around, worshiping the physician who was believed to have mysterious power. MT saw a parallel between the response of "these simple, superstitious, disease-tortured creatures" and "the multitude" who had flocked around Jesus the healer.[141]

MT was eager to discover reliable history in Palestine about the ancient Israelites and the early Christians. At Jacob's well, one of the sites he considered authentic, he noted: "This is an interesting spot. Jesus rested here. . . . The customs of the inhabitants remain the same—women with waterpots on their heads. This well, these mountains, yonder city were looked on by the Savior." Other places he considered genuine included the Garden of Gethsemane, and the ruined wall of Jericho.[142]

Bible stories surfaced in MT's memory when he noticed that old friends "ran and fell upon each other's necks and kissed each other's grimy, bearded faces upon both cheeks."[143] Previously he thought it far-fetched to claim that men ever embraced one another in that manner, but "old Scriptural phrases that never possessed any significance for me before take to themselves a meaning." He could now understand the breach of custom when a Pharisee host failed to welcome Jesus with a kiss.[144]

On the other hand, MT found preposterous much that tourists were told: "Sat under the tree whereon Judas hanged himself"; "Place where 20,000 children beheaded by Herod were buried";[145] "We looked every where, as we passed along, but never saw grain or crystal of Lot's wife."[146] At Jerusalem's Mosque of Omar, which was constructed over a

---

[140]IA 526; Isaiah 55:1.
[141]IA 473-75.
[142]MTN 99, 101, 107.
[143]IA 545; cp. Genesis 33:4; Luke 15:20.
[144]Luke 7:45.
[145]MTN 97, 101.
[146]IA 597.

rock from which the prophet of Islam allegedly ascended to Heaven, he remarked: "In the place on it where Mahomet stood, he left his foot-prints in the solid stone. I should judge that he wore about eighteens."[147]

A mature person, MT believed, respects not only the authentic shrines of one's own religion but also those of other peoples. Consequently, he was chagrined when the pilgrims arrogantly profaned a mosque by stepping on prayer carpets with their boots and breaking off souvenirs from the surroundings. He claimed he was more afraid of being shot by his trigger-happy companions who were fearful of assault by "infidels" than by the unoffensive Arabs.[148]

Like most visiting Christians, MT anticipated that he would find the Church of the Holy Sepulchre impressive, but he found it "scandalized by trumpery gewgaws and tawdry ornamentation."[149] As he looked at "imaginary holy places created by the monks," he pondered, "One is grave and thoughtful when he stands in the little Tomb of the Saviour— he could not well be otherwise in such a place—but he has not the slightest possible belief that ever the Lord lay there."[150] With a touch of wistfulness he wrote, "Oh for the ignorance . . . that could enable a man to kneel at the Sepulchre and look at the rift in the rock, and the socket of the cross, and the tomb of Adam and feel and know and never question that they were genuine."[151] As a Protestant, he found the ecclesiastical surroundings distracting, "When one stands where the Saviour was crucified, he finds it all he can do to keep it strictly before his mind that Christ was not crucified in a Catholic Church."[152]

MT pretended to be a naive tourist when he visited Adam's alleged tomb, and he carried a guidebook similar to one still available that describes the Chapel of Adam in the Church of the Holy Sepulchre.[153] There he made this note: "Navel of the world in the Greek chapel, where

---

[147]IA 579.
[148]IA 540-43.
[149]IA 560.
[150]IA 570.
[151]MTN #7, 40.
[152]IA 572.
[153]G. S. Freeman-Grenville, *The Basilica of the Holy Sepulchre* (Jerusalem: Cana Carta, 1993) 51.

Adam's dust came from. . . . Adam's grave."[154] Greek Christians evidently thought it was more appropriate to designate the place where Adam died as the center of the earth than to hallow the omphalos at Delphi's Temple of Apollo that had been so designated in pagan Greek mythology.

*MT grieving for his earliest ancestor
at the reputed tomb of Adam in Jerusalem.*

Most excursionists relied less on their own observations than on the romantic descriptions created by previous Protestants who had written

---

[154]MTN 98.

guidebooks. "Our pilgrims have brought their verdicts with them," MT noted:

> I can almost tell, in set phrase, what they will say when they see Tabor, Nazareth, Jericho, and Jerusalem—because I have the books they will "smouch" their ideas from. These authors write pictures and frame rhapsodies, and lesser men follow and see with the author's eyes instead of their own, and speak with his tongue.[155]

In MT's opinion, the worst guidebook author was William Prime, whom he sometimes called "Grimes." He commented: "Prime was a gushing pietist; religion was his daily tipple; he was always under the influence of religion. Seldom actually and solidly drunk with holiness but always on the verge of it, always dizzy, boozy, twaddlesome."[156] Prime's guide to Palestine opens melodramatically:

> There lay Holy Land and thither my pilgrim feet would carry me. . . . I trembled lest the nerves and sinews should fail me and the delicate thread of life break before I could kneel at the Tomb! How I looked earnest, longing, clinging gazes at my wife, lest some dire mishap should prevent that perfect joy of our glad lives and forbid our standing together on the Mount of Olives.[157]

In parody of Prime's hysterical prose, MT wrote this about the spot from which the dust of Adam allegedly came and to which it returned:

> How touching it was, here in a land of strangers, far away from home, and friends, and all who cared for me, thus to discover the grave of a blood relation. . . . The fountain of my filial affection was stirred to its profoundest depths, and I gave way to tumultuous emotion. I leaned upon a pillar and burst into tears. . . . Weighed down by sorrow and disappointment, he died before I was born—six thousand brief summers before I was born. . . . Let us take comfort in the thought that his loss is our eternal gain.[158]

MT later supplied more data on his primordial family tree: "After Adam, my ancestor was Cain, who married his sister Mary Ann and had by her a litter of sons and daughters who were also his nephews and

---

[155]IA 511-12.
[156]MTE 349.
[157]William Prime, *Tent Life in the Holy Land* (New York: Harper, 1857) 2.
[158]IA 567.

nieces. It made a good deal of talk."[159] MT was spoofing the biblical literalist's incestuous explanation of how Genesis could refer to Cain building a "city" named Enoch for the vast number of descendents from the sole parents of humankind.[160]

A travesty of true Christianity in Jerusalem, MT thought, was the animosity displayed between its two main divisions, the Greek Orthodox and the Roman Catholic. According to his understanding, the recently ended Crimean War had been provoked by Russia's claim to have the exclusive right to put a new dome on the Church of the Holy Sepulchre. "Sounds as absurd as the crusades," he commented.[161] How ironical, he wrote, for there to be bloodshed out of veneration of "the last resting-place of the meek and lowly, the mild and gentle, Prince of Peace!"[162] At the Church of the Nativity the same "envy and uncharitableness" was found, "The priests and the members of the Greek and Latin churches can not come by the same corridor to kneel in the sacred birthplace of the Redeemer, . . . lest they quarrel and fight on the holiest ground on earth."[163]

MT purchased souvenirs in Jerusalem. At the Bancroft Library in Berkeley I examined a Bible bound in olive wood that he brought back for his mother. He wrote her that he had obtained a flask of water from Jerusalem's Pool of Bethesda when an angel was not watching. He was referring to the place described in John's Gospel where the sick waited for an angel to "trouble the water" and cure their diseases.[164] Tongue-in-cheek, he expressed hope that some angel in Missouri could stir the Bethesda water sample and cure the cripples there.[165] His understanding mother had earlier learned to discount his exaggerations; her indulgence encouraged him to spin tall tales for the rest of his life.[166]

The Holy Land tour dispelled many of the fantasies MT had held since childhood. As a boy, he had envisioned Palestine to be as expansive

---

[159]MT's marginalia in his copy of Rufus Noyes, *Views of Religion*; MTLB 2:511.
[160]Genesis 4:17.
[161]MTN 77.
[162]IA 573.
[163]IA 601.
[164]John 5:4.
[165]LTR 2:130.
[166]MTA 1, 294.

as America, the Sea of Galilee to be one of the largest bodies of water in the world, and the Jordan River to be longer and wider than the Mississippi. Now he realized that "the State of Missouri could be split into three Palestines."[167] Reading as a boy about the "exterminating battles" of Joshua against "all these kings,"[168] he had assumed that the Israelites wiped out an alliance comparable to the armies of all the European powers. But a visit to the site made him aware that each Canaanite realm was only a few miles wide. The "kings," far from being "arrayed in splendid robes ablaze with jewels," were only ragged village chieftains.[169]

One of Gustave Doré's larger-than-life biblical illustrations shows a single cluster of grapes from the Promised Land. It is so huge that two returning spies carry it on a pole swung between them. The artist faithfully represented the story of what the spies brought back to the Israelite camp in the Sinai desert as evidence of a land that "floweth with milk and honey."[170] Probably referring to that story and picture, MT told himself: "I must studiously and faithfully unlearn a great many things I have somehow absorbed concerning Palestine. . . . One gets large impressions in boyhood, sometimes, which he has to fight against all his life."[171] He also contrasted his memory of a charming engraving of the Queen of Sheba's visit from the desert with the uninspiring reality— stinking camels, feasting flies, and dirty people.[172]

Traveling in Palestine toward the end of the dry season, MT viewed the scenery at an unattractive time. "It is the most hopeless, dreary, heartbroken piece of territory out of Arizona," he reported; "I think the sun would skip it if he could make schedule time by going around."[173] As the excursionists moved through the "God-forsaken" barren hills, "a grave gentleman" expressed his longing that Jesus might return there during their visit. To this premillennialist MT countered that the Second Advent

---

[167]IA 479, 486, 596-97.
[168]Joshua 11:5.
[169]IA 484-86.
[170]Numbers 13:23-27.
[171]IA 486.
[172]IA 544.
[173]Daniel McKeithan, ed., *Traveling with the Innocents Abroad* (Oklahoma City: University of Oklahoma Press, 1958) 302.

would take place elsewhere because no sensible person would want to return again to that dismal land.[174] On the same page where he jotted, "Christ been once, will never come again," there is this entry: "Village of Bethany. It is fearfully ratty—some houses—mud—6 ft. square, and others holes in the ground—all windowless."[175] "It is an awful trial to a man's religion to waltz it through the Holy Land," he admitted.[176] Later in life, he quipped that Jesus would not come again anywhere since he made trouble enough the first time.[177]

MT wondered if he might be viewing the fulfillment of biblical prophecies about the plight of a land whose people had been unfaithful. For example, Moses said regarding future generations, "The stranger that shall come from a far land, . . . even all nations shall say, Wherefore hath the Lord done thus unto this land?"[178] MT pondered and questioned:

> Palestine sits in sackcloth and ashes. Over it broods the spell of a curse that has withered its fields and fettered its energies. . . . Palestine is desolate and unlovely. And why should it be otherwise? Can the curse of the Deity beautify a land?[179]

Herman Melville had toured Palesitne a decade earlier, and had MT talked with him in New York about it, he would have been better prepared for what he found there. They both had a similar background of Calvinism followed by honest skepticism, but the Bible continued to be their main literary source. An observation by Walter Bezanson, a Melville specialist, could also be written of MT, "The kinds of questions to which the great religions addressed themselves were precisely those Melville's temperament and training would not let him do without."[180] Traveling alone, Melville preceded MT in visiting Jerusalem shrines and the Mar Saba monastery. He jotted in his journal that "no country will more

---

[174]McKeithan, ed., *Traveling with the Innocents Abroad*, 303.
[175]MTN 99.
[176]LTR 3:101.
[177]MTHL 716.
[178]Deuteronomy 29:22, 24.
[179]IA 607-608.
[180]Walter Bezanson, ed., *Clarel* (New York: Hendricks House, 1960) cviii.

quickly dissipate romantic expectations than Palestine." Judea, he noted, "compares with other regions as skeleton with living and rosy man."[181]

In visiting Egypt, MT found its ancient religion not only impressive but in some ways superior to that of the Hebrews, "We were glad to have seen that land which had an enlightened religion with future eternal rewards and punishment in it, while even Israel's religion contained no promise of a hereafter."[182] He felt awe in the presence of one of the world's wonders:

> The Sphinx is grand in its loneliness; it is imposing in its magnitude; it is impressive in the mystery that hangs over its story. And there is that in the overshadowing majesty of this eternal figure of stone, with its accusing memory of the deeds of all ages, which reveals to one something of what he shall feel when he shall stand at last in the awful presence of God.[183]

Travel Reflections

MT's mind and spirit were nourished by frequent domestic and international travels. He wrote that bigotry cannot be rooted out "by vegetating in one little corner of the earth all one's lifetime."[184] After returning home, he frequently lectured on the topic, "The American Vandal Abroad," urging each listener to travel abroad to diminish narrow-mindedness, and to learn, as he did, a crucial religious and moral message:

> It rubs out a multitude of his old unworthy bias and prejudices. It aids his religion, for it enlarges his charity and his benevolence, it broadens his views of men and things; it deepens his generosity and his compassion for the failings and the short-comings of his fellow creatures. Contact with men of various nations and many creeds teaches him that there are other people in the world beside his own little clique, and other opinions as worthy of attention and respect as his own. . . . Cast into trouble and misfortune in strange lands and being mercifully cared for by those he never saw before, he begins to learn that best lesson all—that one which culminates in the conviction that God put something good and lovable in every man his hands

---

[181]Herman Melville, *Journals* (Evanston IL: Northwestern University Press, 1989) 83, 91.
[182]IA 633.
[183]IA 629.
[184]IA 650.

swearing on the voyage, and signing "Your Improving Prodigal."[193] He gave her credit for this instruction in religious morality:

> One rational way of seeking Christ is to learn to put yourself out of sight when you are meditating an act, and consider how to do it for the comfort and benefit of others, and so take to itself a Christ-like spirit—and that bye and bye when one has made this a habit and it has become a pleasure to consider the weal of others first, that religion will not then be far away.[194]

One of MT's letters to Fairbanks adds to what he previously wrote about the Church of the Nativity, "I touch, with reverent finger, the actual spot where the infant Jesus lay, but I think—nothing."[195] He found it impossible to reflect when he was surrounded by noisy beggars; inspiring thoughts came later, "We do not think, in holy places; we think in bed, afterwards, when the glare, and the noise, and the confusion are gone, and in fancy we revisit alone, the solemn monuments of the past, and summon the phantom pageants of an age that has passed away."[196] Shortly after Phillips Brooks, the most outstanding Episcopal minister of his day, composed "O Little Town of Bethlehem" on the basis of his visit to the village two years earlier, MT wrote Fairbanks his Christmas Eve reflections:

> Don't you realize again, as in other years, that Jesus was born there, and that the angels did sing in the still air above, and that the wondering shepherds did hold their breath and listen as the mysterious music floated by? I do. It is more real than ever. And I am glad, a hundred times glad, that I saw Bethlehem, though at the time it seemed that that sight had swept away forever every pleasant fancy and every cherished memory that ever the City of Nativity had stored away in my mind and heart.[197]

Expressing similar sentiments, MT wrote that same Christmas Day in 1868 to Livy:

> All the night long my memory has been drifting back to Bethlehem, and more and more vividly the reality of what occurred there so many ages ago

---

[193]LTR 2:122.
[194]LTR 2:364.
[195]IA 601.
[196]IA 603.
[197]LTR 2:350.

has seemed to dawn upon me—until now, even I can half comprehend the grandeur of the old first Christmas night."[198]

MT came to realize, as Wilson points out, that holy places are "like Keats's Grecian Urn, they transcend time and space, leave behind the glare, noise, confusion, to assume spiritual importance only after the imagination, through contemplation, discovers their true meaning." Wilson goes on to say, "Although the pilgrim finds genuine revelation at the end of his quest, in so doing he remains isolated from the other Innocents whose pilgrimage, finally, is pretense."[199]

A year after writing letters from Palestine, MT revised them for publication in his "travel book." Memories of his travels there returned to "haunt his reveries," prompting him to add this reflection:

> In the starlight, Galilee has no boundaries but the broad compass of the heavens, and is a theatre meet for great events; meet for the birth of a religion able to save a world; and meet for the stately Figure appointed to stand upon its stage and proclaim its high decrees. But in the sunlight, one says: Is it for the deeds which were done and the words which were spoken in this little acre of rocks and sand eighteen centuries gone, that the bells are ringing today in the remote islands of the sea and far and wide over continents that clasp the circumference of the huge globe?[200]

Back in New York, following a Sunday service at the Plymouth Church, MT was invited to dine with its distinguished pastor, Henry Ward Beecher, and his sisters, Harriet Beecher Stowe and Isabella Beecher Hooker. When MT made his first trip to Hartford shortly afterward, he stayed in the Hooker home. He wrote his mother about meeting members of the Beecher family, reporting that "Henry Ward is a brick" even though the anti-liquor crusader served cider rather than wine.[201] As MT would say, his was a home with six Bibles and no corkscrew. Knowing that Beecher had made much money as a writer and speaker, MT returned to Brooklyn to get his advice on securing a

---

[198]LTR 3:352.
[199]Wilson, "Religious and Esthetic Vision in Mark Twain's Early Career," 163-64.
[200]IA 513.
[201]LTR 2:144.

favorable book contract for his Mediterranean excursion manuscript. The fledgling writer appreciated Beecher's sound judgment:

> "You are one of the talented men of the age . . . but in matters of business, I don't suppose you know more than enough to come in when it rains. I'll tell you what to do and how to do it!" . . . I listened well, and then . . . made a splendid contract for a *Quaker City* book. . . . Puritans are mighty straightlaced and they won't let me smoke in the parlor, but the Almighty don't make any better people.[202]

MT may also have been encouraged by what Beecher had written five years earlier:

> The real lives of boys are yet to be written. The lives of pious and good boys, which enrich the catalogue of great publishing societies, resemble a real boy's life about as much as a chicken picked and larded, upon a spit, and ready for delicious eating, resembles a free fowl in the field.[203]

MT initially considered calling his book "The New Pilgrim's Progress." From childhood he had been acquainted with *The Pilgrim's Progress*, the eighteenth-century allegory by Baptist minister John Bunyan about the struggle of a person named "Christian" to understand how to get to Heaven. But at his publisher's suggestion, they agreed to relegate MT's first title idea to serve as a somewhat ironic subtitle. Since most of the passengers were from the same Puritan stock as the *Mayflower* passengers, this book can be viewed as a reversal, telling of pilgrims going back to the Old World.

The main title became *The Innocents Abroad*, probably because it enabled prospective readers to identify with the naivete of travellers to strange lands. *Innocents Abroad* became MT's first successful book publication and one of the first travel books by an American. He was astute enough to realize that treating hallowed sites with unmitigating reverence would lose the wide readership he was addressing, so he served up a literary concoction that he hoped would satisfy both the impious and the pious. This was easy for him to do, for he was a rich blend of both. Paine describes *Innocents Abroad* in this way:

---

[202]LTR 2:160.

[203]Henry Ward Beecher, *Eyes and Ears* (Boston: Ticknor, 1862) 73.

Passages of it were calculated to take the breath of the orthodox reader; only, somehow, it made him smile, too. It was all so good-natured, so openly sincere. Without doubt it preached heresy—the heresy of viewing revered landmarks and relics joyously, rather than lugubriously; reverentially, when they inspired reverence; satirically, when they invited ridicule, and with kindness always.[204]

§ § §

Shortly after disembarking from the *Quaker City*, MT went to Wash ington to see if a career in government might interest him. Immediately he became secretary to William Stewart, the first senator from Nevada. However, it did not take him much longer to get his fill of the political fighting on Capitol hill than it took for his ardor to cool over Civil War fighting. Or, in comparison with a more recent experience, his disillusionment with the holy city of democracy along the Potomac was as quick as with the holy city of religion along the Tiber. He was disenchanted with President Andrew Johnson, whom the Congress was moving to impeach, and disgusted with the hypocrisy of politicians like Stewart, who pretended to be advocates for the common citizen even as they became wealthy serving the interests of the big mining companies. The months MT spent at the capital would provide him fuel for satire.

MT's best experience in Washington was rooming with William Swinton, whom late in life he referred to as "one of the dearest and loveliest human beings" he ever knew. Together they launched a syndicated column that was carried in a dozen weeklies. Swinton's religion had qualities MT hoped to find in his, and he described his role model this way:

He was a gentleman by nature and breeding; he was highly educated; he was of a beautiful spirit; he was pure in heart and speech. He was a Scotchman and a Presbyterian; a Presbyterian of the old and genuine school, being honest and sincere in his religion and loving it and finding serenity and peace in it.[205]

By way of suggesting why he was unsuited to serve as senatorial secretary, MT wrote a burlesque in which he reported having been asked to reply to a Methodist church request to become legally incorporated in

---

[204]MTB 383.
[205]AMT 154.

Nevada. The senator briefed his secretary that the request was a state rather than federal matter and confided that the religious element in his state was so feeble that the need for incorporation by the Methodists was questionable. In his letter to the Methodist official, MT alleged that he stated, "You will have to go to the State Legislature. . . [for] Congress don't know anything about religion." By way of expressing disdain for both parties of the correspondence he also included this swipe, "This thing you propose to do out in that new country isn't expedient—in fact, it is simply ridiculous. Your religious people there are too feeble, in intellect, in morality, in piety—in everything pretty much."[206]

§ § §

For five years the peripatetic MT moved across areas as far removed as Hawaii and Palestine, giving him a breadth of geographical experience that was without parallel for a writer in his era. He occasionally alluded to a biblical verse to express his experiences: "I have been a stranger in a strange land."[207] His travels enhanced his knowledge of the variety of cultures and religious expressions. MT realized that his grounding in biblical literature gave him a point of contact with people who had read little else. His satirical style of writing was especially effective when he wrote for those who interpreted the Bible literally and supernaturally. At the age of thirty-three he was reaching the apex of a lifespan's curve and was well prepared for a more settled life as an author and family man.

---

[206]CT1 258.
[207]Exodus 2:22; LTR 2:236; 4:96; 6:8, 25.

Chapter 4
Amid Liberal Calvinists

In New York State

Having absorbed the religious and other basic elements of the culture of the American South and the West, Mark Twain was next to encounter cultural challenges at other points of the American compass. During the many years that remained in his life after his *Quaker City* voyage, he was heavily influenced by liberal Calvinism in the Northeast. Both as preacher and friend, he had already learned to appreciate Henry Ward Beecher, the nation's most famous liberal Calvinist. From the time he began to court Olivia ("Livy") Langdon until the last years of his life, he frequently participated in the activities of the lively group of liberal Calvinists that flourished in Elmira, New York, where Livy was born and resided until marriage.

When Livy's parents, Jervis and Olivia Langdon, moved to Elmira from Ithaca in 1845 to establish lumber and coal companies in the region, they found dissent among members of the Presbyterian Church. John Frost, who had been the minister of that oldest church in the town, left in 1839 after being harassed for leading abolitionist rallies. Frost had been influenced by Presbyterian ministers Theodore Weld, who developed the Anti-Slavery Society in New York, and George Bourne, who had written *The Book and Slavery Irreconcilable* in 1816.[1] Some on the church's session who shared Frost's outlook wanted to bar from membership anyone who condoned slavery. Although that ruling board refused to make antislavery conviction a condition for admission to the church fellowship, its abolitionist position was made clear in this resolution, "We regard the holding and treating of human beings as property as inconsistent with the spirit and principles of the gospel and we deplore the fact that members of churches in this country are guilty of this practice."[2]

Jervis Langdon, like MT, grew up in a Presbyterian church. Prior to moving to Elmira, the Langdons helped to start New School Presbyterian

---

[1]William Phipps, "George Bourne," *The Presbyterian Outlook* (13 July 1981): 4-5.

[2]Edward Hoffman, "The First Presbyterian Church" (Elmira NY, privately circulated, 1997) 21-23.

churches in two villages of upstate New York.[3] Believing that the promotion of human liberation was a basic ethical implication of Christianity, they gave sanctuary to Frederick Douglass in 1838 as he was escaping from slavery, and subsequently to hundreds of other fugitives. In a letter to Mrs. Langdon a generation later, Douglass recalled: "(You) made me welcome under your roof in Millport. . . . I have carried the name of Jervis Langdon with me ever since."[4] A few months after settling in Elmira, the Langdons joined with the forty Presbyterians who amiably left their denomination to form "The Independent Congregational Church." Article 10 of its bylaws reads: "No person shall be admitted to the church, or allowed to remain in it, who practices or approves of buying or selling human beings, or holding them in slavery."[5] The new congregation now had a place to "talk and pray antislavery and 'reform.' "[6] To witness that they transcended sectarianism, they decided in 1871 to call themselves simply "Park Church."

In the United States, the Congregationalists and the Presbyterians were the two main branches of Protestantism that had been founded in the sixteenth century by John Calvin of Geneva. The Congregationalists came to emphasize social justice and local autonomy, whereas the Presbyterians tended to be more interested in doctrinal correctness and compliance with regional ecclesiastical directives. The Congregationalists, now the United Church of Christ, remain one of the most socially active denominations in America. Over the years they have been noted for their liberation efforts on behalf of slaves, women, and now, homosexuals.

Writer Max Eastman, who grew up in Park Church, commended the Langdons for being "not only the central pillars but the foundation stones upon which the church had been built."[7] Park Church helped provide temporary sanctuary for the fugitives who assembled in Elmira after fleeing northward on the "underground railway." Their destination was

---

[3]Herbert Wisbey, "Jervis Langdon, Christian Businessman," Mark Twain Lecture Series, Elmira, unpublished tape (March 1989).

[4]LMT 3:428.

[5]*Centennial Album* (Elmira: Park Church, 1946) 46.

[6]Thomas Beecher, "Olivia Langdon Memorial Address" (privately circulated) 7.

[7]Max Eastman, *Heroes I Have Known* (New York: Simon & Schuster, 1942) 16.

Canada because the Fugitive Slave Law prevented their freedom within the United States. The Langdons provided lodging and funding that would enable the fugitives to catch the Northern Central Railway through Elmira and Rochester. Also, William Garrison, Wendell Phillips, and other abolitionists were entertained in the Langdon home when they visited Elmira to speak about the rights of African-Americans. Susan B. Anthony, a leader in the Anti-Slavery Society in Rochester and another underground railway conductor, was probably in contact with the Langdons. Their assistance to fugitive slaves was expensive, socially as well as financially, since being viewed as radicals "cost them social ostracism and contempt,"[8] and caused their "children to be pointed at with a sneer."[9]

Douglass, who became the main African-American leader in the nation, spoke at Elmira in 1848 and returned in 1880 for a commemoration of the Emancipation Proclamation.[10] Due in part to encouragements such as he found among the civilly disobedient whites in Elmira, he expressed confidence that the races in America could enjoy "the inestimable blessings of life, liberty, and the pursuit of happiness, as neighborly citizens of a common country."[11] Numerous liberated slaves chose to settle in Elmira, and Jervis Langdon was no doubt among the "generous white friends" who helped them establish a church there.[12] The Frederick Douglass Methodist Episcopal Zion Church is still prominent in the city.

In Elmira, MT grew to understand better that the Calvinist tradition was not of one mind regarding slavery. Moreover, the abolitionists were as inspired by the Bible as the Hannibal slaveholders had been, but they quoted different texts. They were especially influenced by the verse that Quaker colonists in Pennsylvania had inscribed on the Liberty Bell at the

---

[8]Thomas Beecher at Olivia Langdon's funeral, in Eastman, *Heroes I Have Known*, 111.

[9]Thomas Beecher, "Jervis Langdon Memorial Address" (privately circulated) 27.

[10]Shelly Fisher Fishkin, *Lighting Out for the Territory* (New York: Oxford University Press, 1996) 95.

[11]John Blassingame, ed., *The Frederick Douglass Papers* (New Haven CT: Yale University Press, 1985) 3:576.

[12]Thomas Byrne, *Chemung County 1890–1975* (Elmira NY: Chemung County Historical Society, 1979) 519.

beginning of the antislavery movement. Abolitionists treated as prophetic the Leviticus 25:10 proclamation of freedom to "all the inhabitants" of the land. The Langdons probably introduced MT to the writings of Albert Barnes, the main leader of the New School Presbyterians and an ardent abolitionist. MT had in his library a ten-volume set of New Testament commentaries by Barnes,[13] who attempted to show that early Christian literature could not properly be used to justify slavery. He believed that the apostle Paul, writing a slave master about a fugitive who had come to him for protection, had advocated that he be emancipated. "The principles laid down in this Epistle to Philemon, therefore, would lead to the universal abolition of slavery," Barnes concluded.[14] Even according to the Hebrew Scriptures, fugitive slaves should not be returned to bondage—as then required by the less-humane United States law—but should be permitted to dwell in freedom wherever they had fled.[15] Members of Park Church shared the outlook of Abraham Lincoln who applied the Golden Rule in saying, "As I would not be a slave, so I would not be a master."[16] Late in life, MT referred to early abolitionists, such as Langdon, Bourne, Garrison, Weld, and David Nelson of Missouri as examples of moral courage, "They lived in a storm of vituperation; they were hated, despised, shunned; the whole nation cursed them, not six pulpits in the Union ventured to defend them."[17]

MT had known Jervis Langdon for less than three years when Langdon died of cancer in 1870. In the obituary he wrote, MT called his father-in-law a "noble Christian" because of his eagerness to accept and assist others:

> He had so charitable a nature that he could always find some justification for any one who injured him; and then his forgiveness followed. . . . He stood always ready to help whoever needed help—wisely with advice, healthfully with cheer and encouragement, and lavishly with money. . . . He was an Abolitionist from the cradle and worked openly and valiantly in that

---

[13]MTLB 47.

[14]Albert Barnes, *Notes on the Epistles to the Thessalonians, to Timothy, Titus, and Philemon* (repr.: Edinburgh: Gall & Inglis, 1900) 390.

[15]Deuteronomy 23:15-16.

[16]Roy Basler, ed., *The Collected Works of Abraham Lincoln* (New Brunswick: Rutgers University Press, 1953) 2:532.

[17]WM 495.

cause all through the days when to do such a thing was to ensure to a man disgrace, insult, hatred, and bodily peril.[18]

Jervis Langdon was the wealthiest person in Elmira when he died, but he was remembered mainly for his "fantastic acts of generosity."[19] Those acts manifested the centrality of religion in his life, for he said, "If I cannot do business as a Christian I do not want to do business at all."[20] Before the Civil War, his philanthropy was primarily directed against slavery, the most acute social ill of the nation. At his death he received this tribute, "He formed one of the little band of original abolitionists out of which finally grew that overwhelming and all pervading public sentiment under the steady march of which this relic of barbarism was uprooted."[21] His pastor, Thomas Beecher, extolled the "tender-hearted philanthropy" of the man who had given "many thousand dollars toward the education of whites and blacks in our southern states" after the war. Late in life Langdon spent only a half-hour daily on his own business and devoted the rest of his day to handling charity requests.[22]

Thomas Beecher, the half-brother of Henry Ward Beecher, was another eminent personality in Elmira whom MT greatly admired. He was called to be the pastor of Park Church in 1854 and remained there until his death in 1900. Highly unconventional, he preferred to call himself a "teacher," saying "I do not think good can be done by a preacher's preaching."[23] Earlier, as a pastor in Brooklyn, he had no interest in emulating his brother's oratorical style at the nearby Plymouth Church. "Preaching never really converts anyone, but living does," he opined.[24] Although he paid little attention to preparing sermons, his frank and friendly messages provided simple guidance for applying Christianity. By treating theological talk lightly and by focusing on compassionate deeds, Thomas Beecher attracted a large congregation from all denominations, as well as those who were unchurched and agnostics. He also wrote a

---

[18]LTR 4:183.

[19]Eastman, *Heroes I Have Known*, 109.

[20]Wisbey, "Jervis Langdon: Christian Businessman."

[21](Elmira) *Daily Advertiser*, 8 August 1870.

[22]Thomas Beecher, "Jervis Langdon Memorial Address," 28, 30.

[23]Eva Taylor, *A History of the Park Church* (Elmira NY: Park Church, 1981) 13.

[24]Myra Glenn, *Thomas K. Beecher* (Westport CT: Greenwood, 1996) 79.

weekly column in the local paper where he frequently expressed bold opinions on controversial issues. For example, he advocated cremation and accepted suicide in certain situations.

Thomas Beecher's monument in Elmira
beside the Park Church where he was pastor.

During the Civil War, Beecher organized church members to assist Confederate prisoners at a nearby camp where overcrowding was causing a death rate of eight men per day.[25] For a few months during the War he served as chaplain with the Army of the Potomac. Having gotten to know Lincoln personally while a college student in Illinois, Beecher warned him about a plot by some army dissidents to replace him with General

---

[25]MTCW 69.

McClellan.[26]

Eastman rightly viewed Beecher as a "dominant and molding intellectual and spiritual force" on MT. Beecher's purpose, according to Eastman, "was to live and be helpful in the community as a modern Jesus would, a downright, realistic, iconoclastic, life-loving Jesus with a scientific training and a sense of humor and a fund of common sense." In accord with the Galilean "winebibber,"[27] Beecher hung his personal beer mug in his favorite tavern. Although denounced by teetotalers, Beecher brewed beer and believed that "moderate drinking of wines and beers served a useful function, promoting health and relaxation in some people."[28] Also, in a Jesus-like style, he and his wife Julia took a notorious prostitute into their home, treating her like a daughter until she married.

Beecher was "endowed with a supreme contempt for fame, money, and 'success.' "[29] Harris Starr writes that "Father Tom," as he was affectionately called, was admired by all classes of citizens and that he was "always shabbily dressed, for he impoverished himself by his generosity."[30] Noting his threadbare coat, Jervis Langdon once took him to a tailor and had a new one made. Finding that Beecher had reverted to wearing his old coat some weeks later, he asked what had happened to the new one. Beecher explained that he had met a man who owned no coat and was too embarrassed to give him the badly worn one. Father Bloomer of the Elmira Catholic Church said "Beecher and benevolence are synonymous."[31]

Gretchen Sharlow, who has researched the close ties between the Beechers and Clemens families, and is a member of Park Church, writes, "Beecher was involved in the life of the entire community, active in school administration, politics, planning bridges, even providing everyday

---

[26]Lyman Stowe, *Saints, Sinners, and Beechers* (Indianapolis: Bobbs-Merrill, 1934) 367.

[27]Matthew 11:19.

[28]Glenn, *Thomas K. Beecher*, 142-44.

[29]Eastman, *Heroes I Have Known*, 112-13.

[30]"Thomas Beecher," *Dictionary of American Biography*, ed. Allen Johnson (New York: Scribner's, 1929).

[31]Taylor, *A History of the Park Church*, 23.

chores for the needy such as cutting wood and painting houses."[32]
Fascinated by machines, he not only kept the town clock running but
occasionally was allowed to take over the controls of the locomotive
when he traveled. Dressed like a laborer, he rode around Elmira on a
tricycle he had invented. On the wall of Park Church a commemorative
tablet lists his endeavors: "Workman, citizen, philosopher, minister"—the
order is significant.

MT appreciated the Beecher brothers' interest in integrating theology
with the new science of evolution that was transforming astronomy,
geology, and biology. They were among the first American clergy to
tackle that controversial subject and transform a threat into an asset. The
Beechers taught that Christians should be flexible enough to welcome
scientific findings while retaining the essentials of their religion. An
editorial on brother Henry that MT wrote for the Buffalo *Express* contains
this tribute: "Mr. Beecher has done more than any other man, perhaps, to
inspire religion with the progressive spirit of the nineteenth century, and
made it keep step with the march of intellectual achievement. . . . He has
done as much as any man to keep the people from reading their Bible by
the interpretations of the eighteenth century."[33] Henry Ward Beecher, in
his book *Evolution and Religion*, asserted that God speaks in a unified
way through all creation and that it is artificial to separate natural and
revealed religion.[34] Thomas Beecher supported the then highly controversial theory of biological evolution and even corresponded with Charles
Darwin and Thomas Huxley. He helped establish the Elmira Academy of
Science and became its first president.

Beecher, who had attended theatrical productions in the local Opera
House, held Sunday evening religious services there, because seating was
not adequate elsewhere for the large number who wished to attend. He
was denounced from Elmira pulpits for offering prayers in a "Satanic
edifice." Concerned over declining attendance in their congregations,
some Elmira ministers persuaded the Ministerial Union, which Beecher
had revived, to pass a resolution expelling him from the Union and

[32]"Thomas Beecher," ENC.
[33]Joseph McCullough and Janice McIntire-Strasburg, eds., *Mark Twain at the
Buffalo Express* (DeKalb IL: Northern Illinois University Press, 1999) 59.
[34]Henry Ward Beecher, *Evolution and Religion* (New York: Ford, 1885) 139.

disapproving of Christians who frequented the Opera House. In the Elmira *Advertiser*, MT wryly noted that Beecher's "great mistake was in supposing that when he had the Saviour's endorsement of his conduct, he had all that was necessary." The fulminations of clergy, MT observed, "have crushed a famous Beecher and reduced his audiences from fifteen hundred down to fourteen hundred and seventy-five in one fell blow!" The twenty-five who withdrew, MT commented, preferred that the gospel be preached with "sweet monotonous tranquility" and "impenetrable profundity."[35] The envious local parsons also criticized Beecher for conducting summer services in the city park while wearing a white suit.[36]

To combat sectarianism and to promote an understanding of the variety of beliefs expressed by the seven denominations in Elmira, Beecher gave a series of lectures ranging from Roman Catholicism to Unitarianism. Although he was an evangelical Protestant, he respected the uniform liturgy, the heroic missionaries, and the universality of the Catholic Church, which had the largest congregation in the city.[37] Eventually, most of the area ministers as well as their congregations became more open, enabling joint services at the Opera House to continue for many years. Praising Beecher for his interfaith cooperation, Rabbi Jacob Marcus humbly said, "All I have aimed to be is a worthy assistant minister of Thomas K. Beecher in my pulpit."[38]

Beecher's congregation expanded rapidly, but he was reluctant to promote the construction of a larger edifice. Viewing preaching as secondary in authentic religion, he recognized that he could conduct his ministry as Jesus did—in conversations out-of-doors or by home-to-home and shop-to-shop visits. Even so, Beecher helped plan for the new structure and MT did what he could to raise money for the project by writing an article entitled "The New Beecher Church" for the *New York Times*. The congregation soon pledged a large sum for its construction and the Langdon family matched it. The innovative multipurpose structure was the first of its kind in the nation. "The idea is to make a child look upon a church as only another home, and a sunny one, rather than as a

---

[35]CT1 291-92.

[36]MTCW 105.

[37]Thomas Beecher, *Our Seven Churches* (New York: Ford, 1897) 5-8.

[38]Jacob Marcus, *Thomas K. Beecher* (Elmira NY: Park Church, 1900) 41.

dismal exile or prison," wrote one who recalled his frequent misery in his boyhood church. In addition to areas for traditional functions, MT reported that the plans included a community kitchen, the city's first lending library, a game room for shooting pool and playing cards, a welfare office, bathing rooms for those without such facilities in their homes, and an infirmary for the old and ill. One large area, called the romp room, was designated for dances, basketball, and congregational or civic theater productions. These facilities, virtually unheard of in churches elsewhere, were designed mainly for weekday use, and they were available for any group in the community. MT also endorsed the architectural independence of the church: "There is to be no steeple on the church—merely because no practical use can be made of it. There is to be no bell, because any ignoramus knows what time church service begins without that exasperating nuisance."[39] Beecher designed a mosque-like dome with ventilating windows for what he called an "auditorium," rather than a "sanctuary."

One Elmira citizen remembered that MT was a "faithful attendant at Park Church" during his summers there.[40] His sometimes withering faith seemed to revive in the Elmira religious environment. He treasured the bold and great-hearted Beecher couple and enjoyed stimulating conversations with them. One Sunday morning Father Tom lost track of time as he talked with MT in the Langdon's yard across the street from the church and he had to be fetched to lead the service that had already begun.[41] Apart from his own extended family in the city, the Beechers were MT's closest friends there. They nurtured his passion for Christian humanitarianism and his criticism of materialism.

After Beecher's death in 1900, the city appropriately commemorated "Elmira's First Citizen" with an imposing statue in the public square, which continues to be a central landmark for the city. After pointing to MT's emphasis upon the power of one's mentors, Sharlow says, "His association with the spiritual leader of his Elmira home circle, Thomas K.

---

[39] *New York Times*, 23 July 1871.
[40] *Mark Twain Society Bulletin* (July 1983): 2.
[41] Robert Jerome and Herbert Wisbey, eds., *Mark Twain in Elmira* (Elmira NY: Mark Twain Society, 1977) 190.

Beecher, had a profoundly liberating effect on his philosophical genius."[42]

MT made use of one of his autobiographical dictations when he visited Park Church in 1907 to help dedicate a new organ as a memorial to Beecher.[43] He offered this tribute:

Julia Beecher, wife of the Park Church pastor. The Beechers were role models for the Clemens.

> I knew all the Beecher brotherhood and sisterhood, I believe. The men were all preachers, and more or less celebrated in their day. I knew Rev. Henry Ward, Rev. Thomas K., Rev. Charles, and Rev. James, very well. . . . I knew Rev. Thomas K. Beecher intimately for a good many years. . . . He was deeply versed in the sciences, and his pulpit eloquence fell but little short of that of his great brother, Henry Ward. His was a keen intellect, and he was brilliant in conversation. . . . He was one of the best men I have ever known; also he was one of the best citizens I have ever known. To the end of his days he was looked up to in that town [of Elmira] by both sinners and saints, as a man whose judgment in matters concerning the welfare of the town was better and sounder than anyone else's, and whose purity and integrity were unassailable. He was beloved and revered by all the citizenship.[44]

The ingenuity, wit, and incredible energy of Julia Beecher also fascinated MT. She made dolls to fund foreign and domestic missionary causes, and he assisted her efforts by auctioning them off.[45] He borrowed the word "jabberwocks" from Lewis Carroll to name the grotesque birds

---

[42]Gretchen Sharlow, "Mark Twain's Elmira Teacher: The Reverend Thomas K. Beecher," an unpublished paper presented at the South Central Conference on Christianity and Literature, 31 January 1996.

[43]MTCW 107.

[44]MTP*, autobiographical dictation, 1 March 1907.

[45]MTCW 109.

and beasts she created from dried roots, which he sold at a bazaar in Hartford. He acknowledged that her creatures could "make a body's flesh crawl with pleasure," and expressed relief that she did not breathe life into them![46] Julia was honored in Elmira by what was for many years the only public memorial to a woman in the city. A bronze relief of her kindly face and avant-garde bobbed hair graced the corner of the Federation Building. Together, Julia and Thomas Beecher were the most influential couple in Elmira during the latter part of the nineteenth century. Their legacy endures in their church and in the lore of their community.

Park Church is important to understanding MT's religion not only because he approved of and was informed by its ministry but also because of its impact on the person who was to have the most influence over him. Eastman writes:

> Olivia's gospel, in so far as she learned it from the church in which her mother and father were the central social and financial force, was one of self-reliant revolt against forms and conventions as such. And if she suspected that Mark Twain had unorthodox views about religion, that could only have helped him to fit into the environment in which she had been born and reared. For her own mother was perhaps as unorthodox as anybody in Mr. Beecher's extremely free-thinking congregation.[47]

MT proposed to Livy after courting her for two weeks, but she refused him for six months. A Victorian maiden of twenty-three needed the approval of her parents before becoming engaged. In an effort to reform her suitor so that he would become acceptable to her family, Livy regularly sent him copies of the *Plymouth Pulpit*, a periodical the Langdons subscribed to that featured Henry Ward Beecher's sermons. The Langdons liked Beecher's theology and ethics, especially since he had been an outspoken critic of slavery. After the Fugitive Slave Act was passed, the Plymouth Church became a sanctuary for fleeing slaves. Like his sister Harriet Beecher Stowe, who wrote *Uncle Tom's Cabin*, Henry had urged Lincoln to move more rapidly toward the emancipation of slaves.[48]

---

[46]*Mark Twain Society Bulletin* (February 1978): 1.

[47]Eastman, *Heroes I Have Known*, 128.

[48]Constance Rourke, *Trumpets of Jubilee* (New York: Harcourt, Brace, 1927)

MT's wife, Olivia Langdon Clemens (1845–1904).

In contrast to Calvinism's traditional doctrine of stern judgment and limited atonement for the elect, Beecher preached salvation for all who accepted God's love and worked to reform society. That theme is dramatically expressed in this sermon:

To tell me that back of Christ is a God who for numbered centuries has gone on creating men and sweeping them like dead flies—nay, like living ones—into hell, is to ask me to worship a Being as much worse than the

---

181-84.

conception of any medieval devil as can be imagined. But I will not worship the devil though he should come dressed in royal robes and sit on the throne of Jehovah. I will not worship cruelty, I will worship Love—that sacrifices itself for the good of those who err, and that is as patient with them as a mother is with a sick child.[49]

In his love letters, MT occasionally commented on a sermon Livy had sent. About one, he said he was touched by "the microscopic insight into the secret springs and impulses of the human heart, and the searching analysis of text and subject which distinguish Henry Ward Beecher's wonderful sermons."[50] In another, Beecher impressed him by contrasting the person whose life is based on "Thou shalt not"—steal, swear, murder, and drink—with the Christian who "develops graces into positivity." MT confessed, "I lack . . . that inner sense which tells me that what I do I am doing for love of the Savior."[51]

MT found truth in Beecher's discourses, but more wisdom in Livy, who revealed God in the flesh, "You are a living, breathing sermon; a blessing delivered straight from the hand of God; a messenger, that, speaking or silent, carries refreshment to the weary, hope to the despondent, sunshine to the darkened way of all that come and go about you."[52]

Earthly love and the love of God were intertwined for MT. In courting Livy, he wrote:

> Let us believe that God has destined us for each other. . . . Let us hope and believe that we shall walk hand in hand down the lengthening highway of life, one in heart, one in impulse and one in love and worship of Him—bearing each other's burdens, sharing each other's joys, soothing each other's griefs—and, so linked together—and so journeying, pass at last the shadowed boundaries of time and stand redeemed and saved, beyond the threshold and within the light of that Land whose Prince is the Lord of rest eternal.[53]

In that letter MT showed his familiarity with the ethics of the apostle Paul, and in another letter he echoed what the apostle wrote about the

---

[49]PH 101-102.
[50]LTR 3:46.
[51]LTR 2:353.
[52]LTR 3:63.
[53]LTR 3:11.

ineffable nature of communication with God, "We know not what we should pray for as we ought: but the Spirit itself maketh intercession for us with groanings which cannot be uttered."[54] That view of prayer is similar to MT's devotion that transcends words:

> I am so happy I hardly know what to do with myself—and I bless you, and give honest gratitude to God that it is so. How easy it was to pray when your letter came—for the heart naturally looks upward for something to THANK when a great generous wave of gratitude sweeps over its parched and thirsty deserts. . . . I prayed that at last you might come to love me freely and fully, and that He would prepare me to be worthy of it—which could only be, in utter completeness, through my investment with His spirit. Some of my other prayers have seemed only faint-hearted words, words, words, compared to this, which came surging up out of my heart—a great tide of feeling which scorned set phrase and tricks of speech, and prayed itself![55]

William Pellowe perceives a mystic quality in MT's spirit during those prenuptial months: "During his courtship of Olivia Langdon, Mark came very close to religious ecstasy. His conduct demonstrated the intimate kinship between religion and love, that intermingling of the worship of a beloved partner with expression of devotion to God."[56]

MT had submitted to Livy's parents the names of six prominent San Franciscan professionals as character references, including Charles Wadsworth and Horatio Stebbins. Those two clergymen proved to be appropriate ones for MT's cause for they did not think of him as a reprobate. Stebbins responded, "Mark is rather erratic, but I consider him harmless." However, James Roberts, a deacon in the Calvary Presbyterian Church who was superintendent of the Sabbath School, whose name was not given by MT for vetting, testified that he would "fill a drunkard's grave."[57] "I would rather bury a daughter of mine than have her marry such a fellow," he said.[58] Roberts may have known that MT had once been jailed for public drunkenness in San Francisco or that he had been

---

[54]Galatians 6:2; Romans 8:26, 12:15.
[55]LTR 2:301-302.
[56]PH 110.
[57]AMT 189.
[58]Quoted in MTL 3:57.

called a "Profaner of Divinity" in a Western newspaper.[59] The vetting probably confirmed that MT was not only a frequent imbiber of alcohol, but was a habitual swearer, a financially insecure wanderer, and a poorly educated frontiersman.

As it happened, Jervis Langdon was skilled in judging character; much of his success was due to his willingness to extend business credit only to the trustworthy. Also, he expected others to live as he attempted to live, by the Golden Rule. Livy's parents had come to have so much personal confidence in MT's integrity that they decided to approve him in spite of his bad references. Jervis settled the matter by saying: "I believe in you. I know you better than they do."[60] Livy, it seemed, had so polished her diamond-in-the-rough that the entire Langdon family had come to view him as a valuable addition to the family.

In a letter to a friend, MT told about becoming engaged, "On bended knees, in the presence of God only, we devoted our lives to each other and to the service of God."[61] Afterwards he wrote Livy's mother, "I now claim that I am a Christian."[62] At that same time he also wrote his family about Livy on a lighter note: "She said she never could or would love me—but she set herself the task of making a Christian of me. I said she would succeed, but that in the meantime she would unwittingly dig a matrimonial pit and end by tumbling into it—and lo! the prophecy is fulfilled."[63]

MT's assertion that he became a Christian during his courtship is an exaggeration. Less than two years earlier he referred to himself as a Christian.[64] When he classified himself as a "sinner" on the Mediterranean excursion, he was no more excluding himself from the ranks of Christians than Peter, by calling himself a sinful man, was separating himself from Jesus' disciples. What MT was now professing was a more fastidious observance of Christianity than he had been accustomed to in the years immediately preceding. For a few years he shared Livy's practice of religion, which included setting aside time for daily prayer and the reading

---

[59]MTL 1:253.
[60]MTB 378.
[61]LTR 3:101.
[62]LTR 3:90.
[63]LTR 3:85.
[64](San Francisco) *Alta California*, 7 July 1869.

of religious literature, along with abstaining from liquor and profanity.

Alluding to the story of the prodigal son, his favorite parable, MT offered Livy a long-range perspective on life:

> I do not live backward. God does not ask of the returning sinner what he *has* been, but what he *is* and what he *will* be. . . . Before I began this letter I offered up that prayer which has passed my lips many and many a time during these latter months: that I might be guarded from ever unconsciously or unwittingly saying anything to you which you might misconstrue and be thereby *deceived*—and that I might not be guilty of any taint or shadow of *hypocrisy*. . . . I am striving and shall still strive to reach . . . the highest Christian excellence.[65]

Music helped to cement the bond between the couple. In her only surviving love letter, Livy writes, "I believe dancing and singing is a true way to give praise to God—our whole natures seem to enter in them."[66] Recognizing this mutual interest, MT described to her the "grand explosion of rich sounds" he had heard at a church service he attended in Pittsburgh: "What worship was in the music! How it preached, how it pleaded! And how earthy and merely human seemed the clergyman's poor vapid declamation! He couldn't make us comprehend Christ desolate and forsaken, but the music did."[67] MT was alluding to these lyrics:

> Still near the lake, with weary tread,
> Lingers a form of human kind;
> And on His lone, unsheltered head,
> Flows the chill night-damp of the wind.
>
> Why seeks He not a home of rest?
> Why seeks He not a pillowed bed?
> Beasts have their dens, the bird its nest;
> He hath not where to lay his head.
>
> Such was the lot He freely chose,
> To bless, to save the human race;
> And through His poverty there flows
> A rich, full stream of heavenly grace.[68]

---

[65]LTR 3:74.
[66]LTR 3:394.
[67]LTR 3:380.
[68]William Russell, "O'er the Dark Wave of Galilee."

As MT wooed the genteel Livy, he became devoted to her gentle Christianity, with its less-threatening view of God than the one he had experienced west of the Mississippi. Her religion was also rationally respectable; she, unlike MT, had been able to extend her formal education by taking courses at Elmira Female College as her health permitted.[69] Jervis Langdon was among those who established that evangelical but nonsectarian college, which aimed at standards as high as those of men's colleges. Introducing Livy to his sister, MT boasted, "I take as much pride in her brains as I do in her beauty."[70]

MT's religion was also influenced by other residents of Elmira. Livy's older sister Susan had been adopted as a young child by the Langdons, so the two shared the same home environment. Julia Beecher, who was as bright and unconventional as her husband, was their Sunday school teacher. Susan married Theodore Crane and the two were "pillars" of the Park Church. When MT and Theodore were together, they enjoyed discussing theological and secular literature.

Susan Crane inherited the family's summer cottage from her father, and that became the Cranes' year-round roost for the rest of their lives. MT and his family spent many summers from 1871 to 1903 living there and enjoying their Elmira friends. Some distance from the Crane residence, Susan had an octagonal study built for her brother-in-law that resembled a pilot's cabin on a steamboat. There, hundreds of feet above Elmira, overlooking the peaceful countryside, he wrote some of his novels. The Beechers, who lived on the same East Hill in a house they had designed and built, suggested the Crane residence be called Quarry Farm. MT wrote a friend, "You have never seen any place that was so divine as the Farm. Why don't you come here and take a foretaste of heaven?"[71] "Rest and Be Thankful" was one name he preferred for the Elmira farm.

A daughter of MT has described the lively and affectionate interaction between him and Susan:

Father sometimes called her Saint Sue, and she returned the compliment by

---

[69]MTCW 124-25.

[70]LTR 3:189.

[71]Letter from MT to Joseph Twichell, 2 October 1879, Beinecke Library, Yale University.

baptizing him Holy Samuel. . . . Aunt Sue adored Father's little bursts of temper and would laugh at him most heartily. Often he laughed with her, altering his vehement mood instantaneously to one of childlike mirth. . . . Father often joined my aunt on her morning walk by the flowers, and I am certain now that the subject of their talk was frequently the undying topic of religion. . . . Father loved to fight her on this subject, and she was big enough to be greatly amused by his original way of putting his questions and objections.[72]

Both MT and Susan enjoyed hymn singing, and he recalled this pleasure in one of his letters to her. His favorite hymn, and one that he hoped would be sung at his funeral, had this opening stanza:

Lord, I hear of showers of blessing
Thou art scattering full and free,
Showers the thirsty land refreshing;
Let some droppings fall on me, even me![73]

Shortly before marriage, MT wrote Livy, "I have been reading some new arguments to prove that the world is very old, and that the six days of creation were six immensely long periods." This interpretation of the Genesis account prompted him to meditate on the psalmist's question, "When I consider thy heavens, . . . what is man, that thou art mindful of him?"[74] He realized that astronomy was deflating the grandiose human assumption that man is "the apple of the eye" of God and that all nature was created for one species on "our speck" of the universe.[75] "How insignificant we are," he exclaimed, "with our pigmy little world!" He asked, "Did Christ live 33 years in each of the millions and millions of worlds that hold their majestic courses above our heads?"[76] The tendency of humans to think more highly of themselves than they ought, a Calvinist assessment, had become one of MT's themes and undergirded much of his humor.

§ § §

---

[72]MF 59-61.
[73]LTR 3:181, 184.
[74]Psalm 8:3-4.
[75]Psalm 17:8.
[76]LTR 4:12.

After their wedding in 1870, the Clemenses went to live in Buffalo, New York. Jervis Langdon had provided them a furnished home with servants and had set up his son-in-law as a part owner of a newspaper in the city. During the few remaining months of Jervis's life, MT addressed him as "Father," finding in him a warmth he had never experienced from his own father. MT and Livy regularly attended the Lafayette Street Presbyterian Church,[77] which was probably not the same Buffalo church he had spoken of earlier to his fiancée. About a cerebral sermon he had heard there he made this ironical comment, "There was a sort of Presbyterian frozen-solemnity and stony unfeelingness about church and congregation which cheered me greatly, and brought me peace and satisfaction."[78] A few days after the newlyweds settled in Buffalo, he wrote that he had paraded out to church with Livy, who was dressed in her trousseau finery. They were introduced to the congregation during the Sunday school hour by Lafayette pastor Grosvenor Heacock, whom they found to be "an exceedingly pleasant and hearty man." Using biblical language, MT remarked, "I never can forget his kindness to the stranger within his gates."[79]

When MT was asked to judge compositions at the Buffalo Female Academy to determine graduation prizes, he noticed that the girls appropriately dealt with their themes "from high moral and religious altitudes," but tended to write sermons in the artificial and pretentious styles of their textbooks. Urging simplicity and naturalness, he wrote, "Religion is the highest and holiest thing on earth, and a strained or compulsory expression of it is not gracious, or commendable, or befitting its dignity."[80]

Two articles MT published while he was living in Buffalo illustrate that this "hound of Hannibal," as Daniel Pawley calls him, "had a bloodhound's instinct for sniffing the trails of hypocrites and Pharisees."[81] One was about Brooklyn preacher DeWitt Talmage who, like Beecher, attracted enormous congregations in that city, and his sermons were pub-

---

[77]LTR 4:55.
[78]LTR 3:289.
[79]MTMF 125; Exodus 20:10; Deuteronomy 14:21.
[80]CT1 410.
[81]*Christianity Today* (8 November 1985): 75.

lished in several thousand newspapers internationally.[82] MT owned several books containing Talmage's sermons and listed them for possibile inclusion in an anthology of humor he had been asked to edit.[83] He reacted strongly to a sermon excerpt, later found to be unrepresentative of the full context, that had been published in a Chicago journal. Talmage scemed to warn his high society congregation of the consequence of eliminating rental pews in the much larger "tabernacle" that was being planned. If pews were free, he pointed out, a working man with an offensive odor might sit next to a bonafide member. Moreover, "If you had all the churches free, by reason of the mixing up of the common people with the uncommon, you would keep one-half of Christendom sick at their stomach."[84] In response, MT wrote an article "About Smells" that noted the difference between Talmage's fashionable congregation and the first followers of Jesus, which included stinking fishermen and beggars. The apostles did not say, "Master, if thou art going to kill the church thus with bad smells, I will have nothing to do with this work of evangelization." Is it possible, MT asked sarcastically, that the Christian who once was willing to be burned at the stake with an unpleasant odor now "wilts under an unsavory smell"? He also wondered if Talmage's choir had the nerve to sing the hymn Charles Wesley wrote for workmen, entitled "Son of the Carpenter."[85]

Following this, MT received the complete sermon in question as proof that Talmage was not being serious about the offensive smells. However, MT found it to be "the opaquest sarcasm that ever got into print," and quoted another passage that could as easily be misconstrued: "Do not make all churches free. Some men enjoy the gospel more if they pay a thousand dollars for a pew and have no common people in the house." MT apologized for his misunderstanding of Talmage and acknowledged that he "is a very excellent man and that his heart is really in the freeing of the churches." The pastor's sincerity was manifested, MT noted, when he relinquished his salary until the completion of a new sanctuary for his Central Presbyterian Church. In it the rental of pews

---

[82]William Sweet, *The Story of Religion in America* (New York: Harper, 1950) 386.

[83]N&J 2:362.

[84]CT1 365.

[85]CT1 366.

would not be permitted so that all comers would feel welcomed. MT objected to the principle of charging worshipers for a place to sit in a church.[86]

While living in Buffalo, MT wrote a second article lambasting another leading New York City clergyman for unchristian conduct. William Sabine, rector of the Episcopal Church of the Atonement and later bishop, refused to permit the use of his Madison Avenue church for the funeral of George Holland because the man had been an actor. Sabine thought Christians should shun everything associated with theaters on the presumption that their productions do not teach moral lessons,[87] and he referred Holland's friends to "a little church around the corner" that served as a sanctuary for the poor. Viewing this action as hypocritical, MT condemned the meanness of spirit of any religious leader who would refuse to serve basic human needs. In Sabine's stead, he eulogized Holland "whose theatrical ministry had for fifty years softened hard hearts, bred generosity in cold ones, kindled emotion in dead ones, uplifted base ones, broadened bigoted ones, and made many and many a stricken one glad and filled it brim full of gratitude."

For calling the whole theatrical establishment immoral, MT denounced Sabine as a "crawling, slimy, sanctimonious, self-righteous reptile." "How does a soul like that stay in a carcass without getting mixed with the secretions and sweated out through the pores?" he asked. While crediting pulpits like "The Little Church Around the Corner" (as it is still called) with "disseminating the meat and marrow of the gospel of Christ," he found the theater "just as legitimate an instrument of God." The play *King Lear*, he wrote, surpasses sermons in convincing humans that filial ingratitude is sinful, and *Othello* effectively teaches about the destructiveness of jealousy. MT was convinced that more Christian kindness is transmitted by actors, journalists, and novelists than by preachers with "cancerous piety" who intone "vapid platitudes from the pulpit."[88]

After MT wrote *The Prince and the Pauper*, Livy dramatized it for a family production, with her husband and their daughters playing the

---

[86]McCullough and McIntire-Strasburg, eds., *Mark Twain at the Buffalo Express*, 200-203; LTR 6:519.

[87]*New York Times*, 29 December 1870.

[88]CT1 517-21.

parts. Running counter to the opinions of most respectable Americans, MT advocated participation in theater for all ages. He said, "This is the only school in which can be taught the highest and most difficult lessons—morals. . . . Here the children . . . live through each part."[89]

In Hartford

Soon finding that he did not like the daily duties of a newspaper editor, MT decided he could better pursue his book publishing interests by moving to Hartford. He had learned something about the Connecticut city while he was working with the publisher of *Innocents Abroad*, who lived there. On one business trip he was a guest of John and Isabella Hooker, probably because they were friends of the Langdons, and their daughter Alice was one of Livy's closest companions. John, a descendant of Thomas Hooker who had founded Hartford in 1636, was selling lots from Nook Farm, which he had purchased, to form a colony of literary people with common religious ideals. While MT was staying with the Hookers, he wrote to Mary Fairbanks: "I tell you I have to walk mighty straight. I desire to have the respect of this sterling old Puritan community, for their respect is well worth having."[90]

After a year in Buffalo, the Clemens leased a Nook Farm house from the Hookers in order to become part of a community of liberal Calvinists. Two years earlier, MT had written Joseph Twichell:

> My future wife wants me to be surrounded by a good moral and religious atmosphere (for I shall unite with the church as soon as I am located) and so she likes the idea of living in Hartford. We could make more money elsewhere, but neither of us are much fired with a mania for money-getting.[91]

Twichell, the pastor of the Asylum Hill Congregational Church in Hartford, was the main personal attraction in the city for MT. Twichell was a graduate of Yale College and Andover Theological Seminary. MT had met him shortly after he began to court Livy and immediately respected his outlook on religion and life. At that time MT saw a model of the new Asylum Church and, aware that Hartford was a center for

---

[89]MTS 620.
[90]LTR 2:166.
[91]LTR 3:101.

insurance companies and other risk-taking businesses, he dubbed it "the Church of the Holy Speculators."[92] On his first visit to Hartford, he had helped with the singing when Twichell preached at the almshouse. Of the experience, he wrote Livy, "I have not had anything touch me so since I saw the leper hospitals of Honolulu and Damascus."[93]

Joseph Twichell, pastor of the Asylum Church
in Hartford, and MT's closest friend.

Returning to Hartford a few months later, MT stayed with Joseph Twichell and his wife Harmony. After they "held a long and earnest con-

---

[92]MTB 370; MT was later to become a wild speculator himself, with devastating results.
[93]LTR 2:268.

versation upon the subject of religion," MT wrote Livy: "Now I began clearly to comprehend that one must seek Jesus for himself alone, and uninfluenced by selfish motives."[94] When Livy accepted his marriage proposal, he immediately shared the news with Twichell, who had become, and would continue for life to be his closest male friend. "I am full of gratitude to God this day, and my prayers will be sincere," he wrote him.[95] Twichell co-officiated with Beecher at MT and Livy's wedding service.

MT told his fiancee about Twichell's wisdom in dealing with a baffling person who had quoted obscure New Testament verses as authority for his bizarre ideas. Twichell conveyed what he had learned in seminary about interpreting the Bible in broad context, avoiding the prooftext method. MT wrote Livy about Twichell

> urging me to search the Scriptures for myself and not let one or two vague speeches of the Apostles lift themselves up and overshadow the vast array of evidence which the Testament offers plainly, forcibly and directly in opposition to the doctrines which they *seem* to promulgate.[96]

What did MT and Twichell have in common? Both were about the same age and both had been broadened by travel. Twichell had been through some of the worst Civil War battles as a chaplain, and at Gettysburg he had worked in a field hospital. He laughed over how an abiding friendship had developed when he and a Jesuit chaplain had wrapped themselves tightly together in their blankets to keep from freezing on the Fredericksburg battlefield.[97] Concerning Twichell, Kenneth Andrews writes: "His experience with blood, diseases, death, and pagans in uniform had widened immeasurably his Connecticut horizons, increased his natural gifts as a counselor, and encouraged his development toward a broad tolerance for human failings and a boundless faith in human nature."[98]

Twichell's belief that Henry Ward Beecher was "the greatest man this

---

[94]LTR 2:318.
[95]LTR 2:332.
[96]LTR 3:173.
[97]JHT 32-33.
[98]Kenneth Andrews, "Mark Twain's Hartford" (Urbana IL, thesis abstract, 1950) 4.

country ever produced" exceeded MT's judgment, but both held Beecher in high esteem even after he was charged with adultery.[99] In 1875, Twichell and MT went to Brooklyn to attend one day of the Beecher trial, which was a national front-page sensation for six months and ended with a hung jury. Beecher was later vindicated by his Plymouth Church, but his sister Isabella was convinced he was guilty and MT was inclined to agree with her. Even so, he wrote generously about Beecher to Twichell: "What a pity—that so insignificant a matter as the chastity or unchastity of Elizabeth Tilton could clip the locks of this Samson and make him as other men, in the estimation of a nation of Lilliputians creeping and climbing about his shoe-soles."[100]

Hiking was another interest that MT and Twichell shared, and they tramped many miles together in New England and in Europe. On one woods outing, Twichell suggested to his friend that he write about his days as a river-boat pilot; the result was a section of *Life on the Mississippi*.[101] Andrews, commenting on this enduring friendship, writes, "The two talked endlessly of religion, and every subject, as they walked in the country, and each took sound satisfaction from the other's company and ideas."[102] Once, the two set out to walk from Hartford to Boston. MT reported that after the first day Twichell's "jaw was not tired with twelve hours' wagging" but he was left speechless by someone they met in the bar of the inn where they stopped for the night. Both men were amused by this villager who "oozed . . . incredible smut from every pore" and who was "all ablaze from beginning to end with crimson lava jets of desolating and utterly unconscious profanity."[103]

The closest interaction between MT and Twichell came when they were hiking in Europe. MT frankly told his pastor that he had rejected the traditional assumption that the Bible is the Word of God. He said:

> I don't believe one word of your Bible was inspired by God any more than any other book. I believe it is entirely the work of man from beginning to end—atonement and all. The problem of life and death and eternity and the

---

[99]NF 51.
[100]MTP, letter to Twichell, 14 March 1887.
[101]MTHL 34.
[102]NF 71.
[103]AMT 215-16.

true conception of God is a bigger thing than is contained in that book.[104]

While in Europe, Twichell wrote his wife:

> Mark and I had a good talk after dinner this evening on religion. . . . We get
> into the subject of character and the state of the heart and the application of
> Christ's gospel to the wants of a sinful man. People don't know Mark's best
> side. I am more persuaded of it than ever. . . . And when we kneel down
> together at night to pray, it always seems to bring the spirit of gentleness
> upon him.[105]

After Twichell returned to Hartford, MT adapted a psalmist's rapture
over the deep seas in recalling a mystical experience they had in the
Swiss Alps:

> Alp calleth unto Alp! That stately old Scriptural wording is the right one for
> God's Alps and God's ocean. How puny we were in that awful Presence . . .
> and Lord, how pervading were the repose and peace and blessedness that
> poured out of the heart of the invisible Great Spirit of the mountains![106]

MT appreciated Twichell's openness to viewpoints that deviated from
the general Hartford outlook. When *The Rubaiyat of Omar Khayyam*
became available in English translation, Twichell pointed it out to his
friend. MT testified, "I never yet came across anything that uttered certain
thoughts of mine so adequately." He became ecstatic over that poetry of
a Persian who was skeptical of his traditional theology, and later MT
acknowledged, "No poem had ever given me so much pleasure before,
and none has given so much pleasure since. It is the only poem I have
ever carried about with me."[107] Twichell was also "unorthodox in his
politics," meaning that he had the rare courage to support a candidate of
the Democratic party when most in his congregation were Republicans.[108]
Both men were politically independent and voted for the person they
perceived best for the office. Also, both were authors, and one of
Twichell's books, called *Some Old Puritan Love-Letters*, disclosed a
romantic element in the Protestant heritage. MT described him indirectly

---

[104]MTB 631.

[105]Letter from Joseph Twichell to Harmony Twichell, 30 August 1878,
Beinecke Library, Yale University.

[106]MTL 351; Psalm 42:7 states, "Deep calleth unto deep."

[107]MTB 615, 1295.

[108]MTA 2:25.

in a characterization he gave of a someone he had met on a train:

> I got acquainted with Rev. Mr. Foster, Episcopal City Missionary of
> Syracuse, a noble, splendid fellow—a Twichell. He tells yarns, smokes
> occasionally, has weaknesses and lovable vices, just like a good, genuine
> human being, instead of a half-restored theological corpse like some
> preachers.[109]

Both friends enjoyed earthy diversions. To more readily identify with
nonchurched people while he was on vacation, Twichell took an alias so
that people would not address him as a man of the cloth.[110] On one occasion MT wrote a scatological dialogue to amuse his friend; they laughed
over it later, while they were hiking, until they were "lame and sore."
Twichell then circulated it privately, resulting in its publication in 1882.
About this ribald parody, set in the court of Queen Elizabeth, MT
admitted, "If there is a decent or delicate word findable in it, it is because
I overlooked it."[111] In it, the Queen tries to obtain a confession from the
perpetrator of a "thundergust" fart with a "distressfull stink." And the
nobility tell about widows who, "betwixt the thighs," use simulated
"prickes" that are unwilted, and about an emperor who can "masturbate
until he hath enrich'd whole acres with his seed." Sir Walter Raleigh
concludes with the tale of

> a maid, which being like to suffer rape by an olde archbishoppe, did smartly
> contrive a device to save her maidenhedde, and said to him, *First, my lord,
> I prithee, take out thy holy tool and piss before me*; which doing, lo his
> member felle, and would not rise again.[112]

When MT was in Hartford, the New England newspapers regularly
reported his attendance at the stately gothic church on Asylum Hill. In his
honor a plaque was later placed in the sanctuary at his seat near the front
of the center aisle. "This pew was rented by Samuel L. Clemens,
1872–1891," can still be read in the brownstone church there. Although
MT was never formally confirmed as a church member, he contributed
to missionary work and other church causes. Most of his close Hartford
friends were members of the Asylum congregation, and records show that

---

[109]LTR 4:506.
[110]MTE 248.
[111]MTE 205, 208.
[112]CT1 661-66.

from 1875 to 1888 he occasionally lectured and gave readings there for various purposes.[113] Once his contribution to the Entertainment Committee was a garbled version of Twichell's sermon the previous Sunday.[114] Katy Leary, the Clemens's housekeeper, reported that when MT's attendance at church "dropped off a little bit" and Twichell took notice, MT replied, "Well, Joe, if you weren't so long-winded, I would go more regular."[115] MT explained to his daughter Susy that he did not like church services because "he couldn't bear to hear anyone talk but himself for hours without getting tired." She confirmed that this was true even though he said he was joking.[116]

MT wearied of lengthy prayers as much as long monologues and came up with an alternative kind of self-improvement he might engage in at prayer time. The idea arose when someone gave him a grindstone the size of a watch that could be used for shaving. MT claimed that his whiskers disappeared when he rubbed it on his cheeks. This could protect him from Livy's complaints about his not being ready for church because it took him so long to shave. "I will put this into my vest pocket on Sunday," he spoofed; "then, when I get to church, I'll pull the thing out and enjoy a quiet shave in my pew during the long prayer."[117]

Twichell wrote that MT once accosted him after a Sunday service with this complaint: "The preaching this morning has been of a kind that I can spare. I go to church to pursue my own trains of thought. But today I couldn't do it. . . . You have forced me to attend to you—and have lost me a whole half-hour. I beg that it may not occur again!"[118]

The congregation Twichell attracted was diverse and MT claimed that some of his officers had done time in the penitentiary.[119] During the 1879 Republican campaign, MT testified to the honesty of at least one politician in his parish. In introducing Congressman Joseph Hawley, he said: "He is a member of my church. . . . I have watched him many a time, as the contribution box went by and I never saw him take anything

---

[113]JHT 93, 108.
[114]MTL 314.
[115]LMT 206.
[116]PP 101.
[117]James Pond, *Eccentricities of Genius* (New York: Dillingham, 1900) 202.
[118]Joseph Twichell, "Mark Twain," *Harper's Monthly* (May 1896): 822.
[119]MTA 1:303.

out of it. Would that we had more such men in politics!"[120]

MT often enjoyed making fun of church collections. Edwin Parker, the South Congregational Church minister throughout the Clemenses years in Hartford, told about their occasional visits to his church. MT was attracted there by the fine choir as well as by Parker, whom he ranked him among his top dozen friends.[121] Once, unprepared for the offering plate at the South Church, he whispered to the usher, "Charge it, please!"[122] MT told Owen Wister of another Sunday when a missionary preached in Hartford. Hearing the description of native sufferings, MT decided to double the offering he had been prepared to make. Later, moved to tears by the missionary's pitiful stories, he decided to write a large check because all the cash he brought was not enough. But then, as the missionary went on and on, MT decreased little by little his intended contribution. When the plate was finally passed, MT alleged that he took some money out![123]

MT's favorite story about Twichell concerned hair coloring. One Saturday night he took from his wife's dresser a bottle of what he thought was hair restorer. He saturated his hair with it and found the next morning that his hair was a color never before seen on a man. A substitute preacher could not be found at such a late hour so Twichell took charge as usual. MT reported, "The gravity of the sermon did not harmonize with the gaiety of his head, and the people sat all through it with handkerchiefs stuffed in their mouths." Twichell thought his sermon must have been especially stimulating because so many lined up to greet him afterward, but they only wanted to get a closer look at his hair. New people showed up the next Sunday to see it, which by then had turned reddish green. Looking back on the episode, MT wondered if it was Twichell's clever way of increasing the church's popularity and prosperity.[124]

Twichell and MT were always comfortable with each another because neither one was sanctimonious. MT once wrote his friend, "I wish to gosh you would page your letters and not make me waste profanity which I

[120]MTS 128-29.
[121]"Edwin Parker," ENC.
[122]JHT 96.
[123]*The Family Mark Twain* (New York: Harper, 1972) xvi.
[124]MTA 1:342.

can but ill spare, in helping me hunt my way through."[125] When MT exposed his friend's vanity about his looks and his sermons, Twichell accepted it smilingly, while planning how he might retaliate. The opportunity arose after a Boston acquaintance of Charles Darwin filled MT with pride by telling him that the great man kept by his bedside some books that MT had written. When MT bragged about this, Twichell showed him a passage from Darwin's *Life and Letters* in which he lamented that his total focus on the sciences had ruined his taste for good books in the humanities. Darwin said, "Once I had a fine perception and appreciation of high literature, but in me that quality is atrophied."[126] In spite of this continual mutual twitting, MT told his friend that he thought of him as his pastor. Reciprocally, Twichell wrote, "I'll try to be a better minister than ever to you, Mark."[127]

When Dwight Moody, then the world's preeminent evangelist, came to Hartford, MT attended the final revival meeting. He realized that Moody rivaled Beecher as the most popular Protestant leader and he found their showmanship intriguing. MT liked, and recorded, what Moody had to say on this occasion, as he urged converts to keep their faith alive and growing by participating in local congregations.[128] He also liked the "tempest of indignation [that] swept the town" when someone at the revival criticized a clergyman for drinking a bottle of beer.[129] Abstinence was the response of most church people to the major alcoholism problem in America at that time, so MT was pleased that the epidemic of teetotalism had spared Hartford.[130] In 1875, he wrote his sister: "I hate the very name of total abstinence. I have taught Livy at last to drink a bottle of beer every night; and all in good time I shall teach the children to do the same."[131]

---

[125]Letter from MT to Joseph Twichell, 28 October 1904, Beinecke Library, Yale University.

[126]CT2 814.

[127]Letter from Joseph Twichell to MT, 2 October 1881, Beinecke Library, Yale University.

[128]N&J 2:55.

[129]MTL 326.

[130]NF 46.

[131]Samuel Webster, *Mark Twain, Business Man* (Boston: Little, Brown, 1946) 133.

§ § §

Dr. Horace Bushnell of Hartford was the principal theological mentor for Twichell and the Beecher brothers. Bushnell's broad brand of Protestantism was expressed in those disciples, for "all kept up on current discoveries in science, and felt that a reasonable and compelling religion had to embrace modernity in all its dimensions."[132] Bushnell was largely responsible for Twichell's becoming in 1865 the pastor of the new Asylum Church. Bushnell provided the intellectual foundation for transforming the stern Calvinism that had been dominant in America into a "progressive orthodoxy." He served only the North Congregational Church throughout his career, but his writings have had a profound influence on theology internationally. To honor "the Emerson of Hartford,"[133] his fellow citizens gave his name to the park where the state capitol, at his suggestion, had been located.

MT may have first learned of Bushnell while he was in California, for Bushnell had worked as a surveyor there while recovering his health. In the late 1850s the New Englander had selected the route by which the Southern Pacific would enter San Francisco. He had also recommended Berkeley as the site for a university, but "declined its presidency to return to his Hartford pulpit."[134]

When MT drafted a petition to Congress for copyright protection, Bushnell gave his support. MT commended Bushnell's ethical perspicacity:

> What I want to drive into the congressional mind is the simple fact that the moral law is, "Thou shalt not steal." . . . If we only had some God in the country's laws, instead of being in such a sweat to get Him into the Constitution, it would be better all around. The only man who ever signed my petition with alacrity, and said that the fact that a thing was right was all-sufficient, was Rev. Dr. Bushnell.[135]

MT would have appreciated Bushnell's description of the religious

---

[132]Gregg Camfield, *The Oxford Companion to Mark Twain* (New York: Oxford University Press, 2003) 493.
[133]NF 29.
[134]NF 28.
[135]MTHL 100.

community as "where well-doing is its own end and joy, where life is the simple flow of love, and thought, no longer colored in the prismatic hues of prejudice and sin, rejoices ever in the clear white light of truth."[136]

Bushnell was a generation older than MT, as this comment by MT suggests, "He was feeble in body but his great mind and great heart were as big and full of loving kindness as ever."[137] They exchanged letters in 1872,[138] but Bushnell's death four years later deprived them of an extended friendship. In 1902, MT called Bushnell the "greatest clergyman that the last century produced,"[139] a judgment reinforced by scholars two generations later.[140] Bushnell is widely recognized as the leading spokesperson for theological liberalism in nineteenth-century America. MT admired the biography of Bushnell written by his daughter, Mary Cheney, finding it superior to the acclaimed biography of Bishop Phillips Brooks that he had read.[141] The books have a similar religious perspective, however, since Bushnell had been the theologian who most affected Brooks.

Why did Cheney's biography of Bushnell appeal to MT? Both grew up in a Calvinist church, which caused Bushnell to suffer angst when a terrific thunderstorm followed on the heels of his Sabbath frolicking. MT could also relate personally to Bushnell's account of his mother's love influencing his theological understanding, his skepticism as a youth, his revealing letters to his wife, his untimely children's deaths, his involvement with the development of Hartford, and his struggles against those who charged him with heresy. Moreover, MT must have enjoyed Bushnell's flashes of wit. For example, he once declared it unscriptural to team together two particular ministers "because it is forbidden to yoke an ox with an ass!"[142]

When he was a young bachelor, Thomas Beecher, on Bushnell's recommendation, became the principal of the Hartford Public High

---

[136]Horace Bushnell, *Work and Play* (New York: Scribner, 1984), 38.

[137]MTS 427.

[138]LTR 5:255.

[139]MTS 444.

[140]Shelton Smith, ed., *Horace Bushnell* (New York: Oxford University Press, 1965) ix.

[141]MTL 712.

[142]Mary Cheney, *Life and Letters of Horace Bushnell* (New York: Harper, 1880) 512; Deuteronomy 22:10.

School. Beecher joined Bushnell's church, and several years later, Bushnell preached at his ordination. His mentor helped to liberate Beecher from restrictive creeds and encouraged him to champion iconoclastic ideas and innovative practices. Bushnell convinced him that wrangling over religious dogma was futile, and in appreciation Beecher dedicated to Bushnell his pioneering ecumenical book, *The Seven Churches*. He also helped Beecher realize that a congregation should be a larger-scale family, providing education and fun-filled activities for youth.

Beecher emphasized the central importance of parents conveying religious values through example and precept.[143] Recognizing the importance of the mother as well as the father in a home, he rejoiced when he found Annis Eastman to succeed him as one of the pastors at Park Church.[144] No other church at that time allowed women to be ordained; few churches would even permit women to speak from the pulpit.

Since MT's mature religious outlook was strongly influenced by his Bushnellian friends, it is important to examine Bushnell's basic theology. Whereas the Unitarians rejected the doctrine of the Trinity as irrational, Bushnell made it comprehensible by interpreting it as three expressions of one God. This and other doctrinal restatements helped younger educated Americans who were struggling to relate Christian thought to areas of modernity. Those who were inspired by Bushnell had a religion of "healthy-mindedness," to borrow a classifying term from William James. In his Gifford lectures at the beginning of the twentieth century, James said:

> The advance of liberalism, so-called, in Christianity, during the past fifty years, may fairly be called a victory of healthy-mindedness within the church over the morbidness with which the old hell-fire theology was more harmoniously related. We have now whole congregations whose preachers . . . insist on the dignity rather than on the depravity of man.[145]

Bushnell championed the moral influence theory of Jesus' atonement that views his sacrifice not as compensation paid to a wrathful God for

---

[143]Glenn, *Thomas K. Beecher*, 33-37, 153-56.
[144]"The Park Church Fiftieth Anniversary," 1 January 1896, 24-25.
[145]William James, *Varieties of Religious Experience*, the Gifford Lectures 1901–1902 (New York: Doubleday, n.d. [1900ff.]) 88-89.

the debt of depravity accumulated by Adam and descendants, but as an example to be emulated of God's holy, suffering love. Bushnell modified the Calvinism that had stressed divine majesty and power at the expense of tenderheartedness, eliciting dread rather than affection. MT may have been considering the impact of Bushnell after the mid-nineteenth century when he described religious motivation over the fifteen centuries before 1850: "The fear of Satan and Hell made ninety-nine Christians where love of God and Heaven landed one."[146]

Another seminal idea of Bushnell that influenced liberal Calvinists was his rejection of the traditional teaching about Providence interfering with natural law. He attempted to show that the supernatural and natural realms were complementary and that the doctrine of creation must be reinterpreted in light of scientific knowledge.[147] Bushnell believed that the Genesis story and other religious literature contain metaphors that are an art form; their serious message should be liberated from literalism. He questioned the Protestant attempt to prove truth by merely citing Bible texts. Finding the full truth on religious matters, Bushnell maintained, involves going beyond quoting what is contained in the alleged "word of God." His promoting of a religion that was broadly based on reason and scripture no doubt struck a responsive chord in MT. Sam Portaro writes:

> While Twain was applying the test of human reason to ancient forms of doctrinal expression, men like Bushnell were similarly engaged in bringing new scholarship to bear on scripture, seeking new ways to approach the obscurities of language and imagery that were simply being parroted from pulpits to the detriment of a people who were now equipped to explore with their reason. Twain . . . sought to hold on to tradition and move ahead at the same time. In an age of facile religiosity and popularized piety, the refuge of many who could not take the heat of battle, Twain was an iconoclast who challenged others to join in the fray.[148]

Historian Winthrop Hudson regards Bushnell's *Christian Nurture* as "one of the most influential books ever to be published in America."[149] Emphasis on Christian education in America has been in large measure

---

[146]MTL 817.
[147]Smith, ed., *Horace Bushnell*, 130.
[148]Sam Portaro, "Holiness and Hilarity," *Criterion* (Spring 1983): 23.
[149]Hudson, *Religion in America*, 176.

an outcome of that pioneer work, first published in 1846. Bushnell was critical of Jonathan Edwards, who had been the preeminent New England theologian of the eighteenth century. Edwards had posited that the sovereignty of God and the viciousness of original sin made radical individual change necessary, because religious education that functions incrementally cannot overcome children's depravity and give them salvation status. Edwards gave a boost to hellfire revival preaching and to sudden, emotional adult conversions. The "Great Awakening" in New England sprang from that Edwardian emphasis, and it was especially carried on by followers of George Whitefield.

Bushnell maintained that children raised in Christian surroundings could be expected to experience gradual religious awakenings even though they could not testify to some single transforming experience. A child would develop as a Christian by virtue of being nurtured in a home filled with love, wisdom, and piety.[150] By rejecting the stress on individual conversion that had been prominent in American evangelical Protestantism from the Great Awakening of the 1740s onward, and by emphasizing the power of religious community to help Christian character, Bushnell was returning to traditional Calvinism.[151] Biographer William Bouwsma shows that "Calvin always emphasized the gradualness rather than the suddenness of conversion and the difficulty of making progress in the Christian life."[152]

MT also did not care for revivalism's focus on adult conversion, perhaps because he could never point to some dramatic internal event that gave him confidence that his soul had abruptly been "saved." He explained to Livy why his spiritual growth had been slow, "I would distrust a religious faith that came upon me suddenly—that came otherwise than deliberately, and *proven*, step by step as it came."[153] In particular, MT criticized preachers who had accepted uncritically a conversion tale by a man named Williams who had been imprisoned for armed robbery. While serving time, Williams had composed and

---

[150]Horace Bushnell, *Christian Nurture* (New York: Scribner's, 1861) 10.

[151]See Sandford Fleming, *Children and Puritanism* (New Haven CT: Yale University Press, 1933) 192-208.

[152]William Bouwsma, *John Calvin* (New York: Oxford University Press, 1988) 11.

[153]LTR 3:13.

addressed to himself a letter purported to have been written by a former cellmate. That fictitious ex-prisoner explained how Williams had persuaded him to change his life radically and become a Christian. Now that this convert had been discharged and was holding an honorable job, he claimed that he wanted to help Williams, who was still in prison and suffering from poor health. He said it was his way of expressing his appreciation for the salvation Williams had communicated. Research made on the letter convinced MT that it "was the confoundedest, brazenest, ingeniousest piece of fraud and humbuggery that was ever concocted to fool poor confiding mortals with." The prisoner, a Harvard graduate and preacher's son, had cleverly forged the letter and had it circulated widely to generate petitions for his early release. Naive preachers, who were predisposed to believe in miraculous transformations, did not realize they had been conned when they were extolling Williams from their pulpits.[154]

When the Clemenses were expecting their first child and were planning for Christian family life, MT ordered a copy of Bushnell's *Christian Nurture*.[155] He and Livy recognized from their own personal experiences the significant impact parents had in molding a child's Christian character. They realized that a core statement of religious education in the Bible[156] made transmitting the love of God a basic parental responsibility at all times—when children sit or walk in the home, and when they lie down and rise up. They agreed with Bushnell that the family, not the Sunday school, should be the primary agency for Christian nurture. Albert Stone shows how MT, along with others in the Nook Farm suburb of Hartford, lived in accord with Bushnell's teachings. Stone asserts that MT "accepted the organic unity of the Christian family, and he regarded Susy, Clara, Jean, and their friends as full-fledged members of the social body."[157] The christening ceremony was symbolic of the reception of the child by the caring community. Susy, confused at age five over theological vocabulary, told a visitor about the only visit to the Asylum sanctuary that she could recall, when her sister Clara was

---

[154]LM 333-44.

[155]LTR 4:158.

[156]Deuteronomy 6:4-7.

[157]Albert Stone, *The Innocent Eve: Childhood in Mark Twain's Imagination* (Hamden CT: Archon, 1970) 11.

"crucified."[158]

MT selected a lot near the Asylum Church on which to build the home where children might be properly reared, and he called that home "part cathedral, part cuckoo clock." As to its being a place of worship, prayers were said there, religious songs were sung, and those sharing the Protestant faith gathered there. MT called his Bushnellian household the "Holy Family."[159] The close-knit Nook Farm community created an extended family for the Clemenses that functioned much like a church support group. The Twichell children adored "Uncle Mark" and "Aunt Livy" and in turn the Clemens girls were fond of "Uncle Joe" and "Aunt Harmony." Paine says of the Clemens house, "Friends living near by usually came and went at will, often without the ceremony of knocking or formal leave-taking. They were more like one great family in that neighborhood, with a community of interest, a unity of ideals."[160] Housekeeper Katy Leary, virtually a member of the Clemens family, told about MT's interaction with Hartford children: "He was charming with them. He loved all children and they loved him. . . . He used to sing to them. . . . They had a lovely, happy time. It used to strike me as heavenly."[161]

To comfort Livy over separation from her Elmira home, MT had promised before marriage:

> I shall so strive all the days of my life to make you happy, and shall try so hard to walk as you did in the light and the love of God, that some of the bitterness of your exile shall be spared you. . . . We'll model our home after the old home, and make the spirit of Love lord over all the realm.[162]

Daily reading from the Bible had been customary in the Langdon home, so the Clemenses read a Bible chapter in the morning and said grace before meals in their new home for several years. Widely accepted among Protestants was the prescription that a Bible chapter a day—from any part—kept the devil away. But finding some of the Bible contrary to his values, MT discontinued reading it in a devotional manner. He informed Livy that "in the light of the gospel" he could not accept large

---

[158]AMT 200.
[159]MTB 583.
[160]MTB 476.
[161]LMT 72.
[162]MF 20-21.

portions of it as "the word of God."[163] Subsequently he held that the Bible "was not only not written by God, but was not even written by remarkable capable *men*."[164] To his sister, who seemed to think that being a Christian believer meant to accept the Bible as God's infallible truth, MT asserted that he was "an entire and absolute unbeliever." He sent her a book to help her interpret the Bible according to historical-literary criticism.[165]

Probably resulting mainly from her parental role models, Susy showed religious sensitivity as a child. When four years old she said, "I wish I could sit up all night, as God does."[166] From the age of six, she was able to arrive at moral judgments about fairness that would have been a credit to an adult.[167] At eight, she made a comment at her evening "prayer hour" that made a lasting impression of her father. She had learned about the religions of native Americans and was puzzled by their belief in more than one God. As a result, Susy told her mother that she had modified the way she prayed. She reasoned: "The Indians believed they knew, but now we know they were wrong. By and by it can turn out that we are wrong. So now I only pray that there may be a God and a heaven—or something better." MT wrote down Susy's precise wording and later commented: "My reverence for it has grown with the years. . . . Its untaught grace and simplicity are a child's but the wisdom and the pathos of it are of all the ages that have come and gone since the race of man has lived and longed and hoped and feared and doubted."[168]

MT acted as though the gospel teaching on compassion toward needy humans should be extended to all animals. He lavished affection on the family cats and was also concerned about animals below them on the food chain. William Dean Howells reported MT's distress over a blackbird that had been shot, "He described the poor, stricken, glossy thing, how it lay throbbing its life out on the grass."[169] On witnessing the alleged sport of cockfighting, MT was so upset at the sight of bloody

---

[163]MTB 411.
[164]WM 58.
[165]Webster, *Mark Twain, Business Man*, 131.
[166]MTB 577.
[167]AMT 194.
[168]AMT 192.
[169]William Dean Howells, *My Mark Twain* (New York: Harper, 1910) 43.

birds limping about with their eyes plucked out that he left the performance. He was even more disturbed by to those who "lost themselves in frenzies of delight" at the event.[170] Six-year-old Susy shared her father's sensitivity to the plight of animals. When she heard the story from Genesis of Joseph—how his treacherous brothers had thrown him into a pit, sold him as a slave, and slain a goat to obtain blood to stain Joseph's coat so that their father could be deceived—she wept for the goat.[171]

The Hartford home of the Clemenses was a place for weighing values also extracted from other literature. MT held a Saturday Morning Club for girls in his library, stimulating them by reading literary selections from books that he and others had written.[172] In addition, he presided over a Browning Society for Hartford women where he read poems by Elizabeth and Robert Browning. On his first trip to London, he had visited Robert Browning and had become an ardent admirer of the English poet. He may have identified with Browning because both had semi-invalid wives. Concerning his presumption in attempting to interpret the Brownings' highbrow poetry, he said, "All you need in this life is ignorance and confidence; then success is sure." After that self-deprecating remark, he added: "The poetry never gets obscure till I begin to explain it . . . so I've stopped being expounder. . . . I can read Browning so Browning himself can understand it."[173] Cheney testified to MT's moving renditions of Browning when she visited the Society.[174] Lines from Robert Browning's "Rabbi Ben Ezra," which he often read,[175] express a robust faith:

> Our times are in his hand
> Who saith, "A whole I planned,
> Youth shows but half; trust God: see all, nor be afraid!"

MT recognized how important it was for adults to establish rapport with young people, and advise them in a witty manner that they could

---

[170]LM 297.

[171]AMT 199.

[172]NF 104.

[173]Letter to Mary Foote, 2 Decembner 1887.

[174]Alan Gribben, "A Splendor of Stars and Suns," *Browning Institute Studies* (1978): 93.

[175]MTMF 260.

appreciate and remember. Responding to an invitation to speak to Presbyterian youth in Brooklyn, he sent a card on which he penned: "Always do right. This will gratify some people, and astonish the rest." When he spoke to a Boston youth club in 1882, he treated several of the Ten Commandments in a waggish way. The best policy is to humor your father and mother, he counseled, because parents think they know best. After pointing out how difficult it is to lie consistently over a period of time, he recommended, "You might as well tell the truth at once and be done with it." More seriously, he described situations where Christian kindness should take precedence over the naked truth.[176] He said, "Lies told to injure a person, and lies told to profit yourself are not justifiable, but lies told to help another person . . . that is quite another matter."[177] He also dealt with homicide without jesting, telling his young audience how much domestic sorrow has resulted from playing with guns presumed to be unloaded.[178]

Liberal Calvinists like all other Calvinists, strictly upheld the commandment forbidding adultery, which they understood to include a prohibition against premarital sex, and MT became prudish and anxious when one of his daughters mingled unchaperoned in a mixed-sex gathering. "Familiarity breeds contempt—and children," he harrumphed.[179] An illustration can be given of MT's adherence to the moral code of Hartford Christians. One summer there was a prowler who occasionally entered his home at night. It was discovered that the intruder was not a burglar as presumed but was the lover of his housemaid. She was heartbroken because he had betrayed his promise to marry her. To encourage this nocturnal visitor to fulfill his vow, MT waited with a policeman and a preacher for the next visit, and once the suitor was apprehended gave him the choice of getting married or going to jail for trespassing. As soon as the young man opted for a wedding, Twichell entered from the bathroom with a marriage license and officiated at the ceremony. MT gave the couple a handsome cash start for a successful marriage.[180]

MT and Livy were ever faithful in upholding their marital vows to

---

[176]CT2 527-46.
[177]CT2 136.
[178]CT1 801-803.
[179]MTN 237.
[180]MTB 600-602.

one another. Like the Puritans before him,[181] he and his wife seemed to delight in marital sexuality. Of Livy, he confided, "She poured out her prodigal affections in kisses and caresses and in a vocabulary of endearments whose profusion was always an astonishment to me."[182] Judging from MT's poem that began, "Behold: the penis mightier than the sword,"[183] he apparently valued his sexual potency. Twichell, who was frequently in his home, observed: "His wife's companionship is his perpetual supreme felicity, absence from her his supreme discomfort. He is eminently fond of abiding at home." Livy's affection for MT was only exceeded by her devotion to her children. In describing the Clemens's family relationships, Twichell also quoted from a letter MT wrote to the *Christian Union* about his wife and children:

> They know her for the best and truest friend they have ever had or ever shall have; they know her for one . . . who has always treated them as politely and considerately as she would the best and oldest in the land, and has always required of them gentle speech and courteous conduct toward all, of whatsoever degree, with whom they chanced to come in contact; they know her for one whose promise, whether of reward or punishment, is gold. . . . They know her, and I know her, for the best and dearest mother that lives— and by a long, long way the wisest.[184]

An episode involving six-year-old Jean shows how consistently Livy applied her religious convictions. Speaking up the chimney, Jean petitioned night after night, "Dear Jesus and dear God: I wish you'd bring me a pair of ponies and a nice cart." After listening to her persistent prayer, MT thought that her request should be fulfilled. But Livy advised otherwise, reasoning that doing so might encourage her to pray for something they could not or should not provide, leading her to lose her faith in God.[185]

§ § §

---

[181]See William Phipps, *Recovering Biblical Sensuousness* (Philadelphia: Westminster, 1975) 61, 149.

[182]AMT 185.

[183]Alan Gribben, ed., *Mark Twain's Rubaiyat* (Austin TX: Jenkins, 1983) 21.

[184]Quoted in Joseph Twichell, "Mark Twain," *Harper's Monthly* (May 1896): 826.

[185]LMT 42-43.

Apart from the delight MT had in interacting with his family in Hartford, the most stimulating experiences he had there were associated with "The Monday Evening Club," to which he belonged from 1871 until he left the city in 1891. That club was founded, he wrote, "by that theological giant, Reverend Doctor Bushnell, and some comrades of his, men of large intellectual caliber."[186] One of the other founders was Harriet Beecher Stowe's husband, Calvin Stowe, a Bible exegete. Among the other eminent members were ex-governor Hawley and philologist James Trumbull. Altogether, the Club consisted of about a dozen professional and business men who met fortnightly in members' homes to exchange thoughts on selected themes. Discussion topics included "Calvinism," led by Parker, and "Is this a Regenerate Age?" led by Twichell.[187] Exasperated by the pious way one topic was treated, MT grouched, "These tiresome damned prayer-meetings might better be adjourned to the garret of some church." Even though the membership included only a few ministers, MT joked that "it always had more clergymen in it than good people."[188]

The discussions generally interested him, however, and he used them to test his unconventional ideas. At one meeting, the members discussed the significance of dreams. A retired military officer contended that dreams were used in Bible times for divine warnings or commands but now "dreams merely proceed from indigestion." In the discussion, MT related a dream about his younger brother's funeral, the details of which seemed prophetic.[189] For another meeting, he made these notes: "Club subject—The insincerity of Man—all men are liars [Psalm 116:11], partial or hiders of facts, half tellers of truths, shirks, moral sneaks. When a merely *honest* man appears he is a comet—his fame is eternal—Luther, Christ, and maybe God made two others—or one—besides me."[190]

At the 1876 club meeting in his home, MT read an autobiographical story entitled "The Recent Carnival of Crime in Connecticut." He sketched its theme in his notebook:

---

[186]MTA 1:294.
[187]NF 103.
[188]MTA 1:305-306.
[189]MTA 1:304.
[190]N&J 3:144.

That [story] was an attempt to account for our seeming *duality*—the presence in us of another person. . . . I made my conscience that other person and it came before me in the form of a malignant dwarf and told me plain things about myself and shamed me and scoffed at me and derided me. . . . [Conscience is] the creature of *training*; it is whatever one's mother and Bible and comrades and laws and system of government and habitat and heredities have made it.[191]

The dwarf said, "It is my *business*—and my joy—to make you repent *everything* you do." The narrator exclaimed, "Remorse! Remorse! It seemed to me that it would eat the very heart out of me!"[192] After this personification of the conscience was killed, the narrator enjoyed murder, arson, and stealing.

MT's probe into the divided self recalls the apostle Paul's description of a civil "war" between his "inmost self" and his selfish impulses.[193] Also, it anticipated Robert Louis Stevenson's work, *The Strange Case of Dr. Jekyll and Mr. Hyde*, as well as Sigmund Freud's theory of the "superego" versus the "id." Because of the religious significance of MT's paper, a Club member requested permission to read it for his Sunday sermon at a Hartford church.[194]

Where could a person seeking a fulfilling and reasonable Protestant faith have found more enriching environments than those MT enjoyed in Elmira and in Hartford? Other than Bushnell, Twichell, and Parker, there was still another minister that MT found congenial in Hartford. Rev. Nathaniel Burton was a disciple of Bushnell and became the pastor of the church that he had served. His feeling for MT is expressed in a letter he sent when MT was visiting Europe: "I feel a vague kind of moral support when you are anywhere around. . . . The sooner you come [back] to Hartford the better."[195] Andrews finds in those Congregational ministers a common outlook: "Their devotion to religion was tempered by a wide humanity." Surprised by his camaraderie with the Hartford ministers, MT remarked, "I had not flattered myself before that a part of my mission on

---

[191]MTN 348-49.
[192]CT1 647, 654.
[193]Romans 7:15-23.
[194]MTB 569.
[195]NF 43.

earth was to be a benefactor to the clergy."[196] The clergymen's Hartford churches resembled Beecher's Elmira church, MT's ideal: they were "institutions for community good works and centers of information and appropriate recreation."[197]

While MT and Charles Warner, a *Hartford Courant* editor, were walking into the Asylum Church one Sunday, Warner suggested they combine their talents to write a novel. MT had not previously considered writing a novel but said he would think it over. After church he agreed to write part of what would be entitled *The Gilded Age.*[198] MT took responsibility for the chapters on materialism and political corruption in high places. When a dramatic version of the novel went on tour, after a successful New York run, MT persuaded his clergy friends to attend a Hartford performance in an effort to dispel the general prejudice against the theater among churchgoers.[199]

There is some question as to how pleasant MT's relations were with William Doane, a visiting Hartford preacher who later became an Episcopal bishop. After Doane conducted a service, MT lingered to greet him and give him this mixed message: "I enjoyed your sermon this morning very much. I have a book at home which contains every word of it." Doane was appalled by the implied charge of plagiarism until later that Sunday the impish accuser showed him an unabridged dictionary![200] Joking aside, MT assumed there was little originality in the pulpit, and he had this to say about what he noticed at London's grand library: "Saturdays the great reading room of the British Museum is full of preachers stealing sermons for the next day! . . . They not only copy sermons, but tear them bodily out of the books."[201]

On a brass plate above the fireplace in the Clemenses' library was a sentence from Emerson that captured the spirit of their home, "The ornament of a house is the friends who frequent it." Among the many famous people who visited in their Hartford home, the clergy were well represented. They entertained Scottish evangelical theologian Henry

---

[196]LTR 2:271.
[197]NF 49.
[198]Charles Stoddard, *Exits and Entrances* (Boston: Lothrop, 1903) 70-71.
[199]MTS 92.
[200]*The Independent* (5 May 1910): 962.
[201]LE 143.

Drummond, who integrated evolution with religion.[202] Drummond was especially popular with the younger generation as the author of *Natural Law in the Spiritual World* and *Ascent of Man*. Livy and MT repaid the hospitality of Charles Kingsley, whose historical novels they found a delight. In London, Kingsley had hosted a luncheon in MT's honor and, as canon of Westminster Abbey, had given him a guided tour of the shrine.[203] Darwin had recognized that "divine" in *Origin of Species* as the first clergymen to accept his theory of evolution. Moncure Conway, a noted Unitarian minister, was also a guest in MT's home. He especially enjoyed getting to know Twichell, of whom he said, "His ministerial adventures if printed would add a rich volume to the library of American humour."[204] Adding to the variety, Protap Mazoomdar, a distinguished Hindu Christian prelate, visited with MT in his home.[205]

Thomas Beecher, who had been Livy's pastor since she was a child, wrote her after a visit in Hartford:

> Yours is one of the few restful homes in which intelligence, culture, luxury, and company combine to the compounding of a pleasure which every visitor longs to taste again. . . . Foam over with gladness—my dear Livy—for you are one of the successes in life upon which the Lord lets me look.[206]

Relations with Cable

MT also came to know a Calvinist from New Orleans whose view on African-American rights was so liberal that he eventually became an exile in New England. His name was George Washington Cable, whom MT rated as "the South's finest literary genius."[207] They first met in New Orleans, and MT learned much about postbellum Southern culture from him. Later, on a lecture tour, Cable visited the Clemenses in Hartford. At that time MT wrote Howells, "When it comes down to moral honesty, limpid innocence, and utterly blemishless piety, the Apostles were mere

---

[202]MTB 661.

[203]Howard Baetzhold, *Mark Twain and John Bull* (Bloomington: Indiana University Press, 1970) 200.

[204]Moncure Conway, *Autobiography* (London: Cassell, 1904) 131.

[205]MTB 759.

[206]MTP*, letter to Livy Clemens, 24 May 1884.

[207]LM 287.

policemen to Cable."[208] While staying in the Clemens home, Cable suffered a severe case of mumps. During his lengthy recovery he became more intimately acquainted with his host. Cable wrote his wife about MT's profanity and how he criticized it without effect.[209]

MT and George Cable, billed as "Twins of Genius" on their 1885 tour.

MT was irked that Cable refused to modify some traditional Protestant practices and become a more consistent liberal Calvinist. He differed with Cable on the interpretation and the importance of Moses' commandment pertaining to swearing. Coming from the Western frontier where speech was often as wide open as the landscape, he was character-

---

[208]MTHL 419.

[209]Arlin Turner, *Mark Twain and George W. Cable* (Lansing: Michigan State University) 14.

istically profane. For example, after trying to pour from a pitcher that slopped milk all around, he shouted, "That hell-fired thing; one might as well try to pour milk out of a womb!" Following this outburst, he commented, "I get so damned short of profanity, at a time like this."[210] "Literary louse" Belton Townsend received this treatment, "Let us hope there is a hell, for this poet's sake, who carries his bowels in his skull, and when they operate works the discharge into rhyme and prints it."[211] On another occasion MT used strong language in a theater office and was rebuked. Employing some poetic license, he recorded his response and the outcome:

> "I have often used profane language in the presence of God. As he has always put up with it, I had an idea that maybe a damned theatre manager could stand it." It caught him unexpectedly, and his sudden explosion of laughter shot his false teeth across the corner of his desk, and they fell at my feet like a trophy.[212]

MT showed his appreciation for profanity when he once described the speech of a Captain Wakeman who "wove a glittering streak of profanity thru his garrulous fabric that was refreshing to a spirit weary of the dull neutralities of undecorated speech."[213] He told Twichell about an alternative liturgy: "I warmed to that butcher the moment he began to swear. There is more than one way of praying, and I like the butcher's way because the petitioner is so apt to be in earnest."[214] From Twichell, MT became aware of the old saying, "Some men's oaths are more worshipful than some men's prayers."[215]

MT had a low boiling point and he realized that it was difficult for him to suppress his irritations. "When angry, count four; when very angry, swear," was his dictum.[216] He admitted, "There is not another temper as bad as mine except God Almighty's."[217] Words attributed to

---

[210]MTN 397.
[211]MTHL 488.
[212]N&J 3:524.
[213]CT1 684.
[214]MTL 348.
[215]NF 234.
[216]PW 76.
[217]MTHL 771.

God in the Bible vividly illustrate what MT meant by the wrath of the Almighty: "My fury and mine anger were poured forth, and were kindled in the cities of Judah . . . ; and they are wasted and desolate."[218]

Biographer Paine, who lived with MT for several years, relates that his swearing displayed "a matchless gift of phrase" and that it served as "the safety-valve of his high-pressure intellectual engine. After he had blown off he was always calm, gentle, forgiving, and even tender." After one outburst he said, "Profanity furnishes a relief denied even to prayer."[219] Paine recounted an occasion when MT, out of sorts over something he had misplaced, had trouble restraining his impatience; excusing his female stenographer, he swore with abandon. Later, feeling better, he said: "There ought to be a room in this house to swear in. It's dangerous to have to repress an emotion like that."[220] "If I cannot swear in heaven I shall not stay there," he announced.[221]

When in the company of his wife, however, MT avoided profanity. But one morning, alone in his dressing room he cursed loudly as he threw out the window one shirt after another that was unfit to wear, only to hear his oath repeated, coming from another room in Livy's gentle, firm voice. MT judged her swearing to be "velvety . . . apprentice-like . . . absurdly weak and unsuited to the great language."[222] Aware that her rhythm was off and that she was tone deaf to the art, he said: "It would pain me to think that when I swear it sounds like that. You got the words right, Livy, but you don't know the tune."[223] Feigning repentance, he continued, "Oh Livy, if it sounds like that, God forgive me, I will never do it again!"[224] Their nephew, Jervis Langdon, claimed that MT's swearing "was entirely different from the heavy, guttural, vulgar thing we call profanity" for "it came trippingly, almost musically, from the tongue."[225] Telling about his proofreader, for example, he once said, "I didn't care if he was an archangel imported from Heaven, he couldn't puke his

---

[218] Jeremiah 44:6.
[219] MTB 213.
[220] MTB 1301.
[221] MTN 345.
[222] AMT 212.
[223] MTB 599.
[224] AMT 212.
[225] Jerome and Wisbey 204.

ignorant impudence over my punctuation."[226]

MT did not spare housekeeper Leary either, but she enjoyed his swearing. "Mr. Clemens's swearing really warn't like most people's cussing—it wasn't what you'd call *profane*," she remarked. "I always like to hear it myself, really, 'twas sort of lively and picturesque."[227] What she probably meant was that MT's swearing was occasioned by fleeting disturbances and harbored no deep-seated resentments. As he put it: "The spirit of wrath—not the words—is the sin; and the spirit of wrath is cursing. We begin to swear before we can talk."[228] Leary, a devout Christian, concluded: "Mr. Clemens was really a good Christian man, but people really never understood that. I think he was one of the purest men that I ever knew."[229]

Unchristian deeds, not impious words, concerned MT; true blasphemy came from the hands, not the lips. Thus, much like Jesus, he criticized hypocrites who mouthed religious language but failed to reach out to help those in need.[230] MT observed:

> It is not the word that is the sin, it is the spirit back of the word. When an irritated lady says "Oh!" the spirit back of it is "Damn!" and that is the way it is going to be recorded against her. But if she says "Damn," and says it in an amiable, nice way, it isn't going to be recorded at all. . . . [A man] can swear and still be a gentleman if he does it in a nice and benevolent and affectionate way.[231]

§ § §

Cable caused MT much irritation during their several months tour that involved shared platforms and hotel rooms in many states. At the outset, MT was unaware that Cable had fully retained the Sabbatarianism of their similar religious upbringing. Cable accepted without reservation from the Presbyterian standards that the Sabbath is to be sanctified by a holy resting all that day, even from such worldly employments and recreations

---

[226]LLMT 273.
[227]LMT ,236.
[228]FE 290.
[229]LMT 211.
[230]Matthew 7:21; 25:34-36.
[231]MTS 481.

as are lawful on other days, and spending the whole time in the public and private exercises of God's worship, except so much as is to be taken up in the works of necessity and mercy.[232]

In the year of Cable and MT's joint tour, Rev. James Stacy, who chaired the Southern Presbyterian's Committee for Sabbath Observance,[233] wrote a book to provide guidance to the faithful. In it, he declared that concerts, parades, open museums, newspaper presses, telegraph transmissions, and train operations on Sunday were desecrations and should be banned.[234] He further warned that "this shrieking of locomotives, this lumbering of trains" on Sundays was driving Americans into "open infidelity."[235]

To the great annoyance of his tour partner, Cable refused to use a train on Sunday even in an emergency situation.[236] MT wondered if the legalist would even be willing to travel to heaven on Sunday should he die on the first day of the week! One Saturday while on the tour, Cable abruptly left a reception in order to scurry back to his hotel room before his self-imposed midnight curfew. An elder, choir member, and Sunday school superintendent in a New Orleans Presbyterian church, he attended Sunday school and two church services each Sunday without fail.[237] At the beginning of the tour, he read the Bible aloud to MT each evening.[238] This activity, among others, led MT to call him a "pious ass" and a "Christ-besprinkled psalm-singing Presbyterian."[239] With the strain of the long railway tour showing, he vituperated hyperbolically: "His body is small, but it is much too large for his soul. He is the pitifulest human louse I have ever known."[240] To Howells, he wrote:

---

[232]"Westminster Shorter Catechism," question 60.

[233]*Minutes of the General Assembly of the Presbyterian Church in the United States* (Columbia MO: Presbyterian Publishing House, 1885) 413.

[234]James Stacy, *Day of Rest* (Richmond VA: Whittet, 1885) 226, 280, 298, 306.

[235]Stacy 297.

[236]MTL 450; letter to Livy, 5 February 1885.

[237]Turner, *Mark Twain and George W. Cable*, 53.

[238]MTL 446.

[239]Edward Tinker, "Cable and the Creoles," *American Literature* (January 1934): 322.

[240]LLMT 237.

He is intellectually great—very great, I think—but in order to find room for this greatness in his pygmy carcase, God had to cramp his other qualities more than was judicious.[241]

. . . .

You will never know . . . how loathsome a thing the Christian religion can be made until you come to know and study Cable. . . . In him and his person I have learned to hate all religion. He has taught me to abhor and detest the Sabbath-day and hunt up new and troublesome ways to dishonor it.[242]

Travel in Europe had given MT the opportunity to discover a more appealing observance of the weekly holy day:

Sunday is the great day on the continent. . . . The Germans rest on Sunday, because the commandment requires it. But in the definition of the word "rest" lies all the difference. With us its Sunday meaning is, stay in the house and keep still. . . . We keep it holy by abstaining from work, as commanded, and by also abstaining from play, which is not commanded.[243]

In MT's opinion, American Christians did not realize that recreation might be one of the more effective means of achieving the "rest" God commanded. He thought the Germans abided by religious law and wisely exercised on Sunday, recognizing that physical activity was lacking for many during the secular week. MT devised a way of dealing with a game prohibited on Sunday. After becoming fond of chess and wanting to play every day, he told his family that he had decided to name the chessmen after Bible characters so that the game could qualify as a sanctioned Sunday activity![244]

Some of MT's Sabbath judgments have overtones of the gospel. Jesus was annoyed by Pharisees who gave less attention to human needs on the Sabbath than to the adherence of the burdensome prohibitions of their sect. His principle was that "the sabbath was made to serve humans; they were not made to keep the sabbath."[245] In response to criticism that his compassionate activity on the Sabbath could be postponed to the next

---

[241]MT to Howells, 5 May 1885, Berg Collection, New York Public Library.
[242]MTHL 526.
[243]Mark Twain, *A Tramp Abroad* (New York: Harper, 1907) 1:236-38.
[244]PP 211.
[245]Mark 2:27.

day, Jesus said, "My Father is still working, and I also am working."[246] In the spirit of that teaching, MT observed, "God runs his worldly business just the same on Sunday as he does on week-days, but if you and I break the Sabbath we get damned for it."[247] Not being able to understand why the goodness of an activity depended on whether it was practiced on the first day of the week or at another time, he gibed, "It is not best to use our morals weekdays, it gets them out of repair for Sunday."[248]

MT's disdainful comment on the significance of the Sabbath in Presbyterian history also echoes the gospel. He confessed: "Man's . . . religion does not always adorn him. . . . My ancestors used to roast Catholics and witches and warm their hands by the fire; but they would be blanched with horror at the base thought of breaking the Sabbath."[249] These scornful words recollect those Jesus expressed to some scriptural interpreters, "You strain out a gnat but swallow a camel!"[250] Ironically, MT may have better understood and practiced teachings of the gospel vis-à-vis the Sabbath than Cable, whose religion unwittingly focused on legalistic practices that were more associated with Jesus' opponents.

Despite MT's outspoken denunciations of Cable over his attitude toward swearing and Sunday observances, the two remained amicable. James Pond, the tour manager, remembered that "each was familiar with all the plantation songs and Mississippi River chanties of the negro, and they would often get to singing these together when by themselves."[251] At the close of the tour Cable told his wife that MT had been agreeable, saying "I got him out to church at last!"[252] A decade later, a mellowed MT wrote to Cable, "I have always said, and still maintain, that as a railroad-comrade you were perfect."[253]

What MT especially admired about Cable was his willingness to speak out against Jim Crow laws that were being enacted, even though Cable was a slaveholder's son and a Confederate veteran. He showed that

---

[246]John 5:17.
[247]MT's marginalia in his copy of Rufus Noyes, *Views of Religion.*
[248]CT2 944.
[249]E&E 58.
[250]Matthew 23:24.
[251]Pond 231.
[252]Turner 114.
[253]Turner 122.

become obsessed over how to use the anticipated inheritance to gain status and make more money, and they acquire such mean-spiritedness that they even resort to stealing. In the end, they realize that their love of money did them no good, "Transient were its feverish pleasures; yet for its sake we threw away our sweet and simple and happy life."[4]

In "A Murder, a Mystery, and a Marriage," not widely published until this century (2001),[5] MT drew on his boyhood experience to tell about a Presbyterian minister in a Missouri village who worked to reconcile brothers who mutually hated one another. One was wealthy and, in spite of his contempt for his poor brother, so admired his niece that he willed his estate to her. However, the rich brother learned that she and a youth he despised were in love and planned to marry. The poor brother, motivated by the thought of personal benefits he would indirectly receive when his brother died, prohibited his daughter from marrying the person who would cause his brother to remove her from being his sole beneficiary. In the complex plot, the lust over money by the father and by a rival mysterious suiter of the potential heiress result in the murder of the uncle as well as the distress of a community over injustices motivated by greed.[6]

MT thought that many people everywhere tend to be infatuated with money, but in his own day the craving for wealth was more sinister. Writing to Joseph Twichell, he said:

> All Europe and all America are feverishly scrambling for money. Money is the supreme ideal. . . . Money-lust has always existed, but not in the history of the world was it ever a craze, a madness until your time and mine. This lust has rotted these nations; it has made them hard, sordid, ungentle, dishonest, oppressive.[7]

MT could not recall any obsession with money when he was growing up. He idealized Hannibal in later life as "a little democracy" with economic equality. As he remembered it, "Everybody was poor but didn't

---

[4]CT2 597-626.

[5]There was a limited printing (sixteen copies) in New York in 1945, and in 1983 it was made available on microfilm.

[6]*The Atlantic Monthly* (July 2001): 54-64.

[7]MTL 770.

know it and everybody was comfortable and did know it."[8] It was in the next generation, he thought, that dollar snatching became a craze. He drew a parallel between the degeneration of the American and the ancient Roman republics. Young Rome valued courage and liberty, but over time material prosperity debased public morality. MT, likewise viewing the stupendous wealth of America as bringing with it a moral blight,[9] hit his fellow citizens with this broadside, "Some men worship rank, some worship heroes, some worship power, some worship God, and over these ideals they dispute—but they all worship money."[10] MT himself was among those he indicted, for he prostrated himself to money-making schemes to satisfy his lust for upward mobility in New England society.

The Gilded Age, a novel written by MT and Charles Warner, described American avarice in the period following the Civil War. They gave historians an apt label for that reconstruction era when hungry capitalists took advantage of free enterprise to satisfy their voracious appetites. In MT's opinion, America was becoming increasingly reliant on what Washington Irving had earlier called "the almighty dollar, that great object of universal devotion throughout our land."[11] Justin Kaplan comments:

> All but a few of the characters in *The Gilded Age* worship the golden calf; to possess money is to be religiously possessed. . . . [MT] was notoriously reticent about depicting mature sexual and emotional relationships, but he did write a kind of pornography of the dollar.[12]

Senator Abner Dilworthy, who is found holding an opened Bible upside down, symbolizes the corruption MT depicts in *The Gilded Age*. When Dilworthy campaigns for reelection to Congress, he speaks at prayer meetings, women's church circles, and Sunday schools. From one pulpit he sanctimoniously testifies that as a lad "he would not let bad boys persuade him to go play on Sunday." After being elected to public

---

[8]AMT 28.

[9]MTE 68-69.

[10]MTN 343.

[11]Washington Irving, "Wolfert's Roost," *Knickerbocker Magazine* (November 1836).

[12]Justin Kaplan, *Mr. Clemens and Mark Twain* (New York: Simon & Schuster, 1966) 96.

office, he claims "temptations assailed him on every hand" but he never yielded when "people tried to get him to drink wine, to dance, to go to theaters." His campaign is then wrecked by the revelation that he has been using bribery to get elected.[13]

When MT was writing *The Gilded Age* in the 1870s, he saw firsthand how American business tended to operate. He accused Elisha Bliss, editor of the American Publishing Company in Hartford, of failing to honor contractural arrangements with him. Unethical practices continued, according to MT's overstatement, until "Bliss told the truth once, to see how it would taste, but it overstrained him and he died." MT said the company's board of directors, which he called the Bible Class, "ought to stop opening its meetings with prayer—particularly when it was getting ready to swindle an author."[14]

MT gibed: "The low level which commercial morality has reached in America is deplorable. We have humble God-fearing Christian men among us who will stoop to do things for a million dollars that they ought not to be willing to do for less than two million."[15] The Gettysburg Address, if in accord with postbellum national practice, should have concluded, "Government of the grafter, by the grafter, for the grafter shall not perish from the earth."[16] The "gospel" being heralded by American politicos, MT contended, was that "public office is private graft."[17]

The worship of money that MT denounced might be called "money-theism," or what Jesus called devotion to god Mammon.[18] MT drew a sharp contrast between true and corrupt civilization: in the former, "God enthroned; materially, bread and fair treatment for the greatest number." By contrast, he wrote, corrupt civilization "has invented a thousand useless luxuries, and turned them into necessities; it has created a thousand vicious appetites and satisfies none of them; it has dethroned God and set up a shekel in His place."[19] Common to corrupted humanity,

---

[13]Mark Twain and Charles Warner, *The Gilded Age* (New York: Harper, 1901) 2:46, 234, 239, 284.

[14]MTE 154, 156.

[15]CT2 944.

[16]CT2 947.

[17]CT2 945.

[18]Matthew 6:24.

[19]BMT 75-76.

MT observed, "is the trait which urges a man to sacrifice all his pride, all his delicacy, all his decency, when his eye falls upon an unprotected dollar—a spectacle which sometimes takes the manhood out of him and leaves behind it nothing but the animal."[20]

Attacking Tweed's Tammany Hall machine that controlled New York politics, MT was brazen enough to publish in the *New York Tribune* his "Revised Catechism":

Q. What is the chief end of man?
A. To get rich.
Q. In what way?
A. Dishonestly, if we can, honestly if we must.
Q. Who is God, the one only and true?
A. Money is God. Gold and greenbacks and stocks—father, son, and the ghost of the same—three persons in one: these are the true and only God, mighty and supreme; and William Tweed is his prophet.[21]

Another parody, thirty years later, showed that MT did not think the situation had improved. His version of "The Battle Hymn of the Republic" concluded ingloriously:

In a sordid slime harmonious,
Greed was born in yonder ditch,
With a longing in his bosom—
and for others' goods an itch—
As Christ died to make men holy,
let men die to make us rich—
Our god is marching on.[22]

MT saw tax evasion as an especially widespread manifestation of false worship. He wrote to *Harper's Weekly* this letter on Satan's behalf: "*It makes us smile*—down in my place! Because there isn't a rich man in your vast city who doesn't perjure himself every year before the tax board. . . . When you arrive, I will show you something interesting: a

---

[20]E&E 238.
[21]CT1 539.
[22]CT2 474.

whole hell-full of evaders!"[23] MT also attributed to Satan this motto, "Get what you can, keep what you get."[24]

When a European wondered if there was a single honest man left in the United States, MT said he could not think of any except himself! He then admitted that male honesty had completely vanished because he too had succumbed to temptation:

> I went down, with Rockefeller and Carnegie and a group of Goulds and Vanderbilts and other professional grafters, and swore off my taxes like the most conscienceless of the lot. It was a great loss to America because I was irreplaceable. . . . I believe the entire population of the United States— exclusive of the women—to be rotten, as far as the dollar is concerned.[25]

Concerning the railroad magnate who attempted to corner the gold market by devilish means, MT wrote:

> Jay Gould was the mightiest disaster which has ever befallen this country. The people had *desired* Money before his day, but *he* taught them to fall down and worship it. . . . The gospel [he] left behind . . . is "Get money. Get it quickly. . . . Get it in prodigious abundance."[26]

Gould compounded his evil, in MT's opinion, by spreading a thin veneer of pious philanthropy over his activities:

> When that first and most infamous corrupter of American commercial morals was wallowing in uncountable stolen millions, he contributed five thousand dollars for the relief of the stricken population of Memphis, Tennessee, at a time when an epidemic of yellow fever was raging in that city. Mr. Gould's contribution cost him no sacrifice; it was only the income of the hour which he daily spent in prayer—for he was a most godly man—yet the storm of worshiping gratitude which welcomed it all over the United States in the newspaper, the pulpit, and in the private circle might have persuaded a stranger that for a millionaire American to give five thousand dollars to the dead and dying poor—when he could have bought a circuit judge with it— was the noblest thing in American history, and the holiest.[27]

---

[23]CT2 656.
[24]MTB 1149.
[25]AMT 121.
[26]MTE 77.
[27]MTE 75.

There were robber barons galore in MT's view of America, so he did not limit himself to singling out one or two. Another target of his scorn was Cornelius Vanderbilt, the transportation tycoon. In an apparent attempt to redeem himself, Vanderbilt gave a small percent of his fortune to endow a university in Tennessee that would immortalize his name. At the unveiling of his statue in 1869, Bishop Janes referred to Vanderbilt as someone who had laid up "treasures in heaven."[28] MT did not think that Vanderbilt's giving away a few of his seventy million "greasy green-backs" entitled him to be called "the last and noblest work of God." In a national journal, he exclaimed, "How unfortunate and how narrowing a thing it is for a man to have wealth who makes a god of it instead of a servant." MT asserted that he was richer than Vanderbilt because he was satisfied with the little he possessed, whereas Vanderbilt always craved more.[29]

But the height of hypocrisy, for MT, was for the world's richest family to make it appear in their widely publicized Bible lessons that the gospel sanctioned the cunning methods they used to amass wealth. John D. Rockefeller taught Sunday school in Cleveland, and his son did the same at the Fifth Avenue Baptist Church in Manhattan. MT was amused by the "theological gymnastics" the younger Rockefeller used to jump over Jesus' admonition, "Sell all that thou hast, and distribute unto the poor."[30] Rockefeller offered this sound interpretation: "Whatever thing stands between you and salvation, remove that obstruction at any cost. If it is money, give it away, to the poor; . . . if it is an absorbing infatuation . . . fling it far from you." But MT perceived that Rockefeller wanted his hearers to believe that his family's enormous wealth was incidental and not an obstruction to salvation. Yet, MT observed, billionaire Rockefeller evaded taxes on more than ninety-nine percent of his worth.[31]

John D. Rockefeller Jr. came to the defense of Joseph, the Hebrew patriarch, who took a "corner in corn for the Pharoah."[32] The Genesis saga describes his role as food czar in the court of the Egyptian monarch.

---

[28]SC 156; Matthew 6:20.
[29]CT1 285-88.
[30]Luke 18:22.
[31]MTE 84-85.
[32]*New York Times*, 26 February 1906.

To prepare for future famine, he required his people to store in government silos one-fifth of their grain from bumper crop years. But when the
lean years came, he stripped them of all that they had in exchange for
food.[33] Rockefeller found that action reasonable, MT noticed, even though
Joseph "skinned them of every last penny they had . . . then bought the
whole nation's *bodies* and *liberties* on a 'fair market' valuation for bread
and the chains of slavery."[34] To please his friend Henry Rogers, a
Standard Oil officer, MT spoke to Rockefeller's Bible class in 1902.
Later, invited to a class reunion, he declined, saying, "I am afraid to
come . . . for I am tender in my feelings, and I could not bear it if your
Mr. Rockefeller . . . should get up and go to white-washing Joseph
again."[35]

A stanza of a hymn from the Victorian era expresses a divinely
ordained economic stratification of society that disturbed MT as well as
Karl Marx. In "All Things Bright and Beautiful," by contrast to the
Magnificat of Mary,[36] God sanctions rather than subverts the status quo:

> The rich man in his castle,
> The poor man at his gate,
> God made them, high or lowly,
> And ordered their estate.[37]

Despite MT's denunciation of some of the most prominent capitalists,
Andrew Carnegie became one of his best friends, and they visited
together frequently when both were living in New York City. He called
Carnegie "Saint Andrew" (only partly in honor of the patron saint of
Carnegie's native Scotland), and Carnegie called MT "Saint Mark."[38]
Hearing about one of Carnegie's magnificent gifts to education, MT
quipped: "You can take my halo. If you had told me what you had done

---

[33]Genesis 41:35, 47:13-19.

[34]MTE 91.

[35]Louis Budd, "Mark Twain on Joseph the Patriarch," *American Quarterly*
(1964): 585.

[36]Luke 1:51-53.

[37]Albert Bailey, *The Gospel in Hymns* (New York: Scribner's, 1950) 354.
Most modern hymnals omit this offensive second stanza, and in fact usually print
only two or three of the original six stanzas.

[38]MTS 637.

when at my bedside you would have got it there and then. It is pure tin."
In his autobiography, Carnegie expressed amusement at a letter he had
received from MT: "You seem to be prosperous these days. Could you
lend an admirer a dollar and a half to buy a hymn-book with? . . . P.S.
Don't send the hymn-book, send the money. I want to make the selection
myself." At a banquet, Carnegie compared MT's resiliency after
bankruptcy to the Daniel of Bible legend, "Our friend entered the fiery
furnace a man, and emerged a hero."[39]

Carnegie took Jesus' warning about the peril of riches seriously,
believing that "one of the worst species of idolatry" was making the
amassing of wealth the goal of life. In a startling essay, Carnegie
recognized that the gospel "calls upon the millionaire, while still alive, to
sell all that he hath and give it in the highest and best form to the poor
by administering his estate himself for the good of his fellows."[40]
Accordingly, although he paid few taxes, Carnegie contributed enormous
sums to universities, parks, arts, and international peace. He shared MT's
skeptic outlook on religious doctrine but that did not curtail his giving
millions for the purchase of church organs. At a New York teachers'
meeting, MT said: "Now we have Mr. Carnegie building sixty-five new
libraries. . . . I am glad Mr. Carnegie has done this magnificent thing."[41]
Carnegie probably reminded him of his wealthy father-in-law who was
also devoted to philanthropy.

Make all you ethically can and give all you can to the needy, a motto
of some Protestant capitalists, was MT's notion of economic justice. He
was involved in investment ventures, serving on the board of directors of
the American Publishing Company and the Hartford Accident Insurance
Company.[42] Poverty can be as corrupting as wealth, he noted, citing the
evils of both: "The offspring of riches: pride, vanity, ostentation,
arrogance, tyranny. The offspring of poverty: greed, sordidness, envy,
hate, malice, cruelty, meanness, lying, shirking, cheating, stealing,

---

[39]Andrew Carnegie, *Autobiography* (Boston: Houghton Mifflin, 1920) 295-96.

[40]Andrew Carnegie, *The Gospel of Wealth* (Cambridge MA: Harvard
University Press, 1965) xvi, 49.

[41]MTS 122. Eventually Carnegie financed 2,507 libraries.

[42]CT1 970; MTE 161.

murder."[43] Of both extremes, he concluded, "Nothing incites to money-crimes like great poverty or great wealth."[44]

To curb the excesses of capitalism, MT contributed generously to a New York settlement house that helped slum dwellers achieve skills they needed to rise above poverty.[45] By means of benefit lectures, he raised large amounts of money for children's homes in several states.[46] He enthusiastically promoted fundraising activities to support the Christian humanitarian work of David Hawley, who was the only person employed in Hartford to obtain food and clothing for the most needy. Once asked to participate in a benefit for "Father Hawley's flock," MT replied that his policy was not to appear on a lecture platform again "unless driven there by a lack of bread," but Hawley confronted him with "a lack of bread," so he gladly consented.[47] MT made it clear that the appeal was being made "not in behalf of able-bodied tramps who are too lazy to work, but in behalf of women . . . broken down by illness and lack of food, and children who are too young to help themselves." During the severe winter of 1873, exacerbated by a financial depression, MT was troubled by the many "empty mouths" and "fireless hearths." Writing Livy from London, he asked her to give Hawley a large check and to send to him the "multitude of tramps" who would come to her seeking assistance.[48] Kenneth Andrews notes that the Hartford community was generally reluctant to provide alms, but MT's "generosity was quick, hot, and inexhaustible."[49]

§ § §

MT's convictions on economic justice extended to labor relations in corporations. In 1886, he presented a paper to Hartford's Monday Evening Club entitled "Knights of Labor—the New Dynasty." The biracial and gender-inclusive Knights—the predecessor of the American

[43]MTB 1194.
[44]CT2 945.
[45]MTS 377.
[46]LTR 3:68; 3:377.
[47]LTR 6:392.
[48]LMT 5:480; Paul Fatout, ed., *Mark Twain Speaks for Himself* (West Lafayette IN: Purdue University Press, 1978) 72.
[49]NF 133.

Federation of Labor—had been the first to unionize railroads and had stunned capitalists by winning a strike against Gould's enterprises. At that time the average workman on the prosperous American railroads had no job security and his pay was less than a living wage. A historical review showed, MT argued, that power concentrated in the hands of a few always results in the oppression of many. Workers need to organize, he maintained, in order to protest effectively against seventy-hour work weeks and unsafe conditions that were killing them at the average age of forty. When a labor leader speaks for a large number of skilled workers, MT asserted, "he will see to it that there is fair play, fair working hours, fair wages."[50]

The Hartford buddies of MT were Protestant Republicans and they did not approve of his advocacy of labor, in part because the blue collar workers in New England were mainly Irish Catholics and Democrats. He was not successful in getting his "Knights of Labor" paper published, for those in power recognized it to be subversive. The Protestants in Connecticut were typical for, as church historian Jerald Brauer points out, American Protestants "sided with the railroads against the 'wild beasts turned loose upon society' " even though "the railroads treated their workers in a shameful fashion [and] justice was unknown in dealing with the workers."[51]

The sympathy MT had for the working class resonated with Thomas Beecher more than with Twichell, his two closest clergy friends. In 1880 Beecher ran for Congress on a Labor Party platform. Although he MT called Twichell "the healthiest and heartiest minister that lets me call him friend," he chided him for his lack of "social convictions as to the welfare of the masses" who have been "the bleeding grist of our great financial machine."[52]

Explaining why he did not identify himself with "the thin top crust of humanity," MT wrote in 1889:

> It is not that little minority who are already saved that are best worth trying to uplift . . . but the mighty mass of the uncultivated who are underneath.

---

[50]CT1 883-88.

[51]Jerald Brauer, *Protestantism in America* (Philadelphia: Westminster, 1953) 237.

[52]Milton Rugoff, *The Beechers* (New York: Harper, 1981) 559.

... For all Jonathan Edwards's help they would die in their slums, but the
Salvation Army will beguile some of them up to pure air and a cleaner life.
... I have never tried in even one single instance to help cultivate the
cultivated classes. I was not equipped for it, either by native gifts or training.
And I never had any ambition in that direction, but always hunted for bigger
game—the masses.[53]

George Cable told about the time his traveling companion, looking
out from the train and seeing laborers, "set forth the poetry of toil with
an eloquence so free from false sentiment, yet so reverential to all the
affections and upward strivings of lowliest humanity."[54] MT reminded
those who admired American church buildings that they primarily owed
their construction not to the contributions of the wealthy but to "the back
and forehead and bones of poverty."[55] To the end of his life he championed unions as "the only means by which the workman could obtain
recognition of his rights."[56] At Queen Victoria's Jubilee at the end of the
nineteenth century, he reflected on the international changes she had seen
during a reign that began when MT was one year old:

> She has seen the workman rise into political notice, then into political force,
> then (in some parts of the world) into the chief and commanding political
> force; she has seen the day's labor of twelve, fourteen, and eighteen hours
> reduced to eight, a reform which has made labor a means of extending life
> instead of a means of committing salaried suicide.[57]

We have shown that MT followed in the Calvinistic tradition of
treating money as a good of life while being aware that the founder of
Christianity warned against worshiping it. Not only is the superabundance
of wealth self-destructive to individuals such as the Goulds, Vanderbilts,
and Rockefellers who hoard it, but its inequitable distribution threatens
humane community relations. MT may have been the first American
leader from the middle-class who saw unions as a just way of restraining
capitalistic exploitation.

---

[53]MTL 527.
[54]Arlin Turner, *Mark Twain and George W. Cable* (Lansing: Michigan State
University) 131.
[55]LM 392.
[56]MTB 1557.
[57]E&E 205.

Political Morality

MT had the opportunity to observe the effect of "gilded" politicians not only in Washington but also in the cities of the Northeast that were being transformed by industrial growth. Working as a reporter first in a territorial capital and then in the nation's capital, MT claimed he had come to know "the smallest minds and the selfishest souls and the cowardliest hearts that God makes."[58] Out of that early exposure came his whimsical sketch about men on a train from Washington who become stranded in a blizzard. After a week of hunger, the politicians aboard follow arcane parliamentary procedure to determine who will be cannibalized and in what order.[59] One-liners MT composed over a twenty-five year period convey what he thought of the typical federal officeholder: "To my mind Judas Iscariot was nothing but a low, mean, premature Congressman";[60] "*Senator*: Person who makes laws in Washington when not doing time";[61] and "It could probably be shown by facts and figures that there is no distinctly native American criminal class except Congress."[62]

MT did not mean to suggest that those involved in government outside of Washington were any less corrupt. Recognizing that William Penn had prided himself on paying native Americans for the land that became Pennsylvania, MT noted: "Paid $40 worth of glass beads and a couple of second-hand blankets. Bought the whole state for that. Why you can't buy its *legislature* for twice the money now."[63] Moreover, since representatives mirror the values of their constituencies, MT should not be thought of as intending to blame only lawmakers. One Hartford clergyman, he recalled, spoke to him about a political candidate who was "an unscrupulous scoundrel" but weeks later publicly referred to him in glowing terms.[64] The editors of a book on MT and politics conclude: "Above all else, Mark Twain teaches us that we are the evil that

---

[58]MTL 542.
[59]CT1 269-77.
[60]CT1 549.
[61]CT2 946.
[62]FE 99.
[63]MTN 210.
[64]CT1 857.

surrounds us. When he attacks the legislature, or criticizes the politician, he is commenting on himself—on all of us."[65]

According to MT, a dichotomy exists between private and public morality:

> The American Christian is a straight and clean and honest man, and in his private commerce with his fellows can be trusted to stand faithfully by the principles of home, and honestly imposed upon him by his religion. But the moment he comes forward to exercise a public trust he can be confidently counted upon to betray that trust in nine cases out of ten, if "party loyalty" shall require it.[66]

§ § §

During the Civil War, the federal mint, without legal sanction, began engraving "In God We Trust" on coins. A group of clergymen defended the appropriateness of the slogan, claiming that the United States is a Christian country even though the writers of the Constitution overlooked mentioning that fact. MT's acerbic retort was that they should recognize that Americans also populate hell, for Jesus said most people choose to move down the wide road that leads to destruction.[67] MT put it this way, "It is not proper to boast that America is a Christian country when we all know that five-sixths of our population could not enter in at the narrow gate."[68] The theological propaganda on coins should be removed, MT contended, because it displays that America is lying, since "for nearly half a century almost its entire trust has been in the Republican party and the dollar—mainly the dollar."[69] "The god we trust in" would be—to apply MT's sentiments—more appropriate for embossing on American money. But recognizing that the motto was not likely to be reversed or removed, he suggested a more honest replacement, " 'Within certain judicious limitations we trust in God,' and if there isn't enough room on the

---

[65]David Hodge and Stacy Freeman, eds., *The Political Tales and Truth of Mark Twain* (San Rafael CA: New World Library, 1992) xv-xvi.

[66]WM 396.

[67]Matthew 7:13.

[68]MTE 50.

[69]MTN 394.

coin for this, why, enlarge the coin."[70] He also ventured this qualified approval: "It is the choicest compliment that has ever been paid us, and the most gratifying to our feelings. It is simple, direct, gracefully phrased; it always sounds well—In God We Trust. I don't believe it would sound any better if it were true. And in a measure it is true—half the nation trusts in Him."[71] The public furor over this issue resulted in a congressional mandate to continue placing "In God We Trust" on coinage and currency.

§ § §

In a Fourth of July speech to Britishers about his "progressive" homeland, MT said:

> We have a criminal jury system which is superior to any in the world; and its efficiency is only marred by the difficulty of finding twelve men every day who don't know anything and can't read. And I may observe that we have an insanity plea that would have saved Cain. I think I can say, and say with pride, that we have some legislatures that bring higher prices than any in the world.[72]

MT tended to be more approving of the executive branch of American government. As a Southerner, he did not vote for Lincoln in 1860, but he later lauded "Father Abraham" as American's "greatest citizen" and thought his Gettysburg address articulated the "immortal" hope for democracy.[73] Paraphrasing a Civil War hymn, he showed how the tragic death of Lincoln furthered the work of emancipation: "Christ died to make men holy, / He died to make white men free."[74] In 1867, he wisecracked that when Republicans met, their creed began, "I believe in Abraham Lincoln, the martyr-President of the United States."[75] MT perceived that members of Lincoln's political party adored him postmortem

---

[70]MTS 624.
[71]MTN 394.
[72]CT1 556.
[73]MTB 1124.
[74]FM 418.
[75]MTTB 143.

as incarnating the divine attributes of mercy, justice, suffering, and freedom.[76]

Ulysses Grant was for MT a heroic figure and a warm personal friend. One of MT's proudest accomplishments was assisting Grant, when he was terminally ill, to complete his autobiography and get it properly published. In a letter to Henry Ward Beecher after Grant died, MT described the Christian qualities he had observed in the ex-president, qualities not often associated with military accomplishment, "His patience; his indestructible equability of temper; his exceeding gentleness, kindness, forbearance, lovingness, charity, his *loyalty*."[77]

One issue of injustice associated with Grant displays MT's religious values. MT claimed that John Wanamaker sold Grant's *Memoirs* at his department-store in violation of the copyright held by MT's publishing company. This cheated Grant's widow out of royalties needed to liquidate her debts. MT filed suit, which he lost, against "pirate" Wanamaker who, he said, operated in the guise of a Sunday school superintendent.[78] He referred to the rich business executive as that "unco-pious butter-mouthed Sunday school-slobbering sneak-thief John Wanamaker, now of Philadelphia, presently of hell."[79] Had he been at the scene of Jesus' death and burial, MT conjectured, he would probably have stolen his corpse "in view of the fact that he has been picking Mrs. Grant's pocket in the intervals of keeping Sunday school."[80] Wanamaker was added to MT's list of hypocritical business tycoons who were unjust in dealing with the poor.

When the Hartford Republicans held a rally at the end of Grant's two terms, MT made his first political speech. He supported presidential candidate Rutherford Hayes because of his determination to base the civil service on merit and make it more honest.[81] On learning that Hayes had been elected, he telegrammed his Boston literary crony, William Dean Howells. The entire message was borrowed from the usual Calvinist way of beginning a worship service:

---

[76]AMT 252.
[77]MTL 460.
[78]MTE 348.
[79]MTHL 572.
[80]MTHL 573.
[81]MTS 97.

"Praise God, from whom all blessings flow;
Praise Him all creatures here below;
Praise Him above ye heavenly host;
Praise Father, Son, and Holy Ghost."

"The congregation will rise and sing."[82]

MT was soon to recognize that placing Hayes in the White House was "one of the Republican party's most cold-blooded swindles of the American people, the stealing of the presidential chair from Mr. Tilden, who had been elected, and the conferring of it upon Mr. Hayes, who had been defeated."[83] Samuel Tilden won not only the popular vote but nineteen more unquestioned electoral votes than Hayes, but political manipulations deprived him of receiving what he had earned.

Still a Republican four years later, MT welcomed Grant to Hartford to campaign for James Garfield. After he was elected president, MT petitioned Garfield on behalf of his "personal friend" Frederick Douglass. They first met in 1869 while they were both lecturing in the Boston area.[84] Douglass was now in danger of losing his position as the District of Columbia marshal. MT wrote, "I so honor this man's high and blemishless character and so admire his brave, long crusade for the liberties and elevation of his race."[85] Aided by this testimony, Douglass received an appointment to another federal office.

In 1879, MT informed a New York newspaper that he might become a candidate for president. He boasted that he would not limit campaign financing to "hard money" because "the great fundamental principle of my life is to take any kind I can get." Knowing that a congressional committee might be investigating his past, he admitted that the report he had buried his aunt under a grapevine that needed fertilizing was true, but pointed out that doing so wasn't unconstitutional. "No other citizen was ever considered unworthy of this office because he enriched his grapevines with his dead relatives," he explained. These grounds, plus

---

[82]MTHL 163.
[83]AMT 303.
[84]LMT 3:426.
[85]MTL 394.

desertion in war and hatred of the poor, led him to conclude that he was qualified on "the basis of total depravity."[86]

In 1884, MT began calling himself a mugwump, in effect leaving the party of Lincoln that for two decades he had supported for national offices. He came to believe that Republicans had become toadies of the wealthy, whose monopolies and high tarrifs were squeezing the poor. He justified his political shift to his troubled Hartford friends by citing those in the past who had refused to conform to the tradition. His examples included Jesus, Luther, Galileo, and Washington.[87]

MT campaigned for Grover Cleveland, a Democrat and a Presbyterian minister's son, on the basis of his public integrity and his reforms as governor of New York. At a political rally, he said, "The personality of a man or his character gives immense weight to what he says or does."[88] He ridiculed the bluenoses who refused to support Cleveland because of the charge that he had engaged in sex with a consenting unmarried woman, saying, "Grown men know what the bachelor's other alternative was—and tacitly they seem to prefer that to the widow."[89] He was obviously alluding to prostitution, not abstinence.

Having admiration for Cleveland's honest administration and his opposition to imperialism, MT visited him in Washington. Also, he once wrote Cleveland about an appalling policy of some white citizens toward native Americans. The clipping he enclosed from a New Mexican newspaper announced a $250 reward by Grant County for the scalp of "every hostile renegade Apache killed."[90] MT considered Cleveland exceptional because generally "no matter how healthy a man's morals may be when he enters the White House, he comes out again with a pockmarked soul."[91]

At the time of the New York municipal elections of 1900, MT addressed a mass meeting at city hall and joined in a protest parade down Broadway. He had long opposed the corrupt Tammany Hall but now he was pleased to find "the entire pulpit and almost the entire press against

---

[86]CT1 725-26.
[87]CT1 916.
[88]MTS 186.
[89]MTHL 501.
[90]SC 308.
[91]MF 238.

it."[92] When Tammany boss Richard Croker was soundly defeated, a newspaper gave this credit: " 'Who killed Croker?' 'I,' said Mark Twain, 'I killed Croker, I, the Jolly Joker.' "[93]

Several years later, in another New York City election, MT published this:

> God is an issue in every election; He is a candidate in the person of every clean nominee on every ticket. . . . If Christians should vote their duty to God at the polls, . . . graft would cease. . . . Yet every Christian congregation in the country elects foul men to public office, while quite aware that this also is an open and deliberate insult to God.[94]

MT's views on civic religion can be discerned in his treatment of the American Pilgrims. In a speech to the New England Society, he had the gall to devote most of his remarks to exposing defects of the Puritan settlers, among them killing Indians, driving out Quakers, eliminating Salem "witches," and enslaving Africans. He thought Americans should "cease from varnishing the rusty reputations" of those intolerant people. As he put it, they championed "freedom for every man on this broad continent to worship according to the dictates of his own conscience—and they were not going to allow a lot of pestiferous Quakers to interfere with it." The Puritans "gave the vote to every man . . . except those who did not belong to the orthodox church. . . . They gave us religious liberty to worship as they required us to worship."[95] On another occasion MT asserted that Thanksgiving Day had become "an annual day to compliment God" for assisting Euro-Americans in "exterminating" the native Americans.[96]

In remarks made elsewhere, MT also chided his fellow Americans for not practicing what they profess, "It is by the goodness of God that in our country we have those three unspeakably precious things: freedom of speech, freedom of conscience, and the prudence never to practice either

---

[92]MTS 415.
[93]MTB 1147.
[94]CT2 658.
[95]CT1 783.
[96]MTA 1:292.

of them."[97] Albert Paine accompanied MT to Carnegie Hall and reported on the speech he gave there:

> He talked of politics and of morals—public and private—how the average American citizen was true to his Christian principles three hundred and sixty-three days in the year, and how on the other two days of the year he left those principles at home and went to the tax-office and the voting-booths, and did his best to damage and undo his whole year's faithful and righteous work.[98]

MT's heavy criticism of politicians as a group was due to the exalted moral and religious standards that he thought they should attain in the branches of democratic government. While having some friends among politicians, he was wary that most of them tended to use pious talk as a means of taking advantage of religious people. Believing that a citizen should do more than express scorn toward dishonest government, MT was active in political campaigns, supporting the candidate who practiced Christian principles regardless of party. MT's exhortation on "Christian Citizenship" contained these remarks: "A Christian's first duty is to God. It follows, as a matter of course, that it is his duty to carry his Christian code of morality to the polls and vote them."[99]

Race Relations

MT was concerned with justice issues not only in America's political economy, but also, as an adult, in issues pertaining to racial equality. His first extant letter reveals the mind of a youth bred in a slave state. While job searching in New York, he wrote his mother about "the infernal abolitionists" he encountered, and expressed his homesickness for the "old-fashioned" slave culture. Alarmed that some African-Americans in the free state had better jobs than the whites, he joked, "I reckon I had better black my face."[100] Looking back at those attitudes two decades later, he confessed: "Ignorance, intolerance, egotism, self-assertion, opaque percep-

---

[97]FE 195.
[98]MTB 1272.
[99]CT2 658.
[100]LTR 1:4, 29.

tion, dense and pitiful chuckleheadedness—and almost pathetic unconsciousness of it all. That is what I was at nineteen or twenty."[101]

Transcending his Southern acculturation was a slow process, and a decade later, when MT was in America's Far West, his belief in the inferiority of African-Americans persisted. It was only after moving to the Eastern United States midway through life and becoming part of the Langdon family that his prejudices rapidly dissipated. In 1869 he wrote an indignant editorial about a black man who was lynched after being mistakenly accused of raping a white woman. He sarcastically noted that gentlemen in Memphis with chivalric impulses treated the matter as merely a blunder because only "a nigger" was killed. According to MT, for any black suspected of a major crime, the prevailing attitude was to "wreck a swift vengeance upon him, for the satisfaction of the noble impulses that animate knightly hearts, and then leave time . . . to discover . . . whether he was guilty or no."[102]

From MT's Hartford years onward there is much evidence of his rising above the racism of his times. Beginning in 1882, he made contributions for African-American scholarships at Lincoln University.[103] He viewed assistance to freedmen as a moral obligation owed by a race that had treated them so cruelly. After meeting Warner McGuinn, one of the first of his race at Yale Law School, and learning of his financial difficulties, he became McGuinn's anonymous supporter. MT wrote the Yale Law School dean: "I do not believe I would very cheerfully help a white student . . . but I do not feel so about the other color. We have ground the manhood out of them, and the shame is ours, not theirs, and we should pay for it."[104] After graduating with honors in 1887, McGuinn became the most prominent black lawyer in Baltimore after winning a major civil rights case. He recognized Thurgood Marshall's abilities and became his mentor when Marshall began to practice law in an office next

---

[101]MTL 289.

[102]Joseph McCullough and Janice McIntire-Strasburg, eds., *Mark Twain at the Buffalo Express* (DeKalb: Northern Illinois University Press, 1999) 22.

[103]Arthur Pettit, *Mark Twain and the South* (Lexington: University of Kentucky Press) 125.

[104]Quoted in Geoffrey Ward and Dayton Duncan, *Mark Twain* (New York: Knopf, 2001) 142.

door.[105] MT also underwrote the education of a black Southerner who was studying to become a minister,[106] and assisted Charles Porter, an artist who was born in Hartford. That funding enabled Porter to become the first African-American to study in Paris, where he began his fame for nature paintings. When MT was informed that Porter had gotten into trouble while abroad, he wrote the informant:

> On every sin which a colored man commits, the just white man must make a considerable discount, because of the colored man's antecedents. The heirs of slavery cannot with any sort of justice, be required to be as clear and straight and upright as the heirs of ancient freedom. And besides, whenever a colored man commits an unright action, upon his head is the guilt of only about one tenth of it, and upon your heads and mine and the rest of the white race lies fairly and justly the other nine tenths of the guilt.[107]

Once when a clergyman wrote asking MT to give a benefit lecture to help pay off a church debt, MT scorned the letter's orthography. But when he learned that the preacher was African-American, his attitude completely changed. This understanding of unequal educational opportunity prompted Livy to suggest the following motto, which MT liked, "Consider every man colored till he is proved white."[108] Paine noted that MT discriminated when it came to accepting charity engagements: "Clemens . . . felt that the white man owed a debt for generations of enforced bondage. He would lecture any time in a colored church, when he would as likely as not refuse point-blank to speak for a white congregation."[109]

MT gave enthusiastic support to Booker T. Washington who had risen from slavery to become the foremost African-American educator. At Carnegie Hall in 1906, at the twenty-fifth anniversary celebration of Tuskegee Institute, MT hailed Washington, its president, for educating thousands of Southern blacks.[110] Borrowing imagery John the Baptist had used to refer to Jesus, MT contrasted Washington to the person then

---

[105]Juan Williams, *Thurgood Marshall* (New York: Random House, 1998) 62.
[106]MTB 701.
[107]Pettit 126.
[108]MTHL 510.
[109]MTL 394.
[110]Pettit 136.

occupying the White House. Washington, he said, is "worth a hundred Roosevelts, a man whose shoe-latchets Mr. Roosevelt is not worthy to untie."[111]

After attending an army ceremony, MT jotted in his notebook: "Splendid big negro soldiers; obedient, don't desert, don't get drunk; proud of their vocation, finest and pleasantest soldiers. . . . They all have the look and bearing of gentlemen." He thought that in another century American blacks would deservedly be in command positions and have "whites under foot."[112]

Some family situations reveal much about MT's acceptance of African-Americans as dignified humans. He was grateful to Mary Lewis, the wife of the Quarry Farm tenant; she may have saved Clara's life by serving as her wet nurse.[113] Also, he enjoyed the company of Mary Ann Cord, the elderly cook at the farm, and was indebted to her for heightening his awareness of the emotional trauma of slavery. He immortalized her in "A True Story," his first *Atlantic Monthly* article, by publishing the experiences he had persuaded her to tell his family. She recalled being sold in Richmond along with her husband and seven children, and how forlorn she felt from never seeing or hearing about any of them again— with one exception. "Dey was black," she said of her brood, "but de Lord can't make no chil'en so black but what dey mother loves 'em an' wouldn't give 'em up, no, not for anything dat's in dis whole world." At the auction she clutched to her youngest child, but the slavers tore them apart. The boy assured her, "I gwyne to run away, an' den I work an' buy yo' freedom."[114] He became a fugitive and settled in Elmira as a barber. During the Civil War he found his mother in North Carolina and brought her to live with him. MT was inspired by, and long remembered, this family and their "shameful tale of wrong and hardship."[115]

"Aunty Cord" and MT admired John Lewis, a freeborn African-American who had risked his life to save several Langdon family members in a runaway carriage. MT eavesdropped on disputes between Cord, "a violent Methodist and Lewis, an implacable Dunker-Baptist."

---

[111]MTE 30; John 1:27.

[112]MTN 247; N&J 3:88.

[113]LTR 6:186.

[114]*Atlantic Monthly* (November 1874); CT1 578-79.

[115]MTP, notebook #35.

She said, "Lewis, the Lord sent you there to stop that horse." He responded, "Then who sent the horse there in sich a shape?" MT found commendable the way Lewis humbly said, "Inasmuch as divine providence saw fit to use me as a instrument for the saving of those presshious lives, the honner conferd upon me was greater than the feat performed."[116] MT looked forward year after year to conversing with Lewis in Elmira, and he provided him a pension in his old age. The multiracial culture of Quarry Farm was studied by MT and it appropriately became the gestation place of his novel about Huck and Jim.

MT also considered "invaluable" a former slave named George Griffin, who worked for many years in the Hartford household. Griffin acted as a "peacemaker" among a staff gathered from different religious backgrounds. About him, MT noted:

> He had a remarkably good head; his promise was good; . . . he could be trusted to any extent with money; . . . he was strenuously religious, he was a deacon of the African Methodist Church; no dirt, no profanity, ever soiled his speech, and he neither drank nor smoked. . . . He had the respect and I may say the warm friendly regard of every visiting intimate of our house. . . . Consider the influence of a glory like that upon our little kids in the nursery. To them he was something more than mortal; and to their affection for him they added an awed and reverent admiration.[117]

Having grown up in the South, MT appreciated African-American "spirituals" with their syncopated rhythm, plaintive melodies, and antiphonal forms. He would have agreed with the distinguished sociologist W. E. B. DuBois that the African-American folk songs were "the most beautiful expression of human experience born this side the seas."[118] MT was delighted with the Jubilee Singers from Fisk College in Nashville, which was supported by the American Missionary Association. The highly talented group, mostly former slaves, introduced spirituals in the Northern states. After Beecher's Plymouth Church endorsed the Singers, they were in great demand. Their concerts did much to dispel prejudices

---

[116]MTHL 197-99.

[117]Caroline Harnsberger, *Mark Twain, Family Man* (New York: Citadel, 1960) 114.

[118]W. E. B. Du Bois, *The Souls of Black Folk* (New York: Washington Square, 1970) 206.

of those who had assumed that African-Americans lacked Euro-American sensitivity to the best in religion and art. MT attended many of their performances in America as well as abroad, and after hearing them at his Hartford church he jotted down titles of songs he especially liked.[119] At his home afterward, he sang the tunes with great feeling, accompanying himself on the piano. Housekeeper Katy Leary said:

> And suddenly Mr. Clemens got right up without any warning and begun to sing one of them negro Spirituals. A lady that was there told me he just stood up with both his eyes shut and begun to sing kind of soft like—a faint sound, just as if there was wind in the trees. . . . 'Twas somethin' from another world, she said, and when he got through, he put his two hands up to his head, just as though all the sorrow of the negroes was upon him, and then he began to sing, "Nobody Knows the Trouble I Got, Nobody Knows but Jesus."[120]

Cable said he once had trouble concentrating on his writing when he was rooming with MT because he kept singing a Jubilee song that began, "We shall walk thro' the valley and the shadow of death."[121] Among MT's other favorites were "Swing Low, Sweet Chariot," "Were You There when They Crucified My Lord," "Oh, Dem Golden Slippers," "Rise and Shine and Give God the Glory, Glory," and "Go, Chain the Lion Down." The last spiritual is little known now, but Clara Clemens remembered that he sang it when he was happy.[122] It is a song of triumph, for the "lion" probably originally alluded to the slavemaster. The theme of suffering and deliverance of many spirituals related broadly to religious experience.

The Jubilee Singers toured widely in Europe as well as in the United States. In a letter to publicize their performances in England, MT wrote: "I would walk seven miles to hear them sing again. . . . These gentlemen and ladies . . . reproduce the true melody of the plantations. . . . The so-called 'negro minstrels' simply misrepresent the thing."[123] At Lucerne, Switzerland, expressing their admiration, the Singers sought the Clem-

---

[119]LTR 6:406-08; N&J 3:593.
[120]LMT 213.
[121]Turner 59.
[122]MF 72, 252.
[123]LMT 5:315.

enses out at their lodge to give them a private performance. He noted that
they were "diviner" than when he first listened to them twenty-six years
earlier and that "they are as fine people as I am acquainted with in any
country."[124] "The Jubilee Singers," Edward Wagenknecht comments,
"took him back to his youth and made him see that the same truth holds
in music which he had already discerned in literature, that the finest art
is not exotic."[125] MT wrote Twichell:

> How charming they were—in spirit, manner, language, pronunciation,
> enunciation, grammar, phrasing, matter, carriage, clothes—in every detail
> that goes to make the real lady and gentleman, and welcome guest. . . .
> Away back in the beginning—to my mind—their music made all other vocal
> music cheap, and that early notion is emphasized now. It is utterly beautiful,
> to me; and it moves me infinitely more than any other music can. I think
> that in the Jubilees and their songs America has produced the perfected
> flower of the ages. I wish it were a foreign product, so that she would
> worship it and lavish money on it and go properly crazy over it.[126]

§ § §

The Adventures of Huckleberry Finn (1884) is worthy of close study
for, as John Hays points out, "this masterpiece . . . contains the seeds of
all Clemens's religious thought and speculation."[127] The central characters
of the novel are runaways, Huck from a repressive WASP culture and
Jim from slavery. The interaction of the two reveals MT's agony over
slavery, the prime justice issue of his lifetime. Huck encounters Jim on
an island in the Mississippi River where he has escaped after overhearing
that his owner was planning to sell him to someone from a state where
slaves are treated more cruelly than in Missouri. MT acknowledged that
the character Jim was based on his memory of "Uncle Dan'l," a slave on
the Quarles farm near Hannibal. In 1855, John Quarles freed his fifty-
year-old "faithful servant Dan."[128] MT described Dan'l as one "whose
sympathies were wide and warm and whose heart was honest and simple

---

[124]MTN 336.
[125]MTMW 28.
[126]MTL 645-46.
[127]John Hays, *Mark Twain and Religion* (New York: Lang, 1989) 122.
[128]Monroe County Deed Book "O" Paris, Missouri) 240.

and knew no guile."[129] Dan'l also was the source of MT's favorite ghost story, "The Golden Arm," which he told repeatedly.

Before writing *Huckleberry Finn*, MT portrayed Uncle Dan'l as a character in *The Gilded Age*. His sincerity stands out in the novel, especially in contrast to Senator Dilworthy, who uses religion as a cloak for stealing. One night, while Dan'l is camping with white children by the Mississippi, a fire and smoke belching steamboat thunders nearby. Assuming that the Almighty was approaching, the children's guardian offers himself as a sacrifice with a plea to spare the innocent. He earnestly prays: "Dese chil'en . . . ain't 'sponsible. An' deah Lord . . . it ain't like yo' long-sufferin' lovin'-kindness for to take dis kind o' 'vantage o' sich chil'en. . . . HEAH I IZ. De ole niggah's ready, Lord."[130] Dan'l embodies the gospel teaching of great love, willing as he is to "lay down his life for his friends."[131]

In *Huckleberry Finn* the struggle to rise above conventional values and to act justly is the basic religious issue. An exchange between Huck and Aunt Sally reveals that slaves were considered subhuman in the antebellum South. She inquires about a steamboat explosion:

"Good gracious! anybody hurt?"
"No'm. Killed a nigger."
"Well, it's lucky; because sometimes people do get hurt."[132]

To enable people outside America to understand the relationship between religion and slavery, MT commented:

---

[129]AMT 6.

[130]Mark Twain and Charles Warner, *The Gilded Age* (New York: Harper, 1901) 1:36.

[131]John 15:13.

[132]HF 279. Huckleberry Finn has occasionally been vilified as a racist book because the denigrating and now politically incorrect term "nigger" frequently appears. MT explained at the beginning of the novel that he had used various dialects with which he was personally familiar, including that of Southern negroes and "the extremest form of the backwoods" speech. He realized that it would have been anachronistic to substitute a more dignified word for the word that was then used for a slave in the 1840s, the time of the novel's setting. He intentionally used the linguistically and historically authentic expression to expose the bigotry and cruelty he believed to be the antithesis of religious values.

In those slave-holding days the whole community was agreed as to one thing—the awful sacredness of slave property. To help steal a horse or a cow was a low crime, but to help a trusted slave or hesitate to promptly betray him to a slave-catcher when the opportunity offered was a much baser crime, and carried with it a stain, a moral smirch which nothing could wipe away. . . . It shows that that strange thing, the conscience—that unerring monitor—can be trained to approve any wild thing you *want* it to approve if you begin its education early and stick to it.[133]

Huck becomes aware of Jim as a human with feelings one day on the Mississippi raft after Jim takes Huck's watch so he can sleep longer. On waking up he hears Jim "moaning and mourning" over being separated from his wife and children whom he may never see again. Having once slapped his daughter when he wrongly judged her to be disobedient, he says: "O de po' little thing! de Lord God Amighty fogive po' ole Jim, kaze he never gwyne to fogive hisseff as long's he live!" With amazement, Huck reflects: "I do believe he cared just as much for his people as white folks does for theirn. It don't seem natural, but I reckon it's so."[134]

Jim's compassion is also evident in a discussion he has with Huck over King Solomon. Huck comments on Solomon's large harem and accepts the biblical judgment that he was the wisest man on earth. But Jim thinks "Sollermun" showed a lack of wisdom in having multiple wives and in the way he went about settling the dispute between two mothers.[135] Jim is disturbed over the story " 'bout dat chile dat he 'uz gwyne to chop in two."[136] Like the real mother of the infant, Jim's values are centered in protecting human life from being treated as property that can be divided and destroyed.

In the novel, MT contrasted a slave's anguish over broken family bonds with the feuding between the Grangerford and Shepherdson families. Their names may be an allusion to the archetypical fratricide of Cain, the granger, toward Abel, the shepherd. For decades the two aristocratic white families attacked each other even though the original motiva-

---

[133]MTP, notebook #35.
[134]HF 201-202.
[135]HF 94-96.
[136]1 Kings 3:16-28.

tion for the hatred had been forgotten. Both families attend the same church but take their guns to protect themselves.[137] One Sunday, following preaching on the theme of love, some family members are killed. Huck finds hogs more sincere than these feuders, "Most folks don't go to church only when they've got to; but a hog is different."[138] Hogs like the cool floor of the church and come there to relax in contented togetherness when the Sunday congregation is gone. The sermon on "brotherly love" expresses the congregation's piety but not their practice, whereas such Christian love expresses Jim and Huck's practice but not their piety.

Lionel Trilling provides a helpful analogy for examining the novel's religious meaning, "The boy and the Negro slave form a family, a primitive community—and it is a community of saints."[139] There is depravity all along the river—hypocrisy, slavery, feudings, lynchings, murders—but the two on the raft represent the true church—compassion, forgiveness, loyalty, equality, and freedom. Consider, for example, the scene where Jim confides his hurt feelings after Huck takes advantage of him:

> When I got all wore out wid work, en wid de callin' for you, en went to sleep, my heart wuz mos' broke bekase you wuz los', en I didn' k'yer no' mo' what become er me en de raf'. En when I wake up en fine you back agin, all safe en soun', de tears come, en I could a got down on my knees en kiss yo' foot, I's so thankful. En all you wuz thinkin 'bout wuz how you could make a fool uv ole Jim wid a lie.

Huck then expresses genuine repentance: "It was fifteen minutes before I could work myself up to go and humble myself to a nigger—but I done it, and I warn't ever sorry for it afterwards, neither. I didn't do him no more mean tricks."[140]

The companionship of Huck and Jim on the river provides liberation from bigoted religion:

---

[137]HF 147. This story is based on one MT heard about two families who lived along the Kentucky/Tennessee border. Each had one of their own to stand guard while the others knelt to pray. See LM, 221.

[138]HF 148.

[139]Lionel Trilling, *The Liberal Imagination* (New York: Viking, 1950) 108.

[140]HF 105.

I was powerful glad to get away from the feuds, and so was Jim to get away from the swamp. We said there warn't no home like a raft, after all. Other places do seem so cramped up and smothery, but a raft don't. You feel mighty free and easy and comfortable on a raft.[141]

MT may have been indebted to an ex-slave for his story about Huck wrestling with his conscience when confronted with slavecatchers while on the raft. Should he conform to what he learned to be Christian when growing up and identify a runaway slave or should he provide protection by lying? James Pennington included in his autobiographical *Fugitive Blacksmith* a parallel account of evading recapture by informing suspicious Maryland farmers that he was being taken to Georgia by a slavetrader who died of smallpox after they started out. The gullible and fearful captors then withdrew from the presumed diseased slave. Pennington told about his dilemma of having to choose between two horrors, being returned to his harsh master or being punished by God for dishonesty.[142] MT was probably aware of this widely circulated narrative and of Pennington because of his subsequent prominence as a Presbyterian minister and civil rights leader.[143]

One of the vilest infractions of what Southerners presumed to be the divine order was to assist a runaway slave. Were he to help his good buddy Jim get to a free state, Huck thinks, he would be humiliated by the community that had nurtured him. If he did not tell where Jim was hiding, "people would call me a lowdown Abolitionist and despise me." Huck contemplates having "to get down and lick his boots for shame" the next time he sees one of the townspeople. Those people had cast aside the liberation motif of true Christianity, and viewed a slave as a piece of property legally belonging to its owner. Huck chastises himself:

---

[141]HF 155.

[142]James Pennington, *The Fugitive Blacksmith* (London: Gilpin, 1850) 23-30.

[143]Pennington studied at Yale, became pastor of the Shiloh Presbyterian Church near where MT lived while a printer in Manhattan, and was the first American to receive an honorary doctorate from Heidelberg University in Germany. He wrote a history of blacks in America that was published in Hartford and, in the conclusion of *Uncle Tom's Cabin*, he was commended for his achievements. The *New York Times*, 25 September 1852 and 18 December 1856, told of his civil rights efforts.

The more I studied about this, the more my conscience went to grinding me, and the more wicked and low-down and ornery I got to feeling. And at last, when it hit me all of a sudden that here was the plain hand of Providence slapping me in the face and letting me know my wickedness was being watched all the time from up there in heaven, whilst I was stealing a poor old woman's nigger that hadn't ever done me no harm, and now was showing me there's One that's always on the lookout, and ain't agoing to allow no such miserable doings to go only just so fur and no further, I most dropped in my tracks I was so scared. Well, I tried the best I could to kinder soften it up somehow for myself, by saying I was brung up wicked, and so I warn't so much to blame; but something inside of me kept saying, "There was the Sunday school, you could a gone to it; and if you'd a done it they'd a learnt you, there, that people that acts as I'd been acting about that nigger goes to everlasting fire."[144]

In this vivid depiction of Huck's harsh self-criticism, MT confronts the reader with the perversion of religion by a culture that sanctioned slavery and refused to accept the equal worth of all before God. What people grow up thinking to be "the voice of God" within, MT contended, may be little more than the dictates of bigoted "public opinion."[145] MT did not equate the voice of God with the voice of Huck's conscience, because it is really the defective voice of his boyhood slave community. He urged that one should "keep abreast of his best mental and moral progress," by letting all other loyalties go and gaining confidence when the transformed conscience speaks, "Well done, faithful servant."[146]

Huck painfully moves from an authoritarian conscience, where the internalized voices of his guardians specify his proper conduct, to an autonomous conscience, where he takes individual responsibility regardless of what others may think about him or do to him. Or, as MT described it decades later, "a sound heart is a safer guide than an ill-trained conscience."[147] Huck's negative monitor, the immature I-must-or-be-punished impulse, was gradually replaced by the mature I-ought-in-order-to-attain-an-ideal desire. These internal forces correspond to contrasting outlooks on religion that Huck calls "two Providences." The first

---

[144]HF 268-69.
[145]CT2 511.
[146]CT1 911; Matthew 25:21.
[147]MTP, notebook #35.

is expressed by the stern Miss Watson, Jim's owner, who attempts to use the fear of hell to motivate Huck. The second is expressed by her sister, widow Douglas, who talks about "the good place" to Huck "in a way to make a body's mouth water."[148]

Before writing this novel, MT marked a passage in a book Robert Ingersoll sent him regarding the contaminating effect that images of hell can make on children's minds: "It has been a constant pain, a perpetual terror to every good man and woman and child. It has filled the good with horror and with fear; but it has had no effect upon the infamous and base."[149] MT, who had met Ingersoll in Chicago where they shared the same platform, admired the candor and eloquence with which he attacked superstitions.[150]

Only with the greatest effort is Huck able to transcend his culturally conditioned conscience. Knowing "you can't pray a lie," he believes he cannot be at peace with God until he repents for aiding a fugitive. He writes a letter to Miss Watson disclosing the location of her slave property, then basks in self-righteousness: "I felt good and all washed clean of sin for the first time I had ever felt so in my life, and I knowed I could pray, now." Yet he tears up the letter and says to himself, "All right, then I'll go to hell."[151] He assumes that his decision to go against the approved code will not only bring penalties from members of his Southern culture but will subject him to eternal punishment. But the reader realizes that Huck's redemption began with this resolve.

Huck's struggle with his conscience was exceptionally difficult because it was in part trained by living occasionally with Pap, his rednecked father. After spending a night in the gutter drunk, Pap reminded Huck of "Adam, he was just all mud."[152] Like the biblical postlapsarian Adam,

---

[148]HF 14.

[149]Robert Ingersoll, *Ghosts and Other Lectures* (Washington: Farrell, 1879) 128.

[150]See Thomas Schwartz, "Mark Twain and Robert Ingersoll: The Freethought Connection," *American Literature* (1976): 183-93.

[151]HF 269-71.

[152]HF 33. "The old man," as Huck frequently refers to Pap, may be an allusion to the admonition in Ephesians 4:22-23: "Put off . . . the old man, which is corrupt according to the deceitful lusts; and be renewed in the spirit of your mind."

Pap represents degenerate humanity. The ignorant and directionless man wastes his life in an alcoholic stupor, and he is homicidal when intoxicated. Ragged Pap tells about encountering a well-dressed black college professor from Ohio, who can even vote there. He rages:

> [W]hy he wouldn't a give me the road if I hadn't shoved him out o' the way. I says to the people, why ain't this nigger put up at auction and sold? . . . [T]hey said he couldn't be sold till he'd been in the state six months. . . . Here's a govment that calls itself a govment, . . . and yet's got to set stock still for six whole months before it can take a-hold of a prowling, thieving, infernal, white-shirted free nigger.[153]

Pap not only thinks he is superior to all nonwhites but tries to kill his own loyal son. In spite of Pap's perverse influence on his son, Huck is able to break out of that hereditary and environmental mold and be something other than a chip off the old adamic block.

Huck may have come to the awareness that the greatest stealing involved in slavery is not the keeping of slaves from their owners. Biblical law states regarding property, "Thou shalt not steal;" but it also forbids the kidnapping and selling of persons.[154] Huck's internal monitor wonders if Jim is property. Abolitionists argued that American slavery was essentially the kidnapping of Africans and the trafficking for generation after generation of persons who had been iniquitously stolen from their families and country.[155]

Huckleberry Finn ends with a scene that contains an allusion to Isaiah's description of a suffering servant. Tom Sawyer has become severely injured while engaging in a shenanigan that took advantage of Jim. Yet, in an expression of loyalty and love, Jim comes out of hiding to help a physician save Tom's life. By voluntarily surrendering himself, Jim risks not only the loss of his freedom but also the loss of his life. To

---

[153]HF 36. The Missouri Code of 1825 prohibited a free African-American from remaining in the state for more than six months. MT may have been aware of Dr. John Mitchell, an African-American with Missouri connections, who was then a classic languages and mathematics professor at Wilberforce University in Ohio.

[154]Exodus 20:15, 21:16.

[155]Theodore Bourne, "George Bourne, The Pioneer of American Antislavery," *Methodist Quarterly Review* (January 1882): 74.

keep Jim from a lynching gang, the doctor acknowledges Jim's assistance, adding that "the nigger never made the least row nor said a word, from the start."[156] The account has overtones of a prophecy of a vicarious sufferer that Christians have associated with Jesus, "He was oppressed, and he was afflicted, yet he opened not his mouth."[157]

Tom Sawyer and Huck Finn with their friend Jim.

Jim is the only person in the novel who is unswervingly good, even though he admitted to a peccadillo involving his daughter. In a subsequent novel he continues to accept all people as the Lord's children, and

---

[156]HF 354.
[157]Isaiah 53:7.

asks, "Is he [God] gwine *'scriminate* twixt 'em?"[158] Perceptive interpreters of these novels have discerned that one who is called "nigger" many times is treated by his creator as a noble character. Bernard DeVoto comments: "Jim has all the virtues Mark admired. He is kind, staunch, and faithful, a brave man, a friend who risks his life and sacrifices his freedom for a friend."[159] Robert Cody writes, "Jim is the most truly Christian character in the book: he shows an almost fatherly love in his relationship with Huck; he teaches moral lessons both by word and by deed; and he demonstrates exceptional forebearance throughout his numerous trials and tributations."[160] Booker T. Washington thought that Jim clearly exhibited MT's "sympathy and interest in the masses of the negro people.[161]

Huck also has Christian virtues. For example, Huck emphathizes with killers who are stranded on the sinking steamboat, *Walter Scott*: "I begun to think how dreadful it was, even for murderers, to be in such a fix. I says to myself, there ain't no telling but I might come to be a murderer myself, yet, and then how would I like it?"[162] This recalls the account of a sixteenth-century Calvinist saint who, observing evildoers being led to execution, said, "But for the grace of God there goes John Bradford."[163]

Huck, like Henry Thoreau, is willing to be out of step with most of the church people around him and face their ridicule because he has begun to march to an internal beat. In the end he values loving his neighbor in need more than acting in accord with the Southern norm, and actually fulfills a core biblical teaching. MT shows Huck imitating Jesus; both were disdained for making judgments that ran counter to conventional morality. Jesus denounced the biblical specialists who "neglect justice and the love of God,"[164] and thereby failed to show compassion toward a tax collector, or a prostitute, or a cripple, or a Gentile.

---

[158]Mark Twain, *Tom Sawyer Abroad* (New York: Harper, 1906) 35.

[159]Bernard DeVoto, *Mark Twain at Work* (Cambridge: Harvard University Press, 1942) 96.

[160]Robert Cody, "Providence in the Novels of Mark Twain" (diss., University of Florida, 1978) 51.

[161]*North American Review* (June 1910): 829.

[162]HF 87.

[163]John Bartlett, *Familiar Quotations* (Boston: Little, Brown, 1992) 143.

[164]Luke 11:42.

Huckleberry Finn is in large part a novel about attaining moral and religious maturity, an American "pilgrim's progress" in which the narrator is strengthened by recurring difficulties. As Martin Schockley writes: "The theme is the individual's struggle to know and to do right. Stated in other terms, it is man's universal journey from innocence to wisdom, or, if you prefer, the salvation of the human soul."[165] Also, Francis Carbine comments:

> The religious dimensions of the novel are implicit rather than explicit. . . . The fact that Huck is a wanderer through four states dramatizes for us the fact that he is a pilgrim-searcher. . . . Huck's experience in moral growth— his education in the truth that makes man free—climaxes in the celebrated scene in which Huck battles his conscience. Huck's public conscience was formed by the mores of the slave-owning South. This conscience tells Huck that to help a slave escape is sinful and worthy of damnation. His inner conscience—the unquenchable spark of God in man—tells him that love of neighbor, even of a black, runaway slave neighbor, is not a sin.[166]

Huckleberry Finn is MT's "gospel," sketching as it does Jim and Huck's spiritual journey down the Mississippi River. Hal Holbrook has aptly called it a "hymn to brotherhood."[167] The two rafters learn to express compassion for one another as they encounter the evils of American culture. In mythic terminology, the novel pictures life as both an Eden and a Hell. Stanley Brodwin views it as

> the lay sermon of a preacher who knows how to artistically shape his own comic countertheology. The salvation that Mark Twain offers in Huck's spiritual autobiography is one that neither Bunyan nor Defoe would have easily comprehended, though surely they would have recognized ruefully the lineaments of moral hypocrisy in the New World carried over from the Old. . . . In its pervasive comic and theological realism, *Huckleberry Finn* stands as a unique Protestant-American epic.[168]

---

[165]David Kesterson, ed., *Critics on Mark Twain* (Coral Gables FL: University of Miami Press, 1973) 75.

[166]Francis Carbine, "The Teacher of Religion and the McGuffey Reader," *Dimension* (February 1970): 14, 17, 18.

[167]Hal Holbrook, *Mark Twain Tonight!* (New York: Washburn, 1959) 93.

[168]Stanley Brodwin, "Mark Twain in the Pulpit," in Robert Sattelmeyer and Donald Crowley, eds., *One Hundred Years of Huckleberry Finn* (Columbia: University of Missouri Press, 1985) 372, 385.

§ § §

Pudd'nhead Wilson, the last of MT's Mississippi River writings, describes the decadent aristocracy in an unidyllic Hannibal. The story begins by introducing several members of the "FFV" (First Families of Virginia), each member having this aim, "To be a gentleman—a gentleman without stain or blemish—was his only religion." This rigid code "required certain things of him which his [official] religion might forbid."[169] Characteristic of this way of life was dueling in defense of family honor, adultery with slave women, and being obsessed with accumulating property, including slaves.

MT punctures the Caucasian stereotype of black sexual aggression against white women by making a slave woman the victim of a white master. He wrote boldly of miscegenation—a common practice of the antebellum South that was gossiped about in hushed tones. His story centers on an unusually beautiful and intelligent mulatto slave named Roxana who was "white as anybody, but the one-sixteenth of her which was black outvoted the other fifteen parts and made her a negro."[170] Regardless of her legal classification, she shares virtually the same genes of other Southern whites. However, training has provided her with the same speech and kow-towing demeanor as her fellow slaves. Roxana becomes pregnant by her owner, a member of the "FFV," and gives birth to a blond, blue-eyed son with Caucasian pigmentation. Working as a nanny, she then exchanges him, who is one-thirty-second part negroid, for her mistress's infant son, who was born on the same day.

Roxana justifies switching the children by her interpretation of a sermon by an African-American from Illinois who preached this doctrine of election:

> Nobody kin save his own self—can't do it by faith, can't do it by works, can't do it no way at all. Free grace is de on'y way, en dat don't come fum nobody but jis' de Lord. . . . He s'lect out anybody dat suit him, en put another one in his place, en make de fust one happy forever en leave t'other one to burn wid Satan.[171]

---

[169]PW 3, 102.
[170]PW 12.
[171]PW 22.

Roxana thinks of herself as the Lord's agent in the present age for saving her helpless child from hellish slavery.

Due to dog-like obedience training, the child of the Caucasian couple appears to be to others and himself a docile slave. MT writes: "He could neither read nor write and his speech was the basest dialect of the negro quarter. His gait, his attitudes, his gestures, his bearing, his laugh—all were vulgar and uncouth."[172] At the same time, Roxana's birth child takes on the mean-spirited attitude of the worst slaveholders. He is cruelly overbearing toward his personal slave, even though the slave, who was born of Roxana's mistress, had saved him from drowning. He also mistreats his real mother:

> Tom had long ago taught Roxy "her place." . . . She saw herself sink from the sublime height of motherhood to the somber depths of unmodified slavery. . . . She was merely his chattel now, his convenience, his dog, his cringing and helpless slave, the humble and unresisting victim of his capricious temper and vicious nature.[173]

Tom goes to Yale, where he becomes addicted to alcohol and gambling.

The story was MT's way of affirming the insignificance of racial genes for molding one's character and demonstrating that the distinction between one born free and one born slave was an arbitrary "fiction of law and custom." He wished to show the "idiocy" of racism and a spiritual equality among the races despite dehumanizing conditioning. This is conveyed when Roxana is proving to Tom the truth about his parentage: "Does you know anything dat a mother won't do for her chile? . . . Who made 'em so? De Lord done it. En who made de niggers? De Lord made 'em. In de inside, mothers is all de same."[174]

The conclusion of *Pudd'nhead Wilson* displays that property loss is of more concern than premeditated homicide in the little port along the Mississippi. After Tom murders his foster uncle for money, he is convicted and given a life sentence. But when it is learned that he is the son of a slave, he is pardoned. Lacking civil responsibilities as well as civil rights, the murderer is "sold down the river" because life imprisonment

---

[172]PW 202.
[173]PW 33.
[174]PW 143.

of an expensive animal would cause heavy financial loss to his owner's estate.[175]

There was a consistency between the values MT expressed toward blacks in his novels and in his personal relations. Living in the company of the Langdons and in the community of Nook Farm did a marvelous job of exorcising his boyhood slaveholding prejudices. MT was named for Virginian ancestors whom he called noble,[176] but he became even less bigoted than some of his New England neighbors. Howells, who knew MT and his writings in depth, said:

> He was the most desouthernized Southerner I ever knew. No man more perfectly sensed and more entirely abhorred slavery, and no one has ever poured such scorn upon the secondhand, Walter-Scotticized, pseudochivalry of the Southern ideal. He held himself responsible for the wrong which the white race had done the black race in slavery, and he explained, in paying the way of a negro student through Yale, that he was doing it as his part of the reparation due from every white to every black man.[177]

Women's Rights

As in the case of African-American human rights, MT's awareness of the need for women's rights arose gradually. In "Female Suffrage," an article written when he was twenty-one, he exclaimed, "I never want to see women voting, and babbling about politics, and electioneering."[178] Chivalrous males considered politicking vulgar; they did not want to see virtuous women battling on that sordid level. MT had been brought up to believe that a Christian lady was "the Divinely-appointed civilizer of coarse masculine clay" and that she "occupied that niche of reverent adoration from which the Protestant forebears had expelled the Virgin Mary."[179]

MT's experience in Hawaii made him aware of the influences of Christianity on feminism. With some exaggeration, he described the position of women before and after the coming of Calvinist missionaries:

---

[175]PW 203.
[176]LTR 6:296.
[177]William Dean Howells, *My Mark Twain* (New York: Harper, 1910) 35.
[178](San Francisco) *Alta California*, 19 May 1867.
[179]SCH 176.

In those days woman was rigidly taught to "know her place." Her place was to do all the work, take all the cuffs, provide all the food, and content herself with what was left after her lord had finished his dinner. . . . But the missionaries broke up this satisfactory arrangement of things. They liberated woman and made her the equal of man.[180]

To the New York *Tribune* a few years later, MT wrote approvingly about Hawaii's 1840 constitution: "The missionaries framed a constitution which became the law of the land. It lifted woman up to a level with her lord; it placed the tenant less at the mercy of his landlord; it established a just and equable system of taxation; it introduced the ballot and universal suffrage."[181]

Quakers were defending women's right to speak in public two centuries before MT's time, and there were Quakers among his forebears. On the strength of this, he claimed, "The Quaker woman, Elizabeth Hooton, was an ancestress of mine." She was frequently imprisoned, whipped, and expelled for preaching in Massachusetts, a colony ostensibly established to provide greater religious freedom. MT identified with Hooton and was concerned that she might have adopted the outlook of the Mayflower Pilgrims before she died, which would have qualified her to go to the same place they went.[182]

MT heard Anna Dickinson, a prominent Quaker feminist and protegee of Susan B. Anthony, lecture to a large audience in 1867. He was impressed that she was such a star attraction on the national lecture circuit that she and Henry Ward Beecher commanded the same high fee.[183] An effective abolitionist orator, she had spoken before Congress and in many states. She had become well known because of the 1861 speech she gave as a teenager on the "Rights and Wrongs of Women" and for her advocacy for gender enfranchisement in the Fifteenth Amendment to the U.S. Constitution. MT admired her vim and determination, and had this report published:

> The aim of her speech was to call the attention of the people to the meagre number of avenues to an honest livelihood that are permitted to women, and

[180]RI 459.
[181]LTR 5:564.
[182]CT1 783, 1065.
[183]MTE 215.

the drudging, unintellectual character of those employments, and to demand, as simple justice to her sex, that those avenues be multiplied till women may earn their bread elsewhere than in kitchen and factories without unsexing themselves.[184]

MT became profeminist after becoming attached to Livy. She and other liberal Calvinists in Elmira supported the women's rights movement formally initiated in 1848 at nearby Seneca Falls. Julia Beecher of Park Church was a feminist and, as has been shown, she was a role model for Livy. Laura Skandera-Trombley states, "Throughout her life Olivia was close to women who were dynamic, intelligent, and unapologetic as well as committed feminists—women who had rejected the purely domestic sphere in favor of participation in the world outside."[185] One of Livy's favorite journals was *The Independent*, a Congregational Church publication that advocated women's rights. During their courtship and later, MT expressed interest in that weekly's discussion of women rights.[186]

Dickinson was a friend of the Langdons and visited in their home in 1864 when lecturing on equal rights.[187] Livy, who was only three years younger than Dickinson, shared her religious motivation and wished she had the physical strength to work alongside her. In an 1869 letter to Livy, MT commented on their mutual admiration for Dickinson's activities, but he advised her not to feel compelled to do the same. He said, "Livy you might as well reproach yourself for not being able to win bloody victories in battle, like Joan of Arc."[188]

Andrews writes that feminism "was a crucial issue in Mark Twain's Hartford, absorbing all the reformist energies in the city."[189] MT pleaded for women's suffrage a half-century before it became a constitutional right, and defended the civil disobedience of women who found themselves "voiceless in the making of laws."[190] He contributed to the movement by speaking at rallies and by giving financial support. In his billiard room hung a picture of abolitionist Prudence Crandall, who a generation

---

[184]MTMB 105-106.
[185]MTCW 131.
[186]MTCW 49-52.
[187]MTCW 141-45.
[188]LTR 3:63.
[189]NF 143.
[190]CT1 565.

earlier had established a racially integrated girl's school in Connecticut. The Clemens had provided a retirement residence for Crandall after a mob wrecked her school.[191]

Helen Keller at thirteen, the age when
a mutual admiration with MT began.

MT's desire to raise the status of women went beyond statements of general advocacy. In Helen Keller, he found an individual with talents he was eager to encourage. After meeting Keller when she was fourteen, he used his influence to secure scholarship funds that would enable her to attend college.[192] Spurred by his confidence in her, she passed the Harvard entrance exam with honors. Keller recalled him in this way:

---

[191]MTMW 222; John Lauber, *The Inventions of Mark Twain* (New York: Hill and Wang, 1990) 268.
[192]MTB 1035-37.

He entered into my limited world with enthusiasm just as he might have explored Mars. Blindness was an adventure that kindled his curiosity. He treated me not as a freak, but as a handicapped woman seeking a way to circumvent extraordinary difficulties. There was something of divine apprehension in this so rare naturalness towards those who differ from others in external circumstances.[193]

While Keller was a student at Radcliffe College, from which she would graduate with honors, MT spoke about her at a women's club in New York: "I must mention that beautiful creature, Helen Keller, whom I have known for these many years. I am filled with the wonder of her knowledge."[194] To Keller, he said, "Helen, the world is full of unseeing eyes, vacant, staring, soulless eyes." In turn, she commended him for having no "dull acquiescence" toward "cruelty, unkindness, meanness, or pretentiousness."[195]

For the rest of his life, Keller and MT frequently visited. When he presided at a fundraiser for the blind at the Waldorf-Astoria Hotel, she called him an eloquent "ambassador to the blind."[196] He hailed her "the most marvelous person of her sex that has existed on this earth since Joan of Arc,"[197] and predicted that her fame would continue long into the future.[198] In a letter to Keller, commenting on their years of "affectionate friendship," he remarked, "I suppose there is nothing like it in heaven; and not likely to be, until we get there and show off."[199]

§ § §

Justice for MT was not so much a matter of courtroom judgments but an egalitarian pursuit involving compassion for the downtrodden. For him this was a religious as well as a moral duty. "Father *was* innately *religious*," Clara Clemens wrote; "the most steadfast occupation of his

---

[193]PH 268.
[194]MTS 348.
[195]Helen Keller, *Midstream* (New York: Greenwood, 1968) 49.
[196]MTB 1273.
[197]MTS 642.
[198]MTA 2:297.
[199]MTL 730.

thoughts displayed the urge to help victims of injustice and misfortune."[200] His daughter's assessment is confirmed not only by his works but by a letter MT received late in life from his most intimate literary friend. Howells wrote: "At the right time there is a noble seriousness; and at all times, justice and mercy. . . . For the creature of the Presbyterian deity who did make you, you are very well."[201]

Philip Foner also perceives a moral weight in MT's seemingly light comments on American culture:

> From the beginning, he took the side of the defenseless or oppressed, and fought corruption, privilege and abuse wherever he found them with a fierce humor. . . . [MT exhibited] a burning hatred of all forms of intolerance, tyranny and injustice, an abhorrence of cant and pretension, a passion for human freedom, a fierce pride in human dignity, a love for people and for life, a frank and open contempt for the mean, the cruel, the selfish, the small and petty.[202]

In spite of MT's stringent criticisms of American culture, he considered it the best the world has produced, in large part because many American citizens were trying to combat injustice. From the seeds of "liberty and intelligence" planted in America, he claimed, "has come the Christian world's great civilization."[203] He attributed much of America's goodness to her Christian roots and praised African-American Tuskegee Institute for its efforts to transmit this legacy:

> They thoroughly ground the student in the Christian code of morals; they instill into him the indisputable truth that this is the highest and best of all systems of morals; that the nation's greatness, its strength, and its repute among the other nations, is the product of that system; . . . that whatever is commendable, whatever is valuable in the individual American's character is the flower and fruit of that seed.[204]

---

[200]OMT 8-9.
[201]MTHL 707.
[202]SC 400-401.
[203]CR1 942-44.
[204]MTS 479.

Chapter 6
Ambassador-at-Large

After living overseas for a number of years, MT mused, "I have filled the post—with some credit, I trust—of self-appointed Ambassador-at-Large of the U.S. of America—without salary."[1] A few months before his death he expanded this into a transnational designation when he wrote, "I do not represent a country myself, but am merely Member at Large for the Human Race."[2] He spent a good part of his life abroad: some years before 1891 and most of the next decade. He lived for extensive periods in several European countries and visited three other continents, becoming probably the most widely traveled literary person in history. His fame was such that he received a letter in Australia addressed only, "God knows where."[3] To another addressed, "The Devil knows where," he replied, "*He* did, too."[4] In granting MT an honorary degree from Oxford, the chancellor said, "You shake the sides of the whole world with merriment."[5] That merriment included a great deal of social and religious satire aimed at stirring up cultures from their lethargy.

How could an outspoken critic of injustices at home be eager to represent the best qualities of American life when abroad? MT used his criticisms to promote the positive aspects of American society and advance the global leadership of the United States. He had abundant praise for the American democratic experiment, "The Fourth of July and its results . . . was the noblest and the holiest thing and the most precious that ever happened in this earth."[6] Again, "Men write fine and plausible arguments in support of monarchy, but the fact remains that *where every man in a state has a vote, brutal laws are impossible*."[7] More broadly, in defending the United States from foreign critics in 1890, MT called it the "one real civilization in the world" because it had none of the following:

---

[1]MTP, notebook #32, 20.
[2]Quoted in "Mark Twain's Private Girls' Club," *The Ladies' Home Journal* (February 1912): 54.
[3]MTA 2:241.
[4]MTB 566.
[5]MTB 1394.
[6]MTHL 613.
[7]CY 318.

"Human slavery, despotic government, inequality, numerous and brutal punishments for crimes, superstition almost universal, ignorance almost universal, and dirt and poverty almost universal."[8] But while he celebrated social justice in America, he became increasingly aware of an ugly American movement toward imperialism.

In Europe

Royal families in several European countries were attracted to this American patriot who, as a skilled diplomat, was able to conceal his disdain for monarchy. Once a crowned head of state even loaned MT his private railroad car, and Kaiser Wilhelm II invited him to dinner. His hobnobbing with eminent potentates caused his youngest daughter to remark, "Papa, the way things are going, pretty soon there won't be anybody left for you to get acquainted with but God."[9] Anticipating his visit to the court of the German emperor, MT expressed himself in metaphors from Isaiah, "In that day the Imperial lion and the Democratic lamb shall sit down together."[10]

But in truth—to use another biblical image—MT thought of himself as more like a wolf in sheep's clothing.[11] He fancied that his family had contributed to regicide, tracing his ancestry to Geoffrey Clement, who sentenced Charles I to be decapitated. But some who bore the Clemens name, he admitted, were partners with British monarchs, working as slavers and pirates.[12] However, MT was not sure about his Old World forebears. In a German church he observed statues with names inscribed beneath, one "S.[aint] Peter" and one "S.[aint] Clemens." Feigning pride to find an ancestor in such company who shared even his initial, he said, "This one had on a helmet, probably used to be on the police force before he got promoted."[13]

In *Huckleberry Finn*, the "rapscallions" who impersonate a duke and a king convey MT's take on royalty. Huck says, "You couldn't tell them

---

[8]CT1 942.
[9]MTN 242.
[10]MTB 940; Isaiah 11:6.
[11]Matthew 7:15.
[12]AMT 15-16.
[13]MTN 330.

from the real kind."[14] MT treated sovereigns scathingly for assuming that they rule by divine right:

> The kingly office is entitled to no respect. . . . A monarch when good is entitled to the consideration which we accord to a pirate who keeps Sunday-school between crimes. . . . What a funny thing is monarchy and how curious its assumptions. . . . It assumes that a wrong maintained for a dozen or a thousand years, becomes a right. It assumes that the wronged parties will presently give up and take the same view—that at least their descendants will.[15]

MT had no use for religion that was financed by the royal establishment. In Germany, he noted:

> Here they recognize two sects, Catholic and Lutheran (which appear to differ from each other nearly as much as a red-headed man differs from an auburn-haired man.) These receive state support. . . . I went to church the first Sunday, and on Tuesday came a tax of twelve marks for church support. I have not been since. I can't afford religious instruction at that price. Only the rich can be saved here.[16]

For forty years MT was interested in the Russian emperors. In 1867 he was selected to be the spokesperson for his Mediterranean excursion party when they visited Alexander II at his palace on the Black Sea. MT commended the czar for having distributed land among the twenty million serfs he had freed and for moving his kingdom toward what it professed to be, a land of liberty. But before the Russian Revolution that czar was followed by two more, both of whom returned to the royal family's traditional practice of oppressing commoners. MT addressed Alexander III as "his Satanic Majesty of Russia," in part because he instituted the persecution of religious minorities, especially Jews.[17] World condemnation of Russian royalty did not follow; instead, when Paris was preparing for an autumn visit of Nicholas II in 1896, the adulation was so loud that MT issued, on God's behalf, this order to St. Peter: "I am amazed to find that you have appointed the sixth of October for My Son's Second Advent in the earth, and Paris the place. Do you wish it to

---

[14]HF 201.
[15]MTN 196-97.
[16]MTN 223.
[17]MTN 78; CT2 1, 1017.

go flat? Postpone it at once. I could not get the attention of the French Myself if I appeared in Paris on that date."[18]

At the beginning of the twentieth century, MT was pleased to observe the diminishing power of the Russian royalty. He gleefully explained, in his distinctive way, why the Russians were being beaten by the Japanese:

> The real reason why the Russians are getting licked is because of their niggardly policy. Look at General Kurapotkin! I read in the papers that he has taken out with him only eighty holy images! Just like the Russians! They never make adequate preparations for battle. Why, eighty icons are not half enough.[19]

MT was furious with President Roosevelt for intervening in the Russo-Japanese War to help Russia get favorable peace terms.

MT told a Russian revolutionist, who had come to New York for support, that the Christianity of modern Americans was a sham because "we have lost our ancient sympathy with oppressed peoples struggling for life and liberty."[20] He concluded a letter he sent for a fund-raising effort with his hope that he might live to see the day when a republic would arise in Russia and "when czars and grand dukes will be as scarce there as I trust they are in heaven."[21] MT was especially incensed with Nicholas because he had massacred thousands of his Jewish subjects,[22] and he participated in a benefit for Jewish victims of the Russian pogrom.[23] That dastardly violence prompted MT to send this Yuletide sentiment, "It is my warm and world-embracing Christmas hope that all of us that deserve it may finally be gathered together in a heaven of rest and peace, and the others permitted to retire into the clutches of Satan, or the emperor of Russia, according to preference."[24]

To contribute more substantially to the fomenting revolution, MT wrote "The Czar's Soliloquy" in 1905, after reading that Nicholas was in the habit of meditating after bathing and before dressing. In the soliloquy,

---

[18]MTP, notebook #31.
[19]*The Independent* (5 May 1910): 959.
[20]MTA 2:292.
[21]MTL 795.
[22]OMT 37.
[23]MTS 468.
[24]MTB 1229.

Nicholas comes to realize while standing naked before a mirror that, as he appears there, he is indistinguishable in rank from a common workman. He admits to himself that his people are in awe of him only because of what he wears.[25] The czar illustrates MT's maxim: "Clothes make the man. Naked people have little or no influence in society."[26] Nicholas muses that for centuries the sole purpose of Russia has been to make his family comfortable. He thinks: "Our family is above the law . . . therefore we are outlaws." "No regal tyranny has ever been overthrown except by violence." "For the first time in our history, my throne is in real peril and the nation [is] waking up from its immoral slave-lethargy."[27]

§ § §

In Europe, MT's best service to democracy and religion was his defense of the Jews. He was quick to recognize the trumped up charge of treason against Alfred Dreyfus, a French army officer, who was sentenced to Devil's Island in 1894. "Oh, the French!" he exclaimed, about that famous travesty of justice, "I don't think they have improved a jot since they were turned out of hell."[28] Many conservative Catholics believed that Dreyfus could not be a loyal Frenchman because he was Jewish. The anti-Semitism of that affair convinced Theredor Herzl, whom MT befriended in Vienna, that Jews could not find welcome in Europe and should emigrate to Palestine.

MT spent two years in Vienna, a city with a strong antipathy toward Jews in prominent positions. Adolf Hitler claimed it was only after he came to live there as a young man when he became aware of "the Jewish problem,"[29] which then became the rotten core of his politics. In "Concerning the Jews," an essay written in Vienna, MT showed that he is above racial, caste, and religious prejudice. MT writes, "All that I care to know is that a man is a human being; . . . he can't be any worse." While in Vienna he expressed ethnic equality in this Twainesque way: "We all

---

[25]A similar theme is found in MT's *The Prince and the Pauper*, a story about two boys whose clothes swaps reversed their fortunes.

[26]CT2 942.

[27]CT2 642-45.

[28]MTSP 171.

[29]Adolf Hitler, *Mein Kampf* (Boston: Houghton Mifflin, 1971) 52-62.

belong to the nasty stinking little human race, . . . God's beloved vermin."[30]

MT argued that envy was the fundamental motivation of those Gentiles who were demanding the expulsion of Jews from Europe.[31] "The Jews have the best average brain of any people in the world," he said; "they are peculiarly and conspicuously the world's intellectual aristocracy."[32] It was because of their perspicacity, he pointed out, that Jews had performed as outstandingly in their professions. Another reason MT called the Jews "the most marvelous race the world has ever produced"[33] was that they were the only people who did not let their poor perish from lack of food and shelter.[34] Their charity, he observed, was not limited to aiding their own people. "Suffering can always move a Jew's heart and tax his pocket to the limit," MT said.[35]

Sigmund Freud got to know MT while the two were in Vienna and spoke of him appreciatively in some of his writings. While he was exiled in London, Freud published a summary of MT's "Concerning the Jews" in hopes of lessening bigotry.[36] When a Jew asked MT why he never ridiculed Jews in his writings, he responded that he could not make fun of people suffering from persecution.[37] Because of his bold Jewish advocacy and his Hebrew name, Samuel, the anti-Semitic press in Vienna assumed MT was a Jew.[38]

MT expressed his pro-Jewish sympathies in various ways. Consider these two historical comments: "I hold in just as much reverence that little Jew baby that was born in Bethlehem nineteen centuries ago as if it had been a Christian baby";[39] and "Christianity has deluged the world

---

[30]MTHL 692.

[31]CT2 361.

[32]MTN 151.

[33]MTL 647.

[34]*The American Hebrew* (4 April 1890).

[35]MTA 2:294.

[36]"Sigmund Freud," ENC; *Journal of the American Psychoanalytic Association* (1980): 563-74.

[37]PP 219.

[38]Carl Dolmetsch, *"Our Famous Guest": Mark Twain in Vienna* (Athens: University of Georgia Press, 1992) 250.

[39]MTP, notebook #40, 48.

with blood and tears—Judaism has caused neither for religion's sake."[40] In an effort to accord equal treatment to two great religions, he petitioned New York City to grant equal status to the Jewish and Christian weekly holy days.[41] Also, MT assisted Jewish philanthropy by supporting the Mount Sinai Hospital there. By means of a deduction from a biblical saying he made this appeal: " 'Charity covers a multitude of sins.' Therefore, it is but the plainest and simplest wisdom to keep a supply of it on hand. . . . Take advantage of this present Charity Fair to buy and lay in a real good stock of it."[42]

In his first travel book, MT imagined what an Italian visitor to America might report upon his return:

> Jews, there, are treated just like human beings, instead of dogs. They can work at any business they please; . . . they can even shake hands with Christians if they choose; . . . they can live in any part of a town they like best; . . . there they never have been driven by soldiers into a church every Sunday for hundreds of years to hear themselves and their religion . . . cursed; . . . a Jew is allowed to vote, hold office, yea, get up on a rostrum in the public street and express his opinion of the government if the government don't suit him![43]

MT's Jewish awareness can be traced to his early years. He recalled that two of his Hannibal schoolmates were the first Jews he had ever seen. He was at first awed by them because he had previously thought of Jews only as famous biblical figures.[44] An exchange between MT and his eight-year-old niece suggests that as a young man he knew a Jewish merchant. Showing off her religious knowledge, she told him the biblical story of Moses. Later she informed her father that Uncle Sam lacked good sense because he insisted that he knew Moses well and that he had a store on Market Street.[45] Both MT and his mother had broad religious

---

[40]Lewis Leary, ed., *Mark Twain's Correspondence with Henry Huttleston Rogers* (Berkeley: University of California Press, 1969) 354.

[41]MTSP 200.

[42]1 Peter 4:8; LTR 6:593.

[43]IA 269-70.

[44]AMT 77.

[45]LTR 1:368.

sympathies and when she came to live in St. Louis, where there was a synagogue, she occasionally worshiped there.[46]

When a class of elementary school children visited Quarry Farm one summer, MT identified a Jewish girl because she left uneaten the non-kosher food she had been served. After this he showed special consideration to her, sending his carriage to bring her back several times so that he could learn traditional Jewish stories from her. The girl was greatly impressed by his interest in her as an individual and in his desire to understand her religious culture.[47]

In the last year of his life, MT gave his blessing to the marriage of his daughter Clara to Ossip Gabrilowitsch, a Jewish refugee from Russia. Ossip was at his father-in-law's side when he died and it was fitting that MT's only grandchild had a Jewish and a Christian parent. In 1937 Clara placed a granite monument two fathoms ("mark twain") high at the Langdon-Clemens cemetery plot in Elmira. On it are medallions of her father and her husband, who became an renowned musician.

Global Tour

To liquidate debts incurred, MT set off in 1895 on a round-the-world speaking tour—mainly to Australia, India, and South Africa. On each continent he expressed a strong interest in the impact of the Christianity imported from Europe with the religions of other cultures. In Australia, he remarked on the intelligence of the aborigines, whom he found to be "marvelously interesting creatures." He commented on their high tolerance of pain, their artistry in drawing animals, and their mastery of the boomerang they had invented.[48] The white settlers did not appreciate the aborigines and boasted about "reducing a native population 80 per cent in 20 years."[49] To illustrate one of the ways they carried out that reduction, MT told about a "squatter" who had invited the dark natives living in his area to a Christmas feast, and then exterminated them by

---

[46]Doris Webster and Samuel Webster, "Whitewashing Jane Clemens," *Bookman* (July 1925): 532.

[47]Robert Jerome and Herbert Wisbey, eds., *Mark Twain in Elmira* (Elmira NY: Mark Twain Society, 1977) 181-82.

[48]FE 193-94, 218-24.

[49]FE 208.

lacing the pudding with arsenic. He then penned this devastating comment:

> In many countries we have taken the savage's land from him, and made him our slave, and lashed him every day, and broken his pride, and made death his only friend, and overworked him till he dropped in his tracks; . . . yet a quick death by poison is lovingkindness [by comparison]. . . . There are many humorous things in the world; among them the white man's notion that he is less savage than other savages.[50]

The practices of some early European settlers in Australia provided MT with other examples to show why they hardly deserved to be called civilized. Sugar planters had kidnapped Pacific islanders who, cut off from their native area, died on plantations at an annual rate as high as eighteen percent. MT commended the efforts of missionaries to publicize the illegal operation, noting that one highly paid kidnapper had charged that "missionaries have poisoned his life." He sympathized with Rev. William Gray who asserted, "What I am concerned about is that we as a Christian nation should wipe out these races to enrich ourselves." MT publicized to the world Gray's grim indictment of the forced labor, which read in part:

> It generally demoralizes and always impoverishes the Kanaka [Polynesian], deprives him of his citizenship, and depopulates the islands fitted to his home. . . . The whole system is contrary to the spirit and doctrine of the Gospel of Jesus Christ. The Gospel requires us to help the weak, but the Kanaka is fleeced and trodden down. The bedrock of this Traffic is that the life and liberty of a black man are of less value than those of a white man.[51]

MT told about a raw example of British imperialism that occurred in the early decades of the nineteenth century on the Australian island of Tasmania. He was chagrined that European settlers had exterminated the thousands of aborigines there, mainly by gunfire. He thought that miscegenation would have been more humane, commenting caustically, "They should have been crossed with the Whites. It would have improved the Whites and done the Natives no harm."[52] He praised one attempt to replace kindness for killing, even though it came too late to avert the

---

[50]FE 212-13.
[51]FE 89-90.
[52]FE 265.

genocide. George Robinson, a Methodist missionary, gained the confidence of several hundred surviving Tasmanians and took them to a reserve where they could live without fear of annihilation.

On the Australian continent, MT found inspiring other records of missionary activity by Westerners, "When we first landed here the natives lived only to fight, and the victory was celebrated by a cannibal feast." But he reported that after decades of Christian witness "there has been no fighting or killing all along the coast."[53] He forecast that "All the savage lands in the world are going to be brought under subjection to the Christian governments of Europe. I am not sorry, but glad."[54]

MT was also impressed that Australia had welcomed a wide variety of non-Christian religions as well as Christian denominations. After naming them, he remarked: "About 64 roads to the other world. You see how healthy the religious atmosphere is."[55] Illustrating this is a note he made concerning a fellow train traveler there: "For comrade, a Catholic priest who was better than I was, but didn't seem to know it—a man full of graces of the heart, the mind, and the spirit; a lovable man."[56] MT hoped that the good father would rise through the ecclesiastical hierarchy and someday become an archangel!

§ § §

India was the country that most interested MT on his global tour, mainly because of its exotic religions. Large portions of the chapters on India in *Following the Equator* are focused on India's amazing variety. Having had difficulty relating to one God, MT was overwhelmed by Hinduism's plethora of divine beings: "India has 2,000,000 gods, and worships them all. In religions all other countries are paupers; India is the only millionaire."[57] He found that the fantastic stories of the deeds of the Hindu gods made it difficult for missionaries to convince Hindus of the superiority of Christianity. One missionary reported that, while the credulous Hindus had no trouble believing in the biblical miracles, they were not as grand as their own supernatural tales. For example, the story

---

[53]MTN 286.
[54]FE 625.
[55]FE 183.
[56]FE 241.
[57]FE 397.

of Samson carrying away Gaza's city gate to a far hill paled beside that
of Hanuman who carried mountains from the Himalayas to Ceylon. MT
began the chapter on mythology with this quip: "There are those who
scoff at the schoolboy, calling him frivolous and shallow. Yet it was the
schoolboy who said, 'Faith is believing what you know ain't so.' "[58]

At Benares, MT visited with the famous Swami Saraswati, a naked
ascetic who had attained the "state of perfection" after many rein-
carnations, and was adored as a god. In exchange for his book of Hindu
meditations, MT gave him a copy of *Huckleberry Finn*. The encounter
provided an opportunity for MT to reflect on the reverence he attempted
to express for the commitments of others:

> The reverence which is difficult, and which has personal merit in it, is the
> respect which you pay, without compulsion, to the political or religious
> attitude of a man whose beliefs are not yours. You can't revere his gods or
> his politics, and no one expects you to do that, but you could respect his
> belief in them if you tried hard enough. . . . We hardly ever try. If the man
> doesn't believe as we do, we say he is a crank, and that settles it. I mean it
> does nowadays, because now we can't burn him. . . . We despise all
> reverences and all objects of reverence which are outside the pale of our
> own list of sacred things. And yet . . . we are shocked when other people
> despise and defile the things which are holy to us.[59]

MT viewed the funeral practices he saw in Benares in North India
with understanding. Much of his information about them came in oral and
written form from Arthur Parker, a Christian missionary living there. MT
appreciated the "touching picture" of Hindu devotion he found in Parker's
lucid handbook on Benares.[60] Commenting on cremation, in contrast to
Western burials, MT wrote: "We are drifting slowly—but hopefully—
toward cremation in these days. . . . When cremation becomes the rule we
shall cease to shudder at it; we should shudder at burial if we allowed
ourselves to think what goes on in the grave."[61]

The responses of MT to the historic holy cities of Benares and
Jerusalem were similar. In both he sought to understand the meaning of

---

[58]FE 132.
[59]FE 509-15.
[60]FE 480-83.
[61]FE 377.

religious practices he found strange, and while appreciating the spirituali-
ty of the devotees he was repelled by some of their practices. For
example, he tells of boating along the Ganges at Benares where pilgrims
were washing and drinking from the sacred river amid "a random corpse
slopping around" and where "the foul gush from a sewer was making the
water turbid."[62]

In Bombay, MT visited the Parsee Tower of Silence where the flesh
of human corpses is consumed by vultures. Our "ambassador" inserted in
a notebook there, "One marvels to see here a perfect system for the
protection of the living from the contagion derivable from the dead."[63] He
generally admired the Parsees, saying "They have a pure and lofty
religion, and they preserve it in its integrity and order their lives by it."[64]
They were also, he claimed, even more lavishly benevolent than the Jews.

In his book, MT quoted the first stanza of a hymn by Bishop
Reginald Heber, a missionary to India, that his travels brought to mind:

> From Greenland's icy mountains,
> From India's coral strand;
> Where Afric's sunny fountains
> Roll down their golden sand;
> From many an ancient river,
> From many a palmy plain,
> They call us to deliver
> Their land from error's chain.

MT commented: "Those are beautiful verses, and they have remained in
my memory all my life. But if the closing lines are true, let us hope that
. . . [we will] at the same time borrow some of its pagan ways to enrich
our high system with."[65] He judged those lines to be presumptuous and
claimed that the "deeply religious heathen" on the globe vastly outnumber
genuine Christians.[66]

MT compared the division of labor in India, where men always work
the fields, with his recollection of Catholic shrines in Bavaria amid "the

---

[62]FE 497.
[63]Quoted in *The Hindoo Patriot*, 4 February 1896, 3.
[64]FE 378.
[65]FE 525.
[66]MTN 277.

shameful spectacle of gray and venerable old grandmothers . . . mowing and binding in the fields, and pitchforking the loads into wagons." In Austria, he often saw "a woman and a cow harnessed to the plow, and a man driving." In France, amid symbols of religious devotion, he witnessed peasant women in virtual slavery. There, men would issue orders but would refuse to assist women with heavy lifting. One Frenchman in charge, MT noted, was "enlightening himself with the histories of French saints who used to flee to the desert in the Middle Ages to escape the contamination of woman." The inhumane treatment of women in continental Europe convinced him that churchmen failed to make any connection between Christianity and the merciful treatment of women. Quoting from the second stanza of Heber's hymn, his "favorite poem," he wrote, "Every prospect pleases, / And only man is vile."[67] Heber's generic "man" becomes for MT the chauvinistic "male."

There were Hindu customs pertaining to women that MT also abhorred. He approved of the colonial policy that prohibited the practices of female infanticide and widow suicide. Before discontinuance by the British government, he reported, 800 widows annually threw themselves on pyres beneath their husbands' corpses and burned themselves to death.[68] That change by the British illustrates why MT believed that the Indians were fortunate to be no longer under Hindu and Muslim rulers.[69] "The handful of English in India govern the Indian myriads with apparent ease," he observed, "and without noticeable friction, through tact, training, and distinguished administrative ability, reinforced by just and liberal laws—and by keeping their word to the native whenever they give it."[70]

Aga Khan III came to MT's hotel to meet him and to discuss Huck Finn's philosophy. "God wants to see you," is the way MT's servant introduced him.[71] The Persian prince, a descendant of Muhammad's family and the Shah of Iran, was being educated to lead the Ismailian Muslims. Khan later remembered MT as having godly attributes, "He

---

[67]FE 526-28.
[68]FE 397, 462.
[69]FE 626.
[70]FE 518.
[71]FE 366.

seemed to me dear, gentle and saintly, sad and immensely modest for so great and famous a genius."[72]

Incidentally, MT found that some people in India had such a false impression of the Western world that they referred to Chicago, the site for the 1893 World Congress of Religions, as "the Holy City." To provide another perspective, he began a chapter on India in *Following the Equator* with an impatient Satan informing some newcomers to hell, "The trouble with you Chicago people is, that you think you are the best people down here; whereas you are merely the most numerous."[73]

MT revealed in India that he had transcended his cultural conditioning concerning race and skin color. There he noted, "nearly all black and brown skins are beautiful, but a beautiful white skin is rare. . . . Where dark complexions are massed, they make the whites look bleached-out, unwholesome, and sometimes frankly ghastly." As a result, he said, white ladies paint their faces in a vain attempt to make themselves more attractive.[74] He reasoned that "white was not a favorite complexion with God" since humanity is two-thirds dark-skinned. Recalling that he found the Nazareth townspeople dark, he extrapolated that the family of Jesus was likewise not lily white.[75] But he recognized that people's inward core signified more than their outward appearance, "The hearts of men are about alike, all over the world, no matter what their skin complexion may be."[76]

§ § §

As MT traveled about South Africa, the last stop on his world tour, the acceptance of imperialism that he had in India began to reverse. His sympathies lay first with the native Africans, the ultimate underdogs, next with the Boers, who had settled in South Africa two centuries earlier, and last with the British, then the mightiest of global imperial powers. At that time the government of South Africa was divided between British and Boer territories. Descended from Dutch Calvinists, the Boer, according to MT, "is grim, serious, solemn, and is always diligently fitting himself for

---

[72]Mohammed Shah, *The Memoirs of Aga Khan* (London: Cassell, 1954) 3:32.
[73]FE 519, 582.
[74]FE 381, 383.
[75]Quoted in *The Ladies' Home Journal* (February 1912): 54.
[76]MTLB 653.

heaven, suspecting that they couldn't stand him in the other place."[77] Both groups with a European heritage oppressed the black Africans. The Boer "patriots," assuming they had God's approval, "stole the land from the feeble blacks, and then re-stole it from the English robber."[78]

MT could sense that war was brewing between the Boers, who were farmers, and the British, who lusted after the incredible deposits of gold and diamonds recently discovered there. Although he had high regard for Rudyard Kipling, who had come to Elmira just to meet him, he opposed his imperialistic sympathies. In 1899, MT wrote a parody of a poem by Kipling that praised British patriots for volunteering to fight the Boers.[79] Also, MT observed that "the holy ones air their smug pieties" from British pulpits but "show their contempt for the pieties of the Boer."[80] When the war erupted, he commented, with Lincolnian wit: "I notice that God is on both sides in this war. . . . I am the only person who had noticed this; everyone here thinks He is playing the game for this side, and for this side only."[81] MT estimated the comparative strength of the ecclesiastical artillery:

> At a signal from the Primate of all England the eighty thousand English pulpits thundered forth a titanic simultaneous supplication to their God to give the embattled English in South Africa the victory. The little Boer battery of two hundred and ten guns replied with a simultaneous supplication to the same God to give the Boers the victory.[82]

Knowing that the British popularly called the Boers uncivilized, MT countered with his own impressions of Boer culture:

> Happiness, food, shelter, clothing, wholesale labor, modest and rational ambitions, honesty, kindliness, hospitality, love of freedom and limitless courage to fight for it, composure and fortitude in time of disaster, patience in time of hardship and privation, absence of noise and brag in time of victory, contentment with a humble and peaceful life void of insane excite-

---

[77]MTN 298.
[78]MTN 296.
[79]Arthur Scott, *On the Poetry of Mark Twain* (Champaign: University of Illinois Press) 34.
[80]MTL 694.
[81]MTHL 716.
[82]BMT 324.

ments—if there is a higher, better form of civilization than this, I am not aware of it.[83]

MT informed the world that Cecil Rhodes, the prime minister of the Cape Colony, and his fellow capitalists were behind the current fighting with the Boers. He called Rhodes, who coveted the mineral-rich Boer land, a Cain, a Judas, and a Golden Calf,[84] and said of his "gang":

> They are chartered to rob and slay, and they lawfully do it, but not in a compassionate and Christian spirit. . . . They issue "regulations" requiring the incensed and harassed natives to work for the white settlers, and neglect their own affairs to do it. This is slavery. . . . Rhodesia is a happy name for that land of piracy and pillage.[85]

Two religious groups operating in South Africa impressed MT. He saluted the Salvation Army, which was founded in London a generation earlier: "They are the missionaries for me. They feed the poor, they employ the idle, and ex-prisoner, they reform the drunkard and the wanton."[86] (He was later to meet the Army's founder, General William Booth, on the day when both were honored at Oxford University.) MT also expressed admiration for the Trappist Catholics after visiting their community. He was amazed that any humans would be willing to live in their somber surroundings without tasty food, comfortable beds, stimulating conversation, and family intimacy. Yet, the silent Trappists were contented and he praised them for "christianizing and educating and teaching wage-yielding mechanical trades to 1,200 boys and girls."[87] Mohandas Gandhi, who had visited the same monastery a year earlier, was also inspired by the personal self-discipline and effective labors of those monks and nuns.

The Anti-Imperialist

The Declaration of Independence's paraphrase of a verse from the Bible's opening chapter, that God created all humans equal, was basic to MT's religion. Accordingly, he was ever alert to the way in which Americans

---

[83]MTL 694.
[84]MTN 84.
[85]FE 691.
[86]MTP, notebook #30, 39.
[87]FE 652.

disregarded either its international or its national implications. He advocated a higher patriotism that gave no favoritism to one's native country.

In the last years of the nineteenth century, Cuba and the Philippines rebelled against Spanish colonial rule. In 1898, MT cheered when President McKinley obtained from Congress a declaration of war on Spain, because America intended to assist Cubans in their independence movement. He wrote Twichell: "I have never enjoyed a war—even in written history—as I am enjoying this one. . . . It is a worthy thing to fight for one's freedom; it is another sight finer to fight for another man's. And I think this is the first time it has been done."[88] In a speech after the three-month war, he said: "We have turned aside from our own comfort and seen to it that freedom should exist not only within our own gates, but in our own neighborhood. We have set Cuba free and placed her among the galaxy of free nations of the world."[89]

By contrast, MT detected an ulterior motive in his country's efforts to assist the Filipinos in their efforts to free themselves from Spanish colonialism. America began suppressing their movement for self-government, causing MT to feel betrayed: "When the United States sent word to Spain that the Cuban atrocities must end, she occupied the highest moral position ever taken by a nation since the Almighty made the earth. But when she snatched the Philippines she stained the flag."[90] Beginning in 1899, he let his fury fly against the American aggression in the Philippines, which was a popular and religious cause among his fellow citizens. While running for reelection, McKinley justified the American capture of the Filipinos in this way, "There was nothing left for us to do but to take them all . . . and civilize and Christianize them, and by God's grace do the best we could by them, as our fellow-men for whom Christ also died."[91] Protestant churches, recognizing that the acquisition of Catholic areas would open the door for their evangelistic missionaries, advocated an "Imperialism of Righteousness."[92] MT's considerable international

---

[88]MTL 663.

[89]MTS 350.

[90]MF 213.

[91]Lewis Gould, *The Spanish-American War and President McKinley* (Lawrence: University Press of Kansas, 1982) 109.

[92]William Sweet, *The Story of Religion in America* (New York: Harper, 1950) 358.

experiences enabled him to see that the American government principally wanted a naval base and a coaling station in the Philippines that would give America military and trade advantages in East Asia. He imagined the Filipinos coming to this conclusion, "There must be two Americas: one that sets the captive free, and one that takes a once-captive's new freedom away from him, . . . then kills him to get his land."[93]

A cartoon displaying MT's awareness that President McKinley was preoccupied with imperialism and unconcerned over lynchings in America.

An imperialist newspaper treated MT's criticisms patronizingly: "We are sorry to say that Mark is on a spree. . . . He is in a state of mortifying

[93]CT2 467.

intoxication from an overdraught of seriousness, something to which his head has not been hardened. Wait, and welcome the prodigal as of old on his return." That prompted the reminder by an anti-imperialist paper: "A certain rather famous group of prophets in Jerusalem were explained as 'drunken' by the mockers of their day. And their 'overdraught of seriousness' finally overturned the imperialistic [Roman] world."[94] Reference is made here to the apostles being ridiculed for supporting a leader who had been recently crucified. Peter responded by announcing that God's Spirit would be poured out "upon all flesh," and would be inclusive of genders, classes, and ages.[95]

Jim Zwick demonstrates in his collection of MT's anti-imperialist writings that "Mark Twain was the most prominent opponent of the Philippine-American War."[96] He came to regard leader Emilio Aguinaldo as a modern Joan of Arc, for both were peasant-born, earned their people's trust, pursued liberation, and were harassed by invaders. And he saw in McKinley someone who would repair the chains of bondage that Lincoln had broken.[97]

At that time MT was called upon to introduce Winston Churchill, who was in New York to describe his experiences as a prisoner of the Boers in the South African conflict. MT pointed to the close relationship between Britain and America, "We have always been kin: kin in blood, kin in religion, kin in representative government, kin in ideals, kin in just and lofty purposes; and now we are kin in sin."[98] He maintained that Britain's aggression against the Boers, and America's against the Filipinos, were equally despicable. In spite of his criticism of British action in South Africa, he hoped that the bond between Britain and America would "not be severed in Twain."[99]

American kinship with England included imperialism, MT lamented, for it was an import from Europe. In practice, he said, Euro-American foreign policy could be summed up in a military officer's proclamation,

---

[94]Jim Zwick, ed., *Mark Twain's Weapons of Satire* (Syracuse NY: Syracuse University Press, 1992) xxxvii.

[95]Acts 2:12-18.

[96]Zwick, ed., *Mark Twain's Weapons of Satire*, xvii.

[97]Zwick, ed., *Mark Twain's Weapons of Satire*, 38, 92, 100.

[98]CT2 455.

[99]MTSP 175.

"When the Anglo-Saxon wants a thing *he just takes it*." He interpreted those words to mean that the British and American people are proud to be "thieves, highwaymen, [and] pirates." The officer's words, he noted, set off a "glad storm" of applause at a banquet in 1906 attended by a representative group of Britons and Americans. The boast, MT contended, had been America's private motto, even though "In God We Trust" is heralded in the public propaganda. He reflected, "It has always been a peculiarity of the human race that it keeps two sets of morals in stock—the private and real, and the public and artificial."[100]

At the dawn of what *Time* publisher Henry Luce would call "the American Century," MT, "disgusted by what he saw as an unholy alliance of Christianity, cash, and colonialism,"[101] painted this ugly portrait of

> the stately matron named Christendom, returning bedraggled, besmirched, and dishonored from pirate-raids in Kiao-Chou, Manchuria, South Africa and the Philippines, with her soul full of meanness, her pocket full of boodle and her mouth full of pious hypocrisies. Give her the soap and a towel, but hide the looking-glass.[102]

MT's uncle-in-law, Andrew Langdon, praised the portrait, saying, "In all the books you have written, in all the speeches you have made, I have never seen so much good sense, so much Christianity, so much manhood, so much Godliness as in the ten lines of your salutation speech to the twentieth century."[103]

In 1901, MT provided another blistering cartoon of lady Christendom, who is parading in celebration of the new century:

> A majestic matron in flowing robes drenched with blood, on her head a golden crown of thorns; impaled on the spine the bleeding heads of patriots who died for their country—Boers, Boxers, Filipinos; in one hand a slingshot, in the other a Bible, open at the text—"Do unto others" . . . [along with a] banner with motto—"Love your Neighbor's Goods as Yourself."[104]

---

[100]AMT 346-47.

[101]Justin Kaplan, *Mr. Clemens and Mark Twain* (New York: Simon & Schuster, 1966) 362.

[102]CT2 456.

[103]Hamlin Hill, *Mark Twain: God's Fool* (New York: Harper, 1978) 22, 23.

[104]Quoted in SC 369.

Embittered, MT composed a poem depicting a dying McKinley crying out to God for forgiveness over leading America to become a "Conqueror of helpless tribes, Extinguisher of struggling liberties!" As the president's eyes grow dimmer, he sees a hideous flag:

The Stars are gone, a Skull and Bones
Are in their place; the Red Bars are there,
But soaked with guiltless blood;
The white Bars are Black—
Hide it from my sight![105]

In 1905, MT wrote "The War Prayer," a parody of a wartime worship service, but he was unsuccessful in getting it published. ("None but the dead are permitted to tell the truth," he lamented.)[106] In this service of vengeance, the reading of an unspecified "war chapter from the Old Testament" is followed by the hymn, "God the All Terrible! Thou who ordainest, / Thunder thy clarion and lightning thy sword!"[107] Then, after a prayer for victory, a stranger stalks down the aisle, ascends the pulpit, and announces that he will state the "unspoken part" of what the preacher had in mind:

O Lord, our God, help us to tear their soldiers to bloody shreds with our shells; help us to cover their smiling fields with the pale forms of their patriot dead; help us to drown the thunder of the guns with the shrieks of their wounded, writhing in pain; help us to lay waste their humble homes with a hurricane of fire; help us to wring the hearts of their unoffending widows with unavailing grief; help us to turn them out roofless with their little children to wander unfriended the wastes of their desolated land in rags and hunger and thirst. . . . We ask it, in the spirit of love, of Him Who is the Source of Love, and Who is the ever-faithful refuge and friend of all that are sore beset and seek His aid with humble and contrite hearts. Amen.[108]

With theological profundity, MT exposed that prayers are often phoney because they are no more than expressions of self-interest and

---

[105]Quoted in Scott, *On the Poetry of Mark Twain*, 130.

[106]Quoted in Zwick, ed., *Mark Twain's Weapons of Satire*, 156.

[107]CT2 653. MT's parody is of the first stanza of a popular hymn by Henry Fothergill Chorley that began with "God the Omnipotent!" (or "God the almighty One!") and ended with "Give to us peace in our time, O Lord. "

[108]CT2 654-55.

belligerence. For believers in a God with equal concern for all people, petitions against another people are unworthy.

MT's blunt criticism descended upon McKinley's successor, Theodore Roosevelt, when he approved of an attack on the Moros in the Philippines. That tribe had been hostile first to the Spanish and then to the Americans for suppressing their liberation struggle. To protect themselves, the Moros hid out in the crater of an extinct volcano. When they had been exterminated by artillery fire, General Leonard Wood, Governor of the Philippines, reported: "The enemy numbered six hundred—including women and children—and we abolished them utterly, leaving not even a baby alive to cry for its dead mother. This is incomparably the greatest victory that was ever achieved by the Christian soldiers of the United States."[109]

After this 1906 massacre, President Roosevelt sent a cable to the American troops praising their "brilliant feat of arms" and the excellent way they "upheld the honor of the American flag." MT considered the action a cowardly butchery and said: "This was by all odds the least dangerous battle that Christian soldiers of any nationality were ever engaged in. . . . It was a long and happy picnic with nothing to do but sit in comfort and fire the Golden Rule into those people down there."[110] Edward Wagenknecht, with Twainian irony, comments:

> I am afraid Mark Twain had a very simple mind. It never occurred to him that the Christian virtues apply only to individuals, while nations are wholly exempt from their requirements; he could not grasp the sublime truth that while murder on a retail scale is always murder; murder on a wholesale scale is sometimes a sacred duty.[111]

MT judged the American who viewed patriotism narrowly as blind allegiance to be "a poor sort of Christian—cordial blood-brother to all Americans, but not even second cousin to the rest of the race."[112] In another notebook, he jotted: "Patriotism is being carried to insane excess. I know of men who do not love God because He is a foreigner."[113] He

---

[109]MTA 2:190.
[110]MTA 2:194.
[111]MTMW (first edition, 1935) 258-59.
[112]MTP, notebook #41.
[113]MTP, notebook #36, 14.

remarked further: "From man's point of view patriotism is the noblest thing there is; from God's it is the meanest. . . . A Christian must labor for the breaking down of all walls that interrupt the fusion of the race into a common brotherhood; and one of the most formidable of these is patriotism."[114]

Speaking out against an "unrighteous war" and refusing to fight in it should not be considered unpatriotic, MT asserted. Patriotism should not be defined as making one's conscience conform to the general outlook of the country to whom one pledges allegiance. Echoing what Thoreau wrote in *Civil Disobedience* regarding the American war against Mexico, MT said, "I should still be a patriot [in opposing an unjust war], and, in my opinion, the only one in the whole country."[115]

In spite of his assault upon unjust war, MT rejected pacifism which, to him, unrealistically assumed the basic goodness of human nature. In the last years of his life he predicted that a world war was approaching in the twentieth century.[116] Contributing to that war, MT thought, was the proliferation of arms:

> Anybody but a statesman could invent some way to reduce these vast armaments to rational and sensible and safe police proportions, with the result that thenceforth all Christians could sleep in their beds unafraid, and even the Savior could come down and walk on the seas, foreigner as He is, without dread of being chased by Christian battleships.[117]

§ § §

MT's concern for the rights of other nationals began with his advocacy for the Chinese. He first became acquainted with Chinese aliens while working in San Francisco, and from that time onward he was their advocate whenever the occasion arose. While still a bachelor he thought of applying for a position with American diplomats in China, although he actually never visited there during his life. In 1870, he commended an American diplomat to China who promoted equal justice by insisting that

---

[114]MTP, notebook #42, 54.
[115]MTA 2:17.
[116]MTAL 306.
[117]OMT 40.

an American murderer in China not be exempted from punishment by the Chinese.[118]

In 1880, MT's association with the Asylum Hill Church in Hartford resulted in his becoming involved in diplomacy between the United States and China. Twichell had taken a lead in persuading the Chinese government to establish an educational mission in Hartford to prepare Chinese boys for further study in American colleges. Yung Wing, the Chinese official in charge, attended the Clemenses' church and asked its assistance when he learned that an anti-Western faction in his country was planning to discontinue the program. Recognizing MT's dedication to promoting Chinese-American understanding, Twichell called upon his friend for help. MT had close ties with Ulysses Grant, who was regarded as a hero in China, so he and Twichell met with Grant and asked him to intervene. Grant dispatched a letter to the Chinese government requesting that students might continue to be sent to study in America, and the problem was resolved.[119]

MT thought highly of the Chinese code of ethics, some of which he believed had improved Christianity. He said, "We borrow the Golden Rule from Confucius after it has seen service for centuries."[120] He admired other aspects of traditional Confucianism as well, "The Chinese are universally conceded to be excellent people, honest, honorable, industrious, trustworthy, kind-hearted, and all that—leave them alone, they are plenty good enough just as they are; and besides, almost every convert runs the risk of catching our civilization."[121]

In 1900, MT defended the Boxers, Chinese rebels who were provoked by the arrogance of foreigners toward their nation.[122] Western powers had carved out areas in China where the Chinese were not permitted to rule. He argued that the Boxer aim was parallel to that of the 1882 Chinese Exclusion Act in American law, so "we would be doing the graceful thing to allow China to decide whether she will allow us to go there."[123] Boxer nationalism was only a mirror image of what the majority of

---

[118]E&E 20.
[119]JHT 85-87.
[120]WM 33.
[121]CT2 484.
[122]MTL 699.
[123]MTS 361.

Americans called noble patriotism, he pointed out; thus, we should not demand an open door there when our immigration door was closed. After the Boxer Rebellion failed, some Western governments imposed stiff indemnities on the legitimate Chinese government for lives and property lost. MT thought that such punishment wrongly showed Chinese Christian converts that vengeance was a virtue.

What MT found especially galling was that Christian missions were also compelling compensation from the Chinese government, even though the Boxers had been a rebel society independent of the government. William Ament, a Congregational missionary with the American Board of Foreign Missions, acknowledged that he was using a "mailed fist" rather than a "soft hand" in collecting indemnities.[124] MT responded to Ament's harshness in a satirical essay entitled, "To the Person Sitting in Darkness." That title alludes to Matthew's claim that Isaiah's prophecy had been fulfilled with the coming of a humble Prince of Peace who brought light to a dark world.[125] MT denounced both Ament and the conversion policy operating in a nation where Christians were not welcomed. He remarked that "The Golden Rule distinctly forbids the missionary to ply his trade in China or in any other country whose people he would be unwilling to allow to go to his American home and undermine the religious faith of his family."[126]

Rather than continuing to impose Western civilization on the reluctant Chinese, MT advised that we Westerners should "get our Civilization-tools together and see how much stock is left on hand in the way of Glass Beads and Theology, and Maxim guns and Hymn Books." He noticed that the Chinese were becoming suspicious because containers they were receiving with labels Love, Justice, Liberty, and Equality from the Prince of Peace were filled with weapons, buckets for collecting revenues, and devices to thwart freedom.[127] In a fable he wrote, a bee kingdom accused by a more powerful insect empire of being a "yellow peril" learns from their oppressors how to use powerful weapons to deliver themselves from domination.[128] MT envisioned a reverse move-

---

[124]CT2 458.
[125]Isaiah 9:2; Matthew 4:16.
[126]WM 498.
[127]CT2 461-65.
[128]FM 427-29.

ment of missionaries between America and China that would embody his "hope that some day those excellent people would come here and teach us how to be at peace." But then he acknowledged that would not happen because we have taught them about our reliance on military power.[129]

MT's criticism of missionaries in China elicited commentary in many American and British journals. The editor of a Pennsylvania magazine gave this commendation: "Mark Twain, preacher of righteousness, when the official preachers are dumb, though the oppressed cry in the street."[130] Reacting to the flood of mail that followed, both favorable and unfavorable, he quipped, "Do right and you will be conspicuous."[131] The president of the Congregational Clerical Union attacked MT's roots, saying "he is a man of low birth and poor breeding." Detecting an elitism in this charge, MT responded, "I would prefer to be low-born—in a republic."[132]

Carnegie heralded MT's essay on Christian missions in China as "a new Gospel of Saint Mark" and offered to pay for publishing thousands of copies.[133] When Twichell advised him to be more prudent in publicizing his criticism of American imperialism in China, MT rebuked him:

> I can't understand it! You are a public guide and teacher, Joe, and are under a heavy responsibility to men, young and old; if you teach your people—as you teach me—to hide their opinions when they believe the flag is being abused and dishonored, lest the utterances do them and a publisher a damage, how do you answer for it to your conscience?[134]

MT referred to "Christian pirates like Ament and professional hypocrites and liars like Rev. Judson Smith of the American Board" in another letter to Twichell: "Whenever you ask people to support them [foreign missions] Joe, do bar China. Their presence there is forbidden by the Bible and by every sentiment of humanity—and fair dealing. And they have done vast mischief there. I would bar no other country."[135]

[129]LTR 6:293-94.
[130](Philadelphia) *City and State*, 1 February 1901.
[131]MTP, notebook #44, 1901; MTB 1134.
[132]*New York Sun*, 29 April 1901.
[133]MTB 1133.
[134]MTL 705.
[135]MT to Joseph Twichell, June 1901, Beinecke Library, Yale University.

Earlier MT had recommended a more appropriate focus for mission-ary effort. When an editor in Buffalo, he reported on a New York town where some self-appointed "champions of chastity" had broken into a home. There they stripped and tarred an unmarried woman school teacher who was presumed guilty of having sex. His article, entitled "Domestic Missionaries Wanted," concluded:

> The American Board of Foreign Missions have done a good work in supplying the kindly and refining influences of the gospel to the savages of Asia and the islands of the sea, but let them forward no more missionaries to distant lands for the present. God knows they are needed at home. There are no meaner, mangier, filthier savages in all the wide domain of barbarism than the Christian town of Cohocton, right here at our elbow, can produce.[136]

The retargeting of mission areas continued to be a concern of MT. Responding to the increase of lynchings in America, often sponsored by men of the Ku Klux Klan who claimed they were Christians, he urged:

> Let us import American missionaries from China, and send them to the lynching field. . . . Their motherland supplicates their aid in this her hour of deep distress. They are competent, our people are not; they are used to scoffs, sneers, revilings, danger, our people are not; they have the martyr-spirit; nothing but the martyr-spirit can brave a lynching-mob, and cow it and scatter it; they can save their country, we besseech them to come home and do it. . . . O compassionate missionary, . . . come home and convert these Christians![137]

In *Huckleberry Finn*, MT told about the "masked cowards" in the South who frequently made a mockery of a humane legal system under the cover of darkness.[138] In 1901, he wrote Twichell, "Every lynching account unsettles the brains of another set of excitable white men, and lights another pyre—115 lynchings last year." The crime could be halted, he remarked sardonically, "by extinguishing God's most elegant invention, the Human Race."[139] That same year, after "burning at stakes"

---

[136]CT1 432.

[137]Jack Salzman, ed., *Prospects 25* (New York: Cambridge University Press, 2000) 144-45; Terry Oggel has provided this first accurate text of "The United States of Lyncherdom. "

[138]HF 190.

[139]MTL 715.

had consumed 203 African-Americans, MT wrote an angry article entitled, "The United States of Lyncherdom." In it he optimistically speculated that if all such burnings each year occurred at one time, the shock of such a spectacle might bring about reform. So, he wrote, "Let all the far stretch of kerosened pyres be touched off simultaneously and the glare and the shrieks and the agonies burst heavenward to the Throne." Aware that a mob had besmirched his native state, where religion was generally "more virile and earnest" than in Northern states, he commented, "Those hundred lynchers down in the corner of the state are not real Missourians, they are bastards."[140]

§ § §

MT wanted the public to know that he did not intend his criticism of some missionaries in China to be an attack on all foreign missionaries. When he received a letter suggesting that Christian missionaries should be commended because of their medical work, he responded that there were indeed compassionate ones who are welcomed by natives in Africa and elsewhere.[141] He published a glowing tribute to most missionaries:

> A missionary is a man who is pretty nearly all heart, else he would not be in a calling which requires of him such large sacrifices of one kind and another. He is made up of faith, zeal, courage, sentiment, emotion, enthusiasm; and so he is a mixture of poet, devotee, and knight errant. He exiles himself from home and friends and the scenes and associations that are dearest to him; patiently endures discomforts, privations, discourage-ments, goes with good pluck into dangers which he knows may cost him his life; and when he must suffer death, willingly makes that supreme sacrifice for his cause.[142]

The *Review of Reviews* in London published this discerning editorial:

> Mark Twain is the last man in the world to write a word reflecting upon the self-sacrificing labours of missionaries who are missionaries indeed, to whose labours and martyrdom the world owes many of the best things which it possesses. But of the modern type of missionary who in the name of the

---

[140]Salzman 139-45.

[141]MTB 1420.

[142]Charles Neider, ed., *The Complete Essays of Mark Twain* (Garden City NY: Doubleday, 1963) 311.

Prince of Peace acts often as the precursor of war and conquest, and who insists upon the defense of the Gospel by gunboats and Maxims, excites in Mark Twain somewhat of the same stern and scathing indignation which it would have excited in the Founder of our faith.[143]

MT was perhaps a better missionary than some of the official ones who were unwittingly more caught up in spreading colonialism than they were in offering the message of Jesus. Some missionaries were little more than representatives of Western culture—its clothes, its music, its foods, its family structure, its history, its economic values, and its political power. MT was fully aware, Arthur Scott believes, that many American missionaries "were tools of the government, sent abroad to bully better men into adopting a culture inferior to their own."[144]

MT's last and most intense anti-imperialist efforts were directed toward King Leopold II of Belgium, who privately owned much of tropical Africa. That area had long interested MT because of Henry Stanley, who became Leopold's principal agent in exploring the Congo basin. MT first met Stanley in St. Louis when they were both young journalists and they remained friends for life.[145] After entertaining Stanley in Hartford, MT went to Boston to introduce his lecture on exploring central Africa.[146]

Years later MT became aware that Leopold's Congo property had become a place of severe economic exploitation, and he was convinced that the United States should take the initiative to correct the situation because it had been the first nation to recognize the "Congo Free State." "We occupied the office of midwife to the Congo State and brought it into the world," MT stated.[147] He depicted what the worst of all colonialists was doing:

> The royal palace of Belgium is still what it has been for fourteen years, the den of a wild beast, King Leopold II, who for money's sake mutilates, murders, and starves half a million of friendless and helpless poor natives in the Congo State every year, and does it by the silent consent of all the Christian powers except England, none of them lifting a hand or a voice to stop these atrocities, although thirteen of them are by solemn treaty pledged to the pro-

---

[143]SC 365.
[144]MTAL 263.
[145]MTL 752.
[146]MTHL 573.
[147]*New York World*, 3 December 1905.

tecting and uplifting of those wretched natives. In fourteen years Leopold has deliberately destroyed more lives than have suffered death on all the battlefields of this planet for the past thousand years. . . . It is curious that the most advanced and most enlightened century of all the centuries the sun has looked upon should have the ghastly distinction of having produced this moldy and piety-mouthing hypocrite, this bloody monster whose mate is not findable in human history anywhere, and whose personality will surely shame hell itself when he arrives there—which will be soon, let us hope and trust.[148]

MT acknowledged that "American missionaries of unimpeachable character" had supplied him with detailed testimony of the cruelty of Leopold's agents in the Congo.[149] In particular he stated that Rev. William Sheppard, an African-American Presbyterian, visited an area where many Congolese had been mutilated or killed because they had not met their quota of rubber. He verified that Joseph Conrad's *Heart of Darkness* novel, which had been recently published, was based on horrible reality. It was difficult for Sheppard and his white partner, Rev. William Morrison, to present their case in Europe and America. The libel suit brought against them by Leopold's agents in Leopoldville (Kinshasa) attracted international attention.

Powerful forces were urging Americans to overlook what was going on in the Congo. John D. Rockefeller and some other capitalists had an arrangement with Leopold for sharing in the Congo exploitation. Interested only in the "business character" of the deal, they pressured editors and clergymen to be uncritical of Leopold's administration.[150] By providing subsidies for Catholic missions in Congo, Leopold succeeded in getting the Vatican to disregard Protestants who "imagine" crimes by his agents in Congo. Consequently, none of the many Catholic missions there criticized the King's agents.[151] Leopold also obtained the support of

---

[148]AMT 271. Concerning the millions of Congolese killed by Leopold's agents, see William Phipps, *William Sheppard: Congo's African-American Livingstone* (Louisville: Geneva, 2002) 174-75.

[149]*New York World*, 3 December 1905.

[150]Adam Hochschild, *King Leopold's Ghost* (New York: Houghton Mifflin, 1988) 243-44.

[151]Rene Lemarchand, *Political Awakening in the Belgian Congo* (Berkeley: University of California Press, 1964) 123.

Cardinal James Gibbons, the most influential Catholic in the United States. That prelate sent a letter to Congress urging noninterference with Leopold's business operation in Congo.[152]

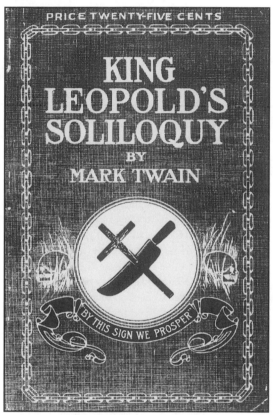

Pamphlet written in 1905
to benefit the Congolese.

The effectiveness of MT's expose of Czar Nicholas in 1905 prompted him to denounce Leopold that same year with similar scornful laughter. As a literary devise, soliloquies are striking because of the presumption that persons honestly speak their mind when they are alone. *King Leo-*

---

[152]Robert Benedetto, *Presbyterian Reformers in Central Africa* (Leiden: Brill, 1996) 221.

pold's Soliloquy focused on his nauseous religiosity and his futile efforts to hide the grim truth. The withering tract contains extended quotations and gruesome illustrations taken from what Sheppard had recorded after visiting a camp where Leopold's flag was flying. MT let the king incriminate himself in this way:

> In these twenty years I have spent millions to keep the press of the two hemispheres quiet, and still these leaks keep on occurring. . . . These meddlesome American missionaries! . . . The natives consider them their only friends; they go to them with their sorrows; they show them their scars and their wounds, inflicted by my soldier police; they hold up the stumps of their arms and lament because their hands have been chopped off, as punishment for not bringing in enough rubber, and as proof to be laid before my officers that the required punishment was well and truly carried out. One of these missionaries [Sheppard] saw eighty-one of these hands drying over a fire for transmission to my officials—and of course he must go and set it down and print it. . . . The kodak has been a sore calamity to us. The most powerful enemy that has confronted us, indeed. In the early years we had no trouble in getting the press to "expose" the tales of the mutilations as slanders, lies, inventions of busy-body American missionaries. . . . Then all of a sudden came the crash! That is to say, the incorruptible kodak—and all the harmony went to hell! The only witness I have encountered in my long experience that I couldn't bribe. Every Yankee missionary and every interrupted trader sent home and got one; and now—oh well, the pictures get sneaked around everywhere, in spite of all we can do to ferret them out and suppress them.[153]

As the soliloquy continues, Leopold kisses the crucifix hanging from his neck to save himself from damnation for cursing those who were publicizing his exploits. He grumbles about those who complain that the Congolese have received nothing for what he has extracted from them, when in fact the Catholic missionaries he had supported have offered them the gospel and the opportunity for salvation. He recalls what he promised two decades earlier when he met with European powers at Berlin for the purpose of carving up Africa into colonies:

> I . . . implored them to place the vast and rich and populous Congo Free State in trust in my hands as their agent, so that I might root out slavery and stop the slave raids, and lift up those twenty-five millions of gentle and

---

[153]CT2 661-82.

harmless blacks out of darkness into light, the light of our blessed Redeemer
. . . and make them comprehend that they were no longer outcasts and
forsaken, but our very brothers in Christ.[154]

Fearful of Leopold's power, journals that had previously been eager
to publish MT's manuscripts refused this satire, even though it was
offered to them without charge. However, it was published and distributed widely in America and Britain by the Congo Reform Association and
by the American Baptist Missionary Union. The cover of the published
satire featured a crucifix with a machete behind it, and this inscription
bcneath it, "By this sign we prosper."

Booker T. Washington joined with MT several times in speaking
about the need for reforms in the Congo at meetings in different cities.
Washington observed: "I have never known him to be so stirred up on
any one question as he was on that of the cruel treatment of the natives
in the Congo Free State."[155] MT became a vice president of the American
Congo Reform Association and made three frustrating trips to Washington to get the United States to act against Leopold. On confronting
Roosevelt about human rights abuses in Congo, MT was told there was
nothing America could do. He got the impression that the president was
trying to please everyone:

> If the twelve apostles should call at the White House, he would say, "Come
> in, come in! I am delighted to see you. I've been watching your progress,
> and I admired it very much." Then if Satan should come, he would slap him
> on the shoulder and say, "Why Satan how do you do? I am so glad to meet
> you. I've read all your works and enjoyed every one of them."[156]

Having failed in his extensive lobbying efforts in Washington to
arouse American government officials, MT decided that church members
might succeed in pressuring American action against Leopold. He told of
his distribution plan for *King Leopold's Soliloquy*: "I intend that the
pamphlet shall go into the hands of every clergyman in America."[157]
Presbyterians and other Protestants effectively petitioned the State

---

[154]CT2 662.
[155]*North American Review* (June 1910): 829.
[156]MTB 1340.
[157]*New York World*, 3 December 1905.

Department to demand that Leopold cease his ruthless exploitation of Congolese natives.[158]

In the end, MT's pen was mightier than Leopold's machete and his "soliloquy" proved to be the most effective writing against imperialism. A London journal noted, "There has not in our time been a fiercer satire or a finer instance of the value of humour as an instrument of reform."[159] African historian Basil Davidson writes: "In 1908, under great international pressure—Mark Twain was foremost in bringing that to bear—and the pressure of its own conscience, the Belgian Parliament brought the Leopoldian system to an end."[160]

§ § §

MT began his mental odyssey with the typical provincial outlook of a child, so his subsequent development was extraordinary. Louis Budd observes, "He ended up a true cosmopolitan and an unpaid yet energetic ambassador to any country, including his own, that would listen."[161] He was a successor to the Stoics, who coined the term "cosmopolitan," teaching that humans are, first, members of the worldwide (*cosmos*) political (*polis*) organization and only second members of local cultures. Because all humans are an expression of divine Reason (*Logos*), some Stoics argued that all ethnics have equal dignity and worth. Even as the Stoics transformed the concept of patriotism, MT pledged allegiance to a fatherland viewed in its broadest scope. He shared with those ancient philosophers the view that world "brotherhood" is a by-product of theology, and said, "The universal brotherhood of man is our most precious possession—what there is of it."[162]

---

[158]Phipps, *William Sheppard: Congo's African-American Livingstone*, 150-57.
[159]*Bookman* (July 1907): 150.
[160]SC 391.
[161]MTSP 190.
[162]MTN 347.

Chapter 7
Biblical Usages

If pioneers heading for the Western frontier of America took only one book with them, it was likely a Bible. In it they had a compact library containing folk tales, moral laws, history, poetry, philosophy, proverbs, short stories, sermons, letters, and prophecy. MT's family possessed a few additional books, but his most careful literature study as a boy was of the Bible. Albert Paine, MT's leading biographer, believes that because of this "something of the stately simplicity of the King James Version crept into his style, and remained there."[1] As an adult, MT found some parts of the King James Version absurd and immoral, other parts reasonable and inspiring. He wrote Livy before their marriage that he anticipated that the wisdom of the Bible would "make our lives an anthem void of discord and our deeds a living worship of the God that gave them."[2] Throughout the rest of his life, when he wished to discuss or to cuss issues, he often resorted to biblical words and ideas.

The Bible MT purchased in Constantinople, with his profuse annotations, is now in an archive at the University of Texas. That was the Bible he studied during his Holy Land excursion in order to become better informed about the sites he was visiting. Eventually his library contained thirty-two different copies of the Bible or of the New Testament, some of which contain his marginalia.[3] Significantly, when he was dealing with family inheritance matters in 1904, the only thing that had belonged to his mother that he wanted to keep was her illustrated family Bible.[4]

MT was dismayed by credulous people who venerate the Bible but do not examine it carefully, preferring to rely on what preachers or biblical commentators want them to believe. He found that most Christians wanted little more than reinforcement for their sectarian indoctrination. In his *Mark Twain and the Bible*, Allison Ensor makes this apt comparison, "Like the pilgrims in the Holy Land, they do not see what is really there but only what someone tells them they should see."[5] MT opined

---

[1]MTN 94.
[2]LTR 3:26.
[3]MTLB 63-64.
[4]MTLB 507.
[5]Allison Ensor, *Mark Twain and the Bible* (Lexington: University Press of

that credulity is not just a common attitude of religious people, "There isn't anything so grotesque or so incredible that the average human being can't believe it."[6] Regarding the lack of independent judgment on matters of importance, he said:

> In religion and politics people's beliefs and convictions are in almost every case gotten at secondhand, and without examination, from authorities who have not themselves examined the questions at issue but have taken them at secondhand from other nonexaminers, whose opinions about them were not worth a brass farthing. . . . You can never find a Christian who has acquired this valuable knowledge, this saving knowledge, by any process but the everlasting and all-sufficient "people say."[7]

Jewish Scriptures

Of the sixty-six books of the the Protestant Bible, MT's favorite was Genesis, and he wrote about it frequently as long as he lived. As an adult he found the prescientific view of the universe with which that book begins to be marvelous but literally preposterous. On the second day of creation, before stars existed, God divided the primeval waters, placing some above a solid astrodome called the "firmament" and some under the undulating surface of the earth;[8] floods occurred when the Lord caused water to burst forth simultaneously from "the great deep" and from firmament sluice gates that he opened.[9] Fruit trees were created on the third day, the day before the source of photosynthesis was created. The firmament contained a track for the sun's daily circuit across the stationary earth, and was a ceiling to which other heavenly "lights" were attached for brightening the darkness.[10]

MT spoofed the biblical notion of the moon being hung on the sky as a decorative ornament for earthlings.[11] He observed that "the difference between that universe and the modern one revealed by science is as the

---

Kentucky, 1969) 94-95.
    [6]OMT 41.
    [7]AMT 369-70.
    [8]Genesis 1:6-7.
    [9]Genesis 7:11.
    [10]Genesis 1:11-17; Psalm 19:1-6.
    [11]CT2 695.

difference between a dust-flecked ray in a barn and the sublime arch of the Milky Way in the skies."[12] He was amused by the ancient account of a four-cornered earth at the center of the world and by the date "4004 B.C." printed in the center column of the opening chapter of Genesis as the year the world was begun, which had been computed by the seventeenth-century Irish Anglican archbishop James Ussher. MT also found that John Lightfoot, a Cambridge professor, had more precisely established the month of creation to coincide with the beginning of the Jewish new year.[13] MT realized that those with scientific understanding recognized that the universe was many thousand times older than traditional biblical interpreters had presumed it to be.[14]

While he was a steamboat pilot, MT became acquainted with Charles Lyell's monumental *Principles of Geology* that stressed the gradual changes in the earth's crust.[15] In 1882, after reflecting on the nature of sandbars, he noted "the biblical absurdity of the Almighty's being only six days building the universe and then fooling away twenty-five years building a towhead in the Mississippi."[16] Neither geology nor astronomy could be reconciled with a literal reading of the Genesis creation account. MT commented:

> [Astronomer] Herschel removed the speckled tent-roof from the world and exposed the immeasurably deeps of space, dim-flecked with fleets of colossal suns sailing their billion-leagued remotenesses. . . . Lyell contributed Geology and spread the six days of Creation into shoreless aeons of time comparable to Herschel's limitless oceans of space.[17]

MT responded jovially to the Genesis account of day-to-day creation units. "Man was made at the end of the week's work, when God was tired," he guessed.[18] The use of the day after that final creation day prompted this lamentation:

[12]MTB 412.
[13]MTB 1506.
[14]LE 22.
[15]MTLB 430.
[16]MTN 161.
[17]FM 378-79.
[18]MTN 381.

The day of rest comes but once a week, and sorry I am that it does not come oftener. . . . It would have been so easy to have two Sundays in a week. . . . The omnipotent Creator could have made the world in three days just as easily as he made it in six. . . . If all-powerful Providence grew weary after six days' labor, such worms as we are might reasonably expect to break down in three.[19]

As to the creation account's repeated refrain, "God saw that it was good," MT claimed that we only give lipservice to that text since there are a number of things we perceive to be not good and attempt to exterminate. Swatting a fly, one of God's creatures, after affirming the goodness of all of them, was like praising a mother's whole family to her face and then slapping one of her children. Among those works of God that people commonly loathe are "the flea, the rat, the snake, the disease germ." Were we more honest, MT said, we would pray, "We praise and glorify many of Thy works, and are grateful for their presence in our earth, Thy footstool, but not all of them."[20]

Jokingly, MT related God's creativity to his own. Confronted with a person who interrupted him before he could complete his train of thought, he said he was glad the person was not present when the Creator said "Let there be light!"[21] He also compared that first chapter of Genesis—which tells of waters above, on, and under the earth—to the verbiage that diluted his creativity:

When the Lord finished the world, he pronounced it good. That is what I said about my first work, too. But time . . . takes the confidence out of these incautious early opinions. It is more than likely that He thinks about the world, now, pretty much as I think about the *Innocents Abroad*. The fact is, there is a trifle too much water in both.[22]

Judging from MT's use of various parts of Christian Scriptures, a Twainian Bible would principally be set in the Garden of Eden. Adam, Eve, and the serpent fascinated him all of his life. Recognizing that the Eden story is one of the best known in human history, he found it an in-

---

[19]CT1 208.

[20]LE 174-75.

[21]AMT 209.

[22]Letter (6 November 1886) in Bernard DeVoto, ed., *The Portable Mark Twain* (New York: Viking, 1946) 764.

exhaustible quarry from which to extract material for both satire and serious insights into the human situation. Concerning the place of Adam in MT's mind, John Tuckey comments, "No other figure appealed more strongly and persistently to his imagination."[23] He envied Adam's primacy, for "when he said a good thing he knew nobody had said it before."[24]

MT's bond with Adam was in part due to hair color, which he could trace genetically at least as far as his red-headed mother. He bragged about his younger appearance, "My hair was as the lurid crimson of the sun."[25] Some nineteenth-century Bible commentaries derived "Adam" from the Hebrew root *ªdamah*, meaning "reddish." When Clemens was seventeen, he began his comic treatment of Adam in an article signed "Son of Adam":

> Although it is not stated in so many words, I have but little doubt that Adam's hair was red—for he was made of "red earth" (as his name indicates), and as the name "Adam" was given to him *after* he was made, it is pretty clear he must have had red hair![26]

To jostle the defenders of a literal Adam and to see how far they would go in affirming his historicity, MT proposed that a monument to the ultimate patriarch of mankind be erected. Statues to commemorate Civil War heroes were then commanding much attention in American cities. A few years after the publication of *The Descent of Man*, "when the storm of indignation raised by it was still raging in pulpits and periodicals," he expressed to some Elmira citizens his feigned consternation over Darwin's disrespect for the founding father of humanity:

> I said there seemed to be a likelihood that the world would discard Adam and accept the monkey, and that in the course of time Adam's very name would be forgotten in the earth; therefore this calamity ought to be averted; a monument would accomplish this, and Elmira ought not to waste their honorable opportunity to do Adam a favor and herself a credit.[27]

---

[23]FM 434.
[24]MTN 67.
[25]MTN 372.
[26](Hannibal) *Journal*, 13 May 1853.
[27]FM 158.

Although MT and Thomas Beecher had treated the monument proposal as so much spoofing, the Elmira city fathers saw it as a way of making their region a destination for pilgrims in search of their roots. Recognizing the commercial advantage of the project, two bankers pledged a substantial sum for its promotion. Discussion in the Elmira newspaper then suggests that they considered asking a sculptor to clothe a statue of Adam with a native leaf rather than a fig leaf, in order to advertise their burgeoning local hardwood business.[28] In 1879, MT drafted a petition to Congress to grant Elmira the exclusive right to erect a national memorial where Adam's descendants could express their respects. He pointed out that it would be dreadful if our common progenitor were eclipsed by some simian exalted by evolutionists. More-over, he wrote, the Father of our Country had a monument under con-struction in the city named for him while "the common father of mankind has been suffered to lie in entire neglect." There were other purple passages in the petition, "All races and all colors and all religions are interested in seeing that his name and fame shall be placed beyond the reach of the blight of oblivion." It is appropriate that "this testimonial of affection and gratitude shall be the gift of the youngest of the nations that have sprung from his loins, after 6,000 years of unappreciation on the part of its elders."[29] Ninety-four of Elmira's leading citizens, including the governor of New York, signed the petition and MT's Hartford friend Joe Hawley agreed to present it to Congress. Upon further reflection, Hawley lost his nerve to carry out the joke because he feared that his fellow congressmen might take it seriously and pass it!

Speaking in Ottawa to the Royal Literary and Scientific Society several years later, MT related his failed monumental effort. When he solicited in behalf of the only celebrity in his family tree, he claimed that most people were irritated and exploded "A-dam," stressing the second syllable. He offered sober reasons for bestowing honor on humanity's first parent:

> To him we owe the two things which are most precious—life, and death. Life, which the young, the hopeful, the undefeated hold above all wealth and

---

[28]Robert Jerome and Herbert Wisbey, eds., *Mark Twain in Elmira* (Elmira NY: Mark Twain Society, 1977) 83-86.

[29]MTB 1648-49.

all honors; and death, the refuge, the solace, the best and kindliest and most prized friend and benefactor of the erring, the forsaken, the old, and weary, and broken of heart, whose burdens be heavy upon them, and who would lie down and be at rest.[30]

In 1883, when excavation for the Statue of Liberty pedestal had begun, MT was asked for a letter that could be raffled to support the construction. He sent some money along with a letter that may have been counterproductive to the intended purpose. It read:

What you want of a monument is to keep you in mind of something you haven't got—something you've lost. Very well; we haven't lost liberty; we've lost Adam. . . . Evolution is steadily and surely abolishing him; and we must get up a monument, and be quick about it, or our children's children will grow up ignorant that there ever was an Adam.[31]

At the beginning of the twentieth century, MT was truly disgusted to learn that two candidates for the Presbyterian ministry were turned down because they classified the story of Adam as a myth. Tongue-in-cheek, he stated that the action gave him encouragement to "try once more to get justice done to our common ancestor—justice in the form of a monument." He maintained that Adam should rank higher than Socrates, Shakespeare, Darwin, and other heroes of the human race.[32]

In 1905, when brontosaurus bones were featured at the American Museum of Natural History, MT wrote "Adam's Soliloquy." It tells of Adam's surprise, on visiting the fossil hall in New York, to see an enormous skeleton. Realizing that he had been given the task of naming animals, he admitted: "I have no recollection of him; neither Eve nor I had heard of him until yesterday. We spoke to Noah about him; he colored and changed the subject."[33]

Using Genesis 2:20 as a springboard, MT treated Adam as a biologist who both named and classified the flora and fauna for his scientific dictionary. Also, he had fun with the assumption in Genesis that all animals were originally vegetarians.[34] Eve notes in her diary, "I found

---

[30]CT1 846.
[31]CT1 847-48.
[32]FM 451.
[33]CT2 635.
[34]See Genesis 1:30, 9:3.

some tigers and nestled in amongst them and was adorably comfortable, and their breath was sweet and pleasant, because they live on strawberries."[35] There were also lions who relished turnips and buzzards who feasted on bananas.

The implications of a literal Adam and Eve tickled MT, including their not having been belly-buttoned babies. "Adam and Eve had many advantages," he wrote, "but the principal one was, that they escaped teething."[36] When Eve informs Adam that she was made out of a rib taken from his side, he is doubtful because by his count, not one is missing. Having enjoyed his solitude, Adam finds it takes time to overcome the irritation caused by the new companionship.[37]

Regarding the baneful legacy of Adam to his posterity, MT noted: "He invented sin—he was the author of sin. . . . I wish he had taken out a copyright on sin—just for the sake of the parties who would infringe it."[38] MT remarked, ironically: "Let us be grateful to Adam our benefactor. He cut us out of the 'blessing' of idleness and won for us the 'curse' of labor."[39]

When treated as actual history, MT judged the Eden story to be absurd, but when interpreted as an insightful myth, he found it highly significant. Plato's view, which MT shared, was that imaginative stories (*mythoi* in Greek) contain truth about human relationships that is at least as important as empirical truth. Thus, Shakespeare's dramas contain characters and plots that ring true to human experience even though the plays may not be based on historical fact. The Platonic/Twainian view recognizes that science seeks literal, physical truth, while fiction and art offer truth as metaphor.

In 1879, MT purchased the translation of Henricus Oort's three-volume *Bible for Learners* that introduces the results of the literary-historical biblical criticism that was developing in Germany. He also sent a copy of the work to his brother, and informed his sister Pamela that they should both await Orion's reaction to a book that "may cure him or

---

[35]CT2 696.
[36]PW 26.
[37]BMT 8-10.
[38]N&J 3:16.
[39]FE 305.

kill him."[40] Dutchman Oort treated the Genesis accounts as legends and distinguished between the different accounts of creation in the opening chapters. After dealing with misunderstanding the figurative language pertaining to the births of Adam, Eve, and Jesus as scientific fact, the text concludes on this positive note: "God is Spirit! God is Light! God is Love! And from the bottom of our hearts, we wish that blessing to each one of our readers!"[41] Also aware that religion and science belonged to different spheres of truth, MT said, "When religion and science elect to live together, it is a plain case of adultery."[42]

MT, as well as modern biologists and astronomers, deserves some credit for indirectly helping release the Eden story from a literal interpretation. Most subsequent biblical interpreters have modified their teachings to accommodate scientific and literary findings. MT realized that the creation myths were intended to be pondered for religious meaning, not for an accurate and detailed description of the physical world. They provide one answer to the questions, "Who made it?" and "Why was it made?" but they do not deal with the scientific questions, "When was it made?" and "How was it made?" The sequence of creation was considered insignificant by the Genesis editors, for in the later version (chapter 1) the wild animals are created before the human (*ha-adam*) and in the earlier version (chapter 2) the reverse is true. Questions of time and development—so essential to scientific truth—are irrelevant to the purpose of the stories.[43] To assume that the storytellers were aware of, and trying to say something about how the organic process evolved is ridiculous.

The biblical myths of creation are central to Judaism, Christianity, and Islam; consequently, they are some of the most influential stories ever told. MT accepted their assumption that equality among all humans is God's purpose, thus making racism and sexism contrary to the divine standard.[44] With regard to human attributes and obligations, he generally

---

[40]MTLB 519.

[41]Henricus Oort, *The Bible for Learners* (Boston: Roberts, 1878) 3:698.

[42]MT's marginalia in his copy of Rufus Noyes, *Views of Religion*; MTLB 511.

[43]See Brevard Childs, *Myth and Reality in the Old Testament*, Studies in Biblical Theology 27 (London: SCM Press, 1962) 74.

[44]Genesis 1:27; see William Phipps, *Genesis and Gender* (New York: Praeger, 1989) 1-35.

accepted these truths: like God, humans have a spiritual nature; they are meant to be free and to have companionship with each other; they are part of an environment that is theirs to enjoy and care for; they are obliged to follow God's instructions and are not to seek God's omniscience. MT said, "I am built . . . in the image of God, but not otherwise resembling him enough to be mistaken for him by anyone but a very nearsighted person."[45]

MT pointed out that all humans, like the representative humans in Eden, enter the world naked and unashamed. Unnatural notions of "modesty" do not foul their minds. By contrast, MT remarked: "The first thing a missionary teaches a savage is indecency. He makes him put clothes on. He is as innocent and clean-minded up to that time as were our first parents when they walked naked before the Lord and were not ashamed."[46] "Man is . . . the Immodest Animal," commented MT further, "for he is the only one who covers his nakedness, the only one with a soiled mind, the only one under dominion of a false shame."[47] He claimed that "nature knows no indecencies; man invents them," using as illustration the Japanese custom of public bathing by both sexes. Although those with Western social mores found that innocent practice contemptible, MT asserted that the Japanese had shown that "all the details of the body were worthy of respect since the gods made them."[48] Edenic fashion apparently appealed to him: "I have seen but one man dressed the way I would like to dress. . . . He was a Sandwich Islander, and he wore—let me see, it was a special occasion—a pair of spectacles."[49]

Ancient people and MT knew about Aesop's fables and recognized that stories about serpents and other animals speaking like people were not intended to be taken literally. He put into Satan's mouth notions of sexuality that originated with some of the church fathers. Satan claims that Adam and Eve were thrown out of Eden because they engaged in sexual intercourse, which God regarded as the principal evil. But MT

----

[45]MTMW 116.
[46]MTN 325.
[47]MTN 242.
[48]MTN 288.
[49](Washington) *Herald*, 8 December 1906.

commented that Adam and Eve found "it was a magnificent discovery, and they stopped idling around and turned their entire attention to it."[50]

The first humans could have acquired a craving for snake meat, MT maintained:

> It is the *prohibition* that *makes* anything precious. There is a charm about the forbidden that makes it unspeakably desirable. It was not that Adam ate the apple for the apple's sake, but because it was forbidden. It would have been better for us . . . if the *serpent* had been forbidden.[51]

In MT's view, Adam was flawed by greediness. He wrote: "What a fool old Adam was. Had everything his own way; had succeeded in gaining the love of the best-looking girl in the neighborhood, but yet unsatisfied with his conquest he had to eat a miserable little apple."[52]

MT recognized that the type of forbidden fruit is not designated in the Eden story. Traditionally the fruit has been associated with a projection in men's necks, produced by an apple getting stuck there when the first man began to fill guilty. But MT asserted that the fruit was a chestnut, a figurative expression for a "mouldy joke." The first chestnut was Adam's response whenever anyone marveled at seeing a waterfall. Unawed by natural gravitation, he would say, "It would be a deal more wonderful to see it tumble *up*!"[53] MT was aware that ancient people were largely unaware of basic scientific law, so readers of the Bible would not expect to find much there that accords with a modern understanding of nature.

A literal reading of the story of the first human creations has implications MT found morally unacceptable. Adam and Eve had not had any personal experiences that would enable them to understand the distinction between "good" and "evil," or the meaning of the word "die." Unable to comprehend the consequence of disobedience, MT regarded capital punishment for stealing fruit unfair.[54] "Death" was unknown until Abel

---

[50]LE 23.
[51]MTN 275.
[52]LTR 1:91.
[53]CT2 103.
[54]LE 22-23, 75-76.

failed to awaken from apparent sleep and became cold with eyes staring after his elder brother attacked him.[55]

MT found in the story of Adam an ahistorical parable of people who live in every generation. "We have had ages and ages of experience," MT said, "and just see what we are when there is any forbidden fruit around."[56] Applications of the psychology of temptation in the Eden myth appear in his writings. Concerning his own urges, he wrote, "There is a fascination about meddling with forbidden things."[57] He grew up along waters dangerous for swimming "which were forbidden to us and therefore much frequented by us. For we were little Christian children and had early been taught the value of forbidden fruit."[58] Accordingly, in the process of getting his fence whitewashed, Tom Sawyer "discovered a great law of human action, . . . that in order to make a man or a boy covet a thing, it is only necessary to make the thing difficult to attain."[59] A vow of abstinence MT once took gave rise to this wry observation, "Taking the pledge will not make bad liquor good, but it will improve it."[60] To encourage the reading of *Huckleberry Finn* as the author intended, the preface threatens banishment and death to anyone finding a moral in the story.

MT appreciated the representative woman in the Eden story at least as much as he did the representative man. She stands out from the male, "From the day that Adam ate of the apple and told on Eve down to the present day, man, in a moral fight, has pretty uniformly shown himself to be an arrant coward."[61] He is also unimaginative, blundering, and aloof; but Eve is beautiful, inquisitive, tenderhearted, resourceful, and gregarious. Observing that water always flows downward and that wood floats, she intuits a purpose in her creation: "I think it was to search out the secrets of this wonderful world and be happy and thank the Giver of

---

[55]BMT 68-69.
[56]MTN 275.
[57]LTR 3:358.
[58]AMT 5.
[59]TS 32.
[60]CT2 946.
[61]CT1 30.

it all for devising it."[62] Eve does not tempt her mate, but she does attempt to humanize him.

In the Eden story, loneliness is the first thing the Lord declares to be not good, and marriage companionship is provided to remedy it. MT followed Calvin who judged partnership—not reproduction—to be the prime purpose of marriage. Adam pays Eve these tributes: "It is better to live outside the Garden with her than inside it without her. At first I thought she talked too much; but now I should be sorry to have that voice fall silent and pass out of my life. . . . Wheresoever she was, there was Eden."[63] Eve responds in kind:

> He loves me as well as he can; I love him with all the strength of my passionate nature. . . . He is strong and handsome, and I love him for that, and I admire him and am proud of him, but I could love him without those qualities. . . . Life without him would not be life. . . . I am the first wife; and in the last wife I shall be repeated.[64]

§ § §

Methuselah was the next biblical character to intrigue MT. At the age of sixty he was still a comparative youth but he was feeling family pressure to find a wife and to begin to "beget."[65] According to Genesis, some of his ancestors had procreated in their seventh decade, but he delayed becoming a father until another century passed.[66] Although he lived for almost a millennium, he died prematurely because he was among those who perished in the great flood. MT cited Methuselah as an example of the independence of technological progress from the mere passage of time. Comparing his life to modern life, MT said: "Our life is not counted by years, but by what has been seen and accomplished. . . . The world did not improve any while he lived—he tended his flocks just as his fathers did, and none of them knew enough to make an iron fence."[67]

---

[62]CT2 706.

[63]BMT 16, 33.

[64]BMT 31-33.

[65]LE 58.

[66]Genesis 5:25.

[67]Quoted in Julia Millikan, ed., *Journal Letters of Emily Severance* (Cleveland: Gates, 1938) 12-13.

MT was amazed that a story about waters submerging the mountains, which the Hebrews borrowed from the Babylonians, was still revered, for "we know that Noah's flood never happened, and couldn't have happened."[68] He was struck by the scriptural assertion that God soon "repented" of having created humans and therefore swept away nearly all of them.[69] Regarding the box-like structure of Noah's ark, former boat pilot MT said: "It was admirably unfitted for the service required of it. Nobody but a farmer could have designed such a thing, for such a purpose."[70] One problem he noted was that the 56,000 cubic-yard structure was too small to accommodate 146,000 types of birds, beasts, and freshwater creatures, plus two million species of insects.[71] Another problem was that the eight members of Noah's family, the youngest of them a hundred years old, could not have handled the gigantic task of feeding all those animals.[72] The reason Noah gave for not including dinosaurs, according to MT, was that their fossils would be needed for museums.[73] The most significant cargo on the ark, he judged, were the microorganisms that lived in the intestines of Noah's family. MT saluted them in a parody, replacing "Salvation, O Salvation" and some other words of his favorite missionary hymn:

> Constipation, O constipation
> The joyful sound proclaim
> Till man's remotest entrail
> Shall praise its Maker's name.[74]

In the saga of Isaac's sons, MT again revealed his penchant for fresh interpretation by suggesting that Esau was nobler than Jacob or Joseph, whom the biblical narrators favored. For MT, forgiveness is a hallmark of the religious spirit, and the circumstances surrounding forgiveness matter. Jacob tricked his twin out of his birthright and blessing, and then, years later, attempted to bribe him with cattle to avoid his revenge. But

---

[68]BMT 322.
[69]BMT 315; Genesis 6:7.
[70]MTN 260.
[71]LE 28.
[72]S&B 138; Genesis 5:32, 7:6-7.
[73]BMT 121.
[74]LE 34; after stanza 3 of "From Greenland's Icy Mountains."

Esau embraced the schemer, insisting that he did not desire compensation from his wealthy brother.[75] Perhaps thinking of his own family situation, MT perceived that it was more difficult for a less successful brother to forgive than the reverse. Yet Esau forgave the more successful Jacob. By the same token, MT judged Esau to be more virtuous than his nephew Joseph, who accepted the brothers who had betrayed him, "Who stands first—outcast Esau forgiving Jacob in prosperity, or Joseph on a king's throne forgiving the ragged tremblers whose happy rascality placed him there?"[76] MT had a comic version of how Joseph identified his younger brother: the Egyptian vizier "fell upon Benjamin's neck and cried: 'Ha! the strawberry upon your left arm!' "[77]

In terms of literary style, some passages of the Bible, in MT's opinion, were in some ways superior to the writings of Shakespeare. Discussing "the exquisite story of Joseph," he asked: "Who taught those ancient writers their simplicity of language, their felicity of expression, their pathos, and, above all, their faculty of sinking themselves entirely out of sight of the reader and making the narrative stand out alone and seem to tell itself?"[78] After criticizing Sir Walter Scott and Charles Dickens for being verbose and using high-flown language, MT commented, "If you wish to see how forcible short words and an unostentatious diction are, glance into the Scriptures." His illustrations included, "Deep calleth unto deep" and "Whither thou goest I will go; and where thou lodgest I will lodge: thy people shall be my people and thy God my God."[79] Charles Stoddard reported staying up most of a night in Liverpool with MT, who was eager to show the rhetorical effectiveness of biblical passages. After quoting the text, "Remember now thy Creator in the days of thy youth,"[80] "the humourist read the book of Ruth with tears in his voice, and selections from the poems of Isaiah in a style that would have melted the hardest heart."[81] MT's friend Joseph Goodman noticed how the Bible

---

[75]Genesis 33:4-9.

[76]IA 494.

[77]MTTB 223; Genesis 45:14.

[78]IA 493.

[79]Jerome and Wisbey, eds., *Mark Twain in Elmira*, 219; Psalm 42:7; Ruth 1:16.

[80]Ecclesiastes 12:1.

[81]Stoddard, *Exits and Entrances*, 73-74.

affected his writing, "The simplicity and beauty of his style are almost without a parallel, except in the common version of the Bible."[82]

MT once seriously suggested a scientific explanation for a bit of biblical supernaturalism, but he later treated the same subject satirically. At Hawaii's Kilauea crater, seeing "a colossal column of cloud towering to a great height in the air immediately above the crater" that "glowed like a muffled torch," he wondered if a volcanic Mount Sinai might have provided direction for the Hebrews during their exodus from Egypt:

> I thought it just possible that its like had not been seen since the children of Israel wandered on their long march through the desert so many centuries ago over a path illuminated by the mysterious "pillar of fire." And I was sure that I now had a vivid conception of what the majestic "pillar of fire" was like, which almost amounted to a revelation.[83]

On a later occasion, MT retold a version of Elijah's contest with the prophets of Baal that originated with a Captain Wakeman, in an effort to show the absurdity of those who "applied natural laws to the interpretation of all miracles, somewhat on the plan of the people who make the six days of creation six geological epochs." In the biblical account of the contest, it was agreed that the winning side would be the one who could by prayer persuade the real divine power to ignite firewood beneath a sacrificial offering.[84] According to MT's version, Presbyterian "Captain Hurricane Jones" opposes the Baal prophets. He pours what appears to be water on the wood at the altar to make his forthcoming performance even more spectacular, but he actually drenches the wood with naphtha. Then, unnoticed during his pretend prayer, he throws in a light that ignites an all-consuming fire![85]

MT quoted from many of the Hebrew scriptures to add historical insight or wit to his writings. (1) He recognized that monotheism is not affirmed in the commandment, "Thou shalt have no other gods before me." Rather, he wrote, "All He [Yahweh] demanded was that He should be ranked as high as the others—not above any of them, but not below any of them. . . . They could march abreast with Him, but none of them

---

[82]MTB 217.
[83]RI 508; cp. Exodus 13:21, 19:18.
[84]1 Kings 18:22-24.
[85]CT1 683-86.

could head the procession."[86] (2) While he was in the Azores, he observed, "Wheat is threshed by oxen in the old scriptural way—''Ye shall not muzzle the ox that treadeth out the grain.' ''[87] (3) In a letter to his brother, he applied a biblical phrase to his own profession, " 'Whoring after strange gods,' which is Scripture for deserting to other publishers."[88] (4) To comfort a despairing friend, he quoted King David's lament over the loss of his closest companion, "How are the mighty fallen in the midst of battle!"[89] (5) In a novel, he created a parallel to prophet Nathan's denunciation of David for arranging a covert killing to cover up his treachery, "He felt as secret murderers are said to feel when the accuser says, 'Thou art the man!' "[90]

MT found Psalm 2 of interest because it portrays God as being highly amused at earthly rulers who operate as though *they* control human destiny. From the psalmist's assertion that God laughs, MT drew this inference: "God made man *in his own image*. Christ, a man, was the *son of God*—and possessed humor, of course."[91] Paine commented on MT's theologizing: "He spoke of humor, and thought it must be one of the chief attributes of God. He cited plants and animals that were distinctly humorous in form and in their characteristics. These he declared were God's jokes."[92]

As MT's mood shifted, he seemed to separate a sense of humor from what is divine. "Everything human is pathetic," he wrote. "The secret of Humor itself is not joy but sorrow. There is no humor in heaven."[93] Again, "We grant God the possession of all the qualities of mind except the one that keeps the others healthy; that watches over their dignity; that focuses their vision true—humor."[94]

While MT was courting Livy, Psalm 27:14 prompted him to ponder:

---

[86]LE 31-32; Exodus 20:3.
[87]MTN 62; Deuteronomy 25:4.
[88]LTR 4:220; Deuteronomy 31:16.
[89]LTR 1:165.
[90]PW 78; 2 Samuel 12:7.
[91]N&J 2:37.
[92]MTB 1556.
[93]FE 119.
[94]MTP, notebook #35, 39-40.

"*Wait* on the Lord"—until selfish motives are gone from you; until your heart is purified of evil passions, . . . until that strength which comes from God's puissance is recognized as the only strength that can avail. . . . With religion to order life, and love to fulfill its decrees, what life could be a failure, what life unworthy?[95]

Other poetic books of the Bible also provided a treasury from which MT drew. (1) He disputed Satan's judgment in the Book of Job: " 'All that a man hath will he give for his life.' . . . Ask a man of 50, 'If you were dead now what would you give to have your life restored?' He wouldn't give a brass farthing."[96] (2) "Man is prone to evil as the sparks fly upward," an adaptation of a verse from Job, expresses MT's view of human nature.[97] (3) In *Tom Sawyer*, an exasperated Aunt Polly uses Job's own words in reference to her foster-son, "Man that is born of woman is of few days and full of trouble, as the Scripture says."[98] Later, on recognizing that Tom might be dead, she affirms with Job, "The Lord giveth and the Lord hath taken away; blessed be the name of the Lord!"[99] (4) One of the tourists with MT in Palestine affirmed confidently that he was in the land where "the voice of the turtle is heard," because it was so stated in the Bible.[100] A traveling companion, eager to hear what he had never heard before, stayed at a pond until he blistered, waiting in vain for a turtle to make a sound. He was then disgusted at the "pilgrim" who insisted on his literal interpretation of a verse in the Song of Songs without making empirical observations.[101] (5) MT adopted a spurious, but then common, allegorization of the Song of Songs, in which Jesus is the handsome bridegroom and is further described as "ruddy, the chiefest among ten thousand."[102] Impressed to read of hair the color of his own, MT wrote, "Jesus Christ, our Savior, 'the chief among ten thousand and

---

[95]LTR 2:329, 333.
[96]MTN 297; Job 2:4.
[97]BMT 310; Job 5:7.
[98]TS 19; Job 14:1.
[99]TS 130; Job 1:21.
[100]Song of Songs 2:12.
[101]IA 490-91.
[102]Song of Songs 5:10, 16.

altogether lovely,' is said to have had 'auburn' or red hair."[103] (6) When MT asked cartoonist Thomas Nast to receive a young admirer, he used a phrase from Ecclesiastes to express the hope that the meeting would be "bread cast upon the waters" and nourish the boy's talents.[104]

Isaiah was MT's favorite prophetic book.[105] He adopted the prophet's broom simile pertaining to devastation by a Mesopotamian army to boast about a book he would launch that would "sweep the world like a besom of destruction (if you know what that is)."[106] When he was traveling in the scorching Palestinian wasteland, he longed for what Isaiah described as "the shadow of a great rock in a weary land." "Nothing in the Bible is more beautiful than that," he said, "and surely there is no place we have wandered to that is able to give it such touching expression as this blistering naked treeless land."[107]

At times, MT considered the portrait of God in the Old Testament to be "the most damnatory biography that ever found its way into print."[108] His best defense of that statement comes from the account in Numbers 31, which he quoted at length, of the warfare Moses conducted against the Midianites at the command of the Lord.[109] MT found appalling that when the One "who is called the Fountain of Mercy" engages in holy war, he makes no distinction between the innocent and the guilty. God has the Israelites slay "all the men, all the beasts, all the boys, all the babies; also all the women and all the girls, except those that have not been deflowered."[110] He was especially indignant that the priests received a share of the virgins to satisfy their lusts. He wrongly assumed that the Israelite priests had accepted a vow of celibacy and that their lechery was like that of some Roman Catholic priests he had read about. Whenever the Old Testament lesson read from pulpits was about "wholesale massacre . . . [and] banishment of the virgins into a filthy and unspeak-

---

[103]ET 105.

[104]LTR 5:249; Ecclesiastes 11:1.

[105]MTLB 63.

[106]LTR 4:263; Isaiah 14:23. "Besom" = KJV for "broom."

[107]Daniel McKeithan, ed., *Traveling with the Innocents Abroad* (Oklahoma City: University fo Oklahoma Press, 1958) 217; Isaiah 32:2.

[108]MTB 1354.

[109]LE 48-49.

[110]LE 52.

able slavery," MT felt that the inconsistency of the "Father of Mercies" should be exposed. To accomplish this, he suggested that the New Testament lesson should be the Beatitudes, so that the congregation could get "an all-round view of Our Father in Heaven."[111] He was probably thinking of those contrasting portraits when he noted, "God, so atrocious in the Old Testament, so attractive in the New—the Jekyl and Hyde of sacred romance."[112]

MT perceived that biblical texts sanctioning violence in ancient times serve to motivate similar acts in the future. Even though preachers with moral sensitivity discreetly pass over such passages, zealots use them to inflame mobs to commit hateful acts. He commented:

> Latter-day Protestantism, by selecting the humaner passages of the Bible, and teaching them to the world, whilst allowing those of a different sort to lie dormant, has produced the highest and purest and best individuals which modern society has known. Thus used, the Bible is the most valuable of books. But the strongly worded authority for all the religious atrocities of the Middle Ages is still in it, and some day or other it may again become as heavy a curse to the world as it formerly was. The devastating powers of the Book are only suspended, not extinguished. An Expurgated Bible would not be an unuseful thing.[113]

The dire consequences of the Torah text commanding death for "witches" was traced by MT from medieval history to early New England's Rev. Cotton Mather:

> The church, after doing its duty in but a lazy and indolent way for eight hundred years, gathered up its halters, thumbscrews, and firebrands, and set about its holy work in earnest. She worked hard at it night and day during nine centuries and imprisoned, tortured, hanged, and burned whole hordes and armies of witches, and washed the Christian world clean with their foul blood. Then it was discovered that there was no such thing as witches, and never had been. . . . At Salem, the parson clung pathetically to his witch-text after the laity had abandoned it in remorse and tears for crimes and cruelties

---

[111]LE 55.
[112]MTN 392.
[113]WM 57-58.

it had persuaded them to do. The parson wanted more blood, more shame, more brutalities; it was the unconsecrated laity that stayed his hand.[114]

The New Testament

MT was unable to accept as historical some of the stories of the Gospels. For example, he doubted if King Herod's slaughter of all children in and around Bethlehem two years old and under had actually happened. Latin historian Tacitus would probably have mentioned it, he thought, had a such a ghastly massacre occurred in the Roman empire. Also, Satan

> wouldn't have led Christ up on a high mountain and offered him the world if he would fall down and worship him. That was a manifestly absurd proposition, because Christ, as the Son of God, already owned the world; and, besides, what Satan showed him was only a few rocky acres of Palestine.[115]

The ethical teachings of Jesus were accepted by MT with less reservation than were some biographical details of the Gospels. Ensor states, "There can be no doubt that Twain considered the teachings of the Sermon on the Mount the most significant part of the whole story of Christ."[116] But MT judged that excellent summary of moral ideals to be too exalted for human nature:

> What a fine irony it was to devise the Christian religion . . . with its golden array of impossibilities: Give *all* thou hast to the poor; if a man smite thee on thy right cheek; if a man borrow thy coat of thee; if a man require thee to go with him a mile; do unto others as you would that others should do unto you; love thy neighbor as thyself. It has supplanted the old religion which went before it—upon men's lips it has. But not in their hearts. That old religion knew men better than this one, and must outlive it: for it says, "Smite those people hip and thigh; burn all they possess with fire; kill the cattle; kill the old men, and the women, and the young children, and the sucklings; spare nothing that has life; for their opinions are not like ours."[117]

---

[114]WM 74-75; Exodus 22:18; Cotton Mather, *The Wonders of the Invisible World* (Boston, 1693).

[115]MTB 1468-69; Matthew 2:16, 4:8-9.

[116]Ensor, *Mark Twain and the Bible*, 90.

[117]WM 589.

Of all Jesus' teachings, MT was most devoted to what has come to be known as the "Golden Rule." Nevertheless he realized that Christians, like the Pharisees, preach the rule without practicing it: "It is Exhibit A in the church's assets, and we pull it out each Sunday and give it an airing. . . . It is strictly religious furniture, like an acolyte, or a contribution plate."[118] He judged church history by the principle of treating others as we would like to be treated, noting ironically that the medieval crusades were "undertaken for the introduction and enforcement of what was known as the Golden Rule."[119]

The Lord's Prayer, recorded in the Sermon on the Mount, appealed to MT. After making light of the long and tedious pastoral prayers he heard in California, he asked, "How would it answer to adopt the simplicity and the beauty and the brevity and the comprehensiveness of the Lord's Prayer as a model?"[120] However, while in Europe he observed that "the average clergyman could not fire into his congregation with a shotgun and hit a worse reader than himself," especially when leading the Lord's Prayer: "He races through it as if he thought the quicker he got it in, the sooner it would be answered. A person who does not appreciate the exceeding value of pauses . . . cannot render the grand simplicity and dignity of a composition like that effectively."[121]

One petition of the Lord's Prayer is central to MT's short story, "The Man That Corrupted Hadleyburg." On the official seal of that "most honest and upright town" are the words LEAD US NOT INTO TEMPTATION.[122] To put into practice that inscription, parents shield their children from every possible temptation. However, because townspeople have never had training in confronting deceitfulness, they have become overly confident of their incorruptibility. A visitor, uncannily like the traditional Satan, gets to know Hadleyburg's civic leaders and discovers that these self-righteous citizens have "the weakest of all weak things, . . . a virtue which has not been tested in the fire."[123] Given a real test they all

---

[118]CT2 369.
[119]FM 326.
[120]CT1 120.
[121]Mark Twain, *A Tramp Abroad* (New York: Harper, 1907) 2:93.
[122]CT2 390, 438.
[123]CT2 426.

succumb, excepting their clergyman. The visitor does not corrupt but merely exposes the greed behind the town's facade of honesty. After this humiliation, the Hadleyburgers decide to strike the NOT from the town motto. In the end, as Pascal Covici notes, "the townspeople show both their acceptance of the sinful nature of men and their readiness to assume the existential dignity which humanity attains by exercising the power of choice that only the acceptance of evil can posit."[124] Like John Milton, MT criticized "cloistered virtue, unexercised and unbreathed, that never sallies out and seeks her adversary."[125] He believed that temptations—like those that tested Jesus—strengthened character, and he thought the Lord's Prayer was wrong to suggest that temptation was an evil to be avoided.

In a lighter vein, MT had fun with the beatitude concerning meekness. At Queen Victoria's Jubilee, he heard many people brag that she reigned over more territory than any sovereign in world history, and that the sun never sets on her empire. England had won the European scramble for colonies and, eager for goods and markets, had gobbled up cultures it considered inferior. This haughtiness prompted MT to write about a British visitor who noticed an open Bible on his writing table. When he was asked if MT was studying the Holy Writ, he answered:

> That's about the most interesting book I ever read. . . . It beats any novel or history or work of science that I ever tackled. It is full of good stories and philosophy. It suggests lots of ideas, and there's news in it. I find things that I never heard of before. Did you ever know that the English people were mentioned in the Bible? . . . I discovered today that Christ spoke of the British people in the Sermon on the Mount. . . . "Blessed are the meek, for they shall inherit the earth."[126]

On other occasions MT used seriously words of Jesus to express comfort. To a bereaved person he had gotten to know on the Mediterranean excursion, he wrote:

> "Come unto me all ye that labor and are heavy laden, and I will give you rest"—*rest*! No words my lips might frame could be so freighted with compassion as are these—so fraught with sympathy, so filled with peace.

---

[124]Pascal Covici, *Mark Twain's Humor* (Dallas: Southern Methodist University Press, 1962) 203.

[125]John Milton, *Areopagitica* (1644) ¶28.

[126]*The Ladies' Home Journal* (October 1898): 6.

Even to me, sinner that I am, this is the most beautiful sentence that graces any page—the tenderest, the softest to the ear.[127]

When MT passed through the ancient site of Caesarea Philippi on his Palestinian tour, he recalled that there Jesus had uttered words "upon which all the vast power and importance the Church of Rome arrogates to itself is founded: 'Thou art Peter and upon this rock I will build my church . . . and what thou shalt bind upon the earth shall be bound in Heaven.' "[128] MT rejected teachings that suggested that some would be excluded from heaven. A clergyman in one of his stories, responding to a question about the inclusiveness of salvation, quotes Jesus' command to "preach the gospel to every *creature*," deducing from this that heaven contains even the smallest of God's creation. Asked if disease germs are included, the clergyman has no answer.[129]

MT's favorite apostle was Thomas, who has often been denounced by preachers because he asked Jesus difficult questions. Jesus had urged people not to accept his way of life until they carefully considered what was expected, and he encouraged Thomas, who relied on observable evidence, to express his doubts in searching for truth.[130] MT thought of Thomas when he read that biologists had generally rejected an announcement that life had been created chemically in a laboratory. Recognizing that even scientific consensus might be wrong, he commented:

It has always been my impression that Thomas was the only one who made an examination and proved a fact. While the others were accepting, . . . Doubting Thomas removed a doubt which must otherwise have confused and troubled the world until now. . . . We owe that hard-headed—or sound-headed witness something more than a slur.[131]

MT occasionally doubted what had been virtually unquestioned by Christian orthodoxy. Not greatly impressed by Jesus' physical suffering on the cross, he suggested that the ordeal was no greater than some

---

[127]LTR 2:137; Matthew 11:28.
[128]MTN 90; Matthew 16:18-19.
[129]John Tuckey, ed., *Mark Twain's Which Was the Dream* (Berkeley: University of California Press, 1967) 496; Mark 16:15.
[130]Luke 14:27-30; John 14:5, 20:24-27.
[131]CT2 651.

women endure in childbirth.[132] Yet he respected the martyrdom of both Jesus and Joan of Arc because of what they stood for. The sacrificial way they lived, more than the final torture inflicted upon them, has given them great significance.

Sometimes MT borrowed a quotation or paraphrased a text from the New Testament and applied it to his own situation. (1) To encourage those who had reluctantly attended his first lecture to return, he sometimes closed with, "If a man compel thee to go with him a mile, go with him Twain."[133] (2) He chuckled over a New Zealand girl's assumption that his pseudonym was scriptural "because Mark is in the Bible and Twain is in the Bible."[134] (3) When Livy accepted his proposal of marriage after months of delay, he wrote Twichell, "I have fought the good fight and lo! I have won!"[135] (4) He concluded one courtship letter by referring to the Hebrews 13:20-21 benediction; in another he wrote out, "The good God that is above us all is merciful to me,—from Whom came your precious love—from Whom cometh all good gifts."[136] (5) He drew on a proverb in a letter to his brother about disposing of some land they had inherited in Tennessee, "I seldom venture to think about our landed wealth, for 'hope deferred maketh the heart sick.' "[137] (6) And when he was suffering from financial ruin, he exclaimed: "Oh Death where is thy sting! It has none. But life has."[138]

MT's knowledge of classic religious texts ranged wider than those included in the canonical books of the Bible, as this paraphrase from the Wisdom of Jesus the Son of Sirach illustrates: "No gross speech is ever harmless. 'A man cannot handle pitch and escape defilement,' saith the proverb."[139] He was not only aware of the Apocrypha but also a book that Anglicans revere. At the end of one of his essays, he cites from the *Book of Common Prayer*, "Read, mark, and inwardly digest," pertaining to

---

[132]MTP, notebook #29, 45.
[133]LTR 2:261; Matthew 5:41.
[134]MTS 341.
[135]LTR 2:293; 2 Timothy 4:7.
[136]LTR 3:164, 220; James 1:17.
[137]LTR 1:72; Proverbs 13:12.
[138]MTN 236; 1 Corinthians 15:55.
[139]LTR 3:133; Sirach (Ecclesiasticus) 13:1.

Bible study.[140] He probably hoped readers would drop the first comma and read his words with understanding!

MT found many New Testament teachings meaningful, but he rejected miraculous elements in it that were contrary to nature. Enchanted by the Christmas story, he wrote Livy: "From the heights of Bethlehem the angels sang Peace on Earth, good will to men! There is something beautiful about all that old hallowed Christmas legend! It mellows a body—it warms the torpid kindnesses and charities into life."[141] But when the fanciful features of the story were taken as fact, he responded with parody. On the star that reportedly "went before" the magi "till it came and stood over where the young child was,"[142] he wrote, "Then the star retired into the sky and they saw it go back and resume its glimmering function in the remote.[143]

In Luke's annunciation story, Mary is puzzled when Gabriel tells her she will conceive without a husband. The angel then assures her, "With God nothing shall be impossible."[144] This set MT off on a yarn about "little Nelly" who tells an audience about twin ladies who want to have a baby and believe that God will answer their prayers. After receiving one baby, they continue to pray and have a dozen more that year. Conflating biblical phrases, Nelly concludes, "Nothing is impossible with God, and whoever puts their trust in Him they will have their reward, heaped up and running over."[145] Reflecting on the irrelevance of Luke's Gospel tracing Jesus' paternal genealogy through many generations back to God, MT thought this simple acknowledgment would have sufficed for one who allegedly had no human father, "Papa up there, is enough for me."[146]

One of MT's skeptical paraphrases of the story of the virginal conception of Jesus (which he confused with the dogma of the Immaculate Conception of Mary that pertains to her own birth) is set in the Southern United States. The parents of a girl who has several suitors approve of

---

[140]BMT 115.
[141]LTR 4:521.
[142]Matthew 2:9.
[143]FM 58-59.
[144]Luke 1:34, 37.
[145]FM 48-49.
[146]Isabel Lyon's journal; MTLB 673.

her becoming engaged to marry one of them, a blacksmith. Soon afterward she becomes noticeably pregnant, causing much gossip. The blacksmith, at first angry over his fiancee carrying some other man's baby, calms down when she explains that an angel came to her when she was alone, dressed in Arkansas fashion—straw hat and blue jeans—to inform her that God has fathered her child. Of course, the villagers "do not believe a word of this flimsy nonsense."[147]

In another parody on the same theme, a bright child named Bessie asks her mother about a pregnant aquaintance who claims she is a virgin. The pregnancy came about, Bessie was told, when the governor's secretary appeared in a dream and announced to the girl that she was going to have a child. The mother treats the story as a silly rationalization, having no doubt that the pregnancy resulted from the girl's illicit sexual intercourse. But when Bessie asks about a similar claim by Mary of Nazareth, her mother is adamant that Mary was an undefiled virgin before Jesus was born. Bessie then learns from a historian of religions that it was common in mythology for gods to impregnate mortal women. When she tells her mother about this, her mother insists that her daughter get interested in something "less awful than theology."[148]

MT made profuse notes in the chapter on Jesus' conception in his copy of *Bible Myths and Their Parallels in Other Religions*.[149] Also, in reading Rufus Noyes's *Views of Religion*, he wrote in the margin, "Gods have always been born out of wedlock—apparently there is no other way to make them respectable." And, "When we reflect upon the origins of Krishna, Buddha, Christ, and the others we are struck with the fact that virgins are not as fertile now as they used to be."

Neither he nor any other prudent person publicly deny that the Virgin Mary bore a child, MT admitted, even though few people accept it privately. In challenging the belief, he hoped to make people aware of the need to deal with reproduction in the context of natural law, "the highest of laws, the most peremptory and absolute of all laws—Nature's laws being in my belief plainly and simply the laws of God, since He insti-

---

[147]FM 53-57.

[148]FM 41-44.

[149]T. W. Doane, *Bible Myths and Their Parallels in Other Religions* (New York: Commonwealth, 1882) 128-35.

tuted them."[150] Although MT did not realize it, the theology he defended here is similar to that of Augustine, the most influential Latin church father. Augustine reasoned that "God, the Author and Creator of all natures does nothing contrary to nature; for whatever is done by him who appoints all natural order and measure and proportion must be natural in every case."[151] But unlike MT, Augustine did not extend this reasoning to the account of the alleged virginal conception of Jesus.

Of supernaturalism in general, MT wrote, "A miracle is by far the most wonderful and impressive and awe-inspiring thing we can conceive of, except the credulity that can take it at par."[152] Besides the story of a virgin conceiving, MT also satirized a New Testament account of physical resurrection. When his publisher wondered if the reissuing of Henry Beecher's *Life of Christ* would be successful, MT "suggested that he ought to have tried for Lazarus, because that had been tried once and we knew it could be done."[153] Had religious people been as quick as MT to question alleged happenings that cannot be explained by the ordinary operations of nature, they would have had an easier time reconciling their faith with modern scientific discoveries.

Scriptural Allusions

In addition to quoting the Bible directly, MT often alluded to it. These allusions are detectable in his writings by the absence of quotation marks. In most cases the borrowing was probably unconscious because many scriptural expressions had so permeated his psyche at an early age that they became his own words and phrases. Alan Gribben has found allusions in MT's writings to more than four hundred biblical passages, 139 to the Gospels and almost as many to the Pentateuch. They are drawn

---

[150]AMT 355-56.

[151]Augustine, *Against Faustus* 26.3.

[152]MTN 393. "Supernaturalism" is used here with this definition: "The theological doctrine that the divine is fundamentally different from the temporal order and cannot be approached through its categories. . . . In this view, faith, revelation, and the authority of Scripture take the place of reason." William Reese, *Dictionary of Philosophy and Religion* (Atlantic Highlands NJ: Humanities Press, 1980).

[153]MTE 188; John 11:44.

from more than half the books of both Testaments.[154] Philip Williams
guesses that there are more than a thousand allusions to the Bible altogether, having found 108 in *The Gilded Age* alone.[155] In MT's writings,
references to the King James Version of the Bible far outnumber those
to Shakespeare or to any other literary corpus. In one sentence of an
essay submitted for the 1881 National Sunday-School Reunion, he strung
together parts of six separate verses from both Testaments to describe the
human condition in a comical manner:

> One day he cometh up as a flower, fair to look upon; but the next day is he
> cut down and trampled under foot of men and cast into outer darkness,
> where the grasshopper is a burden and thieves break through and steal and
> he hath naught of raiment but camel's hair and ashes, and a leathern girdle
> about his loins.[156]

A reader once informed MT that phrases he had used were essentially
the same as those previously published by Oliver Wendell Holmes. Embarrassed, MT recalled that he had read and reread that publication, but
did not realize that some of Holmes's expressions had been stored in his
memory. The same unconscious plagiarism occurred with biblical phrases
that, as he put it, "lay lost in some dim corner of my memory that when
thought of again might be presumed to be one's own original thought."[157]

MT realized that the Bible was the one book most literate and many
illiterate people in his day were familiar with. Today, this is no longer
true, making it difficult for many to detect, understand, and appreciate his
allusions to certain verses and passages. Consider, for instance, Silas
Phelps who is preparing for his Sunday sermon in *Huckleberry Finn*. He
says, "I was a-studying over my text in Acts seventeen."[158] Here, MT
wanted his readers to realize that the sermon to be delivered to fellow
Arkansas slaveholders came from a passage containing a key abolitionist
verse declaring that God "hath made of one blood all nations of men"
(Acts 17:26). For most contemporary readers, reference to a particular

---

[154]MTLB 63.

[155]Philip Williams, *The Biblical View of History* (Ann Arbor MI: University
Microfilms, 1964) 111.

[156]BMT 114; Job 14:1-2; Ecclesiastes 12:5; Matthew 3:4, 6:19, 7:6, 8:12.

[157]AMT 150-51.

[158]HF 316.

chapter of almost any biblical book would not bring any specific recollection.

Joking about a Bible passage is effective only when the reader is familiar with the original meaning and can thereby recognize its incongruity with the novel treatment. Take, for example, MT's conundrum: "Do you know why Balaam's ass spoke Hebrew? Because he was a hebrayist."[159] Readers need to know that a hebraist is a specialist in the Hebrew language, and that Balaam's ass is a talking donkey in the Hebrew Bible. Another pun based on the fable of Balaam is in the episode in which Huck's friend Jim tells of a "chucklehead" named "Balum—Balum's Ass dey call him for short." The allusion is to a donkey who has more sense than his master.[160]

MT often alluded to, as well as quoted from, the creation stories in the opening chapters of Genesis. He suggested that the creation of "man" was a divine afterthought. "Impatient as the Creator doubtless was to see him and admire him," God still permitted more than ninety-nine percent of the world's history to pass before introducing his favorite species. To suggest in another way that humans should be more modest concerning their place in natural history, MT made this analogy, "If the Eiffel tower were now representing the world's age, the skin of paint on the pinnacle-knob at its summit would represent man's share of that age; and anybody would perceive that that skin was what the tower was built for."[161] As to the purpose of human creation, he notes: "Jehovah . . . made man for hell or hell for man. . . . He made it hard to get into heaven and easy to get into hell. He commanded man to multiply and replenish—what? Hell."[162]

With regard to the creation of the archetypical human, MT's Satan says: "I saw him made. . . . He begins as dirt and departs as a stench."[163] MT doubles "the tree of knowledge" of the Eden story and offers his own analysis:

What are the moral qualities? They are but two—love and hate. From each of these trees spring many branches, and the branches bear a variety of

---

[159]N&J 3:235.
[160]HF 56; Numbers 22:28-30.
[161]CT2 573, 576.
[162]MTB 1513; Genesis 1:28.
[163]MSM 55; Genesis 2:7; 3:19.

names; such as Charity, Pity, Forgiveness, Self-sacrifice, and so on, in the one case; and Greed, Envy, Revenge, and so on, in the other. . . . These are the trees of the Knowledge of Good and Evil; Man has eaten of both, the beasts have eaten of neither. This has given man the Moral Sense. The beast has not the Moral Sense. It is this that to a large degree determines what is man and what is beast.[164]

After reading in Andrew White's *History of the Warfare of Science with Theology* about churchmen who denounced the use of chloroform for relieving women's labor pain because God said "in sorrow thou shalt bring forth children,"[165] MT commented:

The church has opposed every innovation and discovery from the day of Galileo down to our own time, when the use of anesthetics in child-birth was regarded as a sin because it avoided the biblical curse pronounced against Eve. And every step in astronomy and geology ever taken has been opposed by bigotry and superstition.[166]

On several occasions, MT appropriated the Genesis description of the sources of flood waters. A stirring letter he received prompted this response, "The fountains of my great deep are broken up and I rained reminiscences for four and twenty hours."[167] Of a talkative fellow stage-coach traveler on his trip to Nevada, he said, "The fountains of her great deep were broken up, and she rained the nine parts of speech forty days and forty nights."[168] It took those same fountains and more to describe his reaction to a humorous story, "The fountains of my great deeps were broken up, and I rained laughter for forty days and forty nights during as much as three minutes."[169] To tell about a monthly investment that never brought a return, he borrowed from the flood story, "That raven flew out of the Ark regularly every thirty days but it never got back anything."[170] From the aftermath of the flood story, he concluded that the "chief joy"

---

[164]WM 468.

[165]Andrew White, *A History of the Warfare of Science with Theology* (New York: Appleton, 1898) 2:63; Genesis 3:16.

[166]MTB 1534.

[167]LTR 4:50.

[168]RI 9; Genesis 7:11-12.

[169]MTB 1300.

[170]AMT 229; Genesis 8:7.

of the "God of the Bible" was "inhaling the odors of burnt meat" from sacrificial altars.[171]

Among certain biblical commentators familiar to MT, the Genesis story of Onan "spilling his seed" on the ground was mistakenly associated with masturbation rather than with coitus interruptus.[172] At a meeting of the Stomach Club in Paris, MT expressed "Some Thoughts on the Science of Onanism."[173] The Onan story, and others no more elevated in the Bible, caused him to muse:

> All indecent books are forbidden by law, except the Bible. Yet it corrupts more young people than all the others put together. For 400 years the Bible has been soiling the minds of Protestant children of both sexes. . . . They have all reveled in the salacious passages secretly.[174]

Recognizing that his published works were only mildly offensive compared to some he had put in his "posthumous trunk," he said of the *Letter from the Earth*, "It would be a felony to soil the mails with it, for it has much Holy Scripture in it of the kind that . . . can't properly be read aloud, except from the pulpit and in family worship."[175] Hearing that a Brooklyn library had banished his novels for the young, he responded that censorship of the corrupting Bible was likewise needed for "unprotected youth."[176] He commented wryly:

> I know this by my own experience, and to this day I cherish an unappeasable bitterness against the unfaithful guardians of my young life, who not only permitted but compelled me to read an unexpurgated Bible through before I was 15 years old. None can do that and ever draw a clean, sweet breath again this side of the grave.[177]

MT's writings contain numerous echoes of the Moses saga in the Torah. (1) "Every quack that is allowed to tread the platform is a small national calamity, like the plague of frogs," he complained.[178] (2) The

---

[171]BMT 316; Genesis 8:21.

[172]Genesis 38:9.

[173]CT1 722.

[174]MT's marginalia in his copy of Rufus Noyes, *Views of Religion*.

[175]MTL 834.

[176]MTL 805.

[177]MTB 1281.

[178]LTR 4:555; Exodus 8:6, 9:14.

coauthor of *The Gilded Age* received this tribute from MT, "Warner has tried to hold up our hands."[179] (3) MT was aware of the Mosaic law granting freedom to a slave after six years in bondage. This could result in a man's separation from his children born in servitude, and from his wife. An antediluvian slavemaster of MT's creation decides to disregard the inconsiderate law and free the entire family of slaves he owns.[180] (4) Of man's crass hypocrisy, MT noted, "He is the only animal who loves his neighbor as himself and cuts his throat if his theology is not straight. He has made a graveyard of the earth in trying to smooth his brother's path to happiness and heaven."[181] (5) In *Huckleberry Finn*, MT cited a phony preacher at a camp meeting who pretended to be inspired by a story of Moses manipulating a magic object in the Sinai desert. He held up an opened Bible and shouted, "It's the brazen serpent in the wilderness! look upon it and live!"[182] (6) While MT was mining the Comstock Lode, he alluded to the Promised Land in writing his mother: "Verily, you shall be satisfied. . . . I have been to the land that floweth with gold and silver."[183]

(7) MT was angered by the flat tax called the tithe that was part of the Mosaic legislation and was continued in British law. In support of a more equitable tax, he said:

> What a pity God didn't levy the tax upon the rich alone. . . . He knew the rich couldn't be forced to pay it and the poor could. With all his brutalities and stupidities and grotesqueries, that old Hebrew God always had a good business head. . . . His commercial satisfaction in the clink of the shekel runs all through the Book—that book whose "every word" he inspired, and whose ideas were all his own; among them the idea of levying a one-tenth income tax upon paupers.[184]

(8) One of MT's favorite poems was "The Burial of Moses," by Cecil Frances Alexander, a famous hymn writer and the wife of an Anglican bishop. Scott notes that "he copied it in his notebook, memorized it, used

---

[179]MTL 317; Exodus 17:12.

[180]LE 60-61; Exodus 21:2-4.

[181]WM 490; Leviticus 19:18; Exodus 32:27.

[182]HF 172; Numbers 21:9.

[183]LTR 1:147; Exodus 3:8.

[184]N&J 3:266; Leviticus 27:30-32.

to recite it with great power all his life."[185] Two stanzas (1 and 8) that he especially liked are in his notebook of the Holy Land trip:

By Nebo's lonely mountain,
  On this side Jordan's wave,
In a vale in the land of Moab,
  There lies a lonely grave.
And no man knows that sepulchre,
  And no man saw it e'er,
For the angels of God upturned the sod,
  And laid the dead man there.

And had he not high honor,—
  The hill-side for a pall,
To lie in state while angels wait
  With stars for tapers tall,
And the dark rock-pines, like tossing plumes,
  Over his bier to wave,
And God's own hand in that lonely land,
  To lay him in the grave?[186]

As for many others in the Judeo-Christian culture, the Book of Psalms was for MT one of the more heavily used parts of the Bible. (1) He knew about the inexpressible gratitude parents feel when they have nursed a sick child "through the Valley of the Shadow and seen it come back to life and sweep night out of the earth with one all-illuminating smile."[187] (2) He combined words from a psalm with other scripture to tell about "the Sunday school boy who defined a lie as 'An abomination before the Lord and an ever present help in time of trouble.' "[188] (3) An evangelist in *Huckleberry Finn* gives a call to repentance that paraphrases lines from a psalm, "Come with a broken spirit! come with a contrite heart!"[189] (4) Having in mind the psalmist who reckoned "threescore and ten" years to be the usual life span, he spoke at his seventieth birthday dinner of the privileges to which he was entitled now that he had passed

---

[185]Arthur Scott, *On the Poetry of Mark Twain* (Champaign: University of Illinois Press) 5.
[186]MTN 69-70; cf. Deuteronomy 34:1-6.
[187]CY 526; Psalm 23:4.
[188]MTS 424; Deuteronomy 7:25; Psalm 46:1.
[189]HF 172; Psalm 51:17.

"the scriptural statute of limitations."[190] (5) He paraphrased a psalmist's line—"In heaven a day is as a thousand years"—to describe the difference between temporal and eternal time.[191] (6) He concluded a talk to young people by lifting phrases from a psalm to express his hope that they might make his instruction a guide to their feet and a light to their understanding.[192] (7) MT's Satan reports to heaven that man "thinks he is the Creator's pet" and that he is such a delight that the Creator "sits up nights to admire him; yes, and watch over him and keep him out of trouble." The claim of Providence's nocturnal protection is based on a psalmist's sentiments.[193]

In the New Testament, MT alluded to the Gospel of Matthew far more frequently than to any other book; accordingly, in the Bible he carried to the Holy Land, that Gospel bears the most markings.[194] Within it, he referred most often to the words and ideas of the Sermon on the Mount. (1) He was aware of how the church leaders, in the course of European history, had preached to commoners from the Beatitudes about meekness and humility in order to gain their support for tyrants who claimed the divine right to exploit them.[195] (2) He talked about the value of exposing one's talents rather than allowing them to be "hidden under a bushel."[196] (3) Jesus appropriated Isaiah's metaphor of the earth as the "footstool" of God's heavenly throne. Adopting the figure, MT once wrote, "If there is one individual creature on all this footstool who is more thoroughly and uniformly happy than I am I defy the world to produce him."[197] (4) He remembered an insane Hannibal youth who had chopped off one of his hands because he believed it had committed a mortal sin, thus taking literally a gospel teaching.[198] (5) Jesus observed that human perversity makes us eager to correct others before we correct ourselves. MT gave the teaching an ironic twist: "I like to instruct people.

---

[190]CT2 718; Psalm 90:10.
[191]LE 14; Psalm 90:4.
[192]MTS 171; Psalm 119:105.
[193]LE 15; Psalm 121:3-8.
[194]MTLB 67.
[195]CY 100; Matthew 5:3, 5.
[196]MSM 190; Matthew 5:15.
[197]MTB 505; Isaiah 66:1; Matthew 5:35.
[198]HH&T 38; Matthew 5:30.

It's noble to be good, and it's nobler to teach others to be good, and less trouble."[199] (6) To discourage ostentation, Jesus said, "When thou prayest, enter into thy closet." Those words help explain a sentence in *Huckleberry Finn*, "Miss Watson she took me in the closet and prayed."[200] (7) Identifying Jesus with God, MT pointed to what seemed to him to be a gross inconsistency, "God himself said, at a time when topics like loving your enemies, and forgiving seventy times seven, and turning the other cheek were taking a rest, that He came into the world not to bring peace but a sword."[201] (8) MT has a child evangelist promising, "Let us seek first the milk of righteousness, and all these things will be added unto us."[202] (9) He lifted metaphors from the concluding parable of the Sermon on the Mount to say, "Friendship . . . is builded upon a rock, and not upon the sands that dissolve away with the ebbing tides."[203]

Apart from the Sermon on the Mount, there are other allusions to the Gospel of Matthew in MT's writings. (1) Bachelor MT was of the opinion that women in politics would lower their holy stature. If suffrage were extended to women, citizens would "consent to take the High Priestess we reverence at the sacred fireside and send her forth to electioneer for votes among a mangy mob who are unworthy to touch the hem of her garment."[204] (2) "I'd noticed that Providence always did put the right words in my mouth, if I left it alone," Huck allows,[205] echoing Jesus' saying, "It shall be given you in that same hour what ye shall speak."[206] (3) MT borrowed phrases from a parable of Jesus to reply to the person who had washed and returned a handkerchief he had left in New York's Central Park, "There is more rejoicing in this house over that one handkerchief that was lost and is found again than over the ninety and nine that never went to the wash at all."[207] (4) He reworked and expanded one of Jesus' hyperboles, "It is easier for a cannibal to enter the

---

[199]MTB 1472; Matthew 7:1-4.
[200]HF 13; Matthew 6:6.
[201]WM 490; Matthew 5:39, 44; 10:34; 18:22.
[202]CT1 262; Matthew 6:33.
[203]LTR 3:124; Matthew 7:24-27.
[204]CT1 211; Matthew 9:20.
[205]HF 277.
[206]Matthew 10:19.
[207]MTB 1416; Matthew 18:13.

Kingdom of Heaven through the eye of a rich man's needle than it is for any other foreigner to read the terrible German script."[208] (5) For a servant who fell asleep over a stove and burned to death, MT punned on Jesus' words in assigning this grisly epitaph, "Well done, good and faithful servant."[209] (6) Speaking seriously, he properly interpreted another teaching of Jesus:

> The spirit of Christianity proclaims the brotherhood of the race. . . . The Christian must forgive his brother man all crimes he can imagine and commit, and all insults he can conceive and utter . . . seventy times seven— another way of saying there shall be no limit to this forgiveness.[210]

(7) Along with the biblical prophets, MT was continually aware of the yawning gap between the profession and the performance of faith. Jesus quoted Isaiah who castigated such pretense, "This people draweth nigh unto me with their mouth, and honoreth me with their lips; but their heart is far from me."[211] MT alluded to this in blasting counterfeit worship:

> We also approve and praise—with our mouths. . . . It is our acts that betray us, not our words. . . . For ages we have taught ourselves to believe that when we hide a disapproving fact, burying it under a mountain of complimentary lies, He [God] is not aware of it. . . . Among ourselves we concede that acts speak louder than words, but we have persuaded ourselves that in His case it is different. . . . Is it not a daring affront to the Supreme Intelligence to believe such a thing?[212]

(8) Near their wedding day, MT asked Livy, "Are not we Twain one flesh?"[213] Here he was alluding to Jesus' paraphrase of the Eden affirmation of the unifying nature of marriage.[214] (9) Pertaining to swearing, he applied to himself Jesus' image of a hypocrite and hoped that his wife would not detect his inward corruption, "I dreaded the day when she

---

[208]MTN 346; Matthew 19:24.
[209]CT1 480; Matthew 25:23.
[210]MTN 332; Matthew 18:22.
[211]Matthew 15:8; cf. Isaiah 29:13.
[212]LE 174.
[213]LTR 3:103.
[214]Matthew 19:5; Genesis 2:24.

should discover that I was but a whited sepulcher partly freighted with suppressed language."[215]

(10) MT saw a parallel between an effort to clean up government and Jesus' action in the Jerusalem temple. After "the Great Republic" of America had decayed by allowing commercial interests to take control, some citizens awoke and "drove the money-changers from the temple, and put the government into clean hands."[216] (11) MT was aware of the way Christians often trivialize Jesus' sacrificial life when they apply his challenge that it be imitated. Thus, when Becky is upset because Tom Sawyer did not return to be with her at school, the narrator says, "She had to . . . take up the cross of a long, dreary, aching afternoon."[217]

Luke's Gospel also appealed to MT, probably because of its emphasis on Jesus' concern for the poor and disreputable outside the community of the righteous. His description of Pudd'nhead Wilson as "a prophet with the kind of honor that prophets generally get at home" echoes Jesus' comment on his rejection at Nazareth.[218] When MT was speaking at a Jewish girls' school, he had Jesus' teaching about sacrificial offering in mind: "When a man with millions gives a hundred thousand dollars it makes a great noise in the world, but he does not miss it. It's noise in the wrong place; it's the widow's mite that makes no noise but does the best work."[219]

Several parables recorded only in Luke made a strong impression on MT. (1) Overtones of the Good Samaritan can be detected in this comment: "There is but one first thing to do when a man is wounded and suffering: *relieve* him. If we have a curiosity to know his nationality, that is a matter of no consequence, and can wait."[220] (2) MT identified with a character of another parable by concluding a letter from San Francisco with "The Prodigal in a far country chawing the husks."[221] A generation

---

[215]AMT 210; Matthew 23:27.
[216]LE 99; Matthew 21:12.
[217]TS 78; Matthew 16:24.
[218]PW 86; Luke 4:24.
[219]MTS 374; Luke 21:1-4.
[220]MTN 344; Luke 10:30-37.
[221]LTR 2:208; Luke 15:16.

later, at a banquet, he referred to himself as a Prodigal Son who had returned from riotous living abroad.[222]

(3) The story of Abraham and Lazarus provided MT, as it had Christians before him, with images of life after death.[223] As Jesus tells it, the greatest honor in the hereafter is to lean on the bosom of Hebrew patriarch Abraham at the heavenly banquet. A rich man in the story is deprived of that reward because of his unconcern for the poor. In MT's story, the rich man is a coal dealer and the greediest man on earth. An angel records that in his many prayers for special Providence, he has asked for such things as an oversupply of miners so that he can reduce wages. But the angel also notes that he once gave fifteen dollars to an impoverished widow out of his $45,000 monthly profit. That generosity put such a heavy strain on his constitution that Abraham "shook out the contents of his bosom and pasted the eloquent label there, 'RESERVED.' "[224] MT also alluded to this parable when he contrasted his compassionate sister-in-law Susie with Abraham, who refused to give water in hell to the rich man who had ignored him. Knowing that the liberal Calvinist could not enjoy heaven if there was suffering in sight, MT gave her this tribute:

> If I do chance to wind up in the fiery pit hereafter, she will flutter down there every day . . . and bring ice . . . and sit there by the hour cheering me up. . . . I can believe a good deal of the bible but I never will believe that a heaven can be devised that will keep Susie Crane from spending the most of her time in Hell trying to comfort the poor devils down there.[225]

MT also alluded to the Acts of the Apostles, Luke's second volume on Christian beginnings. (1) Addressing Simon the sorcerer, Peter charged, "I perceive that thou art in the gall of bitterness and in the bond of iniquity."[226] Similarly MT once described his own situation as, "Being at that time still, as it were, in the gall of sin and bond of iniquity."[227] (2) He likened the wonder of his approaching wedding to Paul's

---

[222]MTS 266; Luke 15:13.
[223]Luke 16:19-26.
[224]CT1 904.
[225]LTR 5:217-18.
[226]Acts 8:23.
[227]LTR 4:548.

marvelous recovery of sight after being struck blind: "Livy, it will give a new revelation to love, a new depth to sorrow, a new impulse to worship. In that day the scales will fall from our eyes and we shall look upon a new world."[228] (3) After seeing the street in Damascus mentioned in Acts, he claimed he had discovered the only facetious remark in the Bible: "The street called Straight is straighter than a corkscrew, but not as straight as a rainbow. St. Luke is careful not to commit himself; he does not say it is the street which is straight, but the 'street which is called Straight.' "[229]

Without source acknowledgement, phrases from the King James translation of Pauline phrases flowed from MT's pen: "Hoping against hope",[230] "Honor to whom honor is due";[231] "Labor of love";[232] "A peace that passeth understanding";[233] "Endure all things, suffer all things";[234] "He [novelist Fenimore Cooper] saw nearly all things as through a glass eye, darkly."[235] Reversing a phrase from a Pauline letter, he wrote, "To the pure all things are impure."[236] Although MT realized that some viewed alcoholic beverages and nudes in a gallery as intrinsic evils, he joined a Pauline writer in criticizing ascetics who failed to recognize that purity was a matter of perception.

MT's borrowings from other biblical books are illustrated by the following. (1) Someone stripped of his specialization was called "a Samson shorn of his locks."[237] (2) To express his doubt that ravens fed Elijah in a desert-like wilderness, he gibed, "The ravens could hardly make their own living, let alone board Elijah."[238] (3) From the Song of Songs: "I used to be terrible as an army with banners";[239] and "Italy is a

---

[228]LTR 3:348.
[229]IA 462; Acts 9:11.
[230]Quoted in Jerome and Wisbey, eds., *Mark Twain in Elmira*, 217.
[231]LE 83; Romans 13:7.
[232]CT1 204; 1 Thessalonians 1:3.
[233]IA 209; Philippians 4:7.
[234]AMT 51; 1 Corinthians 9:12, 13:7.
[235]CT2 184; 1 Corinthians 13:12.
[236]MTN 372; Titus 1:15.
[237]FE 252; Judges 16:19.
[238]MTN 100; 1 Kings 17:4-6.
[239]LTR 1:165; Song of Songs 6:4.

beautiful land and its daughters are as fair as the moon."[240] (4) Speaking to a legislative committee about American liberties, he said, "They didn't come to us in a night, like Jonah's gourd."[241] (5) A woman in *Huckleberry Finn* contends, "the nigger's crazy—crazy's Nebokoodneezer, s'I," which is based of a Bible story of Babylonian king Nebuchadnezzar's temporary insanity.[242] (6) While in mourning, MT wrote Twichell that he was "thankful for my cloud of witnesses, my affectionate and invisible friends."[243] (7) He described Livy "as long-suffering and patient as any Job."[244]

Revelation, the last book of the Bible, also provided MT with images to convey his feelings. Expressing his rapture over having the opportunity to go to Nevada and separate himself from the Civil War, he gushed, "It appeared to me that the heavens and the earth passed away, and the firmament was rolled together as a scroll!"[245] Of a Genoese garden, he rhapsodized, "Through this bright, bold gateway, you catch a glimpse of the faintest, softest, richest picture that ever graced the dream of a dying Saint, since John saw the New Jerusalem."[246]

§ § §

As a child, MT, along with his Hannibal religious community, uncritically accepted the Bible as the literal word of God. But as an adult he came to understand it as containing many stories that should be interpreted as human perspectives on life, which may or may not contain ultimate truth. When in his fifties, he reflected on "the disillusioning corrected angle" of maturity:

People pretend that the Bible means the same to them at fifty that it did at all former milestones in their journey. I wonder how they can lie so. They would not say that of Dickens's or Scott's books. Nothing remains the same: when the man goes back to look at the house of his childhood, it has always

---

[240]LTR 2:76; Song of Songs 6:10.

[241]MTS 386; Jonah 4:10.

[242]HF 346; Daniel 4:32-34.

[243]Letter from MT to Twichell, 8 July 1897, Beinecke Library, Yale University; Hebrews 12:1.

[244]LTR 3:178, James 5:11.

[245]RI 2; Revelation 6:14.

[246](San Francisco) *Alta California*, 9 February 1867; Revelation 21:2.

shrunk . . . to its correct dimensions; the house hasn't altered; this is the first time it has been in focus.[247]

Throughout most of his life, MT engaged in a lover's quarrel with the Bible. Stanley Brodwin observes:

Instead of drawing further and further from the Bible's concepts and characters, he mined them more deeply. Even the language he used to convey his basic attitudes remained biblical and theological rather than secular. . . . There was in him a dark strain of religious anguish and intellectual conflict with the Bible."[248]

With affection mixed with anger MT reflected on many passages of the King James Version that he knew so well. Unfortunately, much of his gentle and caustic wit is lost on those who are not knowledgeable of biblical literature, especially as expressed in that classic English translation. Gregg Camfield concludes his essay on MT and the Bible with this apt sentence.

Whether secretly denouncing it or publicly teasing its devotees, Mark Twain was, like his contemporaries, steeped in the stories and language of the Bible, and his continuous reference, while usually couched in irony, shows how thoroughly the Bible shaped his consciousness whenever he confronted the spiritual, ethical, and scientific questions of his day.[249]

---

[247]MTHL 596.

[248]Stanley Brodwin, "The Theology of Mark Twain," *Mississippi Quarterly* (Spring 1976): 171, 173.

[249]Gregg Camfield, *The Oxford Companion to Mark Twain* (New York: Oxford, 2003) 53.

Chapter 8
Theological Journey

Changing convictions, especially regarding religion, are not often considered a sign of strong character. MT wrote, "When a man who has been born and brought up a Jew becomes a Christian, the Jews sorrow over it and reproach him for his inconstancy; all his life he has denied the divinity of Christ, but now he makes a lie of all his past."[1] MT grumbled about his brother Orion, who "changed his principles with the moon, his politics with the weather, and his religion with his shirt."[2] Appropriating a biblical simile, MT called him as "unstable as water,"[3] and said about his shifting into and out of denominations, "When a man is known to have no settled convictions of his own he can't convict other people."[4] MT even complained, tongue-in-cheek, of God's inconsistency, "What God lacks is conviction—stability of character. He ought to be a Presbyterian or a Catholic or *something*—not try to be everything."[5]

While finding no merit in wishy-washiness, MT did not think it was virtuous to hold beliefs immoveably. "Loyalty to petrified opinions never yet broke a chain or freed a human soul," he observed. In 1887, he reflected on influences over the previous half-century that had modified his Presbyterianism. The discarding of what he had come to view as crude and foolish was attributed to a growth in understanding.[6] Yet occasional shifts in his beliefs are baffling because he sometimes reverted to positions that he had previously set aside.

Views of God

MT's concept of God broadened along with other ideas as he grew to maturity. As a child he believed in special Providence, an outlook widely held in world religions. William Davison provides a standard definition, "The doctrine of special Providence means that God is able and willing, not only to promote general well-being, but also to secure to every one

---

[1]CT1 909.
[2]SCH 229.
[3]Genesis 49:4.
[4]MTL 258.
[5]MTN 344.
[6]CT1 909-16.

who trusts and obeys Him that all things shall work together for his true personal welfare."[7] The concept of special Providence assumes that God directly intervenes in the lives of individuals, often as the result of prayer. Positive or negative sanctions are divinely imposed to modify the behavior of individuals and communities.

In one *Huckleberry Finn* episode, MT essentially wrote about the time in his own childhood when he learned about special Providence and then prayed for gingerbread. After Miss Watson told Huck that he should pray every day and that he would get whatever he requested, he asked for fish hooks, but "couldn't make it work." When he told his Presbyterian guardian about the problem, she explained that answered prayer provides "spiritual gifts" to help people to help one another, and that was different from getting something for oneself.[8] Huck learned not to confuse what he craved with what God was willing to bestow on him, and later commented on a mock evangelist who trusted "Providence to lead him the profitable way—meaning the devil, I reckon."[9]

MT remembered that the news of the villainous real Injun Joe's death was accompanied by an electrical storm and heavy flooding in Hannibal. He described his anguish over the presumed retribution of special Providence:

> I perfectly well knew what all that wild rumpus was for—Satan had come to get Injun Joe. . . . With every glare of lightning I shriveled and shrank together in mortal terror, and in the interval of black darkness that followed I poured out my lamentings over my lost condition and my supplications for just one more chance, with an energy and feeling and sincerity quite foreign to my nature.[10]

While he was working in Nevada, MT credited special Providence with helping to save his life after he had foolishly challenged another journalist to a duel. His opponent, on arriving at the place of mortal contest, noticed that the head of a small bird thirty yards away had been shot off with the Colt revolver MT was holding. Little did the challenger

---

[7]"Providence," James Hastings, ed. *Encyclopaedia of Religion and Ethics* (New York: Scribner's, 1955).

[8]HF 13.

[9]HF 204.

[10]AMT 68-69.

realize that the feat had been accomplished by MT's second, who—unlike MT—was an expert marksman. Assuming that MT had shot the bird, his opponent's courage melted and he withdrew. MT concluded, "I don't know what the bird thought about that interposition of Providence but I felt very, very comfortable over it." In situations like this, he commented, "The proverb says that Providence protects children and idiots. This is really true. I know it because I have tested it."[11]

During his courtship, MT wrote Livy that he was "unspeakably grateful to God for bringing our paths together. The manifest hand of Providence was in it."[12] That "hand" was especially evident as he was taking leave of Livy, who had declined his marriage proposal during his first visit to Elmira. He fell out of the station wagon on his head and had to be returned to her house and her tender care for several days.[13] Circumstances surrounding that occasion caused him to reflect on how Providence can be comprehended: "The real object of it, and the real result, may not transpire till you and I are old, and these days forgotten—and therefore is it not premature to call it bad luck? We *can't tell*, yet."[14] Whereas Providence may provide no specific guidance in facing the future, according to MT, it may help persons to discern a purpose as they look back on one's past.

After their engagement, MT pondered his exclusionary love at first sight:

> If ever a man had reason to be grateful to Divine Providence, it is I. And often and often again I sit and think of the wonder, the curious mystery, the *strangeness* of it, that there should be only one woman among the hundreds and hundreds of thousands whose features I have critically scanned, and whose characters I have read in their faces—only one woman among them all whom I could love with all my whole heart, and that it should be my amazing good fortune to secure that woman's love. And more, that it should be revealed to me in a single *instant* of time, when I first saw you, that you were that woman.[15]

---

[11]AMT 117, 130.
[12]LTR 3:64.
[13]AMT 187-88.
[14]LMT 3:123.
[15]LTR 3:131-32.

Two letters that MT wrote in 1875 affirm special Providence. On Livy's birthday, he wrote, "Six years have gone by since I made my first great success in life and won you, and thirty years have passed since Providence made preparation for that happy success by sending you into the world."[16] Later, writing to Howells about a joint trip, he said, "I will live in the hope that Providence will develop an interest in this expedition, and if that occurs the thing will clip right along to the entire satisfaction of all parties concerned."[17] He admitted to Howells that he was puzzled by "the partialities of Providence," and commented, "There are so many things to attend to and look after in a universe so unnecessarily large as this one, that after all, the real wonder is that more people are not overlooked than are."[18]

In 1878, MT noted, "God does great blessing in such severe methods—instance, Strong's experience in collecting money for his college."[19] James Strong, while visiting Hartford, had been badly injured in a railroad accident. His subsequent amazing recovery induced William Carleton to make a large donation to the Calvinist college in Minnesota—afterward named Carleton College—where Strong was the founding president.

By 1879, both MT and Livy had ceased to believe in the doctrine of special Providence, probably because the personal comforts it had given them were outweighed by the untimely deaths of her father and their son. Livy told her sister that she now accepted a larger God who cared for individuals through the laws of nature. Flora, fauna, and humans were part of a larger scheme of life and love.[20] In 1883, MT wrote about an earlier time in his life "when happenings of life were not the natural and logical results of great general laws, but of special orders, and were freighted with very precise and distinct purposes—partly punitive in intent, partly admonitory; and usually local in application."[21] He wrote a statement of belief that included this disclaimer:

---

[16]LTR 6:597.
[17]MTHL 61.
[18]MTHL 62.
[19]N&J 2:128.
[20]MTB 650.
[21]LM 350.

I do not believe in special providences. I believe that the universe is governed by strict and immutable laws. If one man's family is swept away by a pestilence and another man's spared, it is only the law working: God is not interfering in that small matter, either against the one man or in favor of the other.[22]

By 1886, MT's objection was even stronger: "Special Providence! That phrase nauseates me—with its implied importance of mankind and triviality of God."[23] By then he had come to think of the doctrine, with its presumption that the divine was in petty pursuit of individual happiness or unhappiness, as an affront to the grandeur of God. Looking back as an old man on his belief in a special Providence in earlier years, he marveled at the conceit and superstition that had led him to imagine that God would permit tragedies in order to "beguile" him to a better life.[24] When he heard in 1905 of a friend who had narrowly escaped injury in a railroad accident, he mockingly expressed his gladness "that there is an Ever-watchful Providence to foresee possible results and . . . save our friends." Then he proceeded to give evidence that the surveillance of one Providence was not enough inasmuch as twelve hundred had been killed and sixty thousand injured in railroad accidents just the previous year.[25]

During a blizzard in 1888, which made it impossible for Livy to join MT for a planned trip to Washington, he wrote:

After all my labor and persuasion to get you to at last promise to take a week's holiday . . . this is what Providence has gone and done about it. . . . Pour down all the snow in stock, turn loose all the winds, bring a whole continent to a stand-still; that is Providence's correct idea of the correct way to trump a person's trick. Dear me, if I had known it was going to make all this trouble and cost all these millions, I never would have said anything about your going to Washington.[26]

In 1906, MT took advantage of the San Francisco earthquake, which had destroyed the newspaper building where he had once worked, to ridicule the selfishness implicit in some applications of the doctrine of

---

[22]WM 56.
[23]MTN 190.
[24]AMT 42, 92.
[25]MTL 771.
[26]LLMT 250.

special Providence. In his opinion, the editor of the *Morning Call* had treated him unfairly and MT had—for the only time in his life—been dismissed from his job. He explained:

> I knew the ways of Providence and I knew that this offense would have to be answered for. I could not foresee when the penalty would fall nor what shape it would take but I was as certain that it would come, sooner or later, as I was of my own existence. . . . It was put off longer than I was expecting but it was now comprehensive and satisfactory enough to make up for that. Some people would think it curious that Providence should destroy an entire city of four hundred thousand inhabitants to settle an account of forty years standing, between a mere discharged reporter and a newspaper, but to me there was nothing strange about that, because I was educated, I was trained, I was a Presbyterian and I knew how these things are done. I knew that in Biblical times if a man committed a sin the extermination of the whole surrounding nation—cattle and all—was likely to happen. I knew that Providence was not particular about the rest, so that He got somebody connected with the one He was after.[27]

Biblical writers believed that Providence intervened to protect the righteous and punish the unholy. When small boys made fun of Elisha's bald head, for example, he is said to have "cursed them in the name of the Lord, and bears from the woods mauled forty-two of them."[28] Assuming Elisha's chagrin over the outcome, MT commented: "There is this trouble about special providences—namely, there is so often a doubt as to which person was intended to be the beneficiary. In the case of the children, the bears, and the prophet, the bears got more real satisfaction out of the episode than the prophet did, because they got the children."[29] MT reasoned that the baneful as well as the beneficial effects of Providence should be acknowledged by believers in such. He noted that it is usually applauded when the life of a seaman has been saved by being washed up on an island. Yet there is as much point in blaming Providence for the storm that caused him to be swept overboard in the first place.[30]

---

[27]AMT 122-23.
[28]2 Kings 2:23-24.
[29]PW 26.
[30]MTA 1:209-210.

The doctrine of *special* Providence differs from that of *general* Providence, which pertains to God creating and providing for the universe in an orderly way. John Calvin illustrated the latter when he wrote, "Although it is by the operation of natural causes that infants come into the world . . . yet therein the wonderful providence of God brightly shines forth."[31] In an unfinished novelette written in 1898, MT treated general Providence positively. The final page of what has posthumously been entitled "The Great Dark" describes a voyage taken by the Edwards family. After days on a stormy ocean the captain loses his bearings, and his crew threatens to mutiny, but he pleads with them to courageously accept the wisdom of God's Providence:

> Are we men—grown men—salt-sea men—men nursed upon dangers and cradled in storms—men made in the image of God ready to do when He commands and die when He calls—or are we sneaks and curs! . . . I don't know where this ship is, but she's in the hands of God, and that's enough for me, it's enough for you. . . . If it is God's will that we pull through, we pull through—otherwise not. We haven't had an observation for four months, but we are going ahead, and do our best to fetch up somewhere.[32]

MT's view of general Providence is grounded in some of Jesus' teachings. According to the Sermon on the Mount, the cosmic sun does not discriminate as to the morality of whom it shines on; likewise, God "sendeth rain on the just and on the unjust" alike.[33] In approval of the moral neutrality of nature, MT satirized: "Rain . . . falls upon the just and the unjust alike; a thing which would not happen if I were superintending the rain's affairs. No, I would rain softly and sweetly upon the just, but whenever I caught a sample of the unjust I would drown him."[34] Correspondingly, bolts of lightning hit what is tall even if it happens to be a steeple. "God's lightning strikes more churches than any other property," MT observed.[35]

---

[31]John Calvin, *Commentary on the Book of Psalms* (Grand Rapids MI: Baker, 1981) 1:369.

[32]CT2 343.

[33]Matthew 5:45.

[34]MTB 1441.

[35]MT's marginalia in his copy of Rufus Noyes, *Views of Religion*; N&J 2:511.

Attempts to manipulate God's natural laws were foolish, MT believed. He reported on a controversy that he observed while he was in Australia:

> Rev. Dr. Strong has been trying to explain why prayers for rain are not a proper sort to make. The usual result: a nest of ignorant hornets waked up— violent, vituperative, insulting people. One of them quotes passages from the New Testament to show that what thing soever a righteous Christian prays for, *he will get it*—otherwise God would be violating his contract. . . . This logician [Strong] says—"God reserves the privilege of exercising His own judgment as to which things prayed for He will grant."[36]

Into the mouth of a minister MT put words he thought were all too typical of Christian sermons, "So long as not even the little sparrows are suffered to fall to the ground unnoted, I shall be mercifully cared for."[37] Jesus' sparrow comment had heightened significance among anglophones because in Shakespeare's masterpiece, Hamlet acknowledged, "[T]here's a special providence in the fall of a sparrow."[38] But MT wondered what good it did to have God notice that a sparrow falls if it died just the same.[39]

MT told a story about a flood that came after an Arkansas clergyman prayed for relief from a drought. The resulting devastation caused the citizens of the state to adopt a resolution that concluded, "Since no one can improve the Creator's plans by procuring their alteration, there shall be but one form of prayer allowed in Arkansas henceforth, and that form shall begin and end with the words, *'Lord, Thy will, not mine, be done.'* "[40] MT thought that people should look to the weather bureau for forecasts, relying on it rather than petitionary prayer for knowledge of the future behavior of nature.[41]

MT burlesqued the biblical account of Joshua stopping the river Jordan to make it easier for the Israelites to cross, and staying the sun

---

[36]MTN 262.
[37]CT1 117.
[38]Shakespeare, *Hamlet* 5.2.232; Matthew 10:29.
[39]MSM 65.
[40]FM 63; Luke 22:42.
[41]BMT 324.

and moon to help them complete their slaughter in battle.[42] MT's story concerns several holy children whose motto is, "If ye have faith as a grain of mustard seed . . . nothing shall be impossible unto you."[43] By means of persistent prayer they are able to accomplish the most extraordinary feats. Once, to accommodate a procession, the holy children pray for a river to dam up so that the marchers could cross without getting their feet wet. However, the children failed to take into account that the backed-up water would cause flooding, resulting in loss of farms, livestock, and human life. After the flood, the victims of the disaster met and resolved "that whosoever shall utter his belief in special providences in answer to prayer, shall be adjudged insane and shall be confined." But in spite of that prohibition, the holy children subsequently

> made the sun and moon stand still ten or twelve hours once, to accommodate a sheriff's posse who were trying to exterminate a troublesome band of tramps. The result was frightful. The tides of the ocean being released from the moon's control, burst in one mighty assault upon the shores of all the continents and islands of the globe and swept millions of human beings to instant death.[44]

The presumption of special Providence, MT realized, is often used to claim that people from some places are more important to God than people from other places. This ethnocentricism provided the basis for a humorous tale an Irish comrade told him out West. In the story, an Irish mason falls off a high scaffolding but his descent is broken by hitting someone who happens to be standing underneath. The mason lives but the stranger beneath is killed instantly. The narrator explains:

> There ain't nothing happens in the world but what's ordered just so by a wiser Power than us, and it's always fur a good purpose. . . . There warn't no accident about it; 'twas a special providence, and had a mysterious, noble intention back of it. The idea was to save that Irishman. If the stranger hadn't been there that Irishman would have been killed.[45]

Another one of MT's whimsical stories concerns a couple who are terrified by lightning. The husband thinks that the flashes nearby have

---

[42]Joshua 3:13; 10:13.
[43]Matthew 17:20.
[44]FM 71-77.
[45]AMT 179-80.

been attracted by his lapse in saying bedtime prayers. He explains, "I haven't missed before since I brought on that earthquake, four years ago." His wife believes that lightning can be repelled by ringing church bells.[46]

MT was aware that the setting in which prayers are given sometimes causes a change in the conduct of other humans, even though the prayers do not change nature and nature's God. Women who were successfully crusading against rumsellers in state after state had an effective nonviolent method:

> They only assemble before a drinking shop, or within it, and sing hymns and pray, hour after hour—and day after day, if necessary—until the publican's business is broken up and he surrenders. . . . If I seem to doubt that prayer is the agent that conquers these rumsellers, I do it honestly, and not in a flippant spirit. If the crusaders were to stay at home and pray for the rumseller and for his adoption of a better way of life, or if the crusaders even assembled together in a church and offered up such a prayer with a united voice, and it accomplished a victory, I would then feel that it was the praying that moved Heaven to do the miracle; for I believe that if the prayer is the agent that brings about the desired result, it cannot be necessary to pray the prayer in any particular place in order to get the ear, or move the grace, of the Deity. When the crusaders go and invest a whisky shop and fall to praying, one suspects that they are praying rather less to the Deity than *at* the rum-man.[47]

MT recognized that when God is presumed to micromanage, human responsibility diminishes. When someone says that a murder is "ordained from Above," he noted, "it is no compliment to God. The remark acquits the prisoner— . . . for, if God does a thing His agent is guiltless. . . . It is God's crime."[48] Similarly, he thought it was misleading to put down "by the visitation of God" as the official cause of the suicide of a prominent Nevada citizen who had taken poison, shot himself, and cut his throat before jumping from a fourth-story window.[49] "There are many scapegoats for our blunders," he retorted, "but the most popular one is Providence."[50] He liked the logic of these lines from *The Rubaiyat*:

---

[46]CT1 753-58.
[47]CT1 563-64.
[48]MTN 368.
[49]RI 308.
[50]MTN 347.

O Thou, who didst with pitfall and with gin
Beset the Road I was to wander in,
Thou will not with Predestined Evil round
Enmesh, and then impute my Fall to Sin![51]

Belief in special Providence can so dissolve moral responsibility that thieves can believe that they act with impunity. In *Pudd'nhead Wilson*, robbery is rationalized by that belief. The narrator relates that "even the colored deacon himself could not resist a ham when Providence showed him in a dream, or otherwise, where such a thing hung lonesome and longed for some one to love."[52] Also, Roxana persuades her son to raid villagers' homes while they are all at a reception, since the opportunity for stealing "was like a special providence, it was so inviting and perfect."[53]

Besides special Providence, what other attributes sometimes ascribed to deity did MT find offensive? First, that God solicits through prayers "man's compliments, praises, flatteries." Second, that God is jealous—"a trait so small that even men despise it in each other." Third, that God is boastful, for self-admiration is "unbecoming the dignity of his position." Fourth, that God is revengeful.[54] Fifth, that God "ever sent a message to man by anybody."[55] And last, that all who are designated as gods, in or out of the Bible, deprecate intelligence: "The gods offer no rewards for intellect. There was never one yet that showed any interest in it."[56]

In 1870, for the first time, MT contrasted the God he read about in the Bible and the God he deemed authentic:

To trust the God of the Bible is to trust an irascible, vindictive, fierce, and ever fickle and changeful master; to trust the true God is to trust a Being who has uttered no promises, but whose beneficent, exact, and changeless ordering of the machinery of his colossal universe is proof that he is at least steadfast to his purposes; whose unwritten laws, so far as they affect man,

---

[51]MTP, notebook #27, 37-38; Arthur Scott, *On the Poetry of Mark Twain* (Champaign: University of Illinois Press) 22.

[52]PW 16.

[53]PW 81.

[54]MTN 301-302.

[55]WM 56.

[56]MTN 379.

being equal and impartial, show that he is just and fair; these things, taken
together, suggest that if he shall ordain us to live hereafter, he will still be
steadfast, just, and fair toward us.[57]

What attributes of "the true God," other than constant justice, did MT
admire? In 1891, he wrote about "changes in the Deity—or in men's conception of the Deity" in the era of scientific law:

> Today he is master of a universe made up of myriads upon myriads of
> gigantic suns, and among them, lost in that limitless sea of light, floats that
> atom, his earth. . . . He is governing his huge empire now . . . by applying
> laws of a sort proper and necessary to the sane and successful management
> of a complex and prodigious establishment, and by seeing to it that the exact
> and constant operation of these laws is not interfered with for the accommo-
> dation of any individual or political or religious faction or nation.[58]

In 1898, MT described God as a cosmic artist who created the
world's raw physical stuff and gave it a lovely form:

> The Being who to me is the real God is the One who created this majestic
> universe and rules it. . . . He is the only Originator—He made the materials
> of all things; He made the laws by which and by which only, man may com-
> bine them into machines and other things. . . . Everything which he has
> made is beautiful; nothing coarse, nothing ugly has ever come from his
> hand. . . . The materials of the leaf, the flower, the fruit; of the insect, the
> elephant, the man; of the earth, the crags and the ocean; of the snow, the
> hoarfrost and the ice—may be reduced to infinitesimal particles and they are
> still delicate, still faultless.[59]

In 1906, MT supplemented his earlier reflections on the true divine
character by stressing divine omnipotence and omniscience:

> Let us now consider the real God, . . . that God of unthinkable grandeur and
> majesty, by comparison with whom all the other gods whose myriads infest
> the feeble imaginations of men are as a swarm of gnats. . . . We cannot
> associate with Him anything trivial, anything lacking dignity, anything
> lacking in grandeur. . . . The God that brought this [the universe's] stupen-
> dous fabric into being with a flash of thought and framed its laws with
> another flash of thought is endowed with limitless power. We seem to know

---

[57]BMT 317.
[58]CT2 3.
[59]MTN 361.

that whatever thing He wishes to do He can do that thing without anybody's assistance. We also seem to know that when He flashed the universe into being He foresaw everything that would happen in it from that moment until the end of time.[60]

In 1907, perhaps after reflecting on a psalmist's image of God laughing from heaven at mortals (Psalm 2:4), MT dictated for his autobiography:

I must get that stupendous fancy out of my head. At first it was vague, dim, sardonic, wonderful; but night after night, of late, it is growing too definite. . . . It is the Deity's mouth—His open mouth—laughing at the human race! The horizon is the lower lip; the cavernous vast arch of the sky is the open mouth and throat; the soaring bend of the Milky Way constitutes the upper teeth. It is a mighty laugh, and deeply impressive.[61]

The wonders of nature gave MT moments of religious ecstasy all of his life. After his stagecoach trip through the Rocky Mountains, he spoke about "contemplating the first splendor of the rising sun as it swept down the long array of mountain peaks, flushing and gilding crag after crag and summit after summit, as if the invisible Creator reviewed his grey veterans and they saluted with a smile."[62] While hiking in France he described the alternating sky above Mont Blanc as "the most imposing and impressive marvel I had ever looked upon. . . . If a child had asked me what it was, I should have said, 'Humble yourself, in this presence, it is the glory flowing from the hidden head of the Creator.' "[63] When he saw Switzerland's Jungfrau, the pristine whiteness of the peak caused him to exclaim, "It is as if heaven's gates had swung open and exposed the throne." He found God reflected in things both great and small; the bees and butterflies in the flowers were for him "beautiful creatures that catch the smile of God out of the sky and preserve it."[64]

In 1877 and in 1885 the "longsuffering" God he had read about in the Bible probably prompted these reflections:

---

[60]BMT 322-23.

[61]Gregg Camfield, *The Oxford Companion to Mark Twain* (New York: Oxford, 2003) 622.

[62]RI 77.

[63]Mark Twain, *A Tramp Abroad* (New York: Harper, 1907) 2:30.

[64]CT2 49, 701.

When I think of the suffering which I see around me, and how it wrings my heart; and then remember what a drop in the ocean this is, compared with the measureless Atlantics of misery which God has to see every day, my resentment is roused against those thoughtless people who are so glib to glorify God, yet never to have a word of pity for him.[65]

. . . .

If God is what people say, there can be none in the universe so unhappy as he; for he sees, unceasingly, myriads of his creatures suffering unspeakable miseries—and besides this foresees all they are going to suffer during the remainder of their lives. One might well say "as unhappy as God."[66]

Late in life, embittered by loss, MT sometimes viewed deity differently, as an inflictor of suffering. Judging to be true Isaiah's proclamation, "God's ways are not our ways,"[67] MT claimed the ways of the average human to be more moral! Most humans would not impose pain, misery, and death on innocent life.[68] William Pellowe comments that MT revolted against conceptions of "God less kind at heart than Samuel L. Clemens. . . . His objections were aimed against a doctrine that made God a being who enjoyed sardonic pleasure out of human discomfort."[69] MT contrasted medical missionaries in Africa with God, who invented disease: "Evidently those missionaries are pitying, compassionate, kind. How it would improve God to take a lesson from them!"[70] Of the pitiless God who would decimate human communities with plague or earthquake, he wrote, "God has no special consideration for man's welfare or comfort, or He wouldn't have created those things to disturb and destroy him."[71] By 1903, MT's estimate of divine benevolence had sunk so low that he decided, "None of us can be as great as God, but any of us can be as good."[72] In his most acerbic mood, he wrote Twichell, "God who has no morals, yet blandly sets Himself up as Head Sunday School

---

[65]MTN 128.
[66]N&J 3:149.
[67]Isaiah 55:8.
[68]WM 398-99.
[69]PH 151.
[70]MTMW 199.
[71]MTB 1356-57.
[72]MTN 379.

Superintendent of the Universe; who has no idea of mercy, justice, or honesty, yet obtusely imagines Himself the inventor of these things."[73]

Moral qualities are the sine qua non of MT's genuine God. Despite "the caricature of him which one finds in the Bible," MT believed that God is basically good, and at the same time "there is a large element of Justice and Goodness in His creature man."[74] While on a Caribbean cruise in 1902, he tried to recall these lines from a poem by John Whittier entitled "The Eternal Goodness":

I know not where His hands lift
        Their fronded palms in air;
I only know I cannot drift
        Beyond His love and care.[75]

Several months before he died, MT affirmed the all-powerfulness and foreknowledge of God as before. He also said he would "join the pulpit" and guess "that He is personal." His alliance with a personal God is evident in a poignant note he left with a sick friend, "God and I are sorry that you are so ill."[76]

Views of Jesus

Over the years, MT's thoughts about Jesus remained fairly constant. In 1871 he affirmed, "All that is great and good in our particular civilization came straight from the hand of Jesus."[77] He found the religion of the ancient Israelites to have little "family connection" with "the pure religion of Christ," which he described as "rational and capable of being understood."[78] While most people are tellers of half-truths, Jesus was revered by MT as one of the rare honest persons.[79]

---

[73]Letter from MT to Joseph Twichell, 28 July 1904, Beinecke Library, Yale University.

[74]LLMT 253-54.

[75]MTP, notebook #45; MTLB, 766.

[76]Quoted from the *Boston Post* in Louis Budd, ed., *On Mark Twain* (Durham NC: Duke University Press, 1987) 10.

[77]WM 53.

[78]MTMF xxix.

[79]MTN 181.

On his first trip to England in 1872, MT examined recent work by French painter Gustave Doré that he liked better than any of the many artworks he had seen elsewhere in Europe. His impressions give clues to MT's Christology:

> The Doré gallery has fascinated me more than anything I have seen in London yet. I spent the day there. The main feature is the enormous oil painting 20 by 30 feet, "Christ Leaving the Pretorium" (after judgment has been passed upon him). What a marvelous creation it is! It is the greatest work of art that I have ever seen. . . . In the center of the stairway . . . a Figure with a glory about the head and such a divine sorrow in the face—a face that is saying only one thing, so long as you look—"Father, *forgive* them. . . . [High priest] Caiaphas . . . almost at the Saviour's elbow turns a sneering face upon him. . . . The Christ is the only Christ I ever saw that was divine, except Leonardo da Vinci's. . . . The *real* thing necessary to portray a god is here—not inane gentleness, or sweetness or namby-pamby want of spirit, but that divine *forgiveness*.[80]

In an 1878 letter to Orion, MT backed away from those comments in London on the deity of Christ, "Neither Howells nor I believe in hell or the divinity of the Saviour, but no matter, the Saviour is none the less a sacred Personage, and a man should have no desire or disposition to refer to him lightly, profanely, or otherwise than with the profoundest reverence."[81]

In 1903, MT was curious to discover that church leaders of several denominations were arguing the question, "Did Jesus anywhere claim to be God?" Arguments were cited on both sides but nothing was settled.[82] Had MT joined most modern New Testament scholars in answering that question in the negative, he might have avoided occasionally attributing to God something that Jesus said or did.

The doctrine of Jesus' substitutionary atonement was, in MT's opinion, irrational and morally repugnant. He disputed the traditional view in his inimitable way:

> If Christ was God, He is in the attitude of One whose anger against Adam has grown so uncontrollable in the course of ages that nothing but a sacrifice

[80]LTR 5:614-15.
[81]MTL 323.
[82]WM 309, 568.

of life can appease it, and so without noticing how illogical the act is going to be, God condemns Himself to death—commits suicide on the cross, and in this ingenious way wipes off that old score.[83]

MT's perception of a sharp difference between Jesus and his Christian followers over the centuries was variously expressed: "As concerns Christ there are some uncertainties, but for our solace we know one thing for sure—He was not a Christian."[84] "If Christ were here now, there is one thing he would *not* be—a Christian."[85] "Christianity will doubtless still survive in the earth ten centuries hence—stuffed and in a museum."[86] "There has been only one Christian. They caught and crucified him early."[87] The last epigram states even more sharply what German philosopher Friedrich Nietzsche had asserted a decade earlier, "There has truly been only one Christian, and he died on the cross."[88]

"The Christian's Bible is a drugstore," MT imagined, and for eighteen centuries "the ecclesiastical physician" prescribed from the pharmacy some of its most debilitating drugs. But when patients revolted in the nineteenth century, clergy in English-speaking countries "relinquished the daily dose of hell and damnation." In its place they began to "administer Christ's love, and comfort, and charity and compassion" that all along had been conspicuously shelved in the store.[89]

In 1908, MT was asked to evaluate a letter containing someone's list of the "One Hundred Greatest Men" in history—those who had exerted "the largest visible influence on the life and activities of the [human] race." In responding, he insisted that both Jesus and Satan be added to the list, maintaining that both (Jesus to a greater extent and Satan to a lesser extent) have exerted a greater influence in Western civilization than all other influences combined.[90]

MT admired the human Jesus and rejected the supernaturalism that was associated with him in numerous passages of the Gospels. He

---

[83]MTN 290.
[84]MTP, notebook #35, 23.
[85]MTN 328.
[86]MTN 346.
[87]MTN 344.
[88]Friedrich Nietzsche, *Antichrist* #39.
[89]WM 71-72.
[90]MTL 817.

followed the heresy trials of some Protestant clergy who questioned the virginal conception of Jesus.[91] That alleged miracle stood out for MT as biologically and historically implausible. He also found it theologically repugnant since it suggests that God regards marital intercourse as intrinsically impure.

John Frederick has rightly discerned that "reverence for Christ, as the sole exception to Twain's ruthless iconoclasm, persisted almost until the end of his life."[92] In his last writings there are two criticisms of Jesus that pertain to his alleged teachings and miracles. If it can be assumed that MT's Satan character expressed MT's thinking, then he faulted Jesus for teaching about hell. As Satan put it:

> The first time the Deity came down to earth, he brought life and death. . . . Life was a fever-dream made up of joys embittered by sorrows, pleasure poisoned by pain; . . . death was man's best friend; when man could endure life no longer, death came and set him free. In time, the Deity perceived that death . . . was insufficient; . . . a way must be contrived to pursue the dead beyond the tomb. . . . It was as Jesus Christ that he devised hell and proclaimed it! Which is to say, that as the meek and gentle Savior he [God] was a thousand billion times crueler than ever he was in the Old Testament.[93]

Concerning miracles, MT faulted Jesus—whom he presumed to have equal power with the other divine "half"—for helping only a select few:

> The earthly half—who mourns over the sufferings of mankind and would like to remove them, and is quite competent to remove them at any moment He may choose—satisfies Himself with restoring sight to a blind person here and there instead of restoring it to all the blind; cures a cripple here and there instead of curing all the cripples; furnishes to five thousand famishing

---

[91]OMT 34-36.

[92]John Frederick, *The Darkened Sky* (Notre Dame IN: University of Notre Dame Press, 1969) 151.

[93]LE 46. Had MT looked more carefully into modern biblical scholarship, he would also have recognized that Jesus was not the inventor of hell. The term is based on the Hebrew word "Gehenna" that he borrowed from the Judaism of his day. "Hell" was not intended to describe the everlasting torment of the wicked in the devil's cauldron; rather, it was a metaphor for the extinction of what makes one human. See William Phipps, *The Wisdom and Wit of Rabbi Jesus* (Louisville: Westminster/John Knox Press, 1993) 126-31.

persons a meal and lets the rest of the millions that are hungry remain hungry—and all the time He admonishes inefficient man to cure these ills.[94]

Even so, MT generally rated the theology of the New Testament superior to the theology of Old.

Evil and Freedom

MT was willing to give the Devil his due, "A person who for untold centuries has maintained the imposing position of spiritual head of four-fifths of the human race, and political head of the whole of it, must be granted the possession of executive abilities of the highest order."[95] Concerning this personification of evil, he reserved judgment:

> I have no special regard for Satan, but I can at least claim that I have no prejudice against him. It may even be that I lean a little his way, on account of his not having a fair show. All religions issue bibles against him, and say the most injurious things about him, but we never hear *his* side. We have none but the evidence for the prosecution, and, yet we have rendered the verdict.[96]

Although there is a prejudice against the Prince of Evil, there is nonetheless a human bias toward evil. MT observed: "There is a Moral Sense, and there is an Immoral Sense. History shows us that the Moral Sense enables us to perceive morality and how to avoid it, and that the Immoral Sense enables us to perceive immorality and how to enjoy it."[97] Selfishness is "the mainspring of man's nature," MT claimed, so humans are not naturally oriented to be concerned for God or for a wide circle of people. He made this assessment: "No man that ever lived has ever done a thing to please God—primarily. It was done to please himself, then God next."[98] Moreover, "man is . . . lovable to his own—his family, his friends—and otherwise . . . does his little dirt, commends himself to God, and then goes out into the darkness, to return no more, and send no messages back—selfish even in death."[99]

---

[94]OMT 32.
[95]MTN 343.
[96]CT2 355.
[97]FE 161.
[98]MTN 365.
[99]CT1 858.

Claiming that the sole motivation for all activity is to secure individual satisfaction may have been MT's way of averting self-righteousness when doing good for others. Clara has discussed the disconnect between her father's ethical theory and his emotional responses:

> No subject interested my father more than the incorrigibility of the human race. Even unselfishness was selfish, because whatever the person did, he was doing to please himself. If he gave away his last crust of bread, it was because he would rather see his conscience appeased than his stomach. . . . But the very next moment if some caller entered and recounted an incident picturing the noble conduct of mother, husband, child, his eyes would fill with tears and he would pace the floor, exclaiming: "What noble generosity!"[100]

In 1874, MT hoped to make his debut in the *Atlantic Monthly* with a story about a scientific expedition launched by a variety of small forest critters. They discover fossils of "the long extinct species of reptile called Man." Further exploration discloses a species of God's creation that is lower than Man. Howells rejected the submission, explaining that "a little fable like yours wouldn't leave a single Presbyterian, Baptist, Unitarian, Episcopalian, Methodist, or Millerite paying subscriber."[101] Decades later MT told Howells about his unrewarded efforts to gain acceptance of his view of human nature: "I preached a good sermon to my family yesterday on . . . the human race, that grotesquest of all the inventions of the Creator. It *was* a good sermon, but coldly received, and it seemed best not to try to take up a collection."[102] Disputing the common assumption of humans that they are the capstone of creation, he groused, "If they are the noblest work of God where is the ignoblest!" Yet, his ambivalence on this matter at that last period of his life prompted comments such as this: "In my experience hard-hearted people are very rare everywhere."[103]

The Victorian era was popularly touted as the age of moral and spiritual progress. Those who benefited from the industrial revolution smugly presumed that they were slowly but surely moving away from their barbaric past toward perfection. Afloat was the theory that global

---

[100]MF 182.
[101]CT1 624-30; LTR 6:219.
[102]MTHL 733.
[103]MTA 2:316; MTN 276; AMT 31.

cultures were headed toward WASP supremacy even as nature was eliminating the unfit. MT was skeptical of this self-flattery even as a teenager,
when he chose to comment on the slogan *sic transit gloria mundi*:

> A thousand years from now this race may have passed away, and in its
> stead, a people sprung up, wearing the skins of animals for raiment, and for
> food eating the berries that may grow where now stand the prouder buildings
> of this town. And this people will dig up with their rude instruments some
> memorial of this forgotten race—a steam boiler, perhaps—and gaze with
> astonishment upon it.[104]

While MT usually believed that human understanding of God had
evolved from the Old Testament to the New Testament, he saw no moral
progress in human behavior. Cultural differences aside, human nature has
remained constant. MT noted, crisply, "Difference between savage and
civilized man: one is painted, the other gilded."[105] He also said: "The
heart is just about what it was in the beginning; it has undergone no
shade of change. Its good and evil impulses and their consequences are
the same today that they were in Old Bible Times."[106] Although MT
appreciated the fabulous technological changes taking place and
recognized a degree of material progress, he thought it was unwarranted
to assume that human desires had changed:

> Prodigious acquisitions were made in things which add to the comfort of
> many and make life harder for as many more. But the addition to righteous
> ness? Is that discoverable? I think not. . . . If there has been any progress
> toward righteousness since the early days of Creation . . . I think we must
> confine it to ten per cent of the populations of Christendom."[107]

MT's experiences confirmed his view that belief in cultural progress
was a mere human conceit. He found lawlessness toward Asian aliens in
America's West, indifference to the welfare of immigrants in the
materialistic Northeast, and devices to keep former slaves subservient in
the postbellum South. When a Presbyterian journal lauded humans as "the
Chief Love and Delight of God," MT erupted:

---

[104]N&J 1:25-26.
[105]CT2 942.
[106]MTL 769.
[107]MTL 770.

I watch him progressing . . . higher and higher, sometimes by means of the Inquisition, . . . sometimes by 800 years of witch-burning, . . . sometimes by spreading hell and civilization in China, sometimes by preserving and elevating the same at home by a million soldiers and a thousand battleships; . . . lynching the innocent, slobbering hypocrisies, . . . but always recognizable as the same old Most Sublime Existence in all the range of Non-Divine Beings, the Chief Love and Delight of God; and then I am more gladder than ever that I am it.[108]

MT was one of the first noted Americans to accept Darwin's theory of evolution, but he recognized that it did not support notions of inevitable human progress.[109] Darwin's views so interested him that he owned thirteen of his books.[110] Marginal notes in his copy of Darwin's *The Descent of Man*, show that he read that book carefully. On a visit to England in 1879, he "went up Windemere Lake" and "talked with the great Darwin."[111] The constant process of biological change, MT realized, is independent of moral progress.

MT acknowledged that mankind was distinct among the fauna, albeit the difference was far from commendable. "He is the only Religious Animal," he admitted. "He is the only animal that has the True Religion—several of them."[112] In his essay entitled "The Descent of Man from the Higher Animals" humans are placed on a lower moral plane than other animals because only they act with willful perversity. The human, he claimed, "is the only animal that blushes. Or needs to."[113] Whereas the human intellect has mushroomed in the course of evolution, regression has occurred in one crucial sphere. "There is one thing that always puzzles me," he said; "as inheritors of the mentality of our reptile ancestors we have improved the inheritance by a thousand grades, but in the matter of morals which they left us we have gone backwards as many grades." "If you pick up a starving dog and make him prosperous, he will

---

[108]MTE 383-84.
[109]See William Phipps, *Darwin's Religious Odyssey* (Harrisburg PA: Trinity International, 2002) 131.
[110]MTLB 174-77.
[111]MTN 155.
[112]CT2 211.
[113]CT2 207, 210.

not bite you," MT observed; "This is the principal difference between a dog and a man."[114] But he did liken people to another animal species: "If the sheep had been created first, man would have been a plagiarism. In the make of his soul and in the movements of his spirit, man is nearer to the sheep than to any other creature."[115] We are sheeplike because "we wait to see how the drove is going, then we go with the drove."[116]

MT claimed that he learned about the "descent" of man from a Scotsman (probably a fiction) whose scheme of evolution emerged from much study of the Bible and scientific works:

> Macfarlane considered that the animal life in the world was developed in the course of aeons of time from . . . microscopic seed germ deposited upon the globe by the Creator in the dawn of time, and that this development was progressive upon an ascending scale toward ultimate perfection until man was reached. . . . He said that man's heart was the only bad heart in the animal kingdom; that man was . . . the sole animal that robs, persecutes, oppresses, and kills members of his own immediate tribe, the sole animal that steals and enslaves the members of any *tribe*.[117]

MT feigned that he performed an experiment to discover whether humans tend to be more peaceful than other animals. In one cage he put a cat and a dog, and soon taught them to be friends. During the next two days he added some other species and they learned to accept, and even to be affectionate toward one another. Then, in a separate cage, he put a representative from each of the main global religions. The group included, among others, an Irish Catholic, a Scottish Presbyterian, a Mediterranean Muslim, and an Indian Brahman. Within two days they had all killed one another because they "had disagreed on a theological detail."[118]

In real life, MT argued for the moral superiority of animals. He had read about a hunt organized to entertain an English earl in which seventy-two buffalo were killed and only part of one was eaten. He contrasted that account with an experiment that placed some calves with an anaconda; one of the calves was crushed and swallowed but the satisfied reptile

---

[114]MTL 804; PW 142.
[115]MTP, notebook #45.
[116]MTA 2:10.
[117]AMT 97.
[118]CT2 212.

had no disposition to harm the rest. No other species can match the avaricious and miserly *Homo sapiens*, MT contended, in accumulating more food than can be consumed. He also compared the difference among the species in fighting: "The higher animals engage in individual fights, but never in organized masses. Man is the only animal that deals in that atrocity of atrocities, War. He is the only one that gathers his brethren about him and goes forth in cold blood and with calm pulse to exterminate his kind."[119]

For MT, nothing so reveals the old Adam in us as perennial warfare. His brief tenure as a Civil War officer gave him a keen personal awareness of the tendency to violent behavior in humankind. Believing him to be a war veteran, an editor asked him to contribute an essay in 1885 to a series on notables who had engaged in military service during America's most costly conflict. The article he submitted, entitled "The Private History of a Campaign That Failed," so undercut the journal's intended heroic portrayal of war that it was excluded from the subsequent published collection of essays.

With considerable fictitious embellishment, MT told about joining a unit of the Missouri State Guard to defend his county from invasion by the Union army. The unit organizer was "full of romance and given to reading chivalric novels." However, what started out as a romp with hometown buddies and inane drills soon became "a repulsive nightmare." He was among those on night guard when a stranger, who happened to ride by, was shot. MT then allegedly went up to the gruesomely bloody civilian who carried no weapon and witnessed his agonizing death. Not having been subjected to the usual military propaganda that demonizes the enemy, MT found himself in a war where he was supposed to be "killing strangers against whom you feel no personal animosity" and whom "you might otherwise help if you found them in trouble." After two weeks with the militia, he accepted the Union commander's amnesty to those who relinquished their hostility toward the federal government. MT noted ironically that "those among us who . . . learned to obey like machines, became valuable soldiers."[120]

---

[119]CT2 208, 210.

[120]CT1 863-82. Generations later, a prominent member of the House of Representatives was applauded when he denounced MT as a coward for abandoning those who had fought and died in the Civil War. Joseph Shannon of Missouri

In MT's judgment, the "sham grandeurs" found in *Ivanhoe*, and in other novels of Sir Walter Scott, had done much to glorify the knightly code of honor in the South; dueling was the gentlemanly way to settle an argument. An American Cervantes, MT lampooned the pretensions of chivalry that created a "reverence for rank and caste." He viewed the era of English feudalism as a time of "decayed and swinish forms of religion,"[121] and was infuriated with Scott for romanticizing an era filled with human abuse. Finding that even in New York contests imitating the medieval knights were still being staged, MT suggested a reinactment scenario:

> Let us have a fine representation of one of those chivalrous wholesale butcheries and burnings of Jewish women and children, which the crusading heroes of romance used to indulge in their European homes, just before starting to the Holy Land, to seize and take to their protection the Sepulchre and defend it from "pollution."[122]

MT's Satan, speaking in the eighteenth century, traced the escalation of destructive instruments and prophesied:

> Cain did his murder with a club; the Hebrews did their murders with javelins and swords; the Greeks and Romans added protective armor and the fine arts of military organization and generalship; the Christian has added guns and gunpowder; two centuries from now he will have so greatly improved the deadly effectiveness of his weapons of slaughter that all men will confess that without the Christian Civilization, war must have remained a poor and trifling thing to the end of time. . . . Two centuries from now it will be recognized that all competent killers are Christian; then the pagan world will go to school to the Christian; not to acquire his religion, but his guns.[123]

---

made this attack in 1940 when Congress was considering issuing a commemorative stamp in MT's honor. Shannon asserted that MT was not a "real Missourian" because he "took the oath of allegiance to the Confederacy" and then "deserted." "He was a dismal failure as a belligerent," Shannon remarked. *The Congressional Record* (25 January 1940) 86:698-99. Actually, MT never swore allegiance to the Confederacy. Also, the Congressman did not point out that if the Confederate rebellion had succeeded there would be no Federal Union and Missouri supporters of slavery would not be meeting in Washington.

[121]LM 304-304.
[122]CT1 420.
[123]MSM 135-37.

An Armageddon ends a novel MT helped write about a Connecticut Yankee who introduces scientific technology into King Arthur's realm. After thousands are destroyed by an electrical shock, the rest of the enemy are annihilated by machine guns that "vomit death."[124] Military weaponry is the means by which the Dark Ages moves into modernity. MT later wrote, "The surest way to get rich quickly in Christ's earthly kingdom is to invent a gun that can kill more Christians at one shot than any other existing kind."[125] Given the depravity of human nature, he thought that warfare would never cease. In 1906, he wrote: "Man was created a bloody animal and I think he will always thirst for blood and will manage to have it. I think he is far and away the worst animal that exists; and the only untamable one."[126]

§ § §

MT gave much attention to describing the appalling cruelties of Christians after they had achieved political power in Europe. Visiting the Roman Coliseum, he reflected on an irony of church history. The pagan Romans enjoyed watching Christians being torn limb from limb by beasts, while centuries later Inquisition leaders received sadistic pleasure from tormenting people whose religion differed:

> When the holy Mother Church became mistress of the barbarians, she . . . pointed to the Blessed Redeemer, who was so gentle and so merciful toward all men, . . . and they did all they could to persuade them to love and honor him—first by twisting their thumbs out of joint with a screw; then by nipping their flesh with pincers . . . and finally by roasting them in public.[127]

The perversity of churchmen was illustrated by MT in this sketch of medieval history he wrote while traveling in France:

> The Christians displaced the Saracens [Muslims], and it was these pious animals who built these strange lairs [crusader castles] and cut each other's throats in the name and for the glory of God, and robbed and burned and

---

[124]CY 565.
[125]OMT 39.
[126]MF 264.
[127]IA 274-75.

slew in peace and war; and the pauper and the slave built churches, and the credit of it went to the bishop who racked the money out of them.[128]

MT provided many illustrations of Pascal's dictum, "Men never do evil so completely and cheerfully as when they do it from religious conviction."[129] He recognized, as did some biblical leaders, that religiously motivated people sometimes "beat spears into pruning hooks" but are often eager to do the opposite, converting materials needed for a peaceful life into instruments of alleged holy wars.[130]

Accordingly, the narrator in *Connecticut Yankee* has this to say about sixth century England:

> I will say this much for the nobility: that, tyrannical, murderous, rapacious, and morally rotten as they were, they were deeply and enthusiastically religious. Nothing could divert them for the regular and faithful performance of the pieties enjoined by the church. More than once I had seen a noble who had gotten his enemy at a disadvantage, stop to pray before cutting his throat.[131]

Despite the many accounts of human evil in *Connecticut Yankee*, MT wrote Howells on its completion about his frustration over having to omit other examples. "They burn in me," he acknowledged, but to tell all "would require a library—and a pen warmed up in hell."[132]

MT faulted the medieval Catholic hierarchy not only for its treatment of non-Catholics, but for its persecution of some who considered themselves devout Catholics. An outstanding example was Dominican Friar Giordano Bruno, who shattered the biblical cosmology by positing that the universe has neither center nor circumference.[133] Bruno thought the excellence of God was magnified by innumerable planets revolving about countless suns; but in 1600 he became a martyr to astronomy at the hands of the Inquisition. MT caustically commented, "The Church has burned

---

[128]MTL 553.

[129]Pascal, *Pensees* #894.

[130]Isaiah 2:4; Micah 4:3; Joel 3:10.

[131]CY 202.

[132]MTHL 613.

[133]Dorothea Singer, *Giordano Bruno* (New York: Greenwood, 1968), 58.

many other men besides Bruno for denying lies which it got out of the great source of lies, the Bible."[134]

John Hawkins, Protestant England's first successful slave-hunter, was knighted by Queen Elizabeth. His work, as MT described it

> was to remain a bloody and awful monopoly in the hands of Christians for a quarter of a millenium, was to destroy homes, separate families, enslave friendless men and women, and break a myriad of human hearts, to the end that Christian nations might be prosperous and comfortable, Christian churches be built, and the gospel of the meek and merciful Redeemer be spread abroad in the earth; and so in the name of his ship, unsuspected but eloquent and clear, lay hidden prophecy: she was called "The Jesus."

MT recognized that the eventual leader in the fight against slavery was William Wilberforce, a member of an evangelical movement that the English establishment did not like. In 1888 a pope declared the enslavement of Africans to be wrong, MT noted, long after most slaves had been freed.[135]

European rulers had succumbed to the primeval serpent's temptation and had played God, MT believed. He was relieved, therefore, that the democratic revolutions of modern Europe had "so completely stripped the divinity from royalty that, whereas crowned heads in Europe were gods before, they are only men since, and can never be gods again, but only figureheads, and answerable for their acts like common clay."[136] Once "divine rights" had been removed from secular royalty, MT observed, the Vatican arrogantly claimed more power. He treated the papal infallibility dogma Pius IX proclaimed in 1870 as too ludicrous for rational debate. MT's Satan harangues:

> Look at the Pope's infallibility. . . . Look at his loosing-and-binding authority—which is not confined to earth, but which even God on His Throne is obliged to submit to. . . . Will a day come when the race will detect the funniness of these juvenilities and laugh at them—and by laughing at them destroy them?[137]

---

[134]MT's marginalia in his copy of Samuel Bayne, *The Pith of Astronomy*; MTLB 53.
[135]WM 72-74.
[136]LM 303.
[137]MSM 165.

MT repeatedly used the account of the 1572 massacre of Protestants on St. Bartholomew's Day in France to illustrate just how immoral professed Christians could be. He had probably first heard of the massacre through Hannibal Presbyterians, because the event was of major significance in the history of Calvinism. The slaughter was instigated by Catherine de Medici and ordered by her son, King Charles IX. Huguenots (French Calvinists) were attacked in cities and towns while they were engaged in Sunday worship. MT accurately told how Catholics "sprang a surprise upon the unprepared and unsuspecting Protestants, and butchered them by thousands—both sexes and all ages." He echoes the indignation of François Voltaire, "Half of the nation butchered the other, with a dagger in one hand and a crucifix in the other."[138] "Children were brained against the wall," MT's description of the fanaticism was probably appropriated from a psalmist's blessing on those who would smash Babylonian babies against the rocks.[139] Afterward there was great joy in Rome; Pope Gregory XIII had a commemorative medal struck featuring his portrait on one side and an angel slaughtering Huguenots on the other. MT's detailed account of the event concluded:

> Seventy thousand lives were taken in those two or three days in France, and the true religion retired from its exploit so much strengthened that the other side was never able to seriously threaten its supremacy afterward. There have been French massacres since . . . but none of these are half such matters of pride to the French as their peerless St. Bartholomew's.[140]

MT was also well aware of the reciprocal persecution of Catholics by his fellow Protestants in Northern Ireland. He wrote in 1875:

> A week ago a vast concourse of Catholics assembled at Armagh to dedicate a new Cathedral; and when they started home again the roadways were lined with groups of meek and lowly Protestants who stoned them till all the region round about was marked with blood. . . . Every man in the community is a missionary and carries a brick to admonish the erring with. . . . The usual cry is, "To hell with the Pope!" or "To hell with the Protestants!" according to the utterer's system of salvation.[141]

---

[138]CT2 207; Francois Voltaire, *Works* (New York: Fertig, 1988) 15.2.62.
[139]LE 148; Psalm 137:9.
[140]LE 149.
[141]CT1 633.

Religious massacres were discussed in one of MT's favorite books, *Memoirs* by the French social philosopher Louis Saint-Simon. In a margin of that book, MT noted:

> So much blood has been shed by the church because of an omission from the Gospel: "Ye shall be *indifferent* as to what your neighbor's religion is." Not merely tolerant of it, but indifferent to it. Divinity is claimed for many religions; but no religion is great enough or divine enough to add that new law to its code.[142]

In spite of his searing criticism of the medieval church, MT acknowledged that "the great majority" of Catholic priests even in that era "were sincere and right-hearted, and devoted to the alleviation of human troubles and sufferings."[143] A hero in *Connecticut Yankee* is a priest who befriends a young woman whose supportive husband has been shanghaied. She is sentenced to hang for a bit of shoplifting she engaged in to keep her starving infant alive. At the scaffold, the priest denounces the injustice of British law that is more concerned with protecting property than providing for the needy. When the noose is placed around the mother's neck, he takes the infant from her arms and promises to care for it.[144] That hanging actually happened in eighteenth-century England,[145] but the priest's intervention was the novelist's benevolent addition.

§ § §

Recognizing MT's thesis that evil has always been pervasive in society, what hope did he have for individuals avoiding being over-whelmed by its force? At the age of fifty, he wrote, "A but little considered fact in human nature: that the religious folly you are born in you will die in, no matter what apparently reasonabler religious folly may seem to have taken its place meanwhile and abolished and obliterated it."[146] At the age of seventy he observed that those who persist in a particular faith do so "because they are born and reared among that sect,

---

[142]MTB 1537.

[143]CY 215.

[144]CY 461-63.

[145]William Lecky, *A History of England in the Eighteenth Century* (New York: Appleton, 1882) 3:582-83.

[146]MTHL 461.

not because they have thought it out."[147] Those general comments relate to MT's situation, as Paul Boller shows, "Intellectually Twain had been chafing at the orthodox Christian conception of things since early manhood; but emotionally he was never able to emancipate himself from the teachings of his boyhood Calvinism."[148] Finding a residual Calvinism in the marrow of MT bones, DeLancey Ferguson has even claimed that "all his life he thought of theology and philosophy in terms of the Hannibal Presbyterian Church."[149]

What essentially does it mean to be a Calvinist? Philosopher Vergilius Ferm has provided this concise definition: "Calvinistic thought is a system in which God is made the center of all that is and happens, God's will pervading human and cosmic events, and upon whom man is utterly and cheerfully dependent."[150] That accurate description does not emphasize the judgment of God, because Calvin's teaching focused more on divine mercy.[151] For example, Calvin asserted that "God declares that he adopts our babies as his own before they are born. . . . How much injury the dogma that baptism is necessary for salvation . . . has entailed."[152] Although Calvin did not believe that unbaptized infants were damned, some "Calvinists" betrayed him on this matter. MT "told an anecdote of an old minister who declared that Presbyterianism without infant damnation would be like a dog on the train that couldn't be identified because it had lost its tag."[153] Countering the wrong assumption of some Presbyterians, MT wrote of God's "grieved disappointment" over the human misunderstanding of his attitude toward children.[154]

The problem of human freedom is raised by the main tenet of Calvinism, the sovereignty of God over all of life. To what extent can people willfully determine their thoughts and actions? Through the ages this

---

[147]WM 95.

[148]Paul Boller, "Mark Twain's Credo," *Southwest Review* (1978): 162.

[149]DeLancey Ferguson, *Mark Twain: Man and Legend* (Indianapolis: Bobb-Merrill, 1943) 25.

[150]"Calvinism," Dagobert Runes, ed., *Dictionary of Philosophy* (Ames IA: Littlefield, Adams, 1958).

[151]John Calvin, *Institutes of the Christian Religion* 2.8.21.

[152]Calvin, *Institutes* 4.15.20.

[153]MTB 1534.

[154]CT2 4.

question has been answered in several ways, including fatalism, predestination, scientific determinism, and self-determinism.

Fatalism is the view that all events are fixed so that neither humans nor gods can alter them. Augustine, one of the main spokespersons for the Latin church, pointed out that Christian theology rejects the fatalism championed by Stoicism and astrology.[155] Calvin found fatalism odious because it posits that even God is controlled by blind and impersonal forces.[156] Although some interpreters of MT have maintained that he was sometimes a fatalist, he did not so designate himself and it is not an appropriate way to describe him.

Predestination is the belief that individual destiny has been decreed by God. Augustine and Calvin championed this theory, arguing that humans are not controlled by irrational fate but by an infinitely wise being who decides what is best for them. During most of MT's lifetime, Presbyterians accepted Calvin's theory that God determined before birth whether an individual would go to Heaven or Hell. Early in life MT was taught that God "hath foreordained whatsoever comes to pass."[157] A few years before death he wrote, "When He flashed the universe into being He foresaw everything that would happen in it from that moment until the end of time."[158] Another statement MT made in the same period also reflected a theological determinism:

> It vexes me to catch myself praising the clean private citizen Roosevelt, and blaming the soiled President Roosevelt, when I know that neither praise nor blame is due to him for any thought or word or deed of his, he being merely a helpless and irresponsible coffee-mill ground by the hand of God.[159]

Henry Van Dyke led Presbyterians to revise their doctrine of predestination,[160] probably with the encouragement of his friend MT. In 1903, changes that Van Dyke had pursued for many years finally resulted in an official modification of Calvinistic theology. The largest Presbyterian denomination in America then approved a doctrinal statement that salva-

---

[155] Augustine, *City of God* 5.9.
[156] Calvin, *Institutes* 1.16.8.
[157] "Westminster Shorter Catechism," queston 7.
[158] BMT 323.
[159] MTL 764.
[160] Tertius Van Dyke, *Henry Van Dyke* (New York: Harper, 1935) 123.

tion had been "freely offered in the Gospel to all; that men are fully responsible for their treatment of God's gracious offer; that His decree hinders no man from accepting that offer; and that no man is condemned except on the ground of his sin." That "Declaratory Statement" expressed views MT frequently advocated. The Presbyterians made clear that the Westminster Confession of Faith "is not to be regarded as teaching that any who die in infancy are lost. We believe that all dying in infancy are included in the election of grace."[161] MT drolly responded: "The Presbyterians extended the Calling and Election suffrage to nearly everybody. . . . Everything is going to ruin; in no long time we shall have nothing left but the love of God."[162]

Scientific determinism, another response to the question of free will, is the assumption that behavior is completely explainable by genetics and conditioning. Those who think they have freedom of action, according to this theory, only display their ignorance of the causal chain over which they have no control. MT first attempted to defend this theory at the Hartford Monday Evening Club but it was completely rejected.[163] Decades later he called it "my Bible—which Mrs. Clemens loathes, and shutters over, and will not . . . allow me to print."[164] The theory was fashionable in some scientific circles, and so after Livy's death he published it under the title, *What Is Man?* MT answered the question by positing that human behavior operates strictly in accordance with the external forces of heredity ("temperament") and environment ("training").[165] Consequently, individuals should not be blamed or praised for their conduct because they are compelled by forces beyond their control. "Sometimes a man is a born murderer; . . . he is only obeying the law of his nature," he contended.[166]

MT provided a straightforward illustration of his scientific determinism theory:

[161]*Minutes of the General Assembly of the Presbyterian Church in the United States of America* (Philadelphia: General Assembly Office, 1903) 125-26.
[162]WM 317.
[163]MTE 240.
[164]MTL 676.
[165]CT2 731-804.
[166]AMT 309.

Mohammedans are Mohammedans because they are born and reared among that sect, not because they have thought it out and can furnish sound reasons for being Mohammedans; we know why Catholics are Catholics; why Presbyterians are Presbyterians; why Baptists are Baptists; why Mormons are Mormons; why thieves are thieves; why monarchists are monarchists; why republicans are republicans, and democrats democrats. We know it is a matter of association and sympathy, not reasoning and examination.[167]

While he was growing up in Hannibal, MT listened to a "black philosopher" who orated from his master's woodpile next door. This was his text, "You tell me whar a man gits his cornpone, en I'll tell you what his 'pinions is." Late in life MT said how "deeply impressed" he was with the way that Hannibal sage had articulated the absence of free will.[168] Stated in sophisticated terms—as MT's older contemporary, Karl Marx had done—people's religious, business, and political ideology is determined by whatever contributes to their livelihood. Whether we are physical slaves or not, according to determinism, we are all totally creatures of outside influences and fashions.

In his article, "The Turning Point of My Life," published a month before he died, MT simplistically traced the circumstances that had caused him to be a writer. When he was twelve his mother apprenticed him as a printer, thus exposing him to publishing. His career in journalism was launched when his brother invited him to go to a Western region where writers were needed. Then, after he returned from an excursion to the Mediterranean he was asked to write a book. He claimed that his will was not a factor in any of this. He said: "Necessarily the scene of the real turning point of my life (and of yours) was the Garden of Eden. It was there that the first link was forged of the chain that was ultimately to lead to the emptying of me into the literary guild."[169] Elsewhere, MT expanded on his theory:

> I positively believe that the first circumstance that ever happened in this world was the parent of every circumstance that has happened in this world since; that God ordered that first circumstance and has never ordered another one from that day to this. Plainly, then, I am not able to conceive of such

---

[167]CT2 510.
[168]CT2 507-509.
[169]CT2 937.

a thing as . . . an *accident*—that is to say, an event without a cause. Each event has its own place in the eternal chain of circumstances, and whether it be big or little it will infallibly cause the *next* event, whether the next event be the breaking of a child's toy or the destruction of a throne.[170]

Pellowe holds that the scientific determinism sometimes espoused by MT is an "inverted Calvinism":

In the place . . . of the Calvinistic Deity who foreordained some souls to happiness and heaven, and foredoomed others to lives of sin and the punishment of hell, Twain had put a machine which determined everything which happened on the earth and above it, in the individual's life and in society, thereby being the cause of joy and woe, of respectability and crime, of diseases and war.[171]

MT can probably best be classified as a self-determinist, even though he was unaware of that twentieth-century designation. Self-determinism assumes that conduct is caused by both antecedent factors and an internal self. Consider MT's wry image of "the serene confidence which a Christian feels in four aces."[172] Each individual has been dealt a hand that represents the external hereditary, environmental, and theological causes of his or her behavior. Even with a good hand, playing it well is needed to win. Dealt a poor hand, skill becomes even more important. Those who use their minds can resist the pressure to conform and can act independently of external influences. The circumstances of birthplace, race, gender, education, wealth, church, and politics have importance, but MT maintained that a person can select from the many factors those that determine whether the game of life will be won or lost.[173]

MT's writings and activities amply demonstrate that people have the freedom to make genuine choices. His analogy of life as a card game appears frequently in the "playing one's hand" motif in *Connecticut Yankee*.[174] Hank Morgan, the Connecticut Yankee in King Arthur's court, thought it would be wrong to require everyone to become a Presbyterian like himself. Corruption was less likely, he held, if a variety of denomina-

---

[170]MTE 380.
[171]PH 214.
[172]CT1 79.
[173]WM 493-94.
[174]CY 66, 72, 507, etc.

tions kept an eye on one another.[175] Positively, variety has grandeur because it provides more freedom of choice. Morgan probably spoke for his literary creators when he said:

> Spiritual wants and instincts are as various in the human family as are physical appetites, complexions, and features, and a man is only at his best, morally, when he is equipped with the religious garment whose color and shape and size most nicely accommodate themselves to the spiritual complexion, angularities, and stature of the individual who wears it.[176]

Other novels of MT also teach that it is imperative to choose the better course. In *Huckleberry Finn*, the protagonist struggles successfully against the dehumanizing environmental forces of Southern culture. Although *Pudd'nhead Wilson* is a novel about cultural determinism, even here Roxana asserts her independence by exchanging her slave baby for a free baby and by escaping from slavery. And MT's *Personal Recollections of Joan of Arc* expresses the self-determinism of one who stands out against the oppression of crown, church, and gender. Her great accomplishments, he noted, came "without shade or suggestion or help from preparatory teaching, practice, environment, or experience."[177] John Tuckey argues that MT's writing about a "spiritualized self" shows that "by the late 1890s he was finding more of a basis for opposing his own reluctantly held deterministic position."[178] The assumption of personal liberty is behind his counsel, "Diligently train your ideals upward, and still upward, toward a summit where you will find your chiefest pleasure in conduct which, while contenting you, will be sure to confer benefits upon your neighbor and the community."[179]

MT often acted independently, and urged others to do the same. He was both religiously and politically unorthodox, if measured by standards of his day. In 1906, he talked with congressmen at the capitol about copyright reforms, on the presumption that they would act responsibly if

---

[175]CY 118, 215.

[176]CY 118.

[177]CT2 593.

[178]John Tuckey, "Mark Twain's Later Dialogue: The 'Me' and the Machine," in *On Mark Twain*, ed. Louis Budd (Durham: Duke University Press, 1987) 129.

[179]MTB 744.

they were informed and reject the status quo.[180] On another occasion, he wrote a New York Senator:

> Dave Hill put up a convicted thief for one of the loftiest places in the judiciary. The people . . . buried him past resurrection under whole mountain ranges of ballots. *Now* you understand why our system of government is the *only* rational one that was ever invented. When we are not satisfied we can *change* things.[181]

It is difficult to discover much of a pattern in MT's shifting viewpoints on human freedom, due in part to his weakness in logical analysis. Arthur Scott, at the conclusion of his study of MT, writes: "With a mind even less analytical than the minds of most artists, he was never quite at home in the realm of ideas. Consequently, many of his attitudes, not being grounded in solid principles, were subject to oscillations."[182] Indeed, MT's own observation is self-incriminating to a degree: "Our judgments are valuable only within the area of our specialized training. Thus lawyers and farmers are incompetent to make clothes without learning the tailor's trade. Yet a large portion of Americans think they can comment on religious matters without any apprenticeship."[183]

There may be a psychological explanation for the determinism that frequently gripped MT as he grew older. One way of rationalizing personal tragedy and guilt is to assume that humans are victims of circumstances over which they have no control. Blaming the external forces of heredity and environment, or claiming that an omnipotent malevolent being (God or Satan) "made me do it" may offer some solace.

Personal Immortality

MT's theological journey also included attempts to discover if there were any human destiny beyond death. All of his life he engaged in an internal and external dialogue on immortality, wavering between hopefulness and despair. As Twainian authority Alan Gribben succinctly puts it, "He was

---

[180]MTL 801.
[181]LLMT 278.
[182]MTAL 304.
[183]WM 260.

suspicious of, but intrigued by, the possibility of life after death."[184] To understand his views on this subject, an important distinction between physical resurrection and spiritual immortality must be made. As an adult, he did not believe in the reassembling of relics when the trumpet sounded on Judgment Day, but he often open-mindedly considered the immortality of the immaterial soul or self. He shared the doubts that he attributed to some Pacific islanders concerning physical resurrection. On his visit to Fiji, he alleged, the islanders informed him why they rejected "the missionary's doctrine." They wondered what would happen to people eaten by sharks that, in turn, were caught and eaten by people. Then, if those people were captured by cannibals and became part of their flesh and bones, "How, then, could the particles of the original men be searched out from the final conglomerate and put together again?"[185]

MT told a story of an undertaker who hoodwinked customers into thinking that his procedure for temporarily arresting decay would preserve the bodies of their loved ones until the final resurrection. The undertaker confided: "You take a family that's able to emba[l]m, and you've got a soft thing. . . . All it wants is physical immortality for [the] deceased, and they're willing to pay for it."[186] The American practice of embalming, introduced during MT's adult years, led him to prefer cremation to burial. "Grotesque, ghastly, horrible" is the way he described the conventional embalming of corpses[187] (which, ironically, would be the way his own dead body would be prepared for exhibition in a church).

When taken literally, MT realized, the traditional notions of the resurrection—with its realm for the redeemed above and for the damned in the netherworld—cannot be reconciled with astronomy, his favorite science. Paine tells how MT examined astronomical models in New York's Museum of Natural History "and lost himself in strange and marvelous imaginings concerning the far reaches of time and space."[188] Recognizing the immensity of the universe caused him to image the earthling as a motherless child:

---

[184]Howard Kerr, ed., *The Haunted Dusk* (Athens: University of Georgia Press, 1983) 177.
[185]FE 98.
[186]LM 286.
[187]LM 280.
[188]MTB 1509.

The lid had been taken off the universe, so to speak, there was vastness, emptiness, vacancy all around everywhere, the snug cosiness was gone, the world was a homeless little vagrant, a bewildered little orphan left out in the cold, a long way from any place and nowhere to go.[189]

To MT, the biblical treatment of man's final abode was farcical if understood literally. The ultimate "city of God" was described in the Book of Revelation as a cube measuring fifteen hundred miles on each side.[190] Above the waters over the earth's lid, the enthroned Creator and his attendant angelic host were in communion with saints in gloryland. The entire geocentric cosmology was stratified, with a paradise above the earth and a hell below in a vast superheated cavern.

On the subject of immortality, MT wrote this serious statement in mid-life:

I think the goodness, the justice, and the mercy of God are manifested in His works; I perceive that they are manifested toward me in this life; the logical conclusion is that they will be manifested toward me in the life to come, if there should be one. . . . There may be a hereafter, and there may not be. I am wholly indifferent about it. If I am appointed to live again, I feel sure it will be for some more sane and useful purpose than to flounder about for ages in a lake of fire and brimstone for having violated a confusion of ill-defined and contradictory rules said (but not evidenced) to be of divine institution. If annihilation is to follow death, I shall not be *aware* of the annihilation, and therefore shall not care a straw about it.[191]

MT received assistance from his often skeptical friend Howells on celestial as well as terrestrial matters. Kenneth Eble, who has extensively studied the relationship between MT and Howells, writes: "The subject of religion was one he shared with Howells through the years. Howells never quite abandoned an essentially Christian position, with the life and example of Christ at the center of it."[192] In his letter of condolence to MT after the death of his brother-in-law Theodore Crane in 1889, Howells inferred human immortality from the nature of God. A good God would

---

[189]FM 360.

[190]Revelation 21:16.

[191]WM 56-57.

[192]Kenneth Eble, *Old Clemens and W. D. H.* (Baton Rouge: Louisiana State University Press, 1985) 201.

want to share eternal life with those who desire it, he reasoned, and a great God would have the power to make it happen. MT thought that argument made sense, and wrote Livy, "The further I get away from the superstitions in which I was born and mis-trained, the more the idea of a hereafter commends itself to me and the more I am persuaded I shall find things comfortable when I get there."[193] At that same time he remarked about the grief of his daughter Jean over the death of her Uncle Ted, "The earned heartbreak of a little child must be high and honorable testimony for a parting spirit to carry before the Throne."[194]

To MT's admission in 1891 that he sometimes feared hell even though he no longer believed in it, Livy responded, "Why, Youth, who then can be saved?"[195] To her husband's bewilderment over immortality, she responded that it begins on this side of death. "How much of immortality you have in your dear blessed self," she assured him.[196] Livy was probably aware that the leitmotif of the Gospel of John is that "eternal life" is a present experience as well as a future hope.[197] But MT never seemed to grasp the New Testament doctrine that those who are in union with the God of love participate in the timeless realm here and now.

During the last decades of his life, MT reflected ambivalently on immortality, often stopping by the Beecher home when he was in Elmira to discuss such matters. There, in 1895, he had a spirited exchange with his good friend Julia as to the likelihood of life after death, finally agreeing that if they later met in heaven, he would gladly admit his error. Following the biblical practice of using stones to seal a covenant, he drew up a "contract" on three stones (which can still be seen in Elmira) as a future reminder. On one of them he inscribed:

If I prove right, by God his grace,
Full sorry I shall be.
For in that solitude no trace

---

[193]LLMT 253-54.

[194]MTMF 264.

[195]Grace King, *Memoirs of a Southern Woman of Letters* (New York: Macmillan, 1932) 173.

[196]LLMT 346.

[197]John 5:24; 17:3.

There'll be of you and me,
Nor of our vanished race.[198]

In 1898, MT noted: "The Bible of Nature tells us no word about any future life, but only about this present one. It does not promise a future life; it does not even vaguely indicate one. . . . The book of Nature tells us distinctly that God cares not a rap for us."[199] But the lack of proof from nature was not for MT tantamount to concluding that life after death does not exist. That same year he reflected on an immaterial self that shares a common memory with the embodied self; it is experienced in dream states and is detachable from "clogging flesh." He mused, "When my physical body dies my dream body will doubtless continue its excursion and activities without change, forever."[200] He appreciated a demythologizing Unitarian who said that "heaven and hell are simply mental conditions—spirits in the former have happy and contented minds, and those in the latter are torn by remorse of conscience." Further, like Socrates, he speculated that souls who engage in learning and teaching might progress to a higher sphere of excellence in another realm.[201] Reviewing a book that describes the New Jerusalem referred to in the final chapters of the Bible, he expressed this longing:

> It would be a wonderful experience to stand there in those enchanted surroundings and hear Shakespeare and Milton and Bunyan read from their noble works. And it might be that they would like to hear me read some of my things. . . . My life is fading to its close, and someday I shall know.[202]

In 1903, MT wrote Livy: "I have been thinking and examining and searching and analyzing, for many days, and am vexed to find that I more believe in the immortality of the soul than disbelieve it. Is this inborn, instinctive, and ineradicable, indestructible? Perhaps so."[203] But a year later he ruminated about his prenatal and postmortem "annihilation":

---

[198]Robert Jerome and Herbert Wisbey, eds., *Mark Twain in Elmira* (Elmira NY: Mark Twain Society, 1977) 198.

[199]MTN 362.

[200]MTN 348-52.

[201]CT1 203; Plato, *Phaedo* 64-70.

[202]Quoted in Ray Browne, ed., *Mark Twain's Quarrel with Heaven* (New Haven CT: College and University Press, 1970) 37.

[203]LLMT 344.

I have long ago lost my belief in immortality—also my interest in it. . . . I have sampled this life and it is sufficient. . . . Annihilation has no terrors for me, because I have already tried it before I was born. . . . There was a peace, a serenity, an absence of all sense of responsibility, an absence of worry, an absence of care, grief, perplexity; and the presence of a deep content and unbroken satisfaction in that hundred million years of holiday which I look back upon with a tender longing and with a grateful desire to resume, when the opportunity comes.[204]

Those close to the elderly MT recognized that he pondered the question of immortality until he died. Clara said of her father: "He never shut up his mind so tight that it would not unfold to the possible mysteries of an invisible world. . . . Sometimes he believed that death ended everything, but most of the time he felt sure of a life beyond."[205] "Mark Twain was immensely interested in his destination after death," observes Hamlin Hill in his careful study of the last decade of the author's life.[206] Also, in his close study of the paradoxes of MT, Edward Wagenknecht concludes:

Immortality was not a dogma with him, but it was a hope. For, as the sorrows of life piled thick and fast upon him, he believed more and more, despite all his skepticism, that there is no sense to the universe if death ends all, and the thought of what lay beyond was often upon his mind.[207]

§ § §

In 1868, Elizabeth Phelps wrote a novel about heaven, entitled *The Gates Ajar*, which became the top Victorian bestseller. MT acknowledged that her conception of a Rhode Island-sized heaven stimulated him to write a burlesque.[208] Phelps's imagination was so earthbound that her portrayal of the afterlife is largely a duplication of the dull, respectable Victorian family in a setting of houses, brooks, fruit trees, flowers, fine horses, dawns, and twilights. She conceived of paradise as a retirement home with all the amenities. The material trappings included the usual

---

[204]AMT 249.
[205]MF 250, 280.
[206]Hill xvii.
[207]MTMW 195.
[208]BMT 181, 205.

books, pictures, and pianos of middle-class living rooms. Less attention was given to the biblically based tradition of pearly gates, golden streets, and harps for continuous worship. Absent from the scene are pain, darkness, and naughty children.[209]

Captain Wakeman shared a dream with MT that gave him the idea of writing a parody of the commonplace view of heaven in his culture. Entitled "Captain Stormfield's Visit to Heaven," he worked on it for decades—longer than on any other work he published. When he submitted it for serial publication in *Harper's Monthly*, his usual magazine outlet, the editor initially rejected it because it was "too damn godly."[210] But two chapters from it were published before he died, and the income it produced caused him to name his last home "Stormfield." The main purpose of this valediction was to picture a humbling, awe-inspiring heaven and to laugh at the vanity of particular human groups who presume such a realm is exclusively theirs. Taking advantage of the vastness of space, petty sectarians are separated and kept peaceful. Earthlings are only one set of the arrivals from the innumerable spheres of the universe; indeed, extraterrestrials are the most numerous.

Stormfield, like Huck Finn, thinks he is going to hell after dying, but winds up in heaven. The clerk there finds his attempts to identify his place of origin meaningless when he mentions San Francisco, then California, then the United States. In desperation Stormfield explains that he has come from the place "the Savior saved," but he is told, "The worlds He has saved are like to the gates of heaven in number—none can count them." Only when he mentions that Jupiter belongs to his planetary system does the clerk have a clue. Finally located after a search for days on a cosmic map of many square miles is the earth, which is a speck designated as "the Wart."[211]

So as not to disappoint former earthlings, souls with a churchgoing background are outfitted with the paraphernalia they expect to receive, "People take the figurative language of the Bible and the allegories for literal, and the first thing they ask for when they get here is a halo and

---

[209]Elizabeth Phelps, *The Gates Ajar* (Cambridge MA: Harvard University Press, 1868) 137-90.

[210]Kent Rasmussen, *Mark Twain A to Z* (New York: Oxford University Press, 1995) 61.

[211]BMT 150-53.

Captain Stormfield travels through space
in MT's fantasy about heaven.

a harp, and so on."[212] While initially satisfied with their angel wings, they quickly discard them, realizing they are only for show and useless for cruising at the speed of light across quadrillion miles. Also, perching on clouds and strumming on harps while crooning psalms is soon found

---

[212]BMT 157-58.

boring by the new arrivals. Moreover, they discover that perpetual idleness does not produce happiness, because without a struggle to overcome pain, pleasure is meaningless. So they turn to self-fulfilling activities they were denied in their former lives. Finding that they can choose their age, they select a year when their minds were functioning well.[213]

Ethnic, religious, and class prejudices are exposed as the story continues. Presbyterian minister DeWitt Talmage had expected heaven to be limited to "the elect," but instead he finds it open for all. "Grand moguls" Moses and Esau arrange a sumptuous reception for a bartender. To Stormfield's surprise, a pagan Native American is the first to greet him. Among the Americans, there are fewer white angels than those with "mud" and "copper" pigments. Arrivals from "the Wart" include Mexicans, Africans, Arabs, Chinese, Eskimos, tramps, cannibals, and politicians. Side by side are Jeremiah and a Tennessee tailor, Muhammad and an Egyptian knife grinder, and Shakespeare and a French shoemaker. Stormfield looks eagerly for the military geniuses, Caesar, Alexander, and Napoleon, but discovers that they have been demoted. Earthly status has no heavenly significance and those honored there may have been unheralded in their previous life. Sir Richard Duffer, "a nobleman from Hoboken," was a low-class butcher before he died, but he had quietly given meat to the poor who would starve before they would beg.[214] MT subtly interjected New Testament messages, "The last shall be first, and the first last"; and "Eye hath not seen . . . the things which God hath prepared for them that love him."[215]

The Stormfield fantasy reveals that MT had returned to the outlook he had on Native Americans as a boy. As a result of reading James Fenimore Cooper's portrayal of their nobility and bravery in *The Last of the Mohicans*, Clemens had romanticized them. But after he personally observed decultured Indians living in Nevada under the domination of white Americans, he began to express the bigotry of fellow Westerners, "Truly he is nothing but a poor, filthy, naked scurvy vagabond, whom to exterminate were a charity to the Creator's worthier insects and reptiles

---

[213]BMT 158-64.
[214]BMT 166-79.
[215]Matthew 20:16; 1 Corinthians 2:9.

which he oppresses."[216] Later in life MT allowed, "We have to keep our God placated with prayers and even then we are never sure of him—how much higher and finer is the Indian's God."[217] On nearing the end of life MT honors Native Americans by having them make up the majority of residents in Stormfield's area of heaven.

MT uses this bit of space fiction to provide a theological and ethical corrective. David Sloane rightly views it as a criticism of

> the self-deluding self-centeredness of prevading notions of Heaven. . . . As in his other published works on religion, Twain's theme revolves around a broad, tolerant, and intelligent application of Christian doctrine. . . . Heaven is seen as ecumenical and universal; narrow doctrines are regarded as inappropriate to a hierarchy far greater than the nationalistic presumptions of American religion.[218]

§ § §

Apart from the Stormfield story, MT's jottings deftly played on traditional Christian stereotypes pertaining to life after death. As his *Quaker City* shipboard experiences illustrate, congeniality with the sanctimonious was not his forte. He expressed a dying person's dilemma in trying to decide where he would like to go next, "Heaven for climate, hell for company."[219] "I would rather be damned to John Bunyan's heaven," MT said about being involved in a situation he strongly opposed.[220] Concerning fellow Americans, he exclaimed, "What a hell of a heaven it will be, when they get all these hypocrites assembled there!"[221] In a similar vein, he quipped, "When I reflect upon the number of disagreeable people who I know have gone to a better world, I am moved to lead a different life."[222] Accordingly, MT had Huck say that he has no interest in what

---

[216]CT1 443; RI 126-29.

[217]MT's marginalia in Richard Dodge, *Our Wild Indians* (Hartford CT: American, 1883) 112; MTLB 197.

[218]David Sloane, *Student Companion to Mark Twain* (Westport CT: Greenwood, 2001) 171]

[219]N&J 3:538.

[220]MTHL 534.

[221]MTL 705.

[222]PW 108.

Miss Watson describes as the "good place" because that is where she plans to go.[223] In a more generous mood, MT gave this reply when asked if he believed in heaven or hell: "I don't want to express an opinion. I have friends in both places."[224] As he grew older he stated: "Travel has no longer any charm for me. I have seen all the foreign countries I want to see except heaven and hell, and I have only a vague curiosity as concerns one of them."[225]

Another play on the stereotypical afterlife had to do with history's first residential telephone that was installed in MT's home in Hartford. The "damned nuisance" disturbed his serenity so much that he had a calendar chart alongside it so he could record and report personally to Alexander Bell the number of "thunder" or "artillery fire" sounds he heard. With this in mind, he sent this holiday greeting to his friends:

> It is my heart-warming and world-embracing Christmas hope and aspiration that all of us, the high, the low, the rich, the poor, the admired, the despised, the loved, the hated, the civilized, the savage may eventually be gathered together in a heaven of everlasting rest and peace and bliss, except the inventor of the telephone.[226]

The images of torture mythologically associated with a subterranean pit in the hereafter were for MT more applicable to some earthly situations. He asserted that the "Holy Inquisition imported hell into the earth,"[227] and he picturesquely referred to prison chain gangs as "invented in hell and carried out by Christian devils."[228] Demythologizing, he maintained that the only hell was "the one we live in from the cradle to the grave."[229] When facing tragedy in his life, he declared, "It is an odious world, a horrible world—it is Hell; the true one, not the lying invention of the superstitious."[230] In short, MT thought it was more

---

[223]HF 4.

[224]Caroline Harnsberger, *Mark Twain's Views of Religion* (Evanston IL: Schori, 1961) 46.

[225]MTHL 645.

[226]*National Geographic* (September 1975): 329.

[227]E&E 223.

[228]MTN 263.

[229]MTN 302.

[230]LLMT 328.

important to focus on coping with torments here and now than to worry about otherworldly punishment.

Studying traditional eschatological mythology, MT noted that it placed value upon sexlessness and exclusiveness. "Of the delights of *this* world man cares most for sexual intercourse," he observed; but "*he has left it out of his heaven*! Prayer takes its place."[231] As to exclusivity, only 144,000 saints will be "redeemed from the earth" at the throne of God according to one book of the New Testament.[232] Of this select few from human population across history, Mollie Clemens apparently considered herself a finalist. Pertaining to his sister-in-law, MT discerned:

> She is saturated to the marrow with the most malignant form of Presbyterianism,—that sort which considers the saving of one's own paltry soul the first and supreme end and object of life. . . . If she ever goes to heaven, she will be likely to say, "I am disappointed; I did not think so many would be saved."[233]

MT was highly suspect of conceptions of heaven that magnified a particular religion. For those who projected into the afterlife their disdain for inclusiveness, he had a tale called "Captain Simon Wheeler's Dream Visit to Heaven." Wheeler was unchurched but "had profound religious views, and their breadth equaled their profundity." Arriving in heaven he noticed that new arrivals, when asked for credentials, placed themselves with their religious group—Baptist, Catholic, Muslim, and the like. Seeing this, Wheeler was fearful for he lacked such identification. However, when he admitted that he had no allegiance to one particular group, he was given a grand welcome. Because he loved all races and religions equally, he was told that instead of being confined to a particular area, he was free to roam among all people and all nations.[234]

§ § §

MT's core convictions resonate with the paradox expressed by Immanuel Kant. Both closely followed developments in astronomy and

---

[231]MTN 397.
[232]Revelation 14:4.
[233]MTHL 256.
[234]BMT 190-04.

both were devoted to the moral law, especially as expressed in the Golden Rule. Kant affirmed:

> Two things fill the mind with ever new and increasing admiration and awe, the oftener and the more steadily we reflect on them: *the starry heaven above and the moral law within.* . . . The former view of a countless multitude of worlds annihilates as it were my importance as an *animal creature*, which after it has been for a short time provided with vital power, one knows not how, must again give back the matter of which it was formed to the planet it inhabits (a mere speck in the universe). The second, on the contrary, infinitely elevates my worth as an *intelligence* by my personality, in which the moral law reveals to me a life independent of animality and even of the whole sensible world.[235]

MT possessed a greater balance of head and heart than Kant. Yet both men shared a common biblical heritage linking the religious with the physical and moral orders, as this psalmist illustrates:

> Thy mercy, O Lord, is in the heavens,
> and thy faithfulness reacheth unto the clouds.
> Thy righteousness is like the great mountains;
> thy judgments are a great deep.[236]

As John Hays recognizes, the mature MT searched for a satisfying alternative to the Christian orthodoxy he had forsaken:

> He could not completely rely upon his reason as the 18th-century Rationalists did. He could not rely upon his feelings as early 19th-century Romantics did for "intimations of immortality." He could not finally accept the scientific determinism his own age came to. He floundered through the options, confused, angry, pained at and in a secular world. This spiritual confusion, however, has an inherent consistency in keeping with someone spiritually alive, someone who persists in asking the big questions of the universe.[237]

---

[235]Immanuel Kant, *Critique of Practical Reason* (1788) conclusion.
[236]Psalm 36:5-6.
[237]John Hays, *Mark Twain and Religion* (New York: Lang, 1989) 12.

Chapter 9
Final Quest

Among MT's contemporaries, it would be difficult to find any cultural leader who was more genuinely engaged in religious seeking. He occasionally flirted with, but refused to adopt, agnosticism, Calvinism, communism, deism, determinism, positivism, transcendentalism, Unitarianism, utilitarianism, or any other doctrine popular in his day. He never became a contented finder, opting for smug pietism or defiant atheism. John Hays, in his book on *Mark Twain and Religion* has soundly shown that "Clemens rages against the world primarily because he is frustrated as he seeks the meaning of existence in a quest for a viable faith."[1] Words of Robert Louis Stevenson, an acquaintance of MT who shared his Calvinist heritage, characterize his continued pursuit of elusive theological truth, "To travel hopefully is a better thing than to arrive."[2] MT's persistent struggle with religious issues gave him a spiritual vitality to the end.

MT's final quest spans the last sixteen years of his life, beginning with his financial failure in 1894 when the Paige typesetting machine in which he had invested a fortune proved a failure. During that period he suffered from nagging illnesses. Finally, after recovering from bankruptcy, nearly all the members of his immediate family died.

Joan of Arc and Susy

Before tragedy occurred in his family, MT completed *Personal Recollections of Joan of Arc*. Different from anything he had written before, the book was about a historical figure who had fascinated him for forty years. When he was a teenager on a Hannibal street, he found a page torn out of a book on the French girl, describing how English soldiers had tormented her.[3] Joan's godliness and bravery instantly appealed to him, which is surprising for someone raised as a Protestant. In the years that followed, as he read more about her in French as well as in English, his sympathy for her idealism and female assertiveness grew. He was motivated to complete his fictionalized history of Joan when he realized that she also interested Susy, the daughter he idolized. When Susy was thir-

---

[1]John Hays, *Mark Twain and Religion* (New York: Lang, 1989) 112.
[2]Robert Louis Stevenson, *Virginibus Puerisque* (London: Chatto, 1922) 120.
[3]MTB 81.

teen she read Friedrich Schiller's *Jungfrau von Orleans* to her mother, and they had both found this drama about another teenager "delightful."[4] Susy and Joan had much in common, according to MT, including "vivacity, enthusiasm, precocious wisdom, wit, eloquence, penetration, [and] nobility of character."[5]

Because MT wanted *Joan of Arc* to be taken seriously, he initially hid behind a French pseudonym. No one reading the book would ever guess that its author doubted supernaturalism. The narrator never questions the priestly exorcism of dragons from the woods near Domremy or Joan's prediction that the wind would change direction and keep English supplies from coming up the river to Orleans. There is no scoffing at Joan's purity of mind and body, or any suggestion that the "voices" she heard might be delusions. MT presented a story of holiness, miracles, and prophecy without satire.

English literary critic Andrew Lang, who later wrote a biography of Joan, contrasted her biography by Anatole France with MT's treatment. Unlike that distinguished French writer, Lang observed, MT had not allowed the story of Joan's spiritual life to become lost in historical detail.[6] MT may even have furthered the ecclesiastical process that resulted in the twentieth-century beatification and canonization of the Maid of Orleans. He described how Joan's community had remained loyal to the Pope in Rome at a time when there were movements against the Pope elsewhere.

The archbishop of Orleans assured MT that anyone who wrote so beautifully about Joan would be welcomed in heaven. MT responded acerbically that such a destiny would satisfy him as long as the place he was assigned was near her and as far away as possible from the church authorities responsible for her death.[7] The narrator in MT's account wonders why "that bastard of Satan, Pierre Cauchon, bishop of

---

[4]Livy's journal, 2 July 1885, 13.
[5]MTP, memorial to Susan Clemens, box 31.
[6]MTL 810.
[7]James Walsh, "To the Editor," *Commonweal* (23 August 1935).

Beauvais,"[8] who presided over Joan's trial, wanted to go to heaven when "he did not know anybody there."[9]

During the trial the heroine sounded like Martin Luther, for both claimed a direct access to God, an outlook unacceptable to the Catholic Church. "Will you submit to the determination of the Church all your words and deeds?" Joan was asked. "I will submit them to Our Lord who sent me," she replied.[10] For both rebels, the authority of the church was secondary to the authority of God. MT referred to Joan and Luther as a "splendid pair equipped with temperaments not made of butter, but of asbestos. By neither sugary persuasions nor by hellfire could Satan have beguiled *them* to eat the apple."[11]

A hidden motif in MT's biography of Joan is the parallel between Jesus and Joan.[12] The "personal recollections" of the narrator, Joan's page, begin by extolling her as "the most noble life that was ever born into this world save only One." Both saviors lived in lands conquered by invaders; both came from simple families and small towns; both were committed to their devout parents' religion; both were humble, yet they stoutly claimed to be messengers from God; both were joyful, serene, compassionate, charismatic, and eloquent speakers; both gave courage to the disheartened and ministered to the sick; both were charged by malignant priests with heresy; and both forgave those who were responsible for their execution. As MT pointed out, Joan "went to her martyrdom with the peace of God in her tired heart, and on her lips endearing words and loving prayers for the cur she had crowned and the nation of ingrates she had saved."[13]

Both Jesus and Joan witness that undeserved suffering and a dramatic death can have a transforming effect on society. After Charles VII—whom she helped crown—permitted her to be burned alive as a witch, it was presumed that her influence would die with her execution. Her tor-

---

[8]Mark Twain, *Personal Recollections of Joan of Arc* (New York: Harper, 1896; repr.: New York: Oxford University Press, 1996) 304.

[9]Twain, *Joan of Arc*, 396.

[10]Twain, *Joan of Arc*, 365-66.

[11]WM 19.

[12]MT's copy of *Jeanne D'Arc* by LaVierge Lorraine contains his notes comparing their trials.

[13]CT2 591.

menters did not realize that her martyrdom "would magnify it and make it permanent."[14] A significant difference between the two mystics is that Jesus was engaged in spreading the message of peace to all people, while Joan participated in the Hundred Years' War between England and France.

MT viewed Joan as a precursor of the leaders in the women's rights movement of his day. She was not content to be a homebody and fulfill her life in the traditional role of taking responsibility for children, cooking, cleaning, and clothes. Rather, she was a soldier dressed like a man who became the youngest person in history, male or female, to command a nation's military forces.

By means of his historical novel about Joan, MT also expressed his affection for Susy. That exceptionally bright girl had written a charming biography of her father a dozen years earlier. Their ties were strong, and when Susy left for Bryn Mawr College they both felt forlorn. MT would think of excuses to visit his pride and joy in Pennsylvania, even if it was just to return her laundry.[15] The longest separation between Susy and her parents came during MT's year-long global lecture tour. In high spirits over their anticipated reunion in a few days, he and Livy learned in London that Susy was dying of spinal meningitis.

MT's main consolation at that agonizing and lonely time was Twichell, who was with Susy during her illness. He was MT's surrogate at her deathbed in Hartford and at her funeral in Elmira, which the elderly Thomas Beecher conducted. MT wrote Twichell from London, where he had remained in seclusion, to express his deep gratitude:

> Through Livy and Katy I have learned, dear old Joe, how loyally you stood poor Susy's friend, and mine, and Livy's; how you came all the way down twice, from your summer refuge, on your merciful errands to bring the peace and comfort of your beloved presence, first to the poor child, and again to the broken heart of her poor desolate mother. It was like you; like your good great heart, like your matchless and unmatchable self. It was no surprise to me to learn that you could still the storms that swept her spirit when no other could; for she loved you, revered you, trusted you, and "Uncle Joe" was no empty phrase upon her lips! I am grateful to you, Joe, grateful to the bottom of my heart, which has always been filled with love for you, and

---

[14]Twain, *Joan of Arc*, 300.
[15]MTHL 636.

respect and admiration; and I would have chosen you out of all the world to take my place at Susy's side and Livy's in those black hours. . . . God bless you, Joe—and all your house.[16]

Howells responded to MT's loss by reaffirming his belief in personal immortality, a view that MT sporadically found plausible:

As for the gentle creature who is gone, the universe is all a crazy blunder if she is not somewhere in conscious blessedness that knows and feels your love. . . . The joint life will go on when you meet on the old terms, but with the horror and pain gone forever. This is the easiest and the most reasonable thing to believe.[17]

Because Howells had himself lost a daughter, the Clemenses were especially comforted by his words. Livy so treasured his letter that she preserved it in her New Testament, where it was found after her death. MT responded to Howells: "Shall we see Susy? Without doubt!"[18]

Still in anguish, MT wrote his spouse:

Do you remember, Livy, the hellish struggle it was to settle on making that lecture trip around the world? How we fought the idea, the horrible idea, the heart-torturing idea. I, almost an old man, with ill health, carbuncles, bronchitis, and rheumatism. I, with patience worn to rags, I was to pack my bag and be jolted around the devil's universe for what? To pay debts that were not even of my making. And you were worried at the thought of facing such hardships of travel, and SHE was unhappy to be left alone. But once the idea of that infernal trip struck us we couldn't shake it. Oh, no: for it was packed with sense of honor—honor—honor—no rest, comfort, joy—but plenty of honor, plenty of ethical glory. And as a reward for our self-castigation and faithfulness to ideals of nobility we were robbed of our greatest treasure, our lovely Susy in the midst of her blooming talents and personal graces. You want me to believe it is a judicious, a charitable God that runs this world. Why, I could run it better myself.[19]

Even though MT had denied special Providence during most of his adult life, he occasionally blamed the dark hand of Providence when in despair. As he put it, "God pours out love upon all with a lavish hand—

---

[16]MTL 636.
[17]MTHL 662.
[18]MTHL 663, 785.
[19]MF 179.

but he reserves vengeance for his very own."[20] On the first anniversary of Susy's death, he penned an outburst entitled "In My Bitterness" in which he complained of divine malevolence. Those who express gratitude to God, he contended, should know that He never provides a lasting kindness. He bestows wealth to heighten the biting pain of the poverty to follow, health to sharpen the anguish over physical decay, and "He gives you a wife and children you adore that through the spectacle of the wanton shames and miseries which He will inflict upon them He may tear the palpitating heart out of your breast and slap you in the face with it."[21] A month later, MT noted that he had been out of his right mind when he expressed those blasphemous feelings.[22]

Susy's death also compounded MT's feelings of personal guilt. Ever since 1872 he had been haunted by his presumed role in the death of his son. When the baby appeared to be convalescing from a serious illness, MT took him out in an open carriage on a frigid morning. He became chilled when the fur blanket slipped off and died of diphtheria soon afterward. He was sure his inattention had inadvertently caused the death of his only son.[23] After Susy's death, he puzzled over God's injustice, telling Livy that she was "a faultless mother" and did not deserve such punishment, while admitting, "I deserve all I get."[24] He irrationally assumed that if he had not left Susy to go on a global lecture tour, she would not have died.

Even though the causes of MT's guilt were imaginary, he was profoundly affected and his pessimism was deepened. He endured a prolonged loss of self-respect, although he was usually able to conceal it from the public. Soon after Susy's death he published this aphorism, "Everyone is a moon, and has a dark side which he never shows to anybody."[25] He confessed: "What a man sees in the human race is merely himself in the deep and honest privacy of his own heart. Byron despised the race because he despised himself. I feel as Byron did, and for the

---

[20]MTN 237.
[21]FM 131.
[22]MTP, letter to Francis Skrine, 18 September 1897.
[23]AMT 190.
[24]MF 180.
[25]FE 654.

same reason."[26] MT's religion had become grace-less; even though he occasionally called himself the prodigal son, he missed the point of Jesus' story, that God's acceptance is unconditional and not dependent on a person's good works.

In 1900, responding to a generous introduction at a banquet, MT revealed something of his inner struggle:

> I enjoy a compliment about as much as any man. But you don't know me. I've got another side unpictured. I've got a wicked side. . . . The truth is that I have led a life full of interior sin. . . . Everyone believes I am just a monument of all the virtues, but it is nothing of the sort. I am leading two lives, and it keeps me pretty busy.[27]

It appears that MT would have welcomed his own death at this time. He wrote then: "Pity is for the living, envy is for the dead";[28] and "All people have had ill luck, but Jairus's daughter and Lazarus [for whom there are resusitation stories] had the worst."[29] To his riddle, "Why is it that we rejoice at a birth and grieve at a funeral?" he answered, "It is because we are not the person involved."[30] He also told a story with a theme similar to that of the Book of Ecclesiastes, about a youth to whom a fairy gave five choices: pleasure, love, fame, riches, and death. The youth tries each of the first four in succession and each is found to be dazzling at the start but empty in the end: pleasure brought ephemeral enjoyments; love was shattered by the death of the beloved; fame provoked derision from the envious; and wealth lacked duration. The youth then chose death, but the fairy had already given it to someone else. All that was left, MT wrote, was "the wanton insult of Old Age."[31]

§ § §

---

[26]MTB 1539.
[27]MTS 357.
[28]FE 184.
[29]MTN 345.
[30]PW 69.
[31]CT2 126.

After Susy's death Livy became interested in spiritualism, and her husband accompanied her to several seances in London.[32] In 1901, MT confided:

> I have never had an experience which moved me to believe the living can communicate with the dead, but my wife and I have experimented in the matter when opportunity offered and shall continue to do so. . . . Mr. Meyers, president of the London Psychical Research Society . . . was a spiritualist. I am afraid he was a very easily convinced man. We visited two mediums whom he . . . considered quite wonderful, but they were quite transparent frauds.[33]

Mrs. Meyers wrote the transcript of one of the seances in which the Clemenses had unsuccessfully attempted to contact Susy. (F. W. Meyers' monograph entitled *Human Personality and Its Survival of Bodily Death* was in MT's library.)

Throughout his life, MT wondered whether there was anything credible about the occult, and he did some investigative reporting on the subject. Alleged mediums were common in Hannibal when he was a boy, and on his first trip to New York he wrote home about visiting "Rochester, famous on account of the 'Spirit Rappings.' "[34] There, in 1848, thirteen-year-old Margaret Fox and her younger sister claimed that spirits responded to questions regarding departed friends by causing one leg of a table on which they had placed their fingers to tap out positive or negative answers. Thus began a national craze in which devotees gathered in parlors and touched table tops while awaiting communications from the other side. While he was in California, MT reported on the performance there of a medium who sat "behind a small deal table with slender legs and no drawers" from which she claimed to receive answers to questions supplied by the audience. He allegedly had this exchange with her when inquiring about the departed: "How many Smiths are present?" "Eighteen million." "What do lost spirits call their dread abode." "The Smithsonian Institute." MT found the "queer mystery" entertaining, but nothing

---

[32]MF 184.
[33]MTL 706.
[34]SCH 90; LTR 1:4.

more.[35] The fad lost vogue when Margaret Fox, as an older adult, admitted that she had hoodwinked the simpleminded.

In 1872, MT had consulted James Mansfield in New York City in an effort to contact his brother Henry who had died years earlier after a steamboat explosion.[36] Ten years later he wrote a thinly disguised account of the experience. In the account, a medium named Manchester cleverly dispensed generalities about the happy abode of spirits and the absence of material things there. But when he asked how Henry died, Manchester revealed his ignorance by denying that he had died young in a catastrophic accident.[37]

Biographer Albert Paine has given a carefully nuanced comment on MT and spiritualism:

> Mark Twain's religion had to do chiefly with humanity in its present incarnation, and concerned itself very little with any possible measure of reward or punishment in some supposed court of the hereafter. Nevertheless, psychic investigation always interested him, and he was good-naturedly willing to explore, even hoping, perhaps, to be convinced that individuality continues beyond death.[38]

In a definitive way Alan Gribben has traced MT's interest in occult phenomena throughout his life. He concludes, "While he privately experimented again and again with the skills of those who claimed extrasensory abilities, publicly he scoffed at most practitioners and their gullible clients."[39]

Search for Healing

Psychic cures with religious overtones interested all members of the Clemens family, in part because of what had happened to Livy as a teenager after she fell and injured her back. The physicians she had consulted in Washington and New York had been unable to relieve her painful spinal paralysis. In desperation, Livy's parents two years later

---

[35]WG 122-25.
[36]LMT 5:42.
[37]LM 312-15.
[38]MTL 706.
[39]Howard Kerr, ed., *The Haunted Dusk* (Athens: University of Georgia Press, 1983) 172.

engaged the services of James Newton, a traveling healer from Rochester whom many considered a quack. Presuming that her mysterious illness was psychosomatic, Newton opened her room to light, prayed over her, raised her up, and gave her the confidence she needed to become active again. He claimed that he could also treat patients at a distance "by means of magnetized letters."[40] MT commented:

> His charge was fifteen hundred dollars and it was easily worth a hundred thousand. For from the day that she was eighteen until she was fifty-six she was always able to walk a couple of hundred yards without stopping to rest. . . . I met Newton once, in after years, and asked him what his secret was. He said he didn't know but thought perhaps some subtle form of electricity proceeded from his body and wrought the cures.[41]

Newton had apparently been influenced, along with a number of other Americans, by the dubious theory of "animal magnetism" that was proclaimed by Franz Mesmer, an Austrian physician. A century earlier, he wrote about an electric energy that penetrates bodies. To cure patients, the "mesmerist" cast a trance-like condition to effect hypnotism.

An essay entitled "Mental Telegraphy" that MT wrote in 1891 was influenced by mesmerism. He believed that the occurrence of similar ideas in different minds, at a physical distance, about the same time was too striking to be coincidental, and for years he collected numerous illustrations of the phenomena. He theorized that "the something which conveys our thoughts through the air from brain to brain is a finer and subtler form of electricity."[42]

In 1886, Susy wrote about a Hartford healer her family trusted: "I shouldn't wonder if we finally become firm believers in Mind Cure. The next time papa has a cold, I haven't a doubt he will send for 'Miss Holden' . . . to cure him of it."[43] In 1893, MT visited a mind-cure therapist to relieve a persistent cough probably related to his heavy smoking. (Of no help were the smoking regulations he had imposed on himself, namely to smoke only one cigar at a time, and never to smoke

---

[40]Alonzo Newton, ed., *The Modern Bethesda* (New York: Newton, 1897) 4, 294.

[41]AMT 184-85.

[42]CT2 42.

[43]PP 203.

when sleeping or refrain when awake!)[44] After being treated by several healers, he agreed with William James that "hypnotism and mind-cure are the same thing."[45] Later, writing Livy in Paris, he seemed to be of two minds: "Do find that Christian Scientist for Susy. . . . I tried the mind-cure out of curiosity. . . . I have coughed only two or three times since. Maybe it was the mind-cure, maybe it was the powders."[46]

When Susy was suffering from anemia and insomnia, MT also recommended that she seek therapy from someone trained by the famous French hypnotist, Dr. Charcot.[47] Who that someone was made little difference, "They do not need to be great and gifted, it is only necessary to make the other person think so—the patient's mind does the real work."[48] In 1896, while her parents were on their world tour, Susy not only received the mind-cure treatment but gave such treatment to others.[49] In a letter to her from India, MT expressed the hope that by replacing unwise ideas with healthy thoughts she would be "permanently saved from the ills which persecute life and make it a burden." About his own situation he also said:

> I am perfectly certain that the exasperating colds and the carbuncles came from a diseased mind, and that your mental science could drive them away, if we only had . . . you here to properly apply it. I have no language to say how glad and grateful I am that you are a convert to that rational and noble philosophy.[50]

MT acknowledged that he, as well as physicians and sorcerers, did not doubt "that the mind exercises a powerful influence over the body."[51] He claimed that the healing power Jesus gave his disciples was intended for any earnest Christian.[52] But it would be a mistake to interpret MT's

---

[44]CT2 715.

[45]MTL 607.

[46]LLMT 285.

[47]MTP, letter to Livy, 30 January 1894.

[48]MT's marginalia in his copy of Andrew White, *A History of the Warfare of Science with Theology* (New York: Appleton, 1898) 2:5.

[49]Caroline Harnsberger, *Mark Twain, Family Man* (New York: Citadel, 1960) 159.

[50]LLMT 316.

[51]WM 231, 241.

[52]WM 356.

endorsement of alternative healing methods as a rejection of standard medical practice. After being treated in Australia, he noted: "It is the loftiest of all human vocations—medicine and surgery. Relief from physical pain, physical distress. Next comes the pulpit, which solaces mental distress; soothes the sorrows of the soul."[53]

The Christian Science movement that originated during this period also intrigued members of the Clemens family. Housekeeper Katy Leary spoke of being with Susy in New York when she was preparing to sail for England to reunite with her family at the end of their round-the-world voyage. She was not feeling well and insisted on seeing only a Christian Scientist, but Katy brought in a medical doctor who accurately diagnosed her illness.[54] Even though Susy's interest in Christian Science may have hastened her death from meningitis, both of MT's surviving daughters continued to get nonmedical treatment for their ailments.

Given the Clemens family's experimentation with Christian Science, it is understandable that MT would investigate its leader, Mary Baker Eddy. He judged that she "is easily the most interesting person on the planet, and, in several ways, as easily the most extraordinary woman that was ever born upon it."[55] Eddy, he acknowledged, "has restored to the world neglected and abandoned features of the Christian religion which her thousands of followers find gracious and blessed and contenting."[56] As we have seen in his treatment of Joan of Arc, MT admired capable and powerful women, so his increasing disappointment with Eddy as he became better acquainted with her was not due to her sex. Also, he was positively disposed to the value of nonphysical therapies.

After studying the crude composition of the works known to be from Eddy's pen, MT became convinced that she had plagiarized Phineas Quimby writings in her principal text, *Science and Health with Key to the Scriptures*. Ever defensive of his own intellectual property rights, MT was also incensed when he detected literary theft. Soon the best-known man in New England at the beginning of the twentieth century was publicly castigating its best-known woman. MT's charge has subsequently been

---

[53]MTN 257.
[54]LMT 134.
[55]WM 394.
[56]WM 361.

confirmed and made more specific. When recovering from a spinal ailment, Eddy was a patient of Quimby, who loaned her his manuscripts that told of the treatment he called Christian Science. Without acknowledgement, she lifted some of his material and published it after his death.[57] Robert Peel, although an Eddy apologist, admits that she also engaged in "unmistakable borrowing" of paragraphs from the writings of Hugh Blair, while denouncing others for plagiarizing.[58]

MT's book entitled *Christian Science* begins with a burlesque, describing how he fell off a cliff and broke every bone. A Bostonian "widow in the third degree" (alluding to thrice-married Eddy) counsels him that cure will come when he acknowledges that his pain is imaginary. But he hears that practitioner shout out when she accidentally brushes her hand against a dress pin. While MT was convinced that the mind plays a part in healing, he did not accept Christian Science's metaphysical claim that physical matter is unreal and sickness is an illusion. He showed sympathy with Christian Science, however, by suggesting that in a perfectly constructed world, evil would not be possible. He wrote: "Evil is the crime of an immoral God. With a moral God it could not exist."[59]

Assuming that a legitimate religion should assist the poor, MT searched for, but could not find, evidence that the Christian Science "church" was making financial contributions to orphans, widows, discharged prisoners, welfare schools, and the like. Instead, the contributions from Eddy's followers were making her wealthy. He contended that she was exploiting for her own advancement the truth that faith healing is legitimate for certain illnesses. Commenting wryly, MT said that she had in effect cancelled the biblical promise that salvation comes "without price."[60] "Science and Wealth, with Key to the Fixtures," was his parody of the title of Christian Science's holy writ.[61]

----

[57]Robert Peel, *Mary Baker Eddy: The Years of Discovery* (New York: Holt, Rinehart and Winston, 1966) 183, 232.

[58]Robert Peel, *Mary Baker Eddy: The Years of Authority* (New York; Holt, Rinehart and Winston, 1977) 107.

[59]MT's marginalia in response to Anatole France; MTLB 673.

[60]WM 253-54; Isaiah 55:1.

[61]John Tuckey, ed., *Which Was the Dream?* (Berkeley: University of California Press, 1967) 491.

Eddy wrote MT to deny that she had engaged in self-promotion and "self-deification," but he demonstrated that writings attributed to her revealed just the opposite.[62] Eddy left herself open to his ridicule when she indulged in this self-glorification:

> I should blush to write of *Science and Health with Key to the Scriptures* as I have, were it of human origin, and I, apart from God, its author; but as I was only a scribe echoing the harmonies of Heaven in divine metaphysics, I cannot be supermodest of the Christian Science textbook.[63]

MT considered Eddy to be even more deluded than the pope in presuming that her main text, which he also called "the Bible-Annex," conveyed the inerrant truth of God. In his view, she had established "a sovereignty more absolute than the Roman Papacy."[64] In a futuristic romp entitled "The Secret History of Eddypus" set in the year A.M. (Anno Matriae) 1001, MT has Christian Science replacing Christianity. In this fantasy world the accepted dogma is that Eddypus Regina, who never grew old, "was caught up into heaven in a chariot of fire." Now the world worships "Mother Mary," celebrates her birth on "Eddymas" day, and studies "Eddygush," her religion, to achieve "Eddyfication."[65]

Several months before he died, when asked if he regretted having made outlandish comments about the revered founder of Christian Science, MT replied that

> Christian Science is valuable; that it has just the same value now that it had when Mrs. Eddy stole it from Quimby; that its healing principle (its most valuable asset) possesses the same force now that it possessed a million years before Quimby was born; that Mrs. Eddy the fraud, the humbug, *organized* that force and is entitled to high credit for that. . . . She has no more intellect than a tadpole—until it comes to *business*—then she is a marvel![66]

Howells found it difficult to say whether MT's "disgust for the illiterate twaddle of Mrs. Eddy's book, or his admiration of her genius for

---

[62]WM 382.
[63]WM 285.
[64]WM 313, 388.
[65]FM 325, 332.
[66]Bernard DeVoto, ed., *The Portable Mark Twain* (New York: Viking, 1946) 786.

organization was the greater."[67] He had written Howells, "If Mrs. Eddy would try martyrdom, it would make her cult permanent; and besides, I would be her friend."[68] Elsewhere he wrote, "The Crucifixion did not make a hundredth part of the stir that the death of Mrs. Eddy would create today."[69] Actually, she and MT died the same year, but she had surpassed him in wealth from book sales. Eddy stimulated MT to do some light theologizing, "When we contemplate her and what she had achieved, it is blasphemy to longer deny to the Supreme Being the possession of a sense of humor."[70] To Twichell, he wrote: "Somehow I continue to feel sure of that cult's colossal future. . . . I am selling my Lourdes stock already and buying Christian Science trust. I regard it as the Standard Oil of the future."[71] Believing as he did that humans were motivated to seek personal happiness and relief from pain, and that hypochondria was common, he understood that Christian Science filled a strong human craving. Ironically, perhaps partly due to his criticisms, Christian Science suffered a decline in membership through much of the twentieth century and has not tyrannized American culture as he had predicted.

Osteopathy, another therapeutic treatment that had become legalized in America at the turn of the twentieth century, interested MT because of its holistic emphasis on the interrelationship of all bodily systems. It was started in his home state by Dr. Andrew Still, who established the first osteopathic college in 1892. MT asserted: "No art of healing is best for all ills. I should distribute the ailments around: surgery cases to the surgeons; . . . nervous prostration to the Christian Scientist; . . . (in my own particular case) rheumatism, gout, and bronchial attacks to the osteopathist."[72] The Clemens family went to Sweden in 1899 to receive treatment from a noted osteopath named Heinrick Kellgren. Livy was cured of a respiratory illness by Kellgren's nonpharmacological method, and Jean received treatment. MT concluded that osteopaths "actually do several of

---

[67]William Dean Howells, *My Mark Twain* (New York: Harper, 1910) 84.
[68]MTHL 849.
[69]MT's marginalia in his copy of Suetonius, *Lives*; MTLB 676.
[70]MTP, letter to Mr. Day, 21 March 1901.
[71]MTB 1076.
[72]MTL 733.

the things the Christian Scientists pretend to do,"[73] and he persuaded William James to try Kellgren's treatment for his heart condition.[74]

In 1901, MT spoke at a committee meeting of New York's General Assembly against a bill that would ban osteopaths as well as Christian Science practitioners. The bill was supported by licensed physicians who, in his opinion, were motivated by self-interest to exclude practitioners of alternative medicine from their state-protected monopoly. He found drug-administering physicians so biased that "to ask a doctor's opinion of osteopathy is equivalent to going to Satan for information about Christianity."[75] To the legislators, he testified:

> When my soul is sick, unlimited spiritual liberty is given me by the state. Now then, it doesn't seem logical that the state shall depart from this great policy, the health of the soul, and change about and take the other position in the matter of smaller consequence—the health of the body. . . . One day my father took me to my uncle's house and he had a picture on the wall of a room showing Christ disputing with the doctors. [According to Luke 2:46, the boy Jesus sat "in the midst of the doctors" to learn about Judaism.] Now, although I was the model Sunday school boy of our section, I couldn't quite understand that. . . . There was an old slave in the house, Uncle Ben by name. . . . I thought perhaps Uncle Ben might be able to enlighten me, for he was a sort of doctor himself, a herb doctor, unlicensed, of course. "Uncle Ben," I asked him, "what does that picture mean? Christ surely didn't begin the dispute, did He?" "Naw, the doctors, they begin it," he said, . . . " 'cause he ain't got no license, dat's why dey say He bust dem up in business." That is it. The objection is, people are curing people without a license and you are afraid it will bust up business.[76]

Bittersweet Last Years

MT's curiosity about various types of therapy was in large part due to his anguish over his wife's persistent debilitation. Livy received osteopathic treatment for a "nervous breakdown" during her last years, but she remained an invalid, bedridden and in pain. Two years before she died he

---

[73]MTL 683, 693.
[74]Jason Horn, *Mark Twain and William James* (Columbia: University of Missouri Press, 1996) 167.
[75]MTN 344.
[76]MTS 386-87.

wrote to Howells, "Life is purgatory at all times— . . . yesterday it was hell."[77] Again MT was tortured by his guilty conscience, believing that he had caused Livy's illness by criticizing her religious faith. Shortly before her death, he sent her this note: "It so grieves me to remember that I am the cause of your being where you are. . . . I drove you to sorrow and heart-break just to hear myself talk. If ever I do it again when you get well I hope the punishment will fall upon me the guilty, not upon you the innocent."[78]

In the winter of 1904 the Clemens family lived in Italy, hoping desperately that its climate would improve Livy's health. MT temporarily lost his own psychic balance during this and other despairing times. His life was centered in his family and he could not bear to watch them suffer. He described his own manic depressive state, "Periodical and sudden changes of mood in me, from deep melancholy to half-insane tempests and cyclones of humor, are among the curiosities of my life."[79] In the last weeks of Livy's life, MT wrote the ending to his bleak "Mysterious Stranger" novel.[80] There, the son of Satan, referred to as "Number Forty-four," declares solipsistically:

> There is no God, no universe, no human race, no earthly life, no heaven, no hell. It is all a Dream—a grotesque and foolish dream. Nothing exists but You. And You are but a *Thought*—a vagrant Thought, a useless Thought, a homeless Thought, wandering forlorn among the empty eternities"[81]

Words of that novel voice MT's feelings then:

> This decaying vile matter . . . in which my spirit is imprisoned. . . . Oh, this human life, this earthly life, this weary life! It is so groveling, and so mean; its ambitions are so paltry, its prides so trivial, its vanities so childish and the glories that it values and applauds—lord, how empty![82]

While in Italy, MT wrote Twichell that for "a *part* of each day" he believed that

---

[77]MTHL 745.
[78]MF 251.
[79]MTE 251.
[80]MSM 11.
[81]MSM 405.
[82]MSM 369.

there is no God and no universe; that there is only empty space, and in it a lost and homeless and wandering and companionless and indestructible *Thought*. And that I am that Thought. . . . I suppose this idea has become a part of me because I have been living in it so long—seven years—and in that time have written so long a story embodying it and developing it in a book which is not finished and is not intended for print.[83]

MT reported Livy's last words before her death in Italy: "I went to the piano and sang the old songs, the quaint negro hymns. . . . I brought up little by little the forgotten words of many songs. . . . She had heard me and had said to the nurse, 'He is singing a good-night carol for me.' "[84] Lines from "Steal Away to Jesus," a spiritual that MT sang then, were prophetic:

> My Lord He call me!
> He call me by the thunder!
> The trumpet sounds with inna my soul!
> I ain't got long to stay here.

(Ken Burns, while claiming to have researched carefully MT's life for his television series, disregarded the plaintive rhythms that meant the most to him throughout his life. Burns excluded spirituals that came out of the sufferings of Southern blacks in the continual background music of that production.)

In Elmira, Twichell officiated at Livy's final rites. From Robert Browning, the Clemenses' favorite poet, he read about love that would never die. Then he read the last stanza of Cardinal Newman's "Lead, Kindly Light":

> So long that power hath blessed me, sure it still
>   Will lead me on;
> O'er moor and fen; o'er crag and torrent, till
>   The night is gone;
> And with the morn, their angel faces smile,
> Which I have loved long since, and lost awhile!

---

[83]Letter from MT to Joseph Twichell, 28 July 1904, Beinecke Library, Yale University.

[84]AMT 344-45.

MT noted poignantly: "Funeral private in the house of Livy's young maidenhood. Where she stood as a bride 34 years ago there her coffin rested; and over it the same voice that had made her a wife then committed her spirit to God now." MT had a German epitaph engraved on the tombstone over her remains. Translated, the epitaph reads, "God be gracious, oh my delight!"[85] Heartbroken, MT wrote to Charles Langdon: "I am a man without a country. Wherever Livy was, that was my country."[86] At that time he gave this cameo depiction, "She was always frail in body and she lived upon her spirit, whose hopefulness and courage were indestructible."[87]

MT's connubial bond to his only true love was not just "till death do us part," but "for time and eternity."[88] Before his wedding, he had written Livy:

> We shall never be separated on earth, Livy; and let us pray that we may not in Heaven. . . . [Marriage] makes of two fractional lives a whole; it gives to two purposeless lives a work, and doubles the strength of each whereby to perform it; . . . it will give a new revelation to love, a new depth to sorrow, a new impulse to worship.[89]

What MT affirmed in his prenuptial love letters, William Pellowe points out,

> was more than the temporary experience pouring into words of honeyed sentimentality—it expressed toward the woman of his heart the attitude that was forever a part of himself. No lover was ever more constant than America's greatest humorist, and it is noteworthy that throughout his writings never did he make jest of honest love between husband and wife.[90]

Much of MT's religion is related to marriage, for he found in marital love qualities that abide forever. He wrote, "Love seems the swiftest but is the slowest of all growths. No man and woman really know what perfect love is until they have been married a quarter of a century."[91]

---

[85]MTB 1222-23.
[86]MTLB 285.
[87]AMT 183.
[88]LTR 3:209.
[89]LTR 3:348.
[90]PH 111.
[91]MTMW 156.

Three decades after his wedding, he made this declaration to someone about to enter the estate of matrimony: "There is nothing in the world that approaches it: . . . a heaven of love, and soft peace and contentment, and serenity. . . . We who have our home in this divine far country, spread wide its hospitable gates to you and say out of heart and mouth, enter in; ye are welcome!"[92]

MT never tired of writing about his love for Livy: "True love is the only heart disease that is best left to 'run on'—the only affection of the heart for which there is no help, and none desired."[93] Shortly after Livy's death he expressed the measure of his love, "What little good was in me I gave to her to the utmost—full measure, the last grain and the last ounce—and poor as it was it was my very best, and far beyond anything I could have given to any other person that ever lived."[94] Of his total devotion to Livy "in sickness and in health," illness claimed the larger portion.

Writing to a groom several years after Livy's death, MT remarked:

> Marriage—yes it is the supreme felicity of life, I concede it. And it is also the supreme tragedy of life. The deeper the love the surer the tragedy. . . . I grieve for you . . . not for the one that shall go first, but for the one that is fated to be left behind. . . . You must consider what I have been through, and am passing through and be charitable with me.[95]

MT's only two siblings to survive to adulthood, who had depended on their brother's generosity over the years, died around the turn of the century. From the age of twenty-eight Pamela had been a widow, and he called her a lifelong invalid. Her talented son Sam, MT's only nephew, also predeceased his uncle in 1908. Orion, who had received much psychological as well as financial support over the years from his younger brother, died in 1897. He and his wife Mollie, who died seven years later, were buried in Mt. Olivet Cemetery in Hannibal alongside Orion's parents and his youngest brother, Henry. MT referred to Orion's death as "his release from the captivity of a long and troubled and pathetic and

[92]MF 237.
[93]MTN 371.
[94]MTCW 16.
[95]MTL 811.

unprofitable life."[96] Just before his death, Orion described to his brother how he planned to write about Judas of Galilee, the leader of a radical Palestinian sect located at a monastery along the Dead Sea. "I imagine those Essenes to have been Buddhists established there about 150 B.C.," Orion wrote; "their secret was the Buddhist worship, as now seen in Roman Catholic Churches."[97] After his brother's death, MT summed up his character: "He was always truthful; he was always sincere; he was always honest and honorable. But in light matters—matters of small consequence, like religion and politics and such things—he never acquired a conviction that could survive a disapproving remark from a cat."[98]

§ § §

In the last decade of his life, MT continued to have clergy friends. Pertaining to his closest companions, Twichell and Livy, he affirmed, "What I am I owe to them."[99] Twichell, writing to MT before his return from Italy after Livy's death, maintained "that for one tempest-tossed in these wide weltering seas there is an Anchorage." Were he at MT's side, he said, "May be, Mark, we would kneel together once in a while, as we have done in times past. Really, it seems to me, that is the posture for a man to take in the midst of these unfathomable realities."[100]

At one birthday party, among the many old friends present, MT singled out his friend from Hartford, where he had lived longer than in any other place: "For five-and-twenty years I was under the Rev. Mr. Twichell's tuition. I was in his pastorate, occupying a pew in his church, and held him in due reverence. That man is full of all the graces that go to make a person companionable and beloved."[101] When Twichell sprained his shoulder shortly before that party, MT teased him as he had in their younger days. Years before, after a church service, MT had commented, "Joe, that's a clever trick of yours to pound the pulpit extra hard when you haven't anything to say." Twichell laughed and replied,

---

[96]AMT 224.
[97]MTP, letter from Orion Clemens to MT, 30 November 1897.
[98]AMT 86.
[99]LLMT 341.
[100]JHT 106-107.
[101]MTS 458.

"Mark, it was clever of you to discover it."[102] So after the old preacher injured his shoulder, MT reminded him that he had once admitted to throwing "artificial power and impressiveness into places . . . by banging the Bible." Claiming that such rigorous arm action was the cause of the sprain, MT cautioned: "You have reached a time of life when it is not wise to take these risks. You would better jump around. We all have to change our methods as the infirmities of age creep upon us."[103]

Paine reported on an occasion in 1902 when MT and Twichell had "one of their regular arguments on theology and the moral accountability of the human race, arguments that had been going on between them for more than thirty years."[104] At this time the issue was the doctrine of strict Calvinism that posited God as the predeterminer of human motivation. Stirred by his reading of Jonathan Edwards's *Freedom of the Will*, MT commented:

> Jonathan seems to hold (as against the Arminian position) that the Man (or his Soul or his Will) never creates an impulse itself, but is moved to action by an impulse back of it. That's sound! Also, that of two or more things offered it, it infallibly chooses the one which for the moment is most pleasing to ITSELF. Perfectly correct!

While he found some of Edwards's determinism acceptable, MT judged him to be "a resplendent intellect gone mad." MT said: "In the last part of the book what I take to be Calvinism and its God begins to show up and shine red and hideous in the glow from the fires of hell, their only right and proper adornment. By God I was ashamed to be in such company."[105] Elsewhere he scorned what he understood to be another aspect of Calvinistic theology: "The halls of heaven are warmed by registers connected with hell; and this is greatly applauded by Jonathan Edwards, Calvin, Baxter, and Company, because it adds a new pang to the sinner's sufferings to know that the very fire which tortures him is the means of making the righteous comfortable."[106]

---

[102]MF 26.
[103]MTL 728.
[104]MTL 719.
[105]MTL 720.
[106]MTB 751.

Twichell twitted MT by accusing him of "getting quite orthodox, on the doctrine of Total Human Depravity anyway."[107] MT had written from Vienna:

> I have been reading the morning paper . . . well knowing that I shall find in it the usual depravities and basenesses and hypocrisies and cruelties that make up civilization, and cause me to put in the rest of the day pleading for the damnation of the human race. I cannot seem to get my prayers answered, yet I do not despair.[108]

When MT informed Twichell that he hoped to be cremated, his impish friend replied, "I wouldn't worry about that, if I had your chances."[109] MT also continued to twitch Twichell, remarking in the last year of his life, "When you are on fire with theology . . . you'll write it to Twichell, because it would make him writhe and squirm and break the furniture."[110] Yet, during his last years, he spoke of him as "my oldest friend—and dearest enemy on occasion—the Rev. Joseph Twichell, my pastor."[111] (Again, in Ken Burns four-hour documentary on MT, this important companionship is given no attention, wrongly suggesting that MT's religious interests can be overlooked by those interested in comprehending his life.)

MT also enjoyed the company of some other Christian ministers he had not met until the twentieth century. While the Clemenses were in Italy, they received the pastoral services of a local Catholic church. MT spoke of "my priest—we are very fond of him. He is a sterling man, and is also learnedly scientific."[112] The priest may have found this relationship of special interest because MT had arranged for the publication of *The Life of Pope Leo XIII* (whose long reign had just ended) by the Charles Webster Company. Named for MT's nephew and manager, the book company had obtained the pontiff's permission to publish his biography, which eventually came out in six languages.

---

[107]Hill 25.
[108]MTL 678.
[109]LM 286.
[110]MTHL 845.
[111]CT2 814.
[112]MTL 753.

In his last trips to London, MT also became friendly with Albert Wilberforce, archdeacon of Westminster Abbey. MT's only problem with him was his gullibility in believing that a recently excavated piece of pottery adorned with flower figures, which he showed MT, was the cup that Jesus had used at the Last Supper. MT said that he would not believe it was the Holy Grail "even if I had gotten it from the twelve apostles in writing, with every signature vouched for by a notary public."[113]

A mutual friendship also developed between MT and several New York City ministers. One was Henry Potter, an Episcopal bishop, who was noted for his social reforms. At a St. Nicholas Society banquet, a Scottish Congregational minister named Donald Mackay, spoke of the similarity between the "genial religion" of St. Nicholas and MT, both of whom were noted for lovingly assisting the needy. Mackay said, "There is a gospel in a smile and in my opinion a man like Mark Twain is as much a preacher of righteousness in this world today as any consecrated bishop, priest, or minister." With a twinkle, MT thanked Mackay "for discovering things in me which I had long before discovered, but which I had begun to fear the world at large would never find out."[114]

Still another friend of MT was Henry Van Dyke, who had fought against political corruption while he was the pastor of New York's Brick Presbyterian Church, and against strict Calvinism while he held the highest elected office of his denomination. Noted for his "Story of the Other Wise Man," and for composing "Joyful, Joyful, We Adore Thee" to fit Beethoven's "Hymn to Joy" melody, he became professor of English at Princeton University in 1900. "I like Van Dyke, and I greatly admire his literary style," said MT, who possessed a number of his "delicious books."[115] Van Dyke's Lyman Beecher Lectures on Preaching at Yale (1896), published as *The Gospel for an Age of Doubt*, dealt with scientific discoveries, determinism, and spiritualism, topics that interested MT. Also, both fought against American imperialism in the Philippines. At a birthday dinner, Van Dyke gave a toast to MT that ended,

> Like the Phoenix, he survives,
> The fires that wreck less noble lives. . . .

---

[113]MTE 342.
[114]*New York Times*, 7 December 1900.
[115]MTLB 722.

And may you keep, at sixty-seven,
The joy of earth, the hope of heaven, . . .
And faith that fights the battle through.[116]

After visiting MT, Methodist minister Fred Adams preached on the biblical text, "Take Mark, and bring him with thee: for he is profitable to me for the ministry."[117] In the sermon, he compared Saint Mark and MT, ministers to humanity, characterizing the latter as "a fearless knight of righteousness."[118] Adams reported that MT "long desired to write a Life of Christ, and only desisted for fear of an entire misunderstanding on the part of the public."[119]

"What was there about Twain that made so many renowned clergymen interested in him?" Pellowe, who raised that question, answered it in this way: "They perceived the sterling worth of a seeker after truth. . . . In the weightier things of justice, good government, intelligent living, and progressive thought, Mark Twain and these clergymen were kindred spirits."[120]

The personal interactions of the elderly MT testify that he was not overwhelmed by family tragedies and continued to be a social activist. While he still had doubts about the goodness of God and of humans, he did not completely lose confidence in either. "I am a moralist in disguise," he wrote in 1902; "it gets me into heaps of trouble when I go thrashing around in political questions."[121] His recognition of the persistence of evil did not prevent him from lending his continued support to a variety of humanitarian causes. Arthur Scott observes:

> In spite of the theoretical pessimism of his late years, Mark Twain's feeling for his fellow man remained one of deep compassion. In practice he could not seem to remember his theory that the human race was too degenerate to be worth saving. He would damn it, then turn around and fight to save it wherever it was in deepest trouble.[122]

---

[116]*Harper's Weekly* (13 December 1902).

[117]2 Timothy 4:11.

[118]MTB 1527.

[119]Fred Adams, "Mark Twain as Preacher," *Methodist Review* (July 1911): 565.

[120]PH 117.

[121]MTL 719.

[122]MTAL 304.

Occasionally MT associated the opposite terms optimism and pessimism with various stages of his life. When he was forty-eight, he wrote, "The man who is a pessimist before he is forty-eight knows too much; the man who is an optimist after he is forty-eight knows too little."[123] Later, he added: "At fifty a man can be an ass without being an optimist, but not an optimist without being an ass"; and "There is no sadder sight than a young pessimist, except an old optimist."[124] Yet, in the last decade of his life, he realized that he had been inaccurate in classifying himself exclusively as a pessimist. He wrote Rev. L. M. Powers: "No man is born either pessimist wholly or optimist wholly; perhaps he is pessimistic along certain lines and optimistic along certain others. That is my case."[125] Optimism was too closely akin to complacency, and pessimism to resignation, for him to devote himself to either.

MT might have more accurately described himself as a meliorist (from the Latin, literally, "better-ist"), as William James called himself, rather than a pessimist ("worst-ist") or an optimist ("best-ist"). Helen Keller wisely discerned that MT was mistaken when he called himself a pessimist, for a pessimist would not, as he did, have exerted leadership in enabling the blind to break down barriers and become productive citizens.[126] As a meliorist he did not consider any situation either so bad or so good that it could not be improved. Ever a reformer, he fulminated against the forces seeking to block the achievement of the international democratic community he envisioned.

In 1902, MT took the opportunity to return to Hannibal for his last hurrah, and the townspeople gave MT an emotional reception at the Presbyterian church. After that occasion, he reminisced: "Often in those days I desired earnestly to stand in that Presbyterian pulpit and give instruction—but I was never asked until today. My ambition of two generations ago has been satisfied at last."[127] Accompanied by his boyhood sweetheart Laura Hawkins he also attended the Baptist church.

---

[123]MTB 744.

[124]CT2 941, 946.

[125]MTL 785.

[126]MTA 2:302.

[127]Quoted in C. J. Armstrong, "Sam Clemens Considered Becoming a Preacher," *The Twainian* (May 1945): 1.

The pastor invited him into the pulpit, "not to preach a sermon but to say a few words." MT responded:

> What I say will be preaching. I am a preacher. We all are preachers. If we do not preach by words, we preach by deeds. . . . Words perish, print burns up, men die, but our preaching lives on. Washington died in 1799, more than a hundred years ago, but his preaching survives, and to every people that is

The Hannibal Presbyterian Church,
still in use, where MT spoke in 1902.
In the steeple is the bell from a sunken
steamboat that he often heard ring.

striving for liberty his life is a sermon. My mother lies buried out there in our beautiful cemetery overlooking the Mississippi, but at this age of mine, she still cheers me. Her preaching lives and goes on with me. Let us see that our preaching is of the right sort, so that it will influence for good the lives of those who remain when we shall be silent in our graves.[128]

As he retraced the roads he had often traveled as a youth, he imagined that he was carrying a spiritual message to those he visited. In St. Louis, Rev. Joseph Newton reported that MT said "he wanted to preach a sermon, since he was as reverend as anybody." MT told about the time St. Francis had asked a brother to go with him into town to preach. Members of the community witnessed the joyful companionship of the friars as they walked through town and back to the monastery. Then the brother asked, "But are we not going to preach today?" Francis said, "We have preached. We have been happy in the love of God and the glory of His sunlight—that is our sermon for the day."[129]

MT admitted, "I, like all other human beings expose to the world only my trimmed and perfumed and carefully barbered public opinions and conceal carefully, cautiously, wisely, my private ones."[130] Two pieces that he may have written on the same day reflect the spirits at war in his aging body. He concluded a birthday commemoration speech by saying:

> I am seventy; seventy, and would nestle in the chimney corner, and smoke my pipe, and read my book, and take my rest, wishing you well in all affection, and that when you in your turn shall arrive at pier No. 70 you may step aboard your waiting ship with a reconciled spirit, and lay your course toward the sinking sun with a contented heart.[131]

Contrast those tranquil remarks intended for public consumption with his unpublished musing at the "troubled and foreboding" beginning of his eighth decade:

> Old Age, white-headed, the temple empty, the idols broken, the worshippers in their graves, nothing left but You, a remnant, a tradition, belated fag-end of a foolish dream, a dream that was so ingeniously dreamed that it seemed real all the time; nothing left but You, center of a snowy desolation, perched

---

[128]*St. Louis Post-Dispatch*, 2 June 1902, 5.
[129]Quoted in Joseph Newton, *River of Years* (Philadelphia: Lippincott, 1946) 89-90.
[130]MTE 317.
[131]CT2 718.

on the ice-summit, gazing out over the stages of that long *trek* and asking Yourself "Would you do it again if you had the chance?"[132]

That description bears a remarkable resemblance to the one given in Ecclesiastes of a hoary-headed oldster who exemplifies the emptiness of life.[133]

During the last four years of MT's life, Paine became his biographer, confidant, and helper. Because MT did not own a home or have family members living with him for some of that time, he relished Paine's companionship, including their frequent billiard games. MT's Hartford home, always a welcome haven after his travels, had been sold because it was haunted by Susy's spirit, and his last home on the outskirts of Redding, Connecticut, was still under construction. Paine described how family suffering and overwhelming loss had affected MT's mood, "One saw the jester, who for forty years had been making the world laugh, performing always before a background of tragedy."[134] A Christmas greeting reflected his bitterness, "Merry Christmas to you, and I wish to God I could have one myself before I die."[135] MT's Boswell also told about an adoring woman who exclaimed: "How God must love you." "I hope so," he replied. After she left, he commented, "I guess she hasn't heard of our strained relations."[136]

MT's bittersweet attitude toward life and religion is mirrored in the lines of a blues spiritual he liked to sing, "Sometimes I'm up, sometimes I'm down, . . . sometimes I'm almost in the ground, oh yes, Lord." Paine commented:

Mark Twain had many moods, and he did not always approve of his own God; but when he altered his conception, it was likely to be in the direction of enlargement. . . . His belief in God, the Creator, was absolute. . . . Mark Twain's God was of colossal proportions—so vast, indeed, that the constellated stars were but molecules in His veins.[137]

---

[132]CT2 719.
[133]Ecclesiastes 12:1-8.
[134]MTB 1300.
[135]MTB 901.
[136]MTB 1292.
[137]MTB 1582.

Reporting in 1908 on activities at his new home, named Stormfield after daughter Clara objected to Innocence at Home, MT said: "I've grown young in these months of dissipation here. And I have left off drinking—it isn't necessary now. Society and theology are sufficient for me." He initiated theological discussion with Paine and reread *A History of the Warfare of Science with Theology in Christendom*,[138] one of his favorite books.

MT's religious views feature significantly in Paine's multivolumed official biography as well as in many of the letters and notebook entries Paine edited. MT confided to Paine that there was no scientific evidence for a future life, but added, "and yet—I am strongly inclined to expect one."[139] Paine summarized MT's faith:

Mark Twain's religion was a faith too wide for doctrines—a benevolence too limitless for creeds. From the beginning he strove against oppression, sham, and evil in every form. He despised meanness; he resented with every drop of blood in him anything that savored of persecution or a curtailment of human liberties. It was a religion identified with his daily life and his work.[140]

During a week in 1906 when MT was despairing, he dictated his "Reflections on Religion"—fleeting ideas and rambling judgments at odds with viewpoints he generally held. He talked about the Creator's "all-comprehensive malice which could patiently descend to the contriving of elaborate tortures for the meanest and pitifulest of the countless kinds of creatures that were to inhabit the earth."[141] Also, he wrongly held Jesus responsible for "inventing a lake of fire and brimstone in which all of us who fail to recognize and worship Him as God are to be burned through all eternity."[142] Moreover, "it is exceedingly likely that there will be a Hell—and it is nearly dead certain that nobody is going to escape it."[143] And again: "Man is a machine and God made it. . . . God alone is

[138]MTB 1470, 1481-83, 1539.
[139]MTB 1431.
[140]MTB 1584.
[141]BMT 325.
[142]BMT 321.
[143]BMT 329.

responsible for every act and word of a human being's life between cradle and grave."[144]

When this bizarre profanity was completed, MT wrote Howells: "I have been dictating some fearful things. . . . I got them out of my system, where they have been festering for years. . . . I feel better now." He warned that his heirs would be burnt alive if this venom against a malevolent deity was released before 2006. Expecting these thoughts to cause a stir even then, he warned, "I shall be hovering around taking notice, along with other dead pals."[145] Clara, MT's sole direct descendant, suppressed his "Reflections" throughout her lifetime. Since there were no heirs left after her death in 1962, they were published by Charles Neider, who comments: "If read superficially they may seem savagely irreverent, yet they are the work of a profoundly religious man. . . . He complains that man's concept of God is a shoddy one, stemming from man's own shortcoming, and that man is presumptuous in thinking he has an inside track with God."[146]

Clara became a devout Christian Scientist and, late in life, she wrote a book about her faith. In it, she testified that her father, when serious, was positive even toward Eddy, calling her "a benefactor to suffering humans." "My father was not a scoffer at the Christian Science religion," she claimed.[147]

Jean's epilepsy, combined with illnesses of his own and of Clara, prompted this outcry: "I cannot think why God, in a moment of idle and unintelligent fooling, invented this bastard human race; and why, after inventing it, he chose to make each individual of it a nest of disgusting and unnecessary diseases, a tub of rotten offal."[148] Of his daughter Jean, he wrote, "She is heavily afflicted by that unearned, undeserved, and hellish disease."[149] Isabel Lyon, a secretary to MT, recorded his reaction to news that Jean's seizures had recurred, "With that fiercest of all his looks in his face, he blazed out against the swindle of life and the

---

[144]BMT 330.

[145]MTHL 811, 815

[146]OMT 2.

[147]Clara Samossoud, *Awake to a Perfect Day* (New York: Citadel, 1956) 16.

[148]Hill 9.

[149]LLMT 331.

treachery of a God that can create disease and misery and crime—create things that men would be condemned for creating."[150]

Jean's love of domestic animals motivated her father to write a short story narrated by a dog named Aileen Mavourneen. Calling herself a Presbyterian, Aileen attends "a dogmatic gathering," where she trots out big words—such as "supererogation"—that she picked up in the house where she lives. She had learned from her mother and from accompanying children to Sunday school that in times of danger whe was supposed to risk her life to help others, even though she, like other animals, will not be rewarded "in another world." When the nursery catches on fire, Aileen drags her master's baby to safety. Initially misunderstanding what happened, he beats her, crippling her for life. Later he marvels that whereas it is intelligence that makes humans privileged to have life after death, some of them have "less of it than this poor silly quadruped that's foreordained to perish."[151] Here MT alluded satirically to the words a psalmist who asserted that "God will redeem my soul from the power of the grave" since humans are not "like the beasts that perish."[152]

On the eve of MT's last Christmas, Jean became the fifth member of his family younger than himself to die. (His three children who predeceased him lived to an average age of eighteen.) Jean drowned during an epileptic seizure while taking a bath. He described her wrenching death but noted that afterward her face had "the Peace of God upon it." His autobiography concluded with "God rest her sweet spirit!"[153] Although he was too infirm to go to Elmira for her burial, he provided an inscription for her headstone; the last line is adapted from Shakespeare:

A most dear daughter
Her desolate father sets this stone
After life's fitful fever she sleeps well.[154]

MT told his housekeeper, "Oh Katy! She's in heaven with her mother." Katy, an Irish-American Catholic, knew MT well, in part because she had daily washed his hair for many years. Although they had

---

[150]FM 125.
[151]CT2 561-71.
[152]Psalm 49:15, 20.
[153]AMT 379-80.
[154]Shakespeare, *Macbeth* 3.2.23.

serious arguments about religion, she concluded that they had the same basic belief in God. She said, "I am sure he believed in the hereafter."[155] Louis Budd, a top Twainian scholar, notes that MT's religious inconsistency increased during his last years—that after his statements of unbelief he "kept adding to the confusion with occasional statements of faith."[156]

Jean's death was in some sense a relief to her father. He knew he was slowly dying of heart failure and feared there would be no one left to take care of her. Clara had recently married and was living in Europe. He referred to his youngest daughter's death as "Jean's emancipation—the only kindness God ever did that poor unoffending child in all her hard life."[157] Two weeks after her death, he held up his cigar and asserted pathetically: "This is my only companion and solace. It is about all I care for now, and I have been warned about making it too constant a companion. I detest the idea of shaking him though, for he and myself have been companions such a long time."[158]

On a visit to London in 1897, MT had been reminded of his own mortality when a foreign correspondent for a New York newspaper filed a story about his death. MT provided the press with this correction, "The report of my death was an exaggeration." From then on he requested ante-mortem obituaries of himself so that he could make corrections—"striking out such clauses as could have a deleterious influence on the other side, and replacing them with clauses of a more judicious character." One of the many responses that especially pleased him was this, "Mark Twain was the only man who ever lived, so far as we know, whose lies were so innocent, and withal so helpful, as to make them worth more than a whole lot of fossilized priests' eternal truths."[159]

Some of MT's religious expressions during the last month of his life typically mix the light and the serious. He sent a letter to a Missouri cousin to acknowledge that prayer helps the recipient, even if no divine assistance is forthcoming. He wrote, "I am grateful for the prayer of those nuns, and for yours; they have already answered themselves in giving me

---

[155]LMT 69-70.
[156]MTSP 188, 207-208.
[157]MTL 838.
[158]*New York World*, 6 January 1910.
[159]MTB 1154-55.

a deep pleasure."[160] Like the smile on the Cheshire cat, his humor was the last thing to go. Perhaps thinking of himself, MT in his last illness advised Paine on "Etiquette for the Afterlife":

> Upon arrival in heaven do not speak to St. Peter until spoken to. . . . Avoid *over*-dressing. A pair of spurs and a fig-leaf is a plenty. Do not try to Kodak him. Hell is full of people who have made that mistake. . . . If you get in don't tip him. That is, publicly.

A more serious part of what he wrote Paine referred once again to the doctrine of the damnation of unbaptized infants that MT presumed some Christians held. Sharing his compassion for the innocent and his contempt for the self-righteous, he counseled Paine that when he leans over the heavenly balusters and sees roasting children he should

> let on to enjoy it; otherwise people will suspect you are not as good a Christian as you look. . . . You will be wanting to slip down at night and smuggle water to those poor little chaps, but don't you try it. You would be caught, and nobody in heaven would respect you after that.[161]

MT is expressing again his disgust at a notion he wrongly thought was part of Presbyterian as well as Catholic theology. Thomas Aquinas, in his medieval summary of Catholic theology, had written about the inhabitants of heaven gazing down at those being tortured in hell: "In order that the happiness of the saints may be more delightful to them and that they may render more copious thanks to God for it, they are allowed to see perfectly the sufferings of the damned."[162]

Clara returned from Europe to be with her dying father. She recorded what she claimed were his last words before he lapsed into a coma, "He opened his eyes, took my hand, and looked steadily into my face. Faintly he murmured, 'Goodbye dear, if we meet—' "[163] He had not taken his own advice on the subject of last words. Forty years earlier he had asserted that a person should write out in advance words of importance for his finale and never "trust to an intellectual spur at the last moment

---

[160]Quoted in Cyril Clemens, "Mark Twain's Religion," *Commonweal* (28 December 1934): 255.

[161]BMT 208-09.

[162]Thomas Aquinas, *Summa Theologica* 3 (supplement): q. 94.1.

[163]MF 291.

to enable him to say something smart with his latest gasp and launch into eternity with grandeur."[164]

Although MT had not written his own obituary or rehearsed his death-bed farewell, he was fully reconciled to dying. He had earlier jotted down, "Death—the only immortal who treats us all alike, whose pity and whose peace and whose refuge are for all—the soiled and the pure—the rich and the poor—the loved and the unloved."[165] When he had visited a Moravian cemetery where all gravemarkers were the same size, he was impressed by "this absolute simplicity, this entire and complete acceptation of Death as a great Leveler—a King, before whose tremendous majesty, shades and differences in littleness cannot be discerned."[166]

Ever spoofing the doctrine of special Providence, MT predicted the time of his death a year before it happened: "I came in with Halley's comet in 1835. It is coming again next year, and I expect to go out with it. . . . The Almighty had said, no doubt, 'Now here are these two unaccountable freaks; they came in together, they must go out together.' Oh! I am looking forward to that."[167] Almost as though God were participating in MT's final joke, he died with the setting sun, when the comet, which had circled around the sun, was beginning to be sighted by earthlings in the night sky of the northern hemisphere.

In his last years of life, MT attracted public attention by wearing white clothing in the winter as well as in the summer. This became not only a hallmark of individuality but also a way of mocking self-righteous-ness. He told reporters that wearing white showed he was a member of the Purity League. "I'm the only one in it," he bragged; "In fact, I'm the only one eligible!"[168] On another occasion he said, "I go out very frequently and exhibit my clothes; Howells has dubbed me the 'Whited Sepulchre.' "[169] Ironically, that biblical expression became literally descriptive of MT's boxed remains. Thousands of mourners saw a

---

[164]CT1 315.

[165]MTN 398.

[166]MF 50.

[167]MTB 1511. To celebrate the sesquicentennial of MT's birth, the United States Post Office issued in 1985 an aerogramme that, in sketches on the cover, associated him with Halley's comet.

[168](London) *Leader*, 19 June 1907.

[169]MF 268.

dazzling white leonine mane, moustache, shirt, tie, and cashmere suit neatly covering what was "full of dead bones."[170]

MT's funeral was conducted by his friends Twichell and Van Dyke at the Brick Presbyterian Church in Manhatten.[171] It was the third time within a few months that Twichell had served at a Clemens ceremony. Earlier at MT's Stormfield villa he had officiated at Clara's marriage and at Jean's funeral. Now, overwhelmed with grief, Twichell prayed "in broken-hearted supplication."[172] After the funeral he wrote this about MT: "Along with his penetrating insight of the weaknesses of humanity went an equally keen appreciation of its nobler aspects and capabilities. . . . He was not wanting in generous tolerations, high admiration, deep reverences, yes, and deep humilities."[173]

Henry Van Dyke, one of the nation's most distinguished religious leaders, eulogized MT's life and values:

> Loyally he toiled for years to meet a debt of conscience, following the injunction of the New Testament, to provide not only things honest, but things "honourable in the sight of all men."[174] . . . Nothing could be more false than to suppose that the presence of humor means the absence of depth and earnestness. There are elements of the unreal, the absurd, the ridiculous in this strange, incongruous world which must seem humourous even to the highest mind. Of these the Bible says: "He that sitteth in the heavens shall laugh; the Lord shall have them in derision."[175] But the mark of this higher humor is that it does not laugh at the weak, the helpless, the true, the innocent; only at the false, the pretentious, the vain, the hypocritical. . . . No one can say that he ever failed to reverence the purity, the frank, joyful, genuine nature of the little children, of whom Christ said, "Of such is the Kingdom of Heaven."[176]

At a later occasion, Van Dyke supplemented his observations about MT's religion:

---

[170]Matthew 23:27.
[171]*New York Times*, 24 April 1910, B3.
[172]Howells, *My Mark Twain*, 84.
[173]JHT 90.
[174]Romans 12:17.
[175]Psalm 2:4.
[176]Quoted in Archibald Henderson, *Mark Twain* (New York: Stokes, 1912) 9-10; Matthew 19:14.

The man who deals justly, loves mercy, and walks humbly with his God[177]
is accepted even though he cannot define deity. Mark Twain was a man of
that type. His honesty, his fidelity, his loving kindness to his neighbor, were
fruits of faith—I will even say of Christian loyalty. No one who heard him
speak with reverence of the simple faith of his dearly loved wife (as he often
spoke to me) could think of him as being indifferent to religion. His sense
of humor made him keenly aware of its perversions and literal misinterpreta-
tions. At these he mocked, even as Elijah mocked at the priests of Baal.[178]
At times, perhaps, his high spirits carried this ridicule to an excess. But of
genuine, simple Christian faith I never heard him speak without loving
reverence. . . . He felt "the mystery of godliness"[179] so much that to deny the
existence of God would have seemed to him the height of impudent folly.[180]

In the parlor in Elmira where MT and Livy had married, Samuel
Eastman, a minister at Park Church, conducted the final rites. (Twichell
could not be there because he had learned after MT's funeral in New
York that his wife was dying.) In his prayer of thanksgiving for MT, he
said, "Our hillside bears witness to the greatness of his heart who sought
to bless even the passing beasts of burden with the joys that enriched his
life."[181] Eastman was alluding to the four stone water troughs MT had
placed along the steep road to Quarry Farm, each inscribed with the name
of one of his children—and they can still be seen in Elmira today.

Woodrow Wilson, with whom MT had become acquainted at Princeton University, where Wilson was president, and in Bermuda, where both
vacationed, published this memorial:

Only those who had the privilege of knowing him personally can feel the
loss to the full: the loss of a man of high and lovely character, a friend
quick to excite and give affection, a citizen of the world who loved every
good adventure of the heart or mind, an American who interpreted much of
America in interpreting himself.[182]

---

[177]Micah 6:8.

[178]1 Kings 18:27.

[179]1 Timothy 3:16.

[180]Quoted in *Commonweal* (28 December 1934): 254-55.

[181]PH 261.

[182]Arthur Link, ed., *The Papers of Woodrow Wilson* (Princeton NJ: Princeton
University Press, 1975) 20:133, 378.

Following his funeral, the *New York Times* associated MT with the inscription on the Statue of Liberty in the city's harbor. Under the headline "Philosopher of Democracy," he was aptly called a champion of "the huddled masses yearning to breathe free." Especially included among those liberty-seeking peoples for whom he was an advocate were Jewish refugees, blacks in Africa or in America, Chinese immigrants, and women in search of equal rights. In 1913, the state of Missouri placed in Riverside Park at Hannibal an imposing statue of MT overlooking the Mississippi. The inscription reads, "His religion was humanity and a whole world mourned for him when he died."

The author beside a two-fathoms-high ("mark twain") monument honoring MT and his Jewish son-in-law, both of whom were buried in this Elmira cemetery.

Chapter 10
Conclusion

After exiting with Halley's comet, MT became the brightest star in the constellation of American historic literary figures. "He is the biggest man you have on your side of the water," Rudyard Kipling wrote to an American; "Cervantes was a relation of his."[1] Nearly a century has passed since he died, but he has social immortality around the globe. His accomplishments belie his epigram, "Fame is a vapor—popularity an accident—the only earthly certainty oblivion."[2] Considering that some of his works are now translated into dozens of languages and published in hundreds of foreign editions, his influence may be even greater now than in "the days of his flesh" and is likely to continue to grow. Because of his continually rising fame, witticisms he never uttered are often attributed to him to help launch a laugh. For example, his alleged quip, "A Pharisee is a good person in the worst sense of the word," expresses his sentiments, but it may well be apocryphal. There is no need to invent comments of MT on religion because his actual insights, as have been shown, are vast and often profound as well as funny. His pen name, which refers to a depth of two fathoms, is not adequate to describe his fathomless penetration into truth about *Homo religiosus*. MT's residual liberal Calvinism has helped to give both a transforming leavening and levity to religious people over the generations that have followed him.

Parallel Lives

Plutarch's classic study of parallel lives shows that comparisons help sharpen one's understanding of the involved personalities. Since Job of Uz and Lincoln of Illinois have charactistics that are generally well known, MT's religion can be viewed from a larger perspective by sketching some similarities and differences between the men.

Job is the best example of the many biblical doubters. As the fictional story of his life begins, Satan is roaming the earth observing human conduct so that he can communicate his findings to the overworld—a literary device that MT adopted in his *Letters from the Earth*. The Lord proudly shows Satan a healthy, successful, and devout man in the prime of life,

---

[1]MTL 747.
[2]MTN 114.

with a loving wife and many children. But the Adversary cynically claims that Job is a fraud, pretending devotion so as to manipulate God into providing him with the things that make him happy. To test whether Job's worship is genuine, the Lord permits a series of disasters that leave Job poverty-stricken and childless. Finally, when smitten with an incurable and painful disease that is presumed to be contagious, Job is ostracized by his community. Initially Job is patient, but soon he begins to scream angrily for God to justify the harsh treatment leveled on his righteous servant, and to end his horrible life.

Several pietists enter the Job story to represent the conventional theological ethics of the ancient Hebrews. Unwittingly they argue the theme of Satan—who has completely disappeared—and try to reinforce the perennial formula of folk religion: God has established the earthly order so that invariably the righteous are rewarded with health, wealth, and a loving family, while the unrighteous are punished with poverty and suffering in proportion to the sins they have committed. The view of Job's "friends" is summarized by this crisp proverb, "Nothing bad happens to good people but the wicked have nothing but trouble."[3] Since wretched things have happened to Job, his interlocutors are convinced that he must be a wicked person who is unwilling to confess secret sins.

Offended, Job argues with these apologists of orthodoxy as they attempt to put the stamp of special Providence on everything that happens. Their theodicy flies in the face of experience. Job has personal proof that not only do bad things frequently happen to good people but good things often happen to bad people. As Job sees it, the wages of sin are pretty good in the unjust scheme God has established. He asks: "Wherefore do the wicked live, become old, yea, are mighty in power? . . . Their houses are safe from fear, neither is the rod of God upon them."[4] On the verge of death, Job is convinced that God pays no attention to suffering. "Oh that one would hear me!" he cries; "my desire is that the Almighty would answer me."[5] Job's God, like a ferocious

---

[3]Proverbs 12:21.
[4]Job 21:7, 9.
[5]Job 31:35.

beast, has power but no kindness, "He teareth me in his wrath, who hateth me: he gnasheth upon me with his teeth."[6]

In the end, Job realizes that the ways of God are vastly more complex than either he or his companions have naively assumed. To operate the natural order, God needs to attend to matters that are bewildering to those whose primary concern is to secure justice in their particular situation. Job sees that an individual's notion of how Providence should operate may be at odds with the general Providence needed to run the universe.

The Book of Job belongs to the "wisdom" writings of the Bible that approach religion from an examination of the complexities of the human situation internationally rather than from hearing a revelation of God's word by Israelite prophets. MT, like the wisdom writers of Job and Ecclesiastes, searches for meaning in life not so much from declarations by spokespersons for the divine that have been transmitted from antiquity as from observing human nature and physical nature. Job's pious "friends" and MT's religious adversaries found little validity in approaching religion in the wisdom literature manner.

The perennial monotheistic problem of apparent injustices in the natural order created by God also greatly troubled MT. For example, he wrote:

> I knew an unspeakable villain who was born rich, remained rich, was never ill a day, never had a bone broken, led a joyous life till 80, then died a painless death by apoplexy. I knew a man who when in his second year in college jumped into an ice-cold stream when he was overheated and rescued a priest of God from drowning; suffered partial paralysis, . . . unable to speak, unable to feed himself, unable to write; . . . he lay and thought and brooded and mourned and begged for death 38 years.[7]

MT also told about Father Damien de Veuster, a Belgian priest and physician, who devoted his life to treating lepers in Hawaii and then died of the disease. After describing this and other cases of self-sacrifice, he lamented: "One great pity of it all is, that these poor sufferers are innocent. The leprosy does not come of sins which they committed."[8] From his youth in the West to his maturity in the East, MT wrestled with the

---

[6]Job 16:9.
[7]MTN 363.
[8]FE 64.

problems associated with the doctrine of a good God who does not remedy the inequities and suffering in the world.

One of MT's short stories concerns adopted orphans who were constantly told, "Be pure, honest, sober, industrious, and considerate of others, and success in life is assured." One child lived by that admonition and "as a man, he was a quiet but steady and reliable helper in the church, the temperance societies, and in all movements looking to the aiding and uplifting of men." The other child, although he was treated with special consideration, developed bad habits and as an adult killed his brother in a bank robbery, was tried, convicted, and sentenced to death. Before his execution, he "experienced religion," which caused much rejoicing in the community. "His grave had fresh flowers on it every day, for a while, and the headstone bore these biblical words, under a hand pointing aloft: 'He has fought the good fight.' "[9]

Both MT and Job quarreled with a seemingly capricious God, and sometimes their reactions showed a trace of paranoia. Even so, both had more religious acumen than those who were appalled by their unconventionality. Frankness in interpersonal relations, human or divine, often signifies a strong bond. For example, a Job-like psalmist who complains that God has abandoned him in his suffering, is nevertheless confident that God's righteous kingdom will come.[10] His cry of dereliction, "My God, my God why hast thou forsaken me?" was also associated with the dying Jesus because paradoxically it expressed a genuine faith.[11]

MT sometimes perceived God to be so preoccupied with the operation of His vast universe that He overlooked human misery. When MT was sequestered in London, mourning the loss of Susy, he said: "I wish the Lord would disguise Himself in citizen's clothing and make a personal examination of the sufferings of the poor in London. He would be moved and would do something for them Himself."[12] Alexander Jones aptly comments, "Twain came to feel that God would do well to devote less of his attention to regulating the circling of comets in outer space and

[9]CT1 747-52; 2 Timothy 4:7.
[10]Psalm 22.
[11]Mark 15:34.
[12]MTN 324.

more to lessening human woe."[13] Cultural historian Howard Jones thinks that "it can be argued with great plausibility that Twain's remote cosmic God is no more than an expansion of the God of Job."[14]

Some have rightly viewed MT's rage in a the context of religion. Mrs. Charles Ives (Twichell's daughter) who was long associated with MT in his Hartford home and church, remarked:

> I feel that Mark Twain was a very sensitive, tenderhearted man who could not solve the problem of pain in the world . . . and couldn't reconcile it with the idea of a loving Father in Heaven. . . . I don't feel that he was an atheist—how could he have got so enraged at the Deity if he thought there was nothing there![15]

In *Mark Twain and Religion*, John Hays observes perceptively:

> Clemens's animus was not so much against religion as it was against the institutions that controlled the religious spirit. His virulent attacks are upon the hypocrites who appropriate the language of religion to achieve an irreligious end. . . . Clemens rages against the world primarily because he is frustrated as he seeks the meaning of existence in a quest for a viable faith.[16]

MT, as well as the writer of the Book of Job, tackled what might be called the problem of "centrism" that constricts psychological, ethical, and religious growth. Centrism in an individual person is first expressed as *ego*centrism; despite socialization, the egocentric infant may never learn as he/she develops to balance the demands of the self with the needs of others. Much of the Book of Job tells about an upright person who is distressed because special Providence has not paid particular attention to him and rescued him from his troubles. *Ethno*centrism, which focuses on a person's group, is also difficult to overcome because trainers of youth themselves often assume that other cultures and nations should revolve about their own. *Anthropo*centrism, which maintains that *Homo sapiens* is at the summit of ecological development, often accompanies the theological presumption that all creation has been made for the exploita-

---

[13]Alexander Jones, "Mark Twain and Religion" (diss., University of Minnesota, 1950) 191.

[14]Howard Jones, *Belief and Disbelief in American Literature* (Chicago: University of Chicago Press, 1967) 111.

[15]PH 219-20.

[16]John Hays, *Mark Twain and Religion* (New York: Lang, 1989) 106, 112.

tion of the species "made in the image of God." *Geo*centrism, which portrays the earth as the pivot around which the heavenly bodies spin, persists in the minds of those who think, as the biblical writers did, that the sun actually rises and sets over their stationary terrestrial habitation.[17]

Like the divine voice Job hears from the whirlwind, many of MT's stories, including the tale of Captain Stormfield, challenge people's sense of their own individual or collective importance in the natural world. In *Connecticut Yankee*, for example, the "boss" eagerly works toward a technological transformation of medieval culture. He says, "I was even impatient for tomorrow to come, I so wanted to . . . be the center of all the nation's wonder and reverence."[18] Yet, in the end, the "new deal" society he develops proves to be a disaster.

MT recognized that many religious people, like characters in the Job drama, act as though the chief end of God is to glorify the righteous, and thereby reverse the first answer in the catechism that he knew from childhood. MT used good-natured parody to attack selfishness, racism, chauvinism, sexism, materialism, capitalism, colonialism, and imperialism—the centrisms of overweening human pride.

§ § §

Another way to clarify MT's religion is to compare him to his older contemporary, Abraham Lincoln. Bostonian William Dean Howells, an outstanding novelist as well as an editor of *Atlantic Monthly*, made this oft-quoted comparison of famous American writers, "Emerson, Longfellow, Lowell, Holmes—I knew them all and all the rest of our sages, poets, seers, critics, humorists; they were like one another and like other literary men; but Clemens was sole, incomparable, the Lincoln of our literature."[19] Lincoln and MT were arguably the two most outstanding men born in the United States during the first half of the nineteenth century.

MT had much in common with Lincoln, especially with respect to religion. Both were descended from WASP grandparents who lived in Virginia, and from parents who migrated beyond the Alleghenies to the

---

[17]Joshua 10:13; Ecclesiastes 1:5.

[18]CY 72.

[19]William Dean Howells, *My Mark Twain* (New York: Harper, 1910) 101.

Mississippi River basin. Both were born in simple cabins to poor pioneers on America's western frontier and were especially affected by the religious outlook of their mothers. They were given names that ultimately were the names of pivotal personalities in the Hebrew Bible. Their formal education consisted of some primary schooling, where the Bible was a main textbook. Its phrases and sentences became embedded in their minds and frequently surfaced to express their ideas. They read the Bible for its literary style as much as for its religious content. In his book on Lincoln's religion, William Wolf states what was equally descriptive of MT: "So much a part of him was the world of the Bible with its stories and characters that much of his humor flowed between its familiar banks."[20] Neither interpreted the Bible in a fundamentalistic manner and both found Henry Ward Beecher's hermeneutics attractive.

MT and Lincoln read widely, mastering written and spoken English. They followed Artemus Ward in developing a comic exaggeration and understatement style. Both used humor to make people laugh at their own inconsistencies and get them to listen to, and often accept, controversial ideas. They mixed genially with cultural leaders even as they exposed defects of their Victorian society. Even though both used homespun yarns and witticisms to take the sting out of criticism, they were both involved in life-threatening duels fueled by their outspoken opinions.

Both Lincoln and MT were occasionally called infidels or scoffers of religion because they had doubts about some dogmas of orthodoxy. As young adults they had been influenced by Thomas Paine's *Age of Reason*, and, like Paine, they came to believe that current social institutions had failed to provide liberty and justice for all. Nevertheless, they were neither religious abolitionists nor political anarchists. Lincoln and MT kept open communication with leaders in both spheres, wistfully hoping and always working for more authentic piety and patriotism.

MT and Lincoln had been imbued with the spirit of the Protestant Reformation. Like their Calvinist forebears, they were devoted to representative democracy, seeing it as the best way to curb the abuse of power inherent in hierarchial governments. Although neither became confirmed as a church member, both expressed an affinity for Presbyteri-

---

[20]William Wolf, *The Religion of Abraham Lincoln* (New York: Seabury, 1963) 133.

anism.[21] Their aristocratic brides brought them back into association with establishment religion even though they always had mental reservations to subscribing to denominational confessional statements. What Martin Marty has said of Lincoln could also be said of MT: "While he was respectful of the churches and shaped by the biblical message that they transmitted, he kept some distance from their doings."[22] Neither showed much concern for traditional orthodoxy or ritual, but both were committed to some teachings of the one they often called "Savior," and they were awed by a God beyond the gods of human creation. As regards theological ethics, MT would have had no difficulty endorsing these immortal phrases: "With malice toward none; with charity for all; with firmness in the right as God gives us to see the right." They viewed reason and faith as companions in the quest for truth, and occasionally they showed theological and religious acuity.

Lincoln is acclaimed as the Great Emancipator, but MT also helped to free from social bondage not only African-Americans, but Asian-Americans, blue-collar workers, Jews, and women. Commenting on MT's animating spirit, social scientist and storyteller Stephen Leacock wrote: "His hatred of tyranny and injustice, his sympathy with the oppressed individual, did more than any other writer toward making the idea of liberty a part of the American heritage."[23] Ironically, some contemporary Americans have accused both Lincoln and MT of being racists, even though they aimed at living by the Golden Rule and did not judge individuals by their pigmentation.

Some basic character qualities that Lincoln and MT shared were a by-product of their faith. In a book on Lincoln's religion, Elton Trueblood shows how his lack of "self-righteousness" resulted from his emphasis upon God's will."[24] Similarly, Clara Clemens said of her father, "He possessed a reverent nature and a humble one, humble in the sense that

---

[21]William Phipps, "Lincoln's Presbyterian Connections," *Journal of Presbyterian History* (Summer 2002): 17-28.

[22]Martin Marty, *Pilgrims in Their Own Land* (New York: Penguin, 1984) 220.

[23]Stephen Leacock, letter to George Ade, 2 January 1941, *The Twainian* (April 1945): 4.

[24]Elton Trueblood, *Abraham Lincoln: Theologian of American Anguish* (New York: Harper, 1972) 123.

he never felt more important than anyone else."[25] Lincoln and MT did not have the arrogance of those who were convinced that they were privy to God's purposes.

Both of these famous men had periods of depression when they despaired of any human effort to make significant changes. Their doleful-ness stemmed in part from the deaths of some of their children, which shook their religious foundations and caused them and their wives to consult mediums in hopes of communicating with the dead. Isaac Arnold borrowed a hallowed text from Isaiah to describe Lincoln, his close friend. What Arnold said of Lincoln could also apply to MT:

> Mirthfulness and melancholy, hilarity and sadness, were strangely combined in him. His mirth was sometimes exuberant. It sparkled in jest, story, and anecdote, while at the next moment, his peculiarly sad, pathetic, melancholy eyes would seem to wander far away, and one realized that he was a man "familiar with sorrow and acquainted with grief."[26]

Verily, Mark Twain was both the Job and Lincoln of American literature.

Ethics and Truth

Samuel Butler, a fellow novelist born the same year as MT, said of his generation, "People in general are equally horrified at hearing the Christian religion doubted, and at seeing it practiced."[27] Disturbed by the chasm between the profession and the practice of faith, MT strove to close the gap by focusing upon the ethical implications of Christianity. His writings may have made many European-Americans aware for the first time that African-Americans and Chinese immigrants were wrongly being treated as inferior. He drew international attention to the despicable treatment of many Jews in Europe as well, and to the exploitation of natives in colonial territories by imperialists who represented some Western governments and churches.

---

[25]MF 45.

[26]Isaac Arnold, *The Life of Abraham Lincoln* (Chicago: Jansen, 1885) 445; Isaiah 53:3.

[27]*Samuel Butler's Notebooks* (New York: Dutton, 1951) 310.

Reading in 1905 that "paganism defiled Christianity," MT altered the phrase to read, "Christianity defiled itself."[28] He found the path of religious truth in the course of American history as elusive as the channel of the muddy Mississippi he feared and loved. Howard Jones calls MT a "foremost Christian," and believes that his indictment of cruelty was "possible only to a man who truly believes he should love his neighbor, fear God, and keep His commandments." Jones continues:

> What Twain asked the world was that it permit Christianity to sit in judgment upon Christianity. How else explain at once his gentleness to most children and all animals, his patience with his invalid wife and his unpredictable brother Orion, and his hatred of hypocrisy, his rages against injustice, inhumanity, and war?[29]

Alexander McKelway, the editor of a Southern Presbyterian journal, had this to say about MT, "He is a Christian man, although such a hater of shams that he sometimes shocks the religious sense of others, or rather the religious non-sense." McKelway defended his evaluation by singling out the way MT dealt with the bankruptcy of his publication business.[30] Although he had no legal obligaton to recompense his creditors, he was persuaded by Livy to pay back $200,000. He set about raising it by lecturing while in shattered health until the debt was liquidated.

Dixon Wecter, a leading MT interpreter of the past generation, said, "Although Mark Twain never lost his deep appreciation for the ethics of Christianity, he stoutly refused allegiance to creeds and churches."[31] In their *New Mark Twain Handbook*, E. H. Long and J. R. LeMaster elaborate on Wecter's opinion: "Ethically he was a Christian; for truth, honor, and lofty ideals were the fabric of his character. No one ever held a greater admiration for the ideals of Christianity than Twain, nor ever felt more remorse when those principles were degraded."[32] The virtues that MT found in President Grant were ones that MT also treasured: "Clarity of statement, directness, simplicity, unpretentiousness, manifest

---

[28]MTLB 748.

[29]Howard Jones, *Belief and Disbelief in American Literature*, 110-111.

[30]*Presbyterian Standard* (14 November 1900): 3.

[31]MTMF xxix.

[32]E. W. Long and J. R. LeMaster, *The New Mark Twain Handbook* (New York: Garland, 1985) 180.

truthfulness, fairness and justice toward friend and foe alike."[33] Philip Foner in his excellent study, *Mark Twain, Social Critic*, views MT in a similar way:

> Twain was deeply interested in the relationship of institutionalized religion to man and society, particularly in reconciling Christian ethics and the social structures of his own day. . . . A sincere, courageous, vital, realistic, dynamic religion for him meant one which would inspire people to create a better world. He urged all churches, as a major step toward this goal, to tear from Christianity all the camouflage of self-deception, hollow sham and hypocrisy, to strip it of the ornamentation of the ages and to return to the original, sound principles of Jesus Christ—the ethics of humanity.[34]

To a cynical politician who had no respect for the truth, Jesus was reported to have said, "For this cause came I into the world, that I should bear witness unto the truth."[35] That comment on veracity in Pontius Pilate's judgment hall points up the significance of comments by H. L. Mencken:

> Mark was the noblest literary artist who ever set pen to paper on American soil. . . . From the beginning of his maturity down to his old age he dealt constantly and earnestly with the deepest problems of life and living, and to his consideration of them he brought a truly amazing instinct for the truth, an almost uncanny talent for ridding the essential thing of its deceptive husks of tradition, prejudice, flubdub, and balderdash. No man . . . ever did greater execution against those puerilities of fancy which so many men mistake for religion.[36]

Like Mencken, William Phelps was impressed with MT's ability to lay bare the essential truth of a matter. Shortly after his death, Phelps offered this tribute to his friend:

> So long as cruelty, snobbism, affectation and the tyranny of convention endure, so long will his powerful attacks on such things be wholesome and

---

[33]AMT 252.
[34]SC 200.
[35]John 18:37.
[36]Frederick Anderson, ed., *Mark Twain: The Critical Heritage* (London; Routledge, 1977) 328.

helpful. For in his wildest exaggerations and most incongruous mirth one can see that what he loved best from first to last was the living truth.[37]

MT once told reporters that whereas some people lie when they pretend to tell the truth, "I tell the truth lying."[38] He was much given to what Huck called "stretchers," zany stories that all but the simplest would accept as enormous exaggerations of the truth. A discerning audience could easily separate the wholesome wheat from the amusing chaff, and take seriously the former.

George Bernard Shaw was amazed that MT could "put things in such a way as to make people who would otherwise hang him believe he is joking."[39] After he met in London the one he considered "by far the greatest American writer," he prophesied, "I am persuaded that the future historian of America will find your works as indispensable to him as a French historian finds the political tracts of Voltaire." Shaw added, "I am the author of a play in which a priest says, 'Telling the truth's the funniest joke in the world,' a piece of wisdom which you helped to teach me."[40]

Sometimes MT put a humorous twist on ancient wisdom, thereby causing readers to consider afresh its importance. His rendering of Jesus' literally absurd saying that one should take the log from one's own eye before removing the speck from another person's eye, came out, "Nothing so needs reforming as other people's habits."[41] To advocate another gospel truth without appearing self-righteous, he asserted, "Revenge is wicked, and unchristian and in every way unbecoming, and I am not the man to countenance it or show it any favor. (But it is powerful sweet, anyway.)"[42]

MT's controlling conviction about religion can be summed up in his epigram, "When in doubt, tell the truth."[43] Like Tennyson who wrote

---

[37]*The Independent* (5 May 1910): 960.
[38]*The Independent* (5 May 1910).
[39]*Harper's Weekly* (20 July 1907): 1054.
[40]MTB 1398.
[41]PW 130; Matthew 7:5.
[42]LMT 3:440.
[43]FE 35.

"There lives more faith in honest doubt, / Believe me, than in half the creeds,"[44] he believed that faith without doubt is dying, if not dead.

MT indicted generic man for his narrowness: "Two things . . . are the peculiar domain of the heart, not the mind—politics and religion. He doesn't want to know the other side. He wants arguments and statistics for his own side, and nothing more."[45] Closed-mindedness prevents consideration being given to fresh viewpoints that enable humans to live together in harmony. MT was called a mugwump and a heretic because of his independent views. Knowing that many in his day unjustly considered him a blasphemer, he filed away many of his writings for posthumous consideration. Only in the past generation, since the death of his daughter Clara, have his religious views been completely available for publication.

To anyone tempted to identify the heart of religion with external appearance, MT cautioned, "Be careless in your dress if you must, but keep a tidy soul."[46] Looking beneath a person's reputation to the real self, he said, "We can secure other people's approval, if we do right and try hard; but our own is worth a hundred of it, and no way has been found out of securing that."[47] Both Jesus and MT advised the less traveled path of religious truth over the "broad way" of popular opinion.[48] "Whenever you find that you are on the side of the majority," MT cautioned, "it is time to reform—(or pause and reflect)."[49] For MT, being good and being lonesome were related.

Humorist and Preacher

In his crusade against human corruption, MT used humor with dazzling effectiveness. He gave it this tribute: "Humor is the great thing, the saving thing, after all. The minute it crops up all our hardnesses yield, all our irritations and resentments flit away, and a sunny spirit takes their

---

[44]Alfred, Lord Tennyson, *In Memoriam* (1850) stanza 3.
[45]MTN 307.
[46]FE 223.
[47]FE 151.
[48]Matthew 7:13; Luke 6:26.
[49]MTN 393.

place."[50] Laughter, conveyed by his fictional and nonfictional writings, was his weapon for exposing human foibles. Commenting on MT's intentions during his last years, Hammond Lamont says:

> His humor has served to keep clear and steady his vision of human relations, has helped him to pierce the sophistries of politicians, and to test the fleeting fashions of a day by eternal principles, has closed his ears to the passing cries of party, and enabled him to stand with courage, and to lift a voice that carries far, for justice and mercy to all men, of all colors, in all lands.[51]

At the beginning of the twentieth century, William James wrote "The Moral Equivalent of War" in which he attempted to deal with what would become the major social problem of the century to follow. In the essay, he contended that nations turn to the momentary thrill of military campaigns when routine life becomes boring, a pattern that will continue unless some constructive means of excitement can be found.[52] For MT, the moral substitute for violence was humor. Armed with serious hilarity, comrades can wage verbal warfare effectively against foolish ideas and dangerous persons. In his last novel, MT wrote, "Power, Money, Persuasion, Supplication, Persecution—these can lift at a colossal humbug—push it a little—weaken it a little, century by century, but only laughter can blow it to rags and atoms at a blast. Against the assault of Laughter nothing can stand."[53]

MT may be likened in some ways to the allegorical figure of the Christian warrior in the New Testament who, having "loins girt about with truth" takes up "the sword of the Spirit."[54] In the fight for equal opportunity for all, MT's mighty pen was his sword, but as Foner writes, "His humor tipped a sword's point. It cuts through social and political pretenses, defended and enriched the democratic heritage of the American people."[55] He used the sword of laughter to stab, if not slay, the sacred cows of white superiority, male dominance, American imperialism, and

[50]CT2 178.

[51]Hammond Lamont, *Nation* (14 December 1905): 479.

[52]William James, *Essays on Faith and Morals* (New York: Longmans, Green, 1949) 311-28.

[53]MSM 166.

[54]Ephesians 6:14-17.

[55]SC 405.

Christian exclusiveness. In accepting an honorary degree from Yale in 1888, MT defended humorists' radically different means of "warfare":

> Ours is . . . a worthy calling; that with all its lightness and frivolity it has one serious purpose, one aim, one specialty, and is constant to it—the deriding of shams, the exposure of pretentious falsities, the laughing of stupid superstitions out of existence; and that whoso is by instinct engaged in this sort of warfare is the natural enemy of royalties, nobilities, privileges, and all kindred swindles, and the natural friend of human rights and human liberties.[56]

Oppression and terrorism have often been associated with the fanaticism that accompanies intolerant religion. Laughter by those adhering to absolute ideologies is only a scornful condemnation of those who think and act differently. On the other hand, freedom can be correlated with comedians who laugh at the pretentions of their own culture. While MT did not spare laughing at other cultures, he mainly laughed at the hypocrisies embedded in the religious, political, and economic values that he had inherited. Positive social changes have resulted from those who have accepted MT's comic vision.

§ § §

Those who knew MT well, however, did not think of him primarily as a humorist. To Fred Adams he was a preacher who used his writings as his pulpit proclamation. He commented, "While his fame has been spread by the infection of his laughter, his real reputation has been made by the seriousness of his moral purpose."[57] Adams's words echo what fourteen-year-old Susy wrote about her father:

> He is known to the public as a humorist, but he has much more in him that is earnest. . . . When he is with people he jokes and laughs a great deal, but . . . when we are all alone at home nine times out of ten he talks . . . not very often about funny things.[58]

---

[56]Paul Fatout, ed., *Mark Twain Speaks for Himself* (West Lafayette IN: Purdue University Press, 1978) 142.

[57]Fred Adams, "Mark Twain as Preacher," *Methodist Review* (July 1911): 566.

[58]PP 207.

Still, MT was not content to be either the typical humorist or preacher. Reflecting on a number of humorists he had known, he recognized that they aimed merely to be jokesters and lacked an abiding influence. He believed that humorists who want to be remembered must subtly inject moral and religious content into the material they prepare. MT maintained that his humor served a solemn purpose:

> Humor is only a fragrance, a decoration. . . . Humor must not professedly teach, and it must not professedly preach, but it must do both if it would live forever. By forever, I mean thirty years. . . . I have always preached. . . . If the humor came of its own accord and uninvited, I have allowed it a place in my sermon, but I was not writing the sermon for the sake of the humor.[59]

MT accepted the common association of preaching with flowery language, annoying harangue, a droning delivery, and condescending advice. Indeed, one definition of "preach" is "to exhort in an officious or tiresome manner."[60] MT charged that "the pulpit . . . bores the people with uninflammable truisms about doing good; bores them with correct compositions on charity."[61] He liked much of what preachers had to say but not the way they said it. He thought that a message served up with humor would be both more memorable and more motivating. His comical stories are often thinly veiled sermons expressing his theological and ethical convictions.

William Thackeray tied humor and preaching together in a way that intrigued MT. In his copy of that Englishman's famous essay on Jonathan Swift, he underlined what Thackeray had written about the religious purpose of humor: "The humourous writer professes to awaken and direct your love, your pity, your kindness—your scorn for untruth, pretension, imposture—your tenderness for the weak, the poor, the unhappy. . . . He takes upon himself to be the week-day preacher." Through humor, Thackeray and MT were able to entice the public to swallow the unpleasant truth and find in it a cure for their personal and corporate sins.

Stanley Brodwin gives this summary of MT's motifs:

---

[59]AMT 273.

[60]*Webster's Ninth New Collegiate Dictionary* (Springfield MA: Merriam-Webster, 1993).

[61]WM 54.

Our brevet Presbyterian, our preacher with a sense of humor, will infuse nearly all his works with these broad but remarkable flexible thematic subjects: providence, reform, and the lies of a fallen civilization. . . . They point to an ideological or theological formation controlling human experience and revealing its inherent comic—or tragic—ironies.[62]

In religious discourse, MT echoed the classic prophets of the Hebrew Bible who proclaimed, "Do not follow the majority when they do wrong";[63] and "The effect of doing right will be peace."[64] He gave American expression to what divine spokesperson Amos declared about religious ritual:

Spare me the sound of your songs;
I will not listen to the melody of your harps.
Instead, let justice flow like a river,
and righteousness like a never-failing stream.[65]

MT's eagerness for social reform was motivated by his prophetic awareness of the painful difference between what a culture is and what it ought to be. A religious work often portrays a paradise to make the deficiencies of the present society stand out in bold relief. The gulf between the ideal and the actual provides the incongruity on which much humor is based. MT's rejection of sordid society emerged from what he imagined a holy society to be. He embraced Isaiah's vision of a righteous and peaceful government and a restored Eden as well as that ancient preacher's condemnation of the phony unethical religion then practiced.[66] MT and Isaiah both brought messsages of hope and of doom to their countrymen.

Comfort the afflicted, and afflict the comfortable was an aim MT shared with Isaiah of Babylonia and some fellow journalists.[67] Isaiah both

---

[62]Stanley Brodwin, "Mark Twain's Theology," in Forrest Robinson, ed., *The Cambridge Companion to Mark Twain* (New York: Cambridge University Press, 1995) 235-36.

[63]Exodus 23:2.

[64]Isaiah 32:17.

[65]Amos 5:23-24.

[66]Isaiah 1:23, 11:4-9.

[67]Finley Dunne, *Observations of Mr. Dooley* (London: Harper, 1906) 240.

assuaged his fellow Jewish exiles and ridiculed idol worship.[68] He told of idolaters who chop down a tree, set aside part of it to make an image, and use the rest as fuel; then they fall down before the carved piece of wood and pray, "Deliver me, for thou art my god!" By similar satire, MT attacked bibliolatry and the worship of the Almighty Dollar. "Disloyalty to the general idols and fetishes" is often required, he asserted, in order to retain "loyalty to one's best self and principles."[69] Zwick calls MT "the most skillful orator of his time" because "he could entertain an audience and damn its idols in the same breath."[70]

The Tolerant Monotheist

"More than most men," Sherwood Cummings observes in *Mark Twain and Science*, "he was preoccupied with religion."[71] He was neither a Bible-banger nor a Bible-basher. Edgar Masters has commented on MT's occasional rejection of the biblical religion, "It seemed to be attached to a rubber band, and was likely to bounce back into his lap at any time. The mythology of Christianity engrossed his imagination. He satirized it to be sure, but it showed that it was always in his thinking."[72] Although MT had no formal theological training, he thought about divine and human nature all of his life. Concerning his chronic predicament, he quipped, "Doubtless theology and dysentery are two of the most enervating diseases a person can have."[73] But this negative assertion should be taken with a grain of salt. In mid-life he claimed, "I detest novels, poetry, and theology,"[74] though in fact he selectively liked them all—especially what he produced himself! He was associated with the major American religious expressions of his lifetime—ranging from the Western frontier revivalists who conducted camp meetings, to the liberal

[68]Isaiah 40:1-2; 44:9-17.

[69]MTN 199.

[70]Jim Zwick, ed., *Mark Twain's Weapons of Satire* (Syracuse NY: Syracuse University Press, 1992) xlii.

[71]Sherwood Cummings, *Mark Twain and Science* (Baton Rouge: Louisiana State University Press, 1988) 26.

[72]Edgar Masters, *Mark Twain: A Portrait* (New York: Scribners, 1938) 15.

[73]MT's marginalia in his copy of Andrew White, *A History of the Warfare of Science with Theology*; MTLB 760.

[74]MTB 512.

Protestants who strove for racial and gender equality, to the New England mind-cure therapists.

MT was aware that God's truth is too vast to comprehend, and was deeply sensitive to the transcendent Being who made the pretensions of human beings appear ludicrous. He exposed the quaintness of the biblical writers' notion of a geocentric universe, surrounded by waters above the firmament and below the earth, that extended several thousand miles in each direction. Finding religious significance in the newer scientific understanding of the world, he opined: "The universe discovered by modern man comports with the dignity of the modern God, the God whom we trust, believe in, and humbly adore. It consists of countless worlds of so stupendous dimensions that, in comparison, ours is grotesquely insignificant."[75] MT's awe of the cosmos showed up the finitude of everything else.

The irreverence of MT drew attention but it did not consistently represent his essential faith. Edward Wagenknecht, in one of the better studies of MT, asserts:

> He never doubted God, and though the Spirit That Denies certainly had a hold upon him in some aspects, he was a seeker and a searcher all his life. . . . Making due allowance for buffoonery, annoyance, and exaggeration, there is less positive irreverence in Mark Twain than many persons believe. He recognizes the power of religion and consistently maintains that he never wishes to interfere with another man's faith.[76]

MT assaulted cherished tradition to disturb the complacent. Even as Jesus' teachings forced his Jewish compatriots to reexamine their unquestioning acceptance of some parts of the Torah,[77] so MT's skepticism of selective doctrines and practices challenged pietistic Christians. He testified, "I can go as far as the next man in genuine reverence of holy things, but this thing of stretching the narrow garment of belief to fit the broad shoulders of a wish, 'tis too much for me."[78] He defended himself from his religious critics, claiming:

---

[75]BMT 317.
[76]MTMW 179, 196.
[77]Matthew 5:21-44.
[78]MTN 108.

I was never consciously and purposely irreverent in my life. . . . The Mohammedan reveres Mohammed—it is his privilege; the Christian doesn't—apparently that is his privilege. . . . They haven't any right to complain of the other. . . . You can't have reverence for a thing that doesn't command it.[79]

Respect for the faith commitments of others ranked high in MT's values. "True irreverence is disrespect for another man's god," he asserted in India.[80] After jotting down notes on Krishna and other "Saviors" of world religions, he said: "I feel an honest reverence for every one of them—on account of their motives. I was only meaning to slur those dull liars, their followers."[81] Elsewhere he remarked:

I would not interfere with any one's religion, either to strengthen it or to weaken it. I am not able to believe one's religion can affect his hereafter one way or the other, no matter what that religion may be. But it may easily be a great comfort to him in this life—hence it is a valuable possession to him.[82]

MT shared the view of John Stuart Mill, who asserted in his important essay *On Liberty*, "The only freedom which deserves the name, is that of pursuing our own good in our own way, so long as we do not attempt to deprive others of theirs."[83] When the widow of Henry Stanley tried to convert MT to spiritualism by testifying that she talked frequently with her husband's spirit, he remarked: "She was as exactly and as comprehensively happy and content in her beliefs as I am in my destitution of them. . . . I would not now try to unsettle any person's religious faith, where it was untroubled by doubt."[84] Or, as he put it in his inimitable irony: "I have no feeling of animosity toward people who do not believe as I do; I merely do not respect 'em. In some serious matters (religion) I would have them burnt."[85]

---

[79]MTB 1313.

[80]FE 507.

[81]MT's marginalia in his copy of Sarah Titcomb, *Aryan Sun-Myths*; MTLB 706.

[82]MTB 1584.

[83]John Stuart Mill, *On Liberty*, chap. 1.

[84]MTE 339-40.

[85]MTB 1514.

MT's acceptance of religion went far beyond a grudging toleration of what he was unable to destroy. His was a tolerance that sought to learn from, and even adopt, the best that a religion could offer. When in the midst of Bushnellian Hartford, the locus of the most creative Protestant theologizing in American history, he responded positively to much of what was being discussed. The breadth of MT's tolerance can be discerned in a letter to Livy about his youngest daughter:

> I am very, very glad Jean is in a convent. . . . If they make a good strong unshakable Catholic of her I shan't be the least little bit sorry. It is doubtless the most peace-giving and restful of all the religions. If I had it I would not trade it for anything in the earth. If I ever change my religion I shall change to that.[86]

Intolerance of the beliefs of others was the one thing the adult MT consistently found intolerable because it necessitated a rigid acceptance of doctrine claimed to be immutable. One widespread viewpoint he adamantly opposed was that the Bible was dictated by God directly to various scribes who passively wrote down words that supplied answers to all significant questions. Indeed, MT thought that God would like to see eliminated some passages in it that are attributed to a divine source. In 1893, Pope Leo XIII declared the Bible to be inerrant, a claim that biblical writers did not make. During the last years of MT's life, some Protestants set down five "fundamentals," beliefs they considered indispensable for true Christians. The verbal infallibility of the Bible was the cardinal dogma of those who referred to themselves as Fundamentalists. They abhorred the presumption of religious liberals that the Bible could contain the fallible ideas of mortals as well as divine truth. MT railed at their lack of moral discernment implicit in equating passages commanding the massacre of Israel's enemies with the "Word of God" expressed in the beatitudes of Jesus. Fundamentalism armed militant reactionaries with simplistic solutions to the complex problems of the "gilded age" and to the increasingly bewildering dilemmas of our scientific/technological era. Although many Christians shared the Fundamentalists' view for centuries, the term itself, coined in the twentieth century, now applies widely to Jews, Christians, and Muslims who believe their respective scriptures to be inerrant.

---

[86]MF 100.

Several other alleged "fundamentals" pertained to the virginal conception of Jesus, his physical resurrection, and the visible return of Jesus to the earth. MT found many scriptural interpreters shackled by a strict literalism on those and other matters, especially as they dealt with myths of human origins and destiny. A literal acceptance of the prescientific stories of Eden, Heaven, and Hell was the background for his rollicking treatment of those realms. MT thought fundamentalists were great fun, even though they were not mental standouts! To make his satire sharper, MT often caricatured all Christians as Fundamentalists even though his close Christian friends also rejected Fundamentalism.

Today, MT's viewpoint on religion is gaining wider acceptance. Despite the reactionary contentions of those who call themselves "creationists," there is a growing awareness that the Bible was never intended as a textbook of science. A Gallup survey indicates that only a third of the American public now accept the Bible as "the actual word of God," down from two-thirds in 1963.[87] Like those liberal Calvinists of Elmira and Hartford, educated people now commonly recognize that the biblical authors were fallible and that it is a sacrilege to attribute their biases to the mind of God.

MT surmised that God is disappointed over the ecclesiastical dogma pertaining to an alleged historical Adam.[88] That notion, which involved Adam's "fall" corrupting all his descendants, has been rejected by liberal Christians. Given that the Hebrew term *adam* means generic man, the Eden story is now interpreted as a timeless parable about every human's struggle with self-centeredness. The composite adamic figure corresponds to what MT said about himself:

> Every man is in his whole person the human race, with not a detail lacking. I am the whole human race; . . . in myself I find in big or little proportions every quality and every defect that is . . . in the mass of the race. . . . The human race is a race of cowards; and I am not only in that procession but carrying a banner.[89]

---

[87]George Gallup and Michael Lindsay, *Surveying the Religious Landscape* (Harrisburg PA: Morehouse Publishing, 1999) 35-36.

[88]CT2 4.

[89]MTE xxix.

For MT, the loving relationships in Eden and the pain over leaving that paradise was an archetype of what he discerned in all humanity. Thomas Werge shows that the familial ties of the primal story fulfilled for MT the classical definition of a sacrament as "a visible sign of a sacred thing."[90] The close relationships he had with his mother, wife, and children were for him an Eden-like sacrament. In MT's fiction it was expressed in the bonding that developed between Huck and Jim, as well as between Tom Sawyer and Aunt Polly.

MT's religion is encapsulated in the New Testament text, "Be ye kind one to another, tenderhearted, forgiving one another, even as God for Christ's sake hath forgiven you."[91] His tour manager James Pond, who had a close relationship with him over many years, said: "Tenderness and sensitiveness are his two strongest traits. He has one of the best hearts that ever beat."[92] Paine, MT's constant companion during his final years, commented:

> In his purely intellectual moments he was likely to be a pessimist of the most extreme type, capably of damning the race and the inventor of it. Yet, at heart, no man loved his kind more genuinely, or with deeper compassion than Mark Twain, perhaps for its very weaknesses.[93]

In reading the Bible for social-justice themes, MT was assisted by Elizabeth Cady Stanton, with whom he was well acquainted. A brilliant person who shared his Calvinist background, Stanton edited a commentary called *Woman's Bible*. By means of a liberal interpretation of the Bible she hoped to subvert traditional sexist practices through showing that Christianity from the beginning should have advocated gender equality.[94] MT supported changes in gender policies that are more in harmony with the teachings and example of Jesus.[95] In addition to

---

[90]Thomas Werge, *Images of Eden* (Notre Dame IN: University of Notre Dame Press, 1979) 2.

[91]Ephesians 4:32.

[92]James Pond, *Eccentricities of Genius* (New York: Dillingham, 1900) 197.

[93]MTL 767.

[94]Elizabeth Cady Stanton, ed., *The Woman's Bible* (New York: European Publishing Co., 1895) 14-15, 21.

[95]See William Phipps, *The Wisdom and Wit of Rabbi Jesus* (Louisville: Westminster/John Knox, 1993) 167-75.

advocating sexual equality, MT's quintessentially American novel *Huckleberry Finn* attests to his longing for racial rapprochement in America. He also respected cultures abroad and was dismayed that some missionaries found no merit in religious traditions indigenous to the areas they served. King Leopold's atrocities in the Congo and President Roosevelt's suppression of the Filipinos illustrated for MT that white men may be the most "savage" of all people.

The complexity of MT should alert his interpreters to be cautious. He was both a funny fellow and a serious thinker, rebel and patriot, unbeliever and believer. His characters' convictions are not necessarily, or even consistently, his own. His commitments must be drawn from the full context of his fictional and nonfictional writings as well as from what those who were near him observed about his behavior.

In his own matchless manner, MT was a feisty herald of ethical monotheism, forever fighting tyranny, intolerance, platitudes, and snobbery. He strove to explain life in ultimate terms on the basis of a reasonable understanding of God. Throughout his life, he confronted moral and religious issues, writing about them in essays, letters, newspaper articles, travelogues, short stories, and novels. His parodies pricked the smug and his scriptural interpretations challenged the comfortably pious. While rejecting biblical teachings he regarded as absurd and morally repulsive, he was engrossed throughout life with Hebrew mythology and he opened a window to healthier winds of the Spirit. Like Calvin, MT had a high respect for using one's brain in the service of religion.

Late in life, MT noted, "The only really important question is, how to be a Christian yet not a fool."[96] But he thought of himself as one kind of fool: "I am a great and sublime fool. But then I am God's fool, and all His works must be contemplated with respect."[97] Hamlin Hill found that self-description so significant that he entitled his book *Mark Twain: God's Fool*. MT discerned a distinction between being God's fool and being a damned fool! He dealt paradoxically with playing the fool as did the apostle Paul, who wrote: "If any man among you seemeth to be wise in this world, let him become a fool, that he may be wise. For the

---

[96]MT's marginalia in his copy of Andrew White, *A History of the Warfare of Science with Theology*; MTLB 760.
    [97]MTHL 215.

wisdom of this world is foolishness with God. . . . We are fools for Christ's sake."[98]

Like a theologian, tragicomedian MT dealt with the joy of life and the significance of death as he shared in the mirth and sufferings of the several religious communities in which he lived. Playing a clown's role in the divine comedy without being a buffoon, he laughed at lesser commitments to Bible and sect. The world will long continue to laugh with him.

§ § §

---

[98]1 Corinthians 3:18-19; 4:10.

Bibliography

Abbreviations of Frequently Cited Works

AMT *The Autobiography of Mark Twain.* Two volumes. Edited by Charles Neider. New York: Harper, 1990.

BMT *The Bible according to Mark Twain.* Edited by Howard Baetzhold and Joseph McCullough. Athens: University of Georgia Press, 1995.

CT1 Mark Twain. *Collected Tales, Sketches, Speeches, and Essays 1852–1890.* New York: Library of America, 1992.

CT2 Mark Twain. *Collected Tales, Sketches, Speeches, and Essays 1891–1910.* New York: Library of America, 1992.

CY Mark Twain. *A Connecticut Yankee in King Arthur's Court.* New York: Webster, 1889. Facsimile reprint: New York: Oxford University Press, 1996.

E&E Mark Twain. *Europe and Elsewhere.* Edited by Albert Bigelow Paine. New York: Harper, 1923.

ENC *Mark Twain Encyclopedia.* Edited by J. R. LeMaster and James Wilson. New York: Garland, 1993.

ET *Early Tales and Sketches 1851–1864.* Volume 1. Edited by Edgar Branch and Robert Hirst. Berkeley: University of California Press, 1979.

FE Mark Twain. *Following the Equator.* Hartford CT: American Publishing Co., 1897. Facsimile reprint: New York: Oxford University Press, 1996.

FM *Mark Twain's Fables of Man.* Edited by John Tuckey. Berkeley: University of California Press, 1972.

HF Mark Twain. *Adventures of Huckleberry Finn.* Edited by Victor Fischer and Lin Salamo. Berkeley: University of California Press, 2001.

HH&T *Mark Twain's Hannibal, Huck, and Tom.* Edited by Walter Blair. Berkeley: University of California Press, 1969.

IA Mark Twain. *The Innocents Abroad or The New Pilgrims' Progress.* Hartford CT: American Publishing Co., 1869. Facsimile reprint: New York: Oxford University Press, 1996.

JHT Leah Strong. *Joseph Hopkins Twichell: Mark Twain's Friend and Pastor.* Athens: University of Georgia Press, 1966.

LE Mark Twain. *Letters from the Earth.* Edited by Bernard DeVoto. Greenwich CT: Fawcett, 1962.

LLMT *The Love Letters of Mark Twain.* Edited by Dixon Wecter. New York: Harper, 1949.

LM Mark Twain. *Life on the Mississippi.* New York: Oxford University Press, 1990. Text from the first complete edition (1883).

LMT   Mary Lawton. *A Lifetime with Mark Twain*. New York: Harcourt, Brace, 1925.

LSI   Mark Twain. *Letters from the Sandwich Islands*. New York: Haskell, 1972.

LTR   *Mark Twain's Letters*. Six volumes. Berkeley: University of California Press, 1988–2002. Volume 1, 1853–1866; 2, 1867–1868; 3, 1869; 4, 1870–1871; 5, 1872–1873; and 6, 1874–1875.

MF   Clara Clemens. *My Father, Mark Twain*. New York; Harper, 1931.

MSM   *Mark Twain's Mysterious Stranger Manuscripts*. Edited by William Merriam Gibson. Berkeley: University of California Press, 1969.

MTA   *Mark Twain's Autobiography*. Two volumes. Edited by Albert Bigelow Paine. New York: Harper, 1924.

MTAL   Arthur Scott. *Mark Twain at Large*. Chicago: Regnery, 1969.

MTB   Albert Bigelow Paine. Three or four volumes with continuous pagination. *Mark Twain, a Biography*. New York: Harper, 1912.

MTCW   Laura Skandera-Trombley. *Mark Twain in the Company of Women*. Philadelphia: University of Pennsylvania Press, 1994.

MTE   *Mark Twain in Eruption*. Edited by Bernard DeVoto. New York: Harper, 1922.

MTHL   *Mark Twain—Howells Letters*. Two volumes with continuous pagination. Edited by Henry Nash Smith and William Merriam Gibson. Cambridge MA: Harvard University Press, 1960.

MTL   *Mark Twain's Letters*. Two volumes with continuous pagination. Edited by Albert Bigelow Paine. New York: Harper, 1917.

MTLB   Alan Gribben, *Mark Twain's Library*. Two volumes with continuous pagination. Boston: Hall, 1980.

MTMF   *Mark Twain to Mrs. Fairbanks*. Edited by Dixon Wecter. San Marino CA: Huntington Library, 1949.

MTMW   Edward Wagenknecht. *Mark Twain: the Man and His Work*. Norman: University of Oklahoma, 1967.

MTN   *Mark Twain's Notebook*. Edited by Albert Bigelow Paine. New York: Harper, 1935.

MTP   *Mark Twain Papers*. The Bancroft Library, Berkeley, previously published in secondary sources. MTP* identifies Mark Twain's previously unpublished words, copyrighted by Chemical Bank as trustee of the Mark Twain Foundation, which reserves all reproduction or dramatization rights in every medium. Quotation is made with the permission of the University of California Press and Robert Hirst, general editor of the Mark Twain Project.

MTS   *Mark Twain Speaking*. Edited by Paul Fatout. Iowa City: University of Iowa Press, 1976.

MTSP   Louis Budd. *Mark Twain: Social Philosopher*. Bloomington: Indiana University Press, 1962.

MTTB   *Mark Twain's Travels with Mr. Brown*. Edited by Franklin Walker and Ezra Dane. New York: Knopf, 1940.

N&J   *Mark Twain's Notebooks and Journals*. Three volumes. Berkeley: University of California Press, 1975–1979. Volume 1, 1855–1873; 2, 1877–83; 3, 1883–1891.

NF   Kenneth Andrews. *Nook Farm: Mark Twain's Hartford Circle*. Cambridge MA: Harvard University Press, 1950.

OMT   *The Outrageous Mark Twain*. Edited by Charles Neider. New York: Doubleday, 1987.

PH   William Pellowe. *Mark Twain, Pilgrim from Hannibal*. New York: Hobson, 1945.

PP   Susy Clemens. *Papa*. Garden City NY: Doubleday, 1985.

PW   Mark Twain. *Pudd'nhead Wilson*. Hartford CT: American Publishing Co., 1899.

RI   Mark Twain. *Roughing It*. Hartford CT: American Publishing Co., 1872. Facsimile reprint: New York: Oxford University Press, 1996.

S&B   *Mark Twain's Satires and Burlesques*. Edited by Franklin Rogers. Berkeley: University of California Press, 1967.

SC   Philip Foner. *Mark Twain, Social Critic*. New York: International Publishers, 1975.

SCH   Dixon Wecter. *Sam Clemens of Hannibal*. Boston: Houghton Mifflin, 1952.

TS   Mark Twain. *The Adventures of Tom Sawyer*. Hartford: American Publishing Co., 1876. Facsimile reprint: New York: Oxford University Press, 1996.

WG   *The Washoe Giant in San Francisco*. Edited by Franklin Walker. San Francisco: Fields, 1938.

WM   Mark Twain. *What Is Man? and Other Philosophical Writings*. Edited by Paul Baender. Berkeley: University of California Press, 1973.

Other Books of Significance

Anderson, Frederick, editor. *Mark Twain: The Critical Heritage*. London: Routledge, 1977.

Baetzhold, Howard. *Mark Twain and John Bull*. Bloomington: Indiana University Press, 1970.

Beer, Thomas. *The Mauve Decade*. New York: Knopf, 1926.

Brashear, Minnie. *Mark Twain, Son of Missouri*. Chapel Hill: University of North Carolina Press, 1934.

Browne, Ray Broadus, editor. *Mark Twain's Quarrel with Heaven; "Captain Stormfield's Visit to Heaven," and Other Sketches*. Masterworks of Literature series. New Haven CT: College and University Press, 1970. Currently: Fox Island WA: New College & University Press, 1970.

Camfield, Gregg. *The Oxford Companion to Mark Twain*. New York: Oxford University Press, 2003.

Cody, Robert. "Providence in the Novels of Mark Twain." Dissertation, University of Florida (Gainesville), 1978.

Cummings, Sherwood. *Mark Twain and Science*. Baton Rouge: Louisiana State University Press, 1988.

DeVoto, Bernard. *Mark Twain at Work*. Cambridge MA: Harvard University Press, 1942.

Duskis, Henry, editor. *The Forgotten Writings of Mark Twain*. New York: Citadel, 1963.

Eastman, Max. *Heroes I Have Known*. New York: Simon & Schuster, 1942.

Emerson, Everett. *The Authentic Mark Twain*. Philadelphia: University of Pennsylvania Press, 1984.

Ensor, Allison. *Mark Twain and the Bible*. Lexington: University Press of Kentucky, 1969.

Fatout, Paul. *Mark Twain on the Lecture Circuit*. Bloomington: University of Indiana Press, 1960.

_____, editor. *Mark Twain Speaks for Himself*. West Lafayette IN: Purdue University Press, 1978.

Ferguson, DeLancey, *Mark Twain: Man and Legend*. Indianapolis: Bobb-Merrill, 1943.

Fishkin, Shelley Fisher. *Lighting Out for the Territory: Reflections on Mark Twain and American Culture*. New York: Oxford University Press, 1996.

Frederick, John. *The Darkened Sky*. Notre Dame IN: University of Notre Dame Press, 1969.

Geismar, Maxwell. *Mark Twain: An American Prophet*. Boston: Houghton Mifflin, 1970.

Gerber, John. *Mark Twain*. New York: Twayne, 1988.

Harnsberger, Caroline. *Mark Twain, Family Man*. New York: Citadel Press, 1960.

_____. *Mark Twain's Views of Religion*. Evanston: Schori, 1961.

Hays, John Q. *Mark Twain and Religion: A Mirror of American Eclecticism*. New York: Peter Lang, 1989.

Henderson, Archibald. *Mark Twain*. New York: Stokes, 1912.

Hill, Hamlin. *Mark Twain: God's Fool*. New York: Harper, 1973.

Hodge, David, and Stacey Freeman, editors. *The Political Tales and Truth of Mark Twain*. San Rafael CA: New World Library, 1992.

Hoffman, Andrew. *Inventing Mark Twain*. New York: Morrow, 1997.

Holcombe, Ira. *History of Marion County*. St. Louis: Perkins, 1884.

Holland, Jeffrey. "Mark Twain's Religious Sense." Dissertation, Yale University, 1973.

Horn, Jason Gary. *Mark Twain and William James: Crafting a Free Self*. Columbia: University of Missouri Press, 1996.

Howells, William Dean. *My Mark Twain*. New York: Harper, 1910.

Hudson, Winthrop. *Religion in America*. New York: Scribner's, 1965.

Howard, Oliver and Goldena. *The Mark Twain Book*. Marceline MO: Walsworth, 1985.

Jerome, Robert, and Herbert Wisbey. *Mark Twain in Elmira*. Elmira NY: Mark Twain Society, 1977.

Jones, Alexander. "Mark Twain and Religion." Dissertation, University of Minnesota, 1950.

Jones, Howard. *Belief and Disbelief in American Literature*. Chicago: University of Chicago Press, 1967.

Kaplan, Justin. *Mr. Clemens and Mark Twain*. New York: Simon & Schuster, 1966.

Kesterson, David, editor. *Critics on Mark Twain*. Coral Gables FL: University of Miami Press, 1973.

Lauber, John. *The Inventions of Mark Twain*. New York: Hill and Wang, 1990.

Long, E. H., and J. R. LeMaster. *The New Mark Twain Handbook*. New York: Garland, 1985.

Masters, Edgar. *Mark Twain: A Portrait*. New York: Scribners, 1938.

McCandless, Perry. *A History of Missouri*. Columbia: University of Missouri Press, 1972.

McCullough, Joseph, and Janice McIntire-Strasbury, editors. *Mark Twain at the Buffalo Express*. DeKalb IL: Northern Illinois University Press, 1999.

McKeithan, Daniel, editor. *Traveling with the Innocents Abroad*. Oklahoma City: University of Oklahoma Press, 1958.

McReynolds, Edwin. *Missouri*. Norman: University of Oklahoma, 1962.

Millikan, Julia, editor. *Journal Letters of Emily Severance*. Cleveland: Gates, 1938.

Neider, Charles, editor. *The Complete Essays of Mark Twain*. Garden City NY: Doubleday, 1963.

Obenzinger, Hilton. *American Palestine: Melville, Twain, and the Holyland Mania*. Princeton NJ: Princeton University Press, 1999.

Pettit, Arthur. *Mark Twain and the South*. Lexington: University of Kentucky Press, 1974.

Rasmussen, Kent. *Mark Twain A to Z*. New York: Oxford University Press, 1995.

Sattelmeyer, Robert, and Donald, editors. *One Hundred Years of Huckleberry Finn*. Columbia: University of Missouri Press, 1985.

Scott, Arthur. *On the Poetry of Mark Twain*. Champaign IL: University of Illinois Press, 1966.

Smith, Henry Nash, editor. *Mark Twain of the Enterprise*. Berkeley: University of California Press, 1957.

Smith, Henry Nash. *Mark Twain: The Development of a Writer*. New York: Atheneum, 1974.

Stoddard, Charles. *Exits and Entrances*. Boston: Lothrop, 1903.

Stone, Albert. *The Innocent Eye: Childhood in Mark Twain's Imagination*. Hamden CT: Archon, 1970.

Sweet, William. *The Story of Religion in America*. New York: Harper, 1950.

Sweets, Henry. *The Hannibal Missouri Presbyterian Church*. Hannibal: Presbyterian Church, 1984.

Tuckey, John, editor. *Mark Twain's Which Was the Dream*. Berkeley: University of California, 1967.

Turner, Arlin. *Mark Twain and George W. Cable*. East Lansing: Michigan State University Press, 1960.

Twain, Mark. *Personal Recollections of Joan of Arc*. New York: Harper, 1896. Facsimile reprint: New York: Oxford University Press, 1996.

Twain, Mark, and Charles Warner. *The Gilded Age*. New York: Harper, 1901.

Webster, Samuel. *Mark Twain, Business Man*. Boston: Little, Brown, 1946.

White, Andrew. *A History of the Warfare of Science with Theology*. New York: Appleton, 1898.

Zwick, Jim, editor. *Mark Twain's Weapons of Satire*. Syracuse NY: Syracuse University Press, 1992.

Index

(Limited to cross-references of names and terms used more than once.)

Adam, 39, 75-77, 123, 174, 224-33, 286, 372
Adams, Fred, 337, 365
Andrews, Kenneth, 113-14, 132, 152, 183
Anthony, Susan B., 91, 182

Baptist, 26, 58, 149, 165, 219, 282, 296, 310, 338
Beecher, Henry Ward, 62-63, 65-66, 85-86, 89, 93, 96, 99-102, 113-14, 143, 158, 166, 182, 248, 357
Beecher, Julia, 95, 99-100, 106, 142, 183, 302
Beecher, Thomas, 93-100, 106, 113, 121, 133-34, 142, 153, 226, 316
Bible, 2-5, 12-14, 19, 22-23, 26-28, 30, 33-34, 36-38, 43, 46-47, 49, 56, 59-60, 71, 74, 78-80, 85-86, 88, 91-92, 107, 113-14, 125-28, 131, 137, 139-43, 145-46, 151, 170, 177, 196, 202, 206, 212, 221-62, 268, 273, 277, 279, 281, 283, 285, 290, 295, 302-03, 305, 322-26, 347-48, 357, 364, 367, 371-73, 375
Brodwin, Stanley, 178, 262, 366
Browning, Robert, 128, 330
Budd, Louis, 4, 220, 345
Buffalo, ix, 96, 108, 110, 213
Bunyan, John, 26, 86, 178, 303, 308
Burns, Ken, 1, 330, 335
Bushnell, Horace, 120-26, 131-32, 371

Cable, George 134-35, 138-42, 154, 167
California, xii, 47-53, 58-59, 103, 120, 209, 242, 267, 305, 320

Calvin, John, and Calvinists, 6, 16, 23, 25, 35, 48, 55, 68, 80, 89-143, 154, 158, 177, 181, 183, 200, 233, 259, 266, 269, 291, 293-94, 297, 313, 334, 336, 351, 357, 372-74
Carnegie, Andrew, 148, 150-51, 212
Catholic, 2-4, 6, 57, 67-71, 75, 78, 95, 97, 113, 153, 189, 191, 196, 198, 202-03, 216-18, 239, 263, 285, 289-92, 310, 314-15, 326, 333, 335, 344-45, 353, 371
Cervantes, 27, 287, 351
Chaney, Mary Bushnell, 121,128
Chinese, 52-53, 209-14, 350, 359
Clemens, Clara, 125, 165, 167, 185-86, 194, 282, 304, 342-43, 345, 348, 358, 363
Clemens, Henry, 16, 21, 37, 131, 321, 332
Clemens, Jane Lampton, 10-15, 18, 21, 24, 29, 32, 51-52. 78, 339
Clemens, Jean, x, 125, 130, 188, 302, 327, 343-45, 348, 371
Clemens, John Marshall, ix, 8-9, 16, 21, 26, 29, 31, 36
Clemens, Livy Langdon, ix, xiii, 84, 89, 100, 102-08, 110-13, 117, 126, 129-30, 134, 137, 142, 164, 183, 221, 237, 245-46, 257, 260-62, 265-66, 295, 302-03, 316-18, 320-23, 327-33, 349, 360, 371
Clemens, Mollie, 37, 43, 48, 53-54, 310, 332
Clemens, Orion, 12, 30, 32, 34, 41-42, 44, 54, 228, 263, 278, 332-33

Clemens, Susy, ix, 117, 125, 127-28, 313-14, 316-18, 320, 322-24, 341, 354, 365

Congregational, 15, 63, 90, 118, 120, 132, 143, 183, 211-12, 336

Crane, Susan Langdon, 106-07, 259

Crane, Theodore, 106, 301

Darwin, Charles, 96, 119, 134, 225, 227, 284

DeVoto, Bernard, 4, 177

Dore, Gustave, 79, 278

Douglass, Frederick, 90-91, 159

Eastman, Max, 1, 90, 95, 100

Eddy, Mary Baker, 324-27, 343

Edwards, Jonathan, 124, 154, 334

Elijah, 71, 236, 260, 349

Elmira, ix, xii, 89-91, 93, 96, 100, 106, 126, 132-33, 142, 165-66, 183, 194, 201, 225-26, 265, 302, 316, 330, 344, 349, 372

Emerson, Everett, xi, 6

Emerson, Ralph Waldo, 120, 133, 356

Ensor, Allison, 60, 221, 241

Episcopal, 46, 50, 58, 61, 84, 91, 110, 116, 133, 201, 245, 282, 336

Fairbanks, Mary, 83-84, 111

Finn, Huckleberry, 168-78, 264, 298, 308, 362, 373

Foner, Philip, 186, 361, 364

Frederick, John, 9, 280

Freud, Sigmund, 132, 192

Fundamentalism, 3, 371-72

Gould, Jay, 148, 159

Grant, Ulysses, 158-59, 210, 360

Gribben,Alan, 4, 248, 299, 321

Hannibal, ix, xiii, 6, 8, 13-39, 41, 51, 55, 63, 83, 144, 168, 179, 193, 255, 261, 164, 191, 293, 296, 313, 320, 338, 350

Hartford, ix, 85, 111-34, 146, 151-53, 155, 158, 163-64, 167, 183, 210, 215, 266, 295, 309, 316, 322, 333, 341, 355, 371-72

Hawaii, ix, 41, 55-59, 68, 88, 112, 181-82, 236, 353

Hawley, Joseph, 117, 131, 226

Hays, John, 36, 39, 168, 311, 313, 355

Hill, Hamlin, 4, 304, 374

Hooker, Isabella Beecher, 85, 111, 114

Howells, William Dean, 4, 127, 134, 139, 158, 181, 266, 278, 282, 289, 301, 317, 326-27, 329, 343, 347, 356

Immortality, 4, 81, 299-310, 314, 317, 321, 331, 345

Isaiah, 12, 175, 188, 211, 239, 255, 257, 276, 359, 367

James, William, 3, 122, 323, 328, 338, 364

Jesus, 3-4, 6, 9, 14, 32, 38, 67-68, 71-75, 78, 80, 84, 95, 97, 101, 105, 107, 109-10, 113, 115, 122, 130-31, 138, 140-41, 143, 146-47, 156-60, 164, 167, 176-77, 189, 192, 195, 200, 211, 214, 219, 229, 237-38, 241-48, 255-58, 263, 269-70, 277-80, 288, 290, 301, 315-16, 323, 328, 337, 354, 358, 361-63, 371-73, 375

Joan of Arc, 3, 183, 185, 205, 245, 298, 313-16, 324

Job 3, 238, 261, 351-56, 359

Jones, Howard, 355, 360

Kant, Immanuel, 49, 311
Kaplan, Justin, 1, 63, 145
Keller, Helen, 184-85, 338

Langdon, Jervis, 89-94, 104, 106, 108, 183
Langdon, Olivia, Mrs., 89-92, 104, 183
Leary, Katy, 117, 126, 138, 167, 316, 324, 344
Lincoln, Abraham, 30, 41, 92, 94, 100, 157, 160, 201, 205, 351, 356-59
Luther, Martin, 131, 160, 315
Lynching, 176, 213-14

McKinley, William, 203-05, 207-08
Methodist, 2, 13-15, 19, 52, 55, 66, 87-88, 91, 165-66, 196, 282, 337
Missionaries, 50, 55-59, 61, 118, 181, 195-98, 202-03, 211-19, 230
Mormons, 41-43, 60, 296
Morticians, 46, 300
Moses, 4, 13, 28, 71, 80, 135, 193, 239, 252-53, 307
Music, 20-23, 48, 56, 58, 66, 83, 105, 107, 109, 150, 166-68, 330
Muslim, 75, 199, 229, 285, 288, 296, 307, 310, 370

Nelson, David, 24, 29, 92
Nevada, ix, 41, 43-47, 87-88, 251, 264, 272, 307
New York City, ix, 46, 58, 60-64, 67, 85, 110, 147, 151, 159-62, 185, 190, 193, 205, 256, 300, 324, 336, 348-50

Paine, Albert, 72, 82, 86, 126, 137, 162, 164, 237, 300, 321, 334, 341-42, 346, 373
Paine, Thomas, 37-39, 221, 357

Palestine, 41, 72-82, 85, 88, 191, 239, 244, 333
Parker, Edwin, 118, 131-32
Paul, apostle, xi, 10, 67, 92, 102, 132, 259-60, 374
Pellowe, William, 103, 276, 297, 331, 337
Peter, apostle, 68, 71, 104, 188-89, 244, 259
Phelps, William, 1, 361
Presbyterian, 5, 9-12, 14-26, 43-44, 48, 54-62, 68, 83, 87, 89-90, 92, 103, 108, 110, 129, 138-39, 141, 143-44, 160, 172, 186, 216, 219, 227, 236, 263-64, 268, 282-83, 285, 291, 293-97, 307, 336, 338, 344, 346, 348, 357, 360, 367

Quaker, 8, 38, 91, 161, 182
Quarles, John, 8, 30, 168

Rising, Franklin, 46-47, 58
Rockefeller, John D., 148-50, 154, 216
Roosevelt, Theodore, 165, 190, 208, 219, 294, 374
Russia, 78, 189-91, 194, 217

Sawyer, Tom, 12-14, 18, 26, 35, 175, 232, 238, 258, 373
Scott, Arthur, 215, 299, 337
Shakespeare, 27, 110, 227-28, 235, 249, 270, 303, 344
Sharlow, Gretchen, xii, 95, 98
Skandera-Trombley, Laura, 4, 183
Slavery and abolition, 5, 16, 24-25, 28-30, 89-93, 100, 161-62, 164-75, 188, 199, 249, 253, 290, 328
Smith, Henry Nash, 2, 4
Stebbins, Horatio, 51, 103
Stevenson, Robert Louis, 132, 313
St. Louis, 12, 30, 60, 191, 215, 340

Stoddard, Charles, 2, 235
Stowe, Harriet Beecher, 85, 100, 131

Talmage, DeWitt, 108-09, 307
Thoreau, Henry, 177, 209
Tuckey, John, 4, 225, 298
Twichell, Joseph, 111-20, 126, 129-30,
    132, 134, 136, 142, 144, 153, 168,
    203, 210, 212-13, 245, 276, 316,
    327, 329-30, 333-35, 348-49, 355

Unitarian, 51, 97, 122, 134, 282, 303,
    313

Vanderbilt, Cornelius, 148-49, 154
Van Dyke, Henry, 294, 336, 348
Voltaire, 27, 291, 362

Wadsworth, Charles, 48-49, 51, 103
Wagerknecht, Edward, 168, 208, 304,
    369
Wakeman, Edgar, 59, 136, 236, 305
Warner, Charles, 133, 145, 253
Washington, Booker T., 164, 177, 219
Washington, George, 18, 160, 226, 339
Wecter, Dixon, 4, 11, 360
White, Andrew, 251, 342
Wilson, James, 69, 82, 85

Zwick, Jim, 4, 205, 368